BECOMING
EUROPE

BECOMING EUROPE

Immigration, Integration, and the Welfare State

PATRICK IRELAND

University of Pittsburgh Press

*55208504

Published by the University of Pittsburgh Press, Pittsburgh, Pa., 15260
Copyright © 2004, University of Pittsburgh Press
All rights reserved
Manufactured in the United States of America
Printed on acid-free paper
10 9 8 7 6 5 4 3 2 1

Library of Congress Cataloging-in-Publication Data
Ireland, Patrick R. (Patrick Richard), 1961–
Becoming Europe ; immigration, integration, and the welfare state / Patrick Ireland.
     p.   cm.
Includes bibliographical references and index.
ISBN 0-8229-5845-7 (pbk. : alk. paper)
    1. Europe—Emigration and immigration—Government policy—Case studies. 2. Europe—
Emigration and immigration—Social aspects—Case studies. 3. Welfare state—Europe. 4.
Immigrants—Cultural assimilation—Europe. 5. Ethnicity—Europe. 6. Turks—Europe. 7.
North Africans—Europe. I. Title.
    JV7590.I74 2004
    325.4—dc22   2004011316

CONTENTS

TABLES

PREFACE

Although it did not occur to me at the time, the work on this book began in the early summer of 1992. The recipient of a German Marshall Fund Fellowship for Younger U.S. Scholars, I had been charged with extending my previous comparative work on immigrant political participation to cover Germany. In that earlier research I had convinced myself, at least, that institutional factors mattered more than ethnicity or social class in explaining how immigrants plugged into French and Swiss politics. It seemed logical to ponder next the relationship between the communities arising from mass migration and the most critical collection of institutions in postwar Europe, the welfare state. The Center for Social Policy Studies at the University of Bremen was kind enough to offer me an office and house privileges. I settled in for a year of quiet study.

Then, that August, right-wing extremists attacked a processing center for asylum seekers outside Rostock, Bremen's eastern "sister" city. A wave of attacks on foreigners rolled across the country, the most horrendous leaving people dead in Mölln, near Hamburg, that fall and in Solingen the next spring. In the interim, German asylum law had grown significantly more restrictive. It seemed as though Germany, suffering through a painful reunification, bore out its poor image in many North American media portrayals: it was a hopelessly closed and xenophobic place. The public meetings and antiracist marches that peppered Bremen's social calendar that year did little to dispel the impression. Long on histrionics, political posturing, and black leather clothing, they had more to do with settling inter-German scores than with reaching out to immigrants.

As I got to know Bremen's working-class neighborhoods, however, a different Germany appeared under those dank, gray North Sea skies. Even in areas dominated by depressing housing projects, all was not hostility, conflict, and despair. Mutual respect, solidarity, and a casual multiethnic rubbing of elbows were just as conspicuous. The closer I looked, the more evident it became that people of goodwill—immigrants, policymakers, and native-stock residents alike—were deeply engaged in an unheralded struggle to build a multicultural society. And it certainly seemed that Germany's welfare state was changing in more dramatic ways than most of the books I was reading in the center's library would have it. Social policy reforms were altering the immigrant integration calculus at the grassroots level, with major ramifications on ethnic relations. That conclusion was confirmed as the present multilayered, cross-national study slowly took shape.

Over the years, many individuals have helped out with information, insights, and moral support, and here I would especially like to thank Thierry Basomboli, George Bitar, Hannelore Bitter-Witz, Jochen Blaschke, Ivo Buchteel, Thomas Faist, Anita Hutner, Ruud Koopmans, Stephan Leibfried, Johan Leman, Jürgen Markwirth, Marco Martiniello, Andrea Rea, B. Schinke, Thomas Schwarz, Paul Statham, Christoph Stefes, Rae Ellen Young, and Tanris Zehle.

My friends in Bremen offered their support at several stages of my research, as did the Berlin Institute for Comparative Social Research during my stays in Germany's once-again capital. Colleagues at the Institute for Migration and Ethnic Studies at the University of Amsterdam convinced me of the wisdom of widening my comparison to include the Netherlands and Belgium. Fieldwork in the Low Countries, as well as follow-up research in Germany, was funded by the University of Denver and the German Academic Exchange Service.

Several institutions also assisted me during the process of turning raw data into this book. I was fortunate enough to begin that ugly task on a fellowship at the Rockefeller Foundation's beautiful Bellagio Center in northern Italy in fall 1999. The rest of the transformation took place across the Mediterranean. Most of the first draft was written while I was a Fulbright Senior Scholar/Lecturer at the Law Faculty of Mohammed V University in Rabat, Morocco, in 2000. The final drafts were completed over the course of my year as a visiting associate professor in the Department of Political Studies and Public Administration at the American University of Beirut in 2002–2003. No one could have asked for more supportive colleagues. My hope is that these experiences of the "other" side of the migration story have contributed nuance and richness to the analysis. I know that my time in the Arab world has greatly influenced my understanding of ethnic relations, Islam, and the human costs of immigration. This end point has not been reached overnight, but the journey has been fascinating.

Beirut, Lebanon
July 2003

ABBREVIATIONS

ABM	Work Creation Mechanisms (Germany)
AWO	Workers Welfare (Germany)
BfA	Federal Labor Office (Germany)
CCCIlg	Consultative Communal Council for Immigrants of Liège (Belgium)
CDA	Christian Democratic Party (Netherlands)
CDU	Christian Democratic Union (Germany)
CRIPEL	Regional Center for the Integration of Foreign or Foreign-Origin Persons (Belgium)
CSU	Christian Social Union (Germany)
DAB	Umbrella Federation of Immigrant Cultural Associations in Bremen (Germany)
DGB	German Trade Union Confederation
DPWV	German Paritative Welfare Confederation (Germany)
DVU	German People's Union
FRG	Federal Republic (Germany)
GSB	Big Cities Policy (Netherlands)
LPF	List Pim Fortuyn (Netherlands)
LR	Livable Rotterdam (Netherlands)
PS	Walloon Socialist Party (Belgium)
PSC	Christian Social Party (Belgium)

PvdA   Labor Party (the Netherlands)

SAMS   Municipal Advisory Council on the Multicultural City (the Netherlands)

SID   Municipal Integration Services (Belgium)

SMC   Municipal Migrants Center (Belgium)

SPD   Social Democratic Party (Germany)

SPIA   Provincial Immigration and Welcoming Center (Belgium)

SPIOR   Associational Platform of Islamic Organizations in the Rijnmond (the Netherlands)

VB   Flemish Bloc (Belgium)

VVD   People's Party for Freedom and Democracy (the Netherlands)

ZAP   Priority Action Zone (Belgium)

BECOMING
EUROPE

INTRODUCTION

Europe's Immigrant
Integration Crisis

Today people are displaying on a daily basis their willingness to risk everything for a job or refuge in Europe, fleeing strife and economic stagnation in the South. The northern Moroccan coast and the small Italian island of Lampedusa, just off the Tunisian coast, have become stepping stones for North and sub-Saharan Africans, Turkish Kurds, and others desperate to cross to the other side of the Mediterranean. The drowned end up snagged in fishing nets and washed up on Sicilian and Spanish beaches. European customs officials uncover suffocated Asians and Africans in cargo containers loaded into the holds of big-rig trucks. Other job seekers and asylum seekers try to enter through the "back door" of central Europe, with the help of mafia-style networks. Stowaways from across Africa and Asia turn up dead or alive in ships plying the Rhine from Switzerland to the Netherlands. Airlines discover frozen African youths in the landing gear of their jumbo jets. Bodies occasionally fall into backyards located under flight paths near major airports. Such appalling events have drawn public, media, and scholarly attention to questions of population movements and border controls.

At the same time, the difficult process of incorporating the millions of immigrants and refugees who have already made it into Europe has generated its own share of challenges. Ostensibly tolerant and peaceful, the Netherlands witnessed in 2002 the meteoric rise and assassination of Pim Fortuyn, the gay social commentator turned politician who won enthusiastic support by calling for stringent restrictions on Muslim immigration. His triumph, however Pyrrhic, merely confirmed the implantation of organized political movements with anti-immigrant messages across Europe—from the National Front in France and Wallonia, to the Flemish Bloc in Flanders, to the Republicans and German People's Union in Germany, and so on. Newspapers across the continent present the sad litany of assaults against people appearing foreign, clashes between immigrant-origin youths and police, and acts of vandalism against mosques and synagogues. Only the most violent and brutal events attract more than passing attention anymore.

How did Europe get to this point? Immigration had seemed like the ideal solution during the economic boom years following World War II, when acute labor shortages compelled Western European employers to import workers from abroad. At first, countries like Switzerland, France, and Belgium turned to their Italian and Iberian neighbors; then they turned to former Yugoslavia and Greece. Before long, France, Britain, and the Netherlands were recruiting from their disintegrating empires in North Africa, South Asia, and the Caribbean. When the Berlin Wall closed off its easy access to German-stock workers from the east, Germany relied on Turkey to fill in the gap. Those inflows differed from those of the prewar era: they occurred on a massive scale and involved an ever more diverse collection of national groups.

When the world economy deteriorated in the early 1970s, it became clear that most of "guests" were not leaving, despite the bans that were imposed everywhere on new immigration. In fact, the influx continued in the form of immigrant workers' family members and refugees. Fierce anti-immigrant reactions were developing. Often with high levels of discomfort, Europeans found themselves living in multiethnic societies. By the early 1990s, there were more than fourteen million nonnationals resident within the twelve-member European Community, concentrated in particular regions and occupations. These immigrant populations were an amalgamation of former migrant and colonial laborers, refugees and asylum seekers, undocumented immigrants and refugees, and their progeny who had become de facto (if not de jure) members of their "host" societies. In each, a growing group of immigrant-origin nationals was emerging alongside true immigrants as the decades passed and stable communities formed.[1] Due to persistent discrepancies between Southern Europeans' socioeconomic, cultural, and political situation and that of native-stock residents, even second- and third-generation Italians, Iberians, and Greeks have been considered part of the immigrant-origin population, notwithstanding their ancestral homelands' membership in the European Union (EU) and new status as countries of immigration in their own right.

Three decades after European host societies ended their mass recruitment of immigrant labor and a decade after they sharply restricted their asylum laws, the presence of large, diverse immigrant-origin communities has moved to the heart of fierce debates over identity, social order, crime, and the use of public resources. These disputes have frequently involved ethnicity, a "collective group consciousness that imparts a sense of belonging derived from membership in a community bound putatively by common descent and culture" (Premdas 1997, 5). Broadly defined, ethnic groups may be based on national identity, language, religion, physical characteristics, or a combination of those attributes (Varshney 2003). Conflict along such lines has steadily intensified, as evidenced by the potency of nationalist political movements and by the policy demands leveled by immigrants, and has reawakened national minorities like the Basques and the Corsicans in the areas of language rights, school curricula, family law, and religious practice. Terrorism and crime, identified in the public mind with particular nationalities, have become continentwide obsessions. Occasionally, ethnic conflict has given way to ethnic violence. Fights between immigrant groups, the most notorious being those pitting Kurds against Turks, have added to concerns.

Islam, especially, has become a lightning rod. Anti-Arab and anti-Muslim sentiment has grown virulent in Europe and was only stoked by the September 2001 terrorist attacks in the United States. Even the call to prayer of the muezzin or the erection of a minaret can provoke upset in many European neighborhoods. The similarities between Islam and Christianity—both worshipping the same one god and propagating universal messages—have for more than a millennium drawn the Muslims and Christians into conflicts that retain their symbolic force: the Muslim conquests in Iberia and the Battle of Poitiers; the Crusades and the recapture of the Holy Land; the Inquisition and the expulsion of the Moriscos; Ottoman hegemony over Eastern Europe and the siege of Vienna; colonial rule and the jihads against it. Policymakers across Europe have sounded the alarm over Islamic fundamentalism and dangerous Islamic "parallel" societies (see Vesting 2003).

The Trouble with Immigrant Settlement

Across Europe the institutions associated with national welfare states—policies, laws, and the actions of institutional gatekeepers—have accounted for the nature and management of ethnic relations, the influence of homeland governments and organizations, the integration processes affecting immigrant-origin minorities and their participation, and the public role of Islam. To varying degrees they have encouraged and politicized ethnic identities. Welfare state restructuring in recent decades has loosened social control and allowed for the release of those ethnic energies. European policymakers have in large part created the ethnic problem with which they feel they are now wrestling.

The implications of that challenge are of critical importance for Europe. The continent's new multiethnic reality means that "tolerance, inclusion, equality, and effective inter-group relations" are not just interesting theoretical issues. They are crucial components of European societies and will determine how democratic and resilient they will be over the long term (Feldblum and Klusmeyer 1999). Although conflict and violence have yet to surpass modest levels overall, Europe's rawer social relations have been altering its political life in troubling ways. Typically overlooked, some neighborhoods meanwhile bear witness to the dynamism and mutual enrichment that immigrants and their cultures have brought to Europe. In any event, the durability of the "push" factors driving people in developing countries to extremes, as well as the abiding "pull"—the demand for immigrant labor in a graying Europe—means that accommodating immigrant-origin populations appears destined to remain at the top of the list of political priorities (United Nations 2000).

According to a prominent line of culturalist argumentation, Europe's future therefore promises to be filled with ethnic conflict. Explicitly or implicitly, ethnic identity is widely assumed to be fundamental; the urge to define and reject "the other" is rooted in human nature (Hardin 1995). In Europe the collapse of the Soviet bloc, German unification, and the opening of national frontiers under the aegis of European integration seem to have given free rein to collective social actors based on primordial ascriptive identities that were once artificially contained. Increasingly popular—certainly since September 11, 2001—have been analyses in which a common religious identity plays an independent, indelible source of identity. Islam, with its allegedly "bloody borders," has appeared as an insuperable barrier to immigrant assimilation and harmonious social relations in liberal democracies (see Huntington 1996).

Long the lodestar for students of immigration, the celebrated Chicago School of Sociology held that at least three generations were necessary for immigrants to become fully assimilated Americans—under circumstances that were more favorable than in today's Europe. Gradual, linear assimilation appearing unlikely, support has built for the notion of segmented assimilation, whereby immigrants and other minority groups in the United States are seen to experience gradual intergenerational socioeconomic improvement, along with the deliberate preservation of cultural membership and values and continued economic attachment to ethnic communities (Portes and Rumbaut 1996; Waters 1999). This approach has gained European adherents as well (see Schmitter Heisler 2000).

Despite their popularity, culturalist approaches suffer from several key shortcomings. Most critically, immigrants with similar ethnic characteristics have achieved divergent levels of labor market, educational, and political access, depending on the country and city in which they live. They have organized in significantly different ways, with important variation in the degree to which ethnic difference finds political expression (Bousetta 2000; Mandel 1991). Nor can arguments that take ethnicity as a given explain why ethnic groups that fight in one place coexist peacefully in another. Labels such as "Turk," "Arab," or "Muslim" gloss over a world of diversity that belies efforts to use such overly broad categories to understand the politics of immigration in Europe.

Ethnicity, in other words, is not so much a category as a dynamic, elastic entity. Its value as a social, economic, and political resource varies; the appraisal depends considerably on institutions and policies. They help to define and create ethnic and other identities—be it intentionally, indirectly, unwittingly, or even in spite of their best efforts not to. They prevent, ease, trigger, and perpetuate ethnic conflict "by structuring incentives in ways that either exacerbate or attenuate the political relevance of cultural identity" (Crawford 1998, 11–12). Ethnic-cultural identities must be negotiated, taking one or another political form in collective action and in their relations with established institutions (Kastoryano 1996). (Non)policies and rules that establish procedures for resource allocation, participation, and accountability have a major influence on identity construction and delineation, as do politicians and other policy actors who cultivate ethnic conflict or cooperation. As Fredrik Barth (1969) noted decades ago, ethnic bonds, if not wholly invented by political leaders and intellectuals for purposes of social manipulation, are linked to specific social and political projects. Hence, if we want to know how immigration affects ethnic identity formation and ethnic maintenance, it is necessary to consider how institutional factors have shaped opportunities for both.

The Transformation of the Welfare State

The most powerful institutions interacting with Europe's resident immigrant-origin populations have been those associated with the welfare state. Concerned first and foremost about meeting their industries' demand for cheap labor, European authorities failed for a long time to implement coherent policies to cope with the social and political fallout of the postwar immigrant and refugee influx. They left the task to their social welfare systems, which divided, combined, and structured immigrants in different ways. When national governments prohibited additional inflows in the 1970s, their avowed mission became to acclimatize to European society the immigrant-origin communities that had formed. Once again, the welfare state was the toolkit with which to achieve that goal.

Immigrants have entered into existing institutional nexuses, therefore, that determine how and where the management of ethnic conflict occurs. How are duties and competencies distributed between levels of government? If ethnic associations are implicated in social policy, are they service delivery agents or the representative hinge between the immigrant-origin populace and the public sector? Given its centrality, the welfare state could reduce or bolster the organizational supports feeding groups based on ascriptive ties, either undercutting or encouraging ethnic and other collective identities in various places and at various times.

Even liberal, residual Anglo-Saxon welfare states have mediated the class, race, ethnic, and gender relations that constitute society. The transformation of the American welfare state in recent decades, for example, has received both credit and blame for giving a fillip to ethnic-based networks of mutual assistance and protection. This development may represent a deliberate plan to contain and defuse protest, provided these associations confine themselves to harmless, localized activity (Jennings 1983; Johnson 1987) and not contest the hold of the co-opted minority elites in the entrenched "regime of race relations management" (Reed 1995). While agreeing that the social programs and urban machine tactics of the New Deal and Great Society siphoned off discontent and isolated minorities from each other and mainstream society, some studies argue that the welfare state's retreat since the early 1980s has renewed collective political activism among minority groups along ethnoracial lines. Has policy change galvanized African Americans and Hispanics and encouraged both middle-class social service providers and poor welfare recipients to mobilize politically (Brown and Erie 1981; Erie 1987)? Assessments of Australian and Canadian experiments with ethnic-based social welfare delivery have generated a similar discussion over their ambivalent influence on ethnic relations and conflict.[2]

What impact has welfare state restructuring had on such phenomena in Europe, where welfare states have been stronger and more cohesive? Social policies there were devised consciously to attenuate the inequalities inherent in unequal market positions and to ensure the integration of all segments of the population (Schmitter Heisler 1992). Even as they have made consensual policymaking processes possible, these welfare states have served not only as purveyors of social protection but also as powerful agents of social control. As the incarnation and guarantor of social citizenship, they have had a powerful say in whether the forces of exclusion or inclusion prevail.

In response to reduced revenues and rising demands after decades of rapid expansion, European welfare states have undergone considerable revamping since the 1970s. Several common themes have emerged across the continent, including greater emphasis on preventing social security systems from impeding the reduction of unemployment, greater pressure for people to arrange their own welfare provisions, and a more dispersed base of funding for public welfare schemes (Barry 2001). By now, Paul Pierson's lament that despite the importance of the subject "we know stunningly little about the politics of social policy retrenchment" (1996, 143) is no longer justified.

Drastic economic changes linked to integrating markets, the decline of manufacturing, and cutbacks in some social welfare programs have produced mass unemployment and a marginalized population of "new" poor. Whether defined objectively (proving unable to obtain to a defined basket of goods), subjectively (falling below a line set on the basis of a self-reporting survey), legally (falling below a set level), or according to the EU poverty line (falling below 50 percent of the average income of a childless household), Western Europe has had relatively less poverty than North America and Oceania. Growth in the ranks of the European poor has been irrefutable, however. The bitter American controversies over an "underclass" and "cultures of poverty," set off by William Julius Wilson (1987, 1996), have taken on a European dimension (see Roelandt and Veenman 1994). The association between disadvantage and minority status has hardened. In its at-risk neighborhoods, Europe now has at-risk population groups. Those of immigrant origin belong to them disproportionately, prompting fears that ethnicity has become a major axis of social exclusion.

When immigrants figure into analyses of European welfare states and their restructuring, what has predominated are cost-benefit analyses of their presence and fiscal contributions for the political economy of social policies in a rapidly aging Europe: are immigrants "useful" or not?[3] They also appear sometimes as passive victims of developments that run against their interests, as when right-wing governments intent on a market-oriented economic strategy have effectively turned them into "internal enemies" in an attempt to comfort native "losers" (Messina 1996, 136–37). Thomas Faist (1994) and Andreas Wimmer (1997) indict "welfare chauvinism" for inciting political mobilization along ethnic-identity cleavages.

In the popular mind, as well as in much of the academic literature, the welfare state's transformation has come largely to signify program cuts and reductions. But the reality is not so simple. Within an institutional setup that has remained recognizable in its general contours, far-reaching, profound alterations have been occurring in policies and internal organization. The process has varied widely from country to country, but virtually everywhere, the welfare state has been undergoing decentralization, privatization, and delegation to nonprofit organizations. In social-policy and social-work circles, simultaneously, the concepts of self-help and empowerment have been gaining ground. The argument here is that all of these developments have interacted in ways that have had major implications for immigrant-origin populations and their collective identities. Together, they have often encouraged ethnic-based mobilization.

Decentralization

National governments have been decentralizing substantial decision-making powers, transferring them to officials at the state and local levels. The thinly disguised intention has been to shed responsibility for facing a range of budget-busting social challenges, even while trumpeting devolution as a way to bring policy closer to citizens. Free-market forces wary of monopolies and big government have fueled the drive to reduce the control of central authorities—and so have communitarians, Greens, and feminists, who wax ecstatic about the value of small-scale politics and organizations (King and Stoker 1996). While decentralization has given regional, state, provincial, and local officials more power, it has also saddled them with tasks for which they lack the experience and administrative capacity. The fragmented funding and personnel resources they receive can fail to compensate for those deficiencies.

Beyond overall similarities in entitlements and benefits programs across

Western Europe, there have been significant differences in the administration and organization of unemployment benefits and in the relationship between them and the safety net of last resort, social assistance programs. These organizational and administrative dissimilarities represent various opportunities for interaction on the part of the long-term unemployed and those on social assistance with the institutions of the welfare state and, therefore, built-in local tendencies toward social cohesion or disconnection. European cities have become a major source of policy innovation, "laboratories of democracy" in the tradition of the American states (King 1999). At the same time, their slim resource base impedes their ability to staunch such major wounds as capital flight and employment losses (Katz 1995).

At the local level, theory meets practice. National models for immigrant settlement run headlong into organizational and practical realities. Municipal institutions have had no choice but to adjust to the presence and needs of resident foreigners and their families. Not surprisingly, the link between urban management and the construction of citizenship has become a budding theme in much writing about local government (Andrew and Goldsmith 1998). Some observers maintain that decentralization exposes minorities to greater discrimination and exclusion (Lieberman 1998), whereas others have found instances where local officials prove more open than their national colleagues (Ireland 1994). Either way, in tinkering with center-periphery relations, national governments have disturbed prevailing mechanisms of social control and, by extension, the state of ethnic relations.

Privatization and Delegation

Even as they have moved to decentralize social policy, national governments have also been contracting out policy formulation and implementation functions to actors in the private and nonprofit sectors. New private-public partnerships have been forged, and policymakers have widely accepted the privatization of certain public services. The ethnic revival that has sometimes looked like the result of inherent cultural animosities or simple policy failure can stem from a conscious decision to delegate responsibility.

Some political economists have made the case that the way in which industrial democracies are organized and integrated into the international political economy affects identity formation. Giving freer rein to competitive economic and political markets fosters ethnic solidarities, distributes economic uncertainty and adjustment along those lines, and pits ethnic and racial subgroups against one another in a struggle over finite economic and political resources (Messina et al. 1992). By all accounts, the growth in residential concentration and segregation in European cities along socioeconomic and ethnic lines has been the by-product of greater resort to market mechanisms in the housing and urban policy sectors (Body-Gendrot 2000). Frequently decried by public officials, this development runs counter to the widely accepted "contact hypothesis." It holds that spatial proximity encourages interaction among members of different racial and ethnic groups, thereby building knowledge and understanding that lead to tolerance and improved relations (Massey and Denton 1993).

Even if spatial concentration and segregation have contributed to the accumulation of social problems in particular neighborhoods, though, it is not certain that they are responsible for ethnic identity construction and conflict. As the contact thesis would have it, neighborhoods with a preponderance of immigrant-origin minorities may reflect a dangerous concentration of social ills, isolation from society at large, and potential ghettoes (Li 1998). Or, as the opposing "conflict hypothesis" maintains, concentration and segregation might reduce the contempt that familiarity breeds among people with different cultural frames of reference and create a safe haven for immigrants to form their own social networks, circumvent linguistic barriers, and incubate small businesses. Ethnic enclaves may compensate for welfare state mechanisms that have not been integrated well enough (see Modood, Beishon, and Virdee 1994). At any rate, the spatial processes at work are the result of foregone policy choices.

Despite high unemployment rates and other persisting problems, immigrants have notched progress in the labor market, education, vocational training, and housing since the 1970s. Neutral or slightly positive general trends could hardly provoke a noticeable sharpening of ethnic-based conflict. Social relations have in fact been notably vibrant and peaceful in a number of ethnic neighborhoods in Europe, where concentrations of any given immigrant group or even immigrant-origin residents overall have only rarely reached the levels found in American ghettoes. Policies may not have provided any panaceas, but they have not suffered general failure or termination. Reductions in social welfare budgets have more often than not spared measures designed to assist immigrants.

In many respects, social policy has grown more like what it once was: the domain of churches, trade unions, the family, and other elements of civil society (Esping-Andersen 1999). More than simply "state divestiture," it has involved the penetration of the state into the nonpublic sector in the hopes not only of saving money but also of guiding it toward collective goals by delegating new tasks to nonprofit organizations that previously received little or no public-sector support.[4] In a timely study of this trend, Claire Ullman (1998) has examined the "other crisis of the welfare state" in France—not the familiar one of fiscal means but that of methods, competence, and problem definition. She contends that savvy political elites from the start have seen the co-optation of nonprofits primarily as a way to strengthen, extend, and fine-tune state power and to foster hearty social partners. They have understood that "state capacity can be threatened rather than promoted by a weak society" (Ullman 1998, 4; see Levy 1999). The popularity of nonprofits derives from their perceived skills in dealing with those social evils that have eluded conventional strategies, most notably the new poverty and new ethnic diversity. Because these areas of concern have widened the scope of recognized social problems, the financial consequences have usually run counter to the objective of slowing growth in welfare state expenditures.

Nor have authorities always achieved their goal of heightened control. Their decision to delegate responsibilities to self-help movements and associations in social policy areas affecting immigrants, combined with spreading notions of "empowerment" among the social workers in firsthand contact with them, has sorely tested that power. Privatization and delegation have released ethnic identities, which earlier policies and nonpolicies unwittingly structured, and have fueled competition and conflict between them. Once again, it is institutional reshuffling that has raised the profile of ethnicity.

Self-Help and Empowerment

Self-reliance, citizen participation, and public consultation have become the sine qua non of revamped social policies in Europe, integrated into planning, formulation, and implementation processes. Nonprofits have served as the instruments with which the state hopes to respond to demands for responsiveness from their most marginalized, disenfranchised clients. Pushing the idea further, self-help movements have stressed the autonomous mobilization of affected groups in a reaction against the welfare state's bureaucratic strong-arming, overly legalistic posture, and fixation on the bottom line. The associated savings in public funds have made self-help popular across the political spectrum (C. Müller 1993). The new left has celebrated the emancipatory possibilities as well. Liberals have hoped to reduce the burden on the individual and the mutual dependence built into social insurance schemes, both seen as lacking trust in individuals' capacities for self-realization. Christian Democrats have harked back to the concept of subsidiarity formulated by Pope Pius XI in his 1891 encyclical Quadragesimo Anno, which stated that no function was to be performed by a higher, more complex, and distant system that could be carried out by more primary groups like the family, neighbors, church, and friends.[5]

The self-help ideology has developed into a solid component of many social policies since the late 1960s, especially in the United States and the Netherlands, yet also in the rest of the Benelux, Britain, Germany, Scandinavia, and Switzerland. Abetting it has been the spread of the empowerment idea in the various fields of social work, the missing link in most analyses of European social policy. Social services have occupied a critical position in the policy response to extreme poverty and other forms of vulnerability and marginalization. Social workers stand on the front lines in the neighborhoods where immigrants and their families live and work. Changes in social policy have translated into far more work for these professionals, along with pressures to adopt scientific management techniques. Clients have metamorphosed into customers. Pedagogical methods focusing on "assistance" have yielded to approaches designed to counter the institutional contexts within which oppression operates (Kulbach and Wohlfahrt 1994).

Behind the new tack is the concept of empowerment. Like self-help and social work in general, it has attracted relatively minor interest from students of social policy.[6] Still an approach that social workers have not always managed to implement, it has generally captured their fancy. Empowerment entails eliciting clients' views as experts on their own situation; it celebrates the "emancipating" effects of self-reliance in daily life and as professional practice. Social workers are to become gatekeepers between people in need and the material and informational resources they require. The cooperation of those politically accountable and the decentralization of social responsibilities are key to realizing successful empowerment processes. A plurality of lifestyles demands a plurality of solutions and an embrace of unconventional strategies, not to mention linkages with broader social movements and social networks that bind the individual to the collective experience of social action. Neighborhood self-help initiatives are taken as the perfect examples of empowerment at work, for they nurture self-understanding and strengthen autonomy. If social work fails to secure a truly democratic process that involves citizens in an active way in policymaking, empowerment and self-help could degenerate into merely a way to free the strong from the discipline of the state and abandon the weak to the will of the market.[7]

There has been wide variation in the employment and effectiveness of voluntary and self-help organizations both as service providers and as nurturers of citizen participation. The substitution of nonprofits for governmental agencies can result in inconsistent and inequitable services, and neighborhood organizations can become just as rigid, unresponsive, and undemocratic as professionalized bureaucracies. Not all voluntary associations will automatically act as effective "schools of liberty"; they can be governed in deeply authoritarian ways (Tocqueville 1969, 195). Even champions of civil society—who laud associations for their flexibility, creativity, and ability to craft civic virtues and civic consciousness—recognize that problems of power and accountability can afflict them.[8]

There has been fierce debate over immigrant associations' potential for incorporating immigrants or for fostering social disintegration. Influenced by American discussions, recent work in Europe has tended to stress the contributions of associational activity to the building of useful social capital. If properly managed and "nested" within broader civic networks, immigrant associations can serve as useful pressure and emancipatory groups (Fennema and Tillie 2001; Thränhardt 2000). Even so, there is acknowledgment that they create social boundaries as much as they generate social capital, and warnings have sounded that parallel societies could emerge out of these associations.

Only a small fraction of immigrants overall ever join an association, with young people and women grossly underrepresented (Huth 2000).

Nowhere has the clash between celebrations of self-help and empowerment, on one hand, and concerns over social control, on the other, proved sharper than in official dealings with Islam. Crucifixes on classroom walls in Bavaria and Italy, the close relationship between Christian churches and democratic states in countries like Poland and the Netherlands, and church taxes in Denmark and Germany have figured on the agenda. Yet Islam has represented the true religious cause célèbre across the continent. Europeans have tended to ignore the diversity within Islam, which they have done much to cultivate, and the contradictory forces that divide the Muslim communities in their midst. Host-society "management" of Islam has been heavily marked by an obsession with security. Government officials in several member states have labored to structure a domestic and domesticated "European" Islam (Ireland 2000; Ramadan 1999).

Despite the mixed track record of such efforts, public policy does shape, even produce, voluntary associations in a variety of ways. Taxes, subsidies, and legal sanctions can be brought to bear on associations in such a way as to render them less factionalized and more amenable to cooperation. Then again, governments can undermine associations through inappropriate regulations, inadequate funding, delays and cutbacks, and outright hostility. The degree of public control also depends on the method of payment: stronger with grants and subsidies than with service contracts or vouchers (Kramer 1981). Reliance on the public teat can encourage associations to focus their attention on government rather than their community. Authorities might actually weaken them in the very attempt to strengthen them, creating financial and other types of dependency.

The welfare state, that bundle of vitally important institutions, has unquestionably helped fashion social citizenship and voluntary associations, including those formed by immigrants (Hein 1993). Associations have in many instances gained in stature, organizational wherewithal, and an official mandate to manage "their" charges. By decentralizing, privatizing, and delegating policy responsibilities, central states have simultaneously drawn such intermediary groups into cooperative relationships with program recipients. Immigrant associations have faced pressure to adopt a more professional profile and conform to established assumptions about how such organizations should behave. The "alliance between voluntarism and vendorism" has threatened to deflect energy and resources everywhere to the "scramble for subsidies" (Wilensky 1981). In addition to devolving more responsibilities onto them, therefore, central and local governments have pitted "native" and immigrant associations against each other and opened up possibilities for mobilization along ethnic lines.

Despite widespread interest in how societies should organize themselves vis-à-vis their states, few studies of civil society have tried to isolate or explain the interaction between changes in the institutions of the welfare state and immigrant associational activity and ethnic-based organization—the two not necessarily being identical—in spite of the repercussions on social control. In today's Europe, outbreaks of urban violence and soaring crime rates have produced appeals for the "zero tolerance" policies made famous by former New York City Mayor Rudolph Giuliani. Frightened and cynical residents nickname distressed neighborhoods "Los Angeles," "the Bronx," and "Cabrini Green." Anxieties over minority populations crystallize in stereotyped images of Islamist and Kurdish terrorists and North African drug dealers. Local officials sometimes find that they have to brandish the term "insecurity" and play on fears in order to pull down grants from national governments for programs to assist immigrants and placate anti-immigrant tensions (Roché 2003).

Decentralization, privatization, and delegation have not characterized all welfare states in Europe to the same degree. Nor have the concepts of empowerment and self-help taken hold equally forcefully everywhere. Even so, across the continent Europeans have been asking themselves the same questions as they contemplate their new multiethnic reality: What do we expect from each other? What rights do we have and what duties? How much difference can and should we tolerate in the public sphere? Where do "our" borders lie?

Much of the discussion that such self-reflection has sparked revolves around competing visions of the multicultural society. In Europe, in contrast to the United States, multiculturalism is primarily considered "something for immigrants" (Glazer 1999). A number of commentators have celebrated the enrichment and effervescence that the coexistence of an assortment of cultural practices brings to the polity (see Cohen 1999; Wieviorka 1996). Many on the traditional political left prize a welfare state in which people are seen in terms of the producer groups to which they belong and between which conflicts are resolved through bargaining and compromise; any special recognition of multiculturalism threatens this process. There has been worry in other quarters that the diversity created by the recent waves of immigration from the developing world may be wearing away the social bonds and shared values that unify European societies (see Rath 1991; Thränhardt 1994). Besides, even if ethnic diversity is to be accommodated, does such incorporation include all claims, including polygamy, child marriage, honor killings, female circumcision, and ritual drug consumption? Which voices from within an identity group should be recognized by the state as representative of the integrity of a group's culture (Shachar 1999)? Will the immigrants' cultural complexity overwhelm European officials, exceeding their "taxonomical capacity"?[9]

Not surprisingly, multiculturalism as policy has become a major bone of contention related to contrasting approaches to welfare state decentralization, privatization, self-help, and empowerment. Different multicultural "levels" and "discourses" have been identified, and policies have varied depending upon the national or local context, time period, and ideology of the actors involved (see Willett 1998). Rinus Penninx and Boris Slijper (1999) have usefully distilled a typology of five "visions of multiculturalism" from the existing literature. They exhaust the full range of perspectives, from those that involve no or only provisional acknowledgment of ethnic diversity in the public sphere to those that make it a fixture of the same, even as they make a key distinction between policies that accept and nurture collective (ethnic) identities and those that do not:

- *Liberal nationalism*—Policymakers stress the complete assimilation of immigrants, leaving room for their cultures of origin only in the purely private realm
- *Liberal neutrality*—Policymakers separate themselves from ethnicity and address individuals only as citizens and with general policies, ignoring what happens in the private realm
- *Liberal multiculturalism*—Policymakers ensure equality for minority ethnic cultures in the public realm, since they recognize that it systematically privileges the dominant culture, but work toward an even playing field and the phasing out of targeted policies
- *Cultural pluralism*—Policymakers accept ethnic identities as constitutive of the individual and the norm even in the public sphere, institutionalizing a role for them in policy debates
- *Communitarian pluralism*—Cultural pluralism becomes an emancipatory variant of older, conservative consociational arrangements, enshrining the principle of "sovereignty in one's own circle"

Whether modest or thoroughgoing, then, welfare state reorganization in the main has reinforced ascriptive identities and unleashed their organizational energies. Officials have responded in contrasting ways to the potential for ethnic turbulence, selecting consciously or not from a range of multicultural policy approaches. A clear connection has appeared between social policy restructuring and the transformation of migration from a widely ignored process into a burning political issue—two of the most momentous developments in recent European politics. Surprisingly, if the strong bonds that tie them have not gone completely unnoticed, then they have been seriously underplayed and oversimplified. By concentrating far too intently on abstract rights, cold statistics, national integration models, and policy discourse, too many immigration scholars have overlooked critical developments and relationships on the ground. To shed light on the more complicated and less black-and-white street-level dynamics of the settlement process is this study's raison d'être. Is the apparent recent revival of ethnic mobilization a product of welfare state evolution?

Causes and Effects

The hypothesized cause, the welfare state, reveals itself to be multifaceted, accommodating a wide variety of providers and policies. The actors include agencies of the state itself, subnational and local officials, nonprofit associations, private markets, and informal networks. In this study, policies in a range of discrete areas—those explicitly geared toward facilitating immigrant settlement, as well as those dealing with issues of employment, education and vocational training, housing, culture, security and crime, and political participation—will come under consideration in turn and in their systemic functioning and cumulative effects. Viewing these social policies as variables structuring processes of congruence and disconnection, I explore whether the postwar European welfare state has promoted and continues to promote peaceful ethnic relations. In careful comparisons across time, ethnic groups, and policy contexts, patterns of ethnic and other forms of mobilization emerge. The spotlight falls on the processes by which immigrants and those of immigrant origin engage with and become part of their host society.

The policies designed to respond to the immigrant presence in European host societies have been variegated and hard to categorize. They can be direct (targeting immigrants) or indirect (intended to affect all members of a community or in a particular sector). Policies against social disadvantage that in principle aim at the general population often target specific groups in practice and can be defined in several ways: according to socioeconomic indicators (compensation programs for persons with low incomes or insufficient education and families with many children), according to national origin or ethnicity (specific policies for immigrants, national groups, religions, or races), or according to territory (problem areas or neighborhoods). To aid in understanding, discussions of policy responses in all of the sectors that affect immigrant settlement will be related throughout this study to the Penninx and Slijper (1999) typology of multicultural visions detailed above.

Those policy effects, which constitute the dependent variable in this study, are not easy to isolate or operationalize. At issue is what immigration scholars and policymakers alike usually call "integration." Almost always announced as a public policy goal, integration rarely has any agreed upon social or political definition. Once defined primarily in terms of how well particular individual immigrants or groups participate in the majority society, integration has come to apply as well to the cohesiveness of the entire host society. It thus becomes the system that is more or less integrated, as much as its components (Westin 2003).

Quantitative approaches that attempt to measure structural factors have had pride of place in assessing integration. An extreme example has been the analysis based on the yearly micro-censuses conducted in Cologne by the local statistical office and in Dortmund by Hartmut Esser (1983). Establishing levels of socioeconomic integration has entailed both objective and subjective assessments of labor market, income, unemployment, education, and housing conditions; ratios of immigrant concentration and spatial distribution; the frequency of immigrants' contact with native-stock inhabitants; and patronage of recreational and cultural offerings. Political integration, when this approach has considered it, has been gauged according to inclusion within host-society institutions and organizations, measured levels of immigrant interest in local legislative and political happenings, and the expressed desire to have the possibility of participating in the same.

There are problems attendant to such an approach. Available data have proved insufficient, ill-suited to comparative analysis, and misleading. Cross-national comparisons present a host of problems. There are differences in definitions and delineations of population categories, the composition of immigrant-origin populations, and scales of analysis. National statistics on assorted aspects of integration are collected on the basis of indicators that vary depending on the particular definition of "integration" that is used. Most of the available data sets on immigration do not allow for cross-tabulation or correlation-drawing in any useful way. The only exceptions are very general surveys like those conducted by Eurostat. Even in Cologne diachronic analysis has been made risky, since investigators have not posed the same questions to the same sample of people. In the German state of Bremen, to cite another telling example, the same methodology has not even been employed to gather information on immigrants in its component cities of Bremen and Bremerhaven (SJS 1991).

The interpretation of measures can present traps as well. For instance, the normative ranking of residents according to selected indices of integration, based on information gathered by a single survey instrument, is an inherently subjective undertaking (Reinsch 2001). Likewise relying on survey data, culturalist studies that focus on interpersonal trust are based on highly debatable assumptions about the positive role of ethnic leaders, the beneficial effects of their integration into local power structures, and the value of associational activity (including that of nationalist and undemocratic groups) in generating that social and political trust (Fennema and Tillie 2001). The suitability of such approaches to comparative analysis is uncertain.

In frequently cited figures relating to immigrant small businesses, moreover, should we see a strategy of self-containment and self-isolation from the host society or an effective, adaptive means of compensating for a lack of alternative employment opportunities (see Bonacich 1988)? And, as mentioned above, a neighborhood with high immigrant-origin concentration could serve to lock individuals within an encapsulated society. Or it could represent a temporary but indispensable incubation stage in a process of integration over time. Like ambiguity attends other indicators commonly cited as evidence of integration, such as numbers of mixed marriages and the popularity of minority fashion and music (Rocheron 1999). It gives pause to remember how lengthy periods of peaceful ethnic coexistence and accommodation, marked by intercommunal amity and numerous intermarriages, preceded general societal breakdown in places like Bosnia, Burundi, Fiji, Guyana, Lebanon, Malaysia, Northern Ireland, Rwanda, and Sri Lanka (Premdas 1997).

By assuming that integration means blending into given host-society structures and institutions, most quantitative studies define any and all forms of segregation, no matter under what circumstances they have arisen, as barriers and therefore negative. The inference is that there exist monolithic ethnonational groups that should fit into undifferentiated societies and cultures. In actuality, it is open to dispute whether an objective difference necessarily implies inequality and exclusion. Does homogeneity perforce mean equality and inclusion? Some scholars have taken to writing about "creolization," where the system of social relations and cultural forms that develops is something completely new, created in a particular economic, political, and social context and affecting the "natives" and their responsiveness as much as immigrants and theirs (Foner 1997).

If quantitative analyses have their difficulties understanding integration, so, too, do those more impressionistic ones at the opposite end of the methodological continuum. Ethnographic studies, single-case studies, descriptive comparisons, and highly theoretical and value-laden discussions certainly contribute to our knowledge of the immigration experience. Whether the policy "lessons" that they derive can be transferred from one context to another is nonetheless subject to doubt (Weiner 1995, 75).

Integration, then, is tricky to define, analyze, and explain. This slippery concept will be conceived throughout this volume in comparative terms along two dimensions. It is advisable to use relational measures, since problematic data sets make it necessary to compare first and foremost the direction of change across time and space when attempting explanation. With an unrealistically homogeneous host society dropped as the benchmark, two trends are possible: when the situation of immigrant-origin populations (of homeland and/or host-society nationality) is converging with that of the native-stock population, there is greater *congruence;* movement in the other direction signifies greater *disconnection.* At issue is thus the extent to which there is a coming together of newer and native residents—examined here both as individuals and as ethnic groups, in keeping with the typology of multicultural policies. Absent is any judgment about the desirability of that convergence or any assumption that the host society remains static and unaffected. As for the dimensions of integration, it is important to distinguish between the *structural* (in terms of the labor market, education and training, housing, and social services) and *political-cultural* (formal and informal modes of participation, inclusion, and cultural exchange) dimensions. The relationship between the two is not straightforward, and policymakers have often stressed one aspect more than or before the other, with major consequences for ethnic relations.

In determining whether congruence or disconnection prevails along the structural and/or political-cultural dimensions, I employ the more reliable data sets and available statistics as general indicators of conditions and trends but not as hard, irrefutable evidence. Instead, I have depended heavily on the comparative method, relational measures (diachronic and spatial), and interviews to round out the analysis and to determine causality. The objects of those tactics include ethnic-based activity and conflict, which are exceptionally challenging to measure. Scoring cannot help but be subjective when it comes to measuring conflict levels, and rankings can only be nominal and not ordinal (Crawford 1998). Supplementing the other sources are evaluations by scholars and other researchers and in-house coding of relevant events as reported in national and local newspapers, in full cognizance of the weaknesses attendant to such increasingly popular methods in immigration research (compare Koopmans and Statham 2000). Determining the extent to which policies have affected outcomes is fraught with difficulty, certainly when it comes to immigrant settlement policies (see Reitz and Breton 1994). To make sure that social policies and not competing factors have caused the observed effects, it is essential to monitor parallels and discrepancies across ethnic groups, trends in social welfare spending, indices of immigrant concentration, and any indicators of attitudes and behavior among immigrant-origin residents of all generations.

The National Cases

The processes of immigrant integration and social policy restructuring are shaping up into a critical two-fisted challenge to welfare states across Europe and the postindustrial North. I have nonetheless found it advisable to construct most-similar comparisons across a set of carefully selected countries and cities over time in order to establish the connection between policy outputs and outcomes, as well as to differentiate between the impact of policies and of developments driven by culture, market forces, or other dynamics. My cases enable me to screen out extraneous and intermediate factors, pointing out trends that have or have not proved liable to manipulation by policies and other institutional factors—my proposed cause—as well as those that can or cannot be explained by competing variables.

The three country cases figuring in this study—Germany, Belgium, and the Netherlands—serve those interests well. In overall terms, these countries have experienced the same migratory trajectory since the war. By 1996 Belgium's resident nonnational population accounted for 9 percent of the total; Germany's for almost 9 percent; and the Netherlands' for around 4.5 percent (SOPEMI 1998, 31–32).[10] By the late 1990s, there were just over 3,000,000

Muslims in Germany, almost 700,000 in the Netherlands, and 370,000 in Belgium. These countries contained significant numbers of asylum seekers as well: 22,800 in Belgium in 1998 (2.2 per thousand inhabitants), 98,700 in Germany (1.2), and 45,200 in the Netherlands (2.9) (Eurostat 2000).

All three host societies have become home to distinct clusters of immigrant-origin communities. Differences of magnitude and composition notwithstanding, each has a settled population of Turkish and North African—in particular, Moroccan—background with roots in the same array of regions (see table 1.1). Turks and Kurds have moved to Germany and the Low Countries from around the Sea of Marmara (including Istanbul) and the nearby western Black Sea, around Izmir along the Aegean, and rural areas of interior Anatolia. Arabs and Berbers have come from Morocco's northern cities—Tangier, Rabat, Casablanca, Tétouan—as well as from small villages in the eastern Rif area between Nador and Oujda (Basfao and Taarji 1994; ZfT 1993). Turks (including many Kurds and other Turkish minorities) have been by far the largest component of the immigrant population in Germany, but the country has gained not insubstantial, fast-growing North African communities. Turks are also the largest immigrant group in the Netherlands, before Moroccans. The order is reversed in Belgium, where Italians have retained their status as the most numerous group overall. The three countries were originally a second-stage destination for many Moroccans from France, and the movements involved sizable numbers of illiterate peasants and few of the intellectuals who have dominated the community there (Chattou 1998).

At least nominally Muslim for the most part, immigrants from Turkey and North Africa serve to illustrate the heterogeneity of Islam. They are divided by an assortment of cross-national and internecine ethnoreligious cleavages. In addition, Islam has been seen as more important to Moroccan immigrants' identity than to Turks', owing to the latter group's experience living under a secular Kemalist state and its general linguistic homogeneity (Bartels 2000).

The presence of both similar and different national groups in the trio of case countries makes it possible to assess culturalist arguments across the cases and across several immigrant generations. No socioeconomic discrepancies

TABLE 1.1

Turks and North Africans, 1990–1995 (in 000s)

	Germany		Belgium		The Netherlands	
	1990	1995	1990	1995	1990	1995
Turks	1612.2	2014.3	81.8	81.7	191.5	182.1
Moroccans	61.8	81.9	138.4	140.3	147.8	158.7
Algerians	5.9	17.7	10.6	9.5	0.6	1.0
Tunisians	24.3	26.4	6.2	5.3	2.4	2.1

Sources: ZfT (1993, 19), Garson (1997/98, 22).

threaten to distort the analysis. A process of class differentiation was visible in immigrant-origin populations by the mid-1980s, meaning growth in the number of ethnic businesses and the emergence of a small cohort of ethnic professionals. In their vast majority, however, immigrants have remained blue-collar and low-level service sector workers in Germany and the Low Countries. Turks and North Africans have traditionally toiled in the energy and manufacturing industries, mining, services (cafés, restaurants, domestic help), trade, and construction. Although their labor participation rates have declined over the years with the formation of families, they still make up some of the biggest immigrant worker contingents in these European countries.

These immigrants have been of no minor importance to Europe in a broader sense. Turkey and the Maghreb have become for Europe the functional equivalent of Mexico for the United States. Because they are so numerous and because they are overwhelmingly Muslim, Turks and North Africans stand as key elements in Europe's new multicultural reality. Owing to bilateral agreements signed decades ago, comparable in their scope and many of their provisions, immigrants from Turkey and Morocco (and Tunisia) also enjoy guaranteed access to most social benefits in EU member states like Belgium, Germany, and the Netherlands.

Critical for the argument here, finally, are the points of convergence and divergence between the Belgian, German, and Dutch welfare states and immigrant settlement (or integration) policies. It is important for the argument here to compare systems whose institutions and policies have been strong and interventionist enough so that any effects that they might have had on the integration processes of Turks, Moroccans, and other national groups can be distinguished. The three countries here have been considered examples of "Rhenish" capitalism—marked by a consensual policymaking and a thickly woven institutional fabric between labor, capital, and the state—and "corporatist" welfare states, falling in an intermediate position between their social democratic Scandinavian and residual, liberal British neighbors (Esping-Andersen 1991). Thus to compare Belgium, Germany, and the Netherlands is to compare apples with apples, not oranges.

Germany and the Low Countries have had among the planet's lowest poverty rates, and social policies have been a major force in reducing social disadvantage (Rainwater 1991). Because they rely heavily on pay-as-you-go social insurance schemes, these systems were particularly quick to come under pressure when unemployment rates began to climb in the late 1960s. Their responses have thus been the herald of changes to come across the continent. In all three countries, welfare reform has entailed a pragmatic but steady approach to decentralization, privatization, and delegation. Those processes have diverged in certain respects, all the same—similar does not mean identical. Consociational Belgium and the Netherlands have maintained more top-down state control than Germany, although the Low Countries have felt comfortable with an interest group universe than has been less structured and more pluralistic than in their much larger, neocorporatist neighbor.

Despite the overall similarities in the structure of their welfare states, Belgium, Germany, and the Netherlands have devised immigrant integration policies and related "caring" strategies that have deviated significantly. Taken together, they exemplify the full range of European policy responses to immigration. France is the only other host society with assessable Turkish- and Moroccan-origin populations and a continental welfare state. By looking at understudied Belgium, however, one is in effect able to examine the French approach to immigrant integration: Wallonia's French-style Republican model has traditionally proved hostile to ethnic identities, a rejection reinforced by the region's socialist leanings—likewise characteristic of neighboring areas in northern France (Schain 1999). Conversely, the Dutch, followed by the Flemish, were quick to embrace an unabashedly multicultural model that took those very ethnic identities as its starting point. Between those extremes, Germany rejected ethnic identities but in effect nourished them through its social policies. Like welfare states on the whole, integration policies have changed in all three countries over the past few decades—the focal period being the twenty-five years after the immigration stoppages of the mid-1970s—with unmistakable effects on ethnic relations and immigrant integration.

The City Cases

Developments at the national level in Belgium, Germany, and the Netherlands present wide variation in the proposed cultural and institutional causal variables. The impact of contrasting integration policies becomes even more visible at the national level. Across Europe immigrant concentrations and the problems associated with them, real and imagined, have varied widely from region to region and city to city. The uneven nature of this distribution robs national-level statistics and comparisons of much of their punch. Policymakers at the local level have had to cope with their cities' new global economic roles even while adjusting to a multiethnic society with its roots in the same transformation. It is in certain urban neighborhoods where the spatial concentration of residents is taking place along socioeconomic and ethnic lines and where multicultural societies are either being built or rendered unworkable. "Processes of identity redefinition and collective strategies" depend increasingly on local-level realities; a complex relationship holds between urban management and both the construction of citizenship and the effective governance of diversity (Le Galès and Harding 1998). In short, it is at the local level that integration models meet reality and where they either succeed or fail in producing desired outcomes. Increasingly, success stories there are adopted as "best practices" by desperate national- and European-level officials.

In the face of similar economic and social pressures, local-level consequences reflect the filtering effects of institutions, intergovernmental relations, and social policies. Within substantial constraints, municipal authorities in Belgium, Germany, and the Netherlands have managed to put their spin on social policies. Local officials and immigrant-origin populations have not enjoyed the luxury of sitting back and philosophizing about what the ideal society might look like. To understand the modi vivendi that they have devised, we need more nuanced treatment than extremely broad "models of incorporation" can provide (compare Brubaker 1992; Castles 2000; and Favell 1998).

With immigrants not spread out uniformly in every host society, it is possible to find cities and neighborhoods that are either alike or dissimilar with respect to their ethnic composition, rates of residential concentration and segregation, and socioeconomic level. The potential for constructing powerful comparisons and undertaking effective tests of competing causal factors is therefore greater than at the national level. Unfortunately, analyses of local-level immigrant integration to date have not fully realized that promise. They have tended to focus on a single case (Reinsch 2001; Schwarz 1992) or to engage in comparison in a rather scattershot, unsystematic manner (Body-Gendrot and Martiniello 2000; Vermeulen 1997). Even the major UNESCO-sponsored Management of Social Transformations Program on multicultural policies and modes of citizenship in European cities follows no cogent method in selecting the cities for which its data templates are developed. Nor do its researchers capture the all-important linkages between "bottom-up" (immigrant-instigated) and "top-down" (municipality-instigated) developments or those between the center and the periphery.

This study tries to avoid such shortcomings. Embedded within the three-country comparison is one among eight cities: Essen, Nuremberg, Bremen, and Berlin in Germany; Ghent (Flanders) and Liège (Wallonia) in Belgium; and Rotterdam and The Hague in the Netherlands. Each metropolis is of major political and economic importance within its national context. The German cities rank among the ten largest in population in their country; their Dutch and Belgian counterparts, among the top three or four in theirs. Most of them have between 450,000 and 600,000 people. Ghent, though smaller, nonetheless stands as a fundamental regional center and participates in several key European urban networks. Quite a bit larger, certainly since the fall of the wall, Berlin has played a critical role in the evolution of immigrant integration policies in Germany and showcases the effects of unification on immigrants. Thanks to the two "outliers," the analysis here can also take into account overall differences in scale between urban areas in Germany and the Low Countries.

More important for this study, the eight case cities have a long history of receiving immigrants and contain several generations of residents of Turkish and North African origin, among others. Their immigrant-origin populations fit in the "average" range for large metropolitan areas in their host society (see Bals 1991; tables 1.2 and 1.3). Each of the eight cities has gained a reputation

TABLE 1.2
German Case Cities

City	% Immigrant, 1995	% Immigrant in the Land, 1996
Berlin	12.2	13.8
Bremen	13.6	12.1
Essen	9.0	11.1
Nuremberg	16.9	9.2

Sources: Thränhardt (1998, 75), ASFS (1997, 19).

TABLE 1.3
Dutch and Belgian Case Cities

City	Nonnational Percentage 1995 (Belgian), 1997 (Dutch)
Ghent (Flanders), Belgium	7.8
Liège (Wallonia), Belgium	18.3*
Rotterdam, The Netherlands	10.7
The Hague, The Netherlands	10.8

*The higher percentage of nonnationals in Liège reflects the greater presence of Southern Europeans in the old mining and steelmaking region of Wallonia.

Sources: VFIK (1995, 17), COS (1998b, 162).

for forward-thinking, interventionist approaches to social problems, including immigrant integration. They have traditionally provided strong, albeit not always dominant, support for mainstream left-wing political parties in local elections. That said, the cities' respective policy responses have not been close to identical or unvarying. The impact of these forceful, distinctive policies becomes apparent when their track records in tackling notably tough social and economic challenges are carefully compared and placed within the context of national developments.

As at the national level, primary and secondary materials and open-ended interviews have represented indispensable sources of information, and secondary analysis of existing data sets and survey results, where appropriate, has added more evidence. Statistics on state/regional and local social spending, while rarely truly comparable, have been taken as suggestive indicators. The research focus is on the point of interface between policymaking systems and the immigrant-origin populations. In conjunction with judicious case selection and use of the comparative method, having access to the assessments of a range of actors and institutions has made it possible to evaluate with a degree of confidence both policy outputs (direct results) and outcomes (the degree to which results can be attributed to outputs). At the local as at the national level in all three countries, the goal has been to chart the evolution of policy, the

degree to which immigrant-origin populations have participated in local social and political life and have organized on the basis of ethnicity or other collective identities, and, ultimately, the state of ethnic relations.

Presaging the Conclusions

Comparative examination demonstrates that European host societies have in
essence been getting the ethnic relations they deserve. Proceeding from institutional setups, the distinctive caring strategies of countries and cities have
tended to be either inclusionary or exclusionary, and they have placed the
emphasis either on the personal needs of an individual or on the collective
needs of particular groups. During the last quarter of the twentieth century,
progressive national and local policymakers in Germany and the Low Countries actively engaged in the struggle to balance claims to distinct ethnic and
cultural traditions with demands for equal treatment irrespective of ethnic
and cultural differences. They availed themselves of the institutions of the
welfare state, powerful tools that could instigate, keep alive, or defuse ethnic
identities and tensions. Some of the policies that authorities devised did not
work as intended. The building pressures of globalizing markets and the worrying durability of the anti-immigrant far right forced them to be very inventive very quickly.

New forms of differentiation and exclusion and new patterns of segregation usually ensued, forcing further adaptation. Whenever ethnicity was dis-
counted, the outcome was the neglect of immigrants' special needs and thus
the continuation of de facto discrimination. Whenever service delivery was
based on ethnicity, conversely, the result was the reification of culturally based
definitions of needs that aggravated the segregation and marginalization of
immigrants. Stressing structural integration did little to bring forth political-
cultural congruence, yet it possibly reduced the likelihood of ethnic conflict.
Stressing political-cultural integration, at least while explicitly championing
ethnic identities, often promoted it. Generally speaking, German and Walloon
officials, who first tried to emphasize the structural integration of individuals,
eventually found themselves compelled to take into account the political-cultural integration of ethnic groups. Their Dutch and Flemish opposite numbers
followed the reverse trajectory. This choice of sequence had implications for
immigrant integration and ethnic relations: starting with policies in the cultural and political realms that called attention to ethnic boundaries guaranteed more friction along those lines. Officials who first stressed structural integration were rarely interested in targeting ethnic groups.

As decentralization, privatization, and delegation progressed differentially
across the cases, social control fluctuated. Diversification by socioeconomic
status, gender, and generation intensified within immigrant-origin communities, as in European society at large, and they experienced even more spatial
concentration than before in Europe's cities. The restructuring of the welfare

state freed and even gave a boost to ethnic identities and mobilization. Even in Germany and Wallonia, previous policies had inadvertently built up their potential. Whether their release resulted in greater ethnic conflict or was channeled in other ways depended on policymakers' responses, locally as well as nationally. Welfare state decentralization raised municipal officials' profile and room for maneuver—even though, again, the degree varied across the cases. In Belgium, Germany, and the Netherlands, policymakers at all levels of government found themselves cornered: too much emphasis on ethnic group diversity could lead to inequality and disparate incorporation; too much emphasis on individual equality of opportunity could lead to a stultifying version of assimilationism. Officials strove, not always successfully, to shape immigrant organizations in ways corresponding to host-society expectations and to overcome cleavages arising from homeland ties and ideologies. Inadequate public resources limited the reach and scope of promising policies. Sometimes, though, financial scarcity put a stop to policies that were in reality feeding undesired developments. Conversely, even when interethnic dialogue was of a nature and level that might have been considered healthy for immigrant integration, it could spook officials fearful of paying a political price if they lost control over developments.

Still, some European policymakers did react gamely to the immigration challenge. Europe's immigrant neighborhoods have not degenerated into the ethnic battlegrounds that they resemble in too many sensational accounts given by journalists, politicians, and scholars. Multicultural synergy may not be the rule, but instances of it do exist. An absence of overt hostility, anyway, is more common than not. That said, sanguine assessments that national citizenship has ceded ground to a more universal model of membership—so much so that social and even political exclusion will soon no longer be a problem for Europe's immigrants (Jacobson 1996; Soysal 1994)—are not borne out here. Rights do not equal practice. Policies matter as much if not more, steering the evolution of capacities and alliances. They determine whether outsider groups gain a toehold in the system or remain fragile and deprived of legitimacy. The organization and administration of the institutional frameworks governing social citizenship create different opportunities for those of immigrant origin to come into contact with the welfare state. They have a major impact on these populations' collective identities and relations with each other and the host society at large.

The implications of such conclusions to Europe should be indisputable, given the centrality that both immigration and the welfare state promise to play in the continent's foreseeable future. There is no need for Europeans to resign themselves to inevitable cultural clashes, avoidable only, one would have to infer, in the unlikely event that immigrant-origin populations were completely assimilated or somehow compelled to return "home." Institutions and policies have the power to shape ethnic relations and, it follows, offer hope of

2

GERMANY

Social Policy and the Construction of Ethnic Identities

Germany, Europe's indispensable country, has occupied a central position in struggles over both social policy and immigrant-origin populations. Since World War II, the German social market economy and, by extension, German prosperity have rested heavily on both. Coming under increasing pressure, the country's welfare state has appeared to confound calls for thorough reorganization by adjusting only incrementally (Cox 2001). When it comes to immigration-related issues, Germany has been seen as closed and irredeemably fixated on blood and "the people" *(das Volk)*. It has been criticized for refusing to accept itself as an immigration country and for making "no attempt to integrate the immigrants or their families into the new environment" (Cesari 2000, 93).

The reality has proved more complicated and, in key respects, has run contrary to those verdicts. Germany's welfare state has been changing in very real ways, with critical implications for ethnic identities and conflicts. And far from failing to devise integration policies, German policymakers' social policy responses have shaped collective ethnic-based identities and kindled intermittent surges in ethnic hostility.

Germany's extended, excruciating struggle to match nation with state, combined with its history of massive emigration, bequeathed an obsession with bloodlines. At the same time, German social democracy has rested on constitutional guarantees of individual human rights, class compromise and bargaining, and the resolution of religious conflict. The combined effect has been a host society finding it easier to extend formal protections to immigrants than to embrace them as members in full. When immigrants entered into German society, they were expected to do so as (temporary) members of the working class and as individuals possessed of a set of fundamental social rights.

Social policies and social work practices endeavored to integrate immigrants only structurally, cast them as passive clients, and encouraged ethnic consciousness. Ethnicity was used to solve problems and then took on a life of its own. The German welfare state relied on a tight network of subsidized nonprofit associations, which had long adhered to an ethnic operating principle. The same was true of most efforts to give immigrants a consultative voice in political decision making. Federal officials also permitted foreign associations to organize immigrants along cleavages found in the homeland. Responsible for modulating the immigrant workers' relationship with the labor movement, the German trade unions were key players in the neocorporatist policymaking system. They were more inclined to contain ethnic energies than to channel them into broader working-class battles.

The German welfare state began to undergo significant decentralization and delegation to self-help associations by the 1980s, belying depictions of being only a pruned entity. Those developments fueled a trend toward political-cultural disconnection along ethnic lines—not a natural outgrowth of immigration, but rather an institutional by-product. When authorities lightened the weight of the welfare state's social control function and simultaneously invoked notions of self-help and empowerment, ethnic mobilization was given freer reign. It escaped its institutional corsets, aided and abetted by public policies. Anti-immigrant sentiment and activity, especially virulent in the wake of unification, profited from and aggravated the situation. Officials have since sought substitutes for their diminished social control and ways to facilitate immigrant integration without heightening ethnic tensions.

Immigrants in a "Nonimmigration Country"

It took longer for Germany to get into the labor-importing game than its European neighbors. After the Second World War, between eleven and twelve million refugees from what had once been part of the *Reich* met most of the labor demands in a rebuilding Germany. In the Federal Republic (FRG), demand soon outpaced even that supply. German officials entered into bilateral labor accords with Italy in 1955 and with Spain and Greece in 1960. Under them, "guest workers," the famous *Gastarbeiter,* came up from Southern Europe on a contractual basis. They tended to concentrate in southern federal-states like Baden-Württemberg and Bavaria, the closest and most advanced German regions.

In August 1961, the East German government closed the last hole in the Iron Curtain and with it the FRG's easy access to eastern labor. Germany's rather marginal colonial experience—considering the modest size of its empire and its short duration—hindered the FRG from relying on that source of workers (Lüsebrink 2002). Instead, officials in Bonn signed a labor recruitment agreement that October with their counterparts in Turkey. The two countries had a relationship dating back at least to the construction by Germans of Middle Eastern railroads and Berlin's alliance with the Ottoman Empire in the nineteenth century. Late in 1969, the one-millionth Turkish guest worker arrived in the Munich train station, where he was warmly greeted by the president of the Federal Labor Office, who presented him with a German television set.[1] Northern Germany had become the region in direst need of workers. By the 1990s, consequently, Turks constituted a far higher percentage of the immigrant population in (city-)states like Bremen, Berlin, and North Rhine–Westphalia than in the south.

By the end of the decade, the Turkish-origin population in Germany comprised just under one-third of the immigrant-origin total and was by far the largest national group. Around 1.4 million (out of 2.5 million in all) had been in the country longer than eight years; almost half were women, and more than half were of the second and third immigrant generations (Sommer 1999). The number of Turks in Germany had grown since the immigration stoppage of the mid-1970s, first due to family reunification and later to the immigration of marriage partners from the homeland, between 30,000 and 40,000 annually (Sen 1999).

Germany had also signed labor agreements with Morocco (1963), Portugal (1964), Tunisia (1965), and Yugoslavia (1968). The treaties with the two North African countries lay largely inactive until the 1980s. Immigration from the Maghreb into Germany has been more recent than immigration into France and the Low Countries. In January 1990, just under 100,000 Moroccans, Tunisians, and Algerians lived in Germany. The vast majority came to work, although the number of asylum seekers was climbing rapidly. Those contingents, albeit modest in absolute terms, constituted a significant share of the fast-growing Arabic-speaking population in Germany. They pointed to the ethnic diversification of Germany's immigrants, a major demographic trend of the past decade. Another trend has been toward the socioeconomic differentiation of immigrant-origin populations, even if in Germany most of them have yet to shed their blue collar. Manufacturing, especially the metals industry, and construction have been the major employers of immigrant-origin workers. Everywhere, they have occupied the least-qualified positions (Krummbacher 1998).

German Policy Evolution

Once German integration policies moved beyond an initial reactive stage, they limited themselves largely to the structural dimension: education and job training, housing, and social welfare. Immigrants could be treated like individual workers in those sectors, and Germany registered true successes in them. Ethnicity entered through the back door, however, as policies in the areas of political participation and social work were stimulating the development of ethnic identities.

Guest workers were by definition supposed to be temporary. The "rotation" principle dictated that they were to leave the FRG within a set period of time (normally two years) after their arrival and be replaced with new contract workers. This impracticable system did not last. Under pressure from employers, who bore the training costs, public officials suspended rotation in the early 1960s. Even then, the general assumption was that most of the foreigners would eventually return home. Any who did not would blend without a trace into German society, just as the "Ruhr Poles" and Italians of an earlier era had done (Murphy 1982). To ensure that nonthreatening outcome, officials put in force a dispersal policy: when the percentage of foreigners in a given district grew too high—12 percent officially made for "overburdening"—no more could settle there (Cohn-Bendit and Schmid 1993, 111).

Structural Integration

By 1974, deteriorating economic conditions compelled German authorities to halt new immigration. Economic forces had converted the guest workers into residents, and their demands on the host society had changed drastically. Settling and integrating them became the expressed goal in Bonn. Restrictions against family reunification fell. As of 1978, immigrants could apply for an unlimited residency permit *(unbefristete Aufenthaltserlaubnis)* after five years in possession of a limited one, and a permanent residency permit *(Aufenthaltsberechtigung)* eight years after that, provided they met three conditions: adequate housing, according to local standards; mandatory school attendance for their children; and "sufficient" knowledge of the German language. Those engaged in gainful employment also needed an appropriate work permit. Exceedingly complex and changeable, the system has always included numerous exceptions and provisions for immigrants from different countries.

The federal government began appointing a commissioner for foreigners in 1978 to make the general guidelines of "aliens" policy more consistent across the country and to enhance the federal government's role. The commissioners (who have all been women to date) eventually became the immigrants' lobbyists within the government.[2] Six of the eleven West German federal-states, together with a number of large cities, had introduced a commissioner before German unification. Then, in September 1979, the federal government's adviser Heinz Kühn issued a memorandum that put the spotlight squarely on the immigrant-origin population's integration into German society. Of particular concern was that of the "first and a half" (those who arrived as youngsters with their parents) and second immigrant generations, characterized ominously by the German Ministry of Labor as "social dynamite on a time fuse" (Radtke 1990, 29).

The question of who was to do the defusing turned into a source of fierce haggling between the different levels of government and political parties. Federal officials control the entry of immigrant workers, refugees, and asylum seekers into Germany. The federal-states *(Länder)* have responsibility for primary and secondary education, police, internal security, the administration of justice, and mass communication. In other areas, too, the federal-states have the last word, including issues relating to family unification and the deportation of rejected asylum seekers. The two levels of government jointly handle housing, higher education, and regional economic development, with the federal-states primarily responsible for implementation. Authorities at the federal-state level have had a margin of maneuver at their disposal that should not be overlooked. For instance, German nationality law, based since 1913 on blood ties *(jus sanguinis),* has set the bar high for immigrants intent on adopting German nationality.[3] Beyond basic requirements on lengths of residency and fees, though, it has been up to the states to determine candidates' worthiness.

The Kühn report ushered in a period when officials launched rearguard actions to boost structural indicators of immigrant integration. Thus a two-pronged strategy toward the education of guest workers' children emerged: integration into the German system (meaning German-language instruction), and, given the inevitability of their departure, preparation for reintegration into homeland schools (and thus supplementary instruction in the mother tongue). Generally, policies in states run by the Social Democratic Party (Sozialdemokratische Partei Deutschlands—SPD) shifted earlier and more insistently toward teaching German and targeting groups in order to address educational deficiencies.

Interpreted in terms of success within the German educational system, integration stayed out of reach nationwide. Students of immigrant stock (11.3 percent of all students in 1990) were overrepresented in those institutions that had gained the stigma as havens for the weaker pupils: the main schools *(Hauptschule,* 18.5 percent immigrant) and comprehensive schools *(Gesamtschulen,* 14.1 percent). The higher up one climbed on the educational ladder in Germany—the intermediate schools *(Realschulen,* 8 percent) and the college preparatory schools *(Gymnasien,* 5 percent)—the fewer immigrant-origin students one encountered. The same was true in the vocational branch (8.2 percent), as well as in Germany's otherwise top-notch apprenticeship system. More youths of immigrant backgrounds failed to complete their formal studies and receive their diplomas. Their linguistic difficulties served as an excuse to shunt a large portion of them (almost 18 percent) into "special" schools for the learning disabled (Schmalz-Jacobsen 1992, 7–10).

As the numbers of immigrant-origin pupils increased, educational officials worried about their concentration in inner-city schools. A number of states introduced segregated classes, and several imposed formal quotas for nonnational pupils. Even so, certain classrooms regularly wound up with concentrations of over 80 percent. Other states, meanwhile, introduced more positive programs, both targeted at immigrant-origin groups and general in scope, in the elementary, secondary, and vocational schools. Some of them worked better than others. Globally in Germany, however, there was steady improvement in most indicators of academic success in the 1980s and 1990s.

Education and training policies in Germany produced outcomes that were uneven yet far from catastrophic, and housing policies advanced the trend. Guest workers first lived in housing provided by employers before they and their families entered the broader market. With an enduring shortage of affordable units, that market revolved far more around apartment rentals than home ownership, and government intervention was less extensive than in countries like France and the Netherlands. Germany's social housing regime entailed government intervention in the private market. Housing allowances, subsidizing renters as well as homeowners, long suffered from serious underutilization. Of equal or greater import in the 1970s and 1980s was public financial assistance for building construction, the provision of which turned the units concerned into social housing. Federal and federal-state governments shared funding responsibility, with the latter overseeing implementation. Local governments could add to the social housing stock as they saw fit and as their budgets permitted. A needs assessment at the time of occupancy determined eligibility, and a tenant whose income rose did not have to move out. In a tight market, such laxity misallocated units, even as it kept native-stock tenants from leaving. In addition, German authorities never encouraged the construction of large housing projects like those surrounding Belgian, Dutch, and French cities. Only a few complexes appeared in industrial cities like Hamburg, Bremen, and Cologne (Osenberg 1987).

The share of immigrant minorities in the population of particular cities and neighborhoods depended on the structure and quality of their housing stock. Immigrants were left with the most dilapidated units at the lowest reaches of the private and social-housing markets, scattered across neighborhoods next to Germans with similar socioeconomic characteristics (Blanc 1991). There were few neighborhoods and individual housing blocks where the native German population completely withdrew, and the spatial dimensions of poor neighborhoods were relatively modest. Segregation levels were thus lower in Germany than in its Belgian and Dutch neighbors (Neef 1992).

Undergirding the structural position of nonnationals was the support of German trade unions. As misgivings about the influx of cheap laborers gave way to acceptance, the German Trade Union Confederation (Deutsche Gewerkschaftsbund—DGB) and in particular its largest member union, IG-Metall, displayed more dependable solidarity than most of their counterparts elsewhere in Europe (Schmitter Heisler 1983). Their loyalty sprang in no small measure from concern about undercutting their own position. Missing the opportunity to organize immigrants under its aegis could weaken the DGB's hand in neocorporatist bargaining with employers, which has stood at the heart of German social democracy. Immigrant participation in worker movements swelled as economic restructuring began to bite in the early and mid-1970s. The joint struggles cemented an alliance between immigrant-origin workers and the DGB and reduced anti-immigrant sentiment within that organization's hierarchy—if not always among the rank and file. The practical advantages of union membership were undeniable to immigrants, whose membership rates climbed to the point where they exceeded those among native-stock workers. Immigrant-origin members of workers' councils grew in number and visibility in factories across the country (Uchatius 1999).

With the trade unions leading the charge on behalf of immigrants, arguments over their presence shifted to "wars by proxy" in the social policy realm (Boos-Nünning and Schwarz 1991). In Germany, the land of jus sanguinis, the persistent legacy of ethnic nationhood made accession to formal citizenship difficult. Germany's constitutional, administrative, and judicial systems offered protection to foreigners, devising a "compensatory" strategy to make up for the difficulties of attaining full membership. The trade unions insisted that nonnational laborers receive the same social rights and benefits as "native" workers. Germany's social market economy, albeit always messier and more differentiated in practice than in many social science renderings, was firmly rooted in the inclusion of individuals through social and economic rights (Baldas, Deufel, and Schwalb 1988). Certain national groups enjoyed protections owing to bilateral treaties that the European Community (EC) signed with labor-exporting countries. Immigrants from Iberia and Greece picked up rights when their homelands joined the EC in the 1980s, and since then, European Union nationals resident in another member state have steadily approached the legal status of nationals. As for non-EU immigrant workers, the 1963 association agreement with Turkey and the 1978 cooperation agreements with the Maghreb countries of Algeria, Tunisia, and Morocco guaranteed them equal economic and social rights and equal treatment in the labor market. These arrangements helped prevent the development of "foreigner colonies" or ghettoes and encouraged structural congruence.

Social Work and Political Integration

Alongside their actions aimed at immigrants' structural integration as individuals and workers, however, German officials had accepted differentiation according to ethnic criteria. Despite widespread qualms about multiculturalism, the policy repertoire in social work and measures to effect political and cultural integration all involved ethnic categorization. This structuring contributed to the formulation and articulation of ethnic-based interests.

Germans have engaged in heated debates over multiculturalism, both at the abstract level and in their assessment of policies to contend with ethnic diversity. Activists in church circles (Gaf 1990; Geissler 1991) and on the new political Left (Gaitanides 1992; Leggewie 1991) have compiled a disjointed laundry list of multicultural demands, including voting rights for resident nonnationals, affirmative action programs, workplace recognition of religious holidays, bilingual education, and so on. Reluctantly in the beginning, the bulk of the SPD eventually adopted a more or less liberal multicultural vision in principle, accepting of ethnicity on a temporary basis.[4] The Greens, for their part, rallied to the cultural pluralist camp, adamant in their demands for ethnic groups' cultural autonomy.

German republicans lionized French nationality codes and their blending of the laws of blood and soil (Oberndörfer 1992), and the traditional left persisted in decrying as misplaced the notion that modern societies divide in the first instance according to the criterion of ethnic membership (Radtke 1990). Both factions rejected policies that endorsed ethnic identities. On that point, if no other, they were in agreement with the far right, which painted a dire picture of a multiethnic Germany, and even some politicians closer to the mainstream right.

While such disputes raged, ethnic-based strategies were developing into accepted practice by public and quasi-public institutions and actors. Liberal multicultural thinking was having an impact on concrete policies in the areas of education, social policy, and social work. In the education field, for example, some local school systems tried to create order out of daily chaos by making use of ethnic differences in preparatory and remedial classes. The same held true when they pegged students' family background and ethnocultural traits as the reason for their lack of scholastic achievement. The role of the German language turned into a major bone of contention (Bommes 1993).

German policymakers, meanwhile, oversaw a system of social welfare that actively constructed ethnic identities. Dominating social policy in Germany have been actors belonging neither to the state, narrowly defined, nor to the private sector. The state co-opted autonomous public-law associations, nonprofits that were awarded a legal preference in the fulfillment of social welfare objectives. These "free carriers" *(freien Träger)* took on the contours of a cartel at the federal level and exercised a monopoly at the local level.

Their roots lay in the confessional traditions of the Reformation and Counter-Reformation, the Catholic solidarity principle, and the struggle against Marxism during the Wilhelmine Empire. After World War I, the Evangelical Lutheran Diakonisches Werk and the Roman Catholic Caritas were joined by the SPD-created Workers Welfare (Arbeiterwohlfahrt—AWO), the independent German Paritative Welfare Confederation (Deutsche Paritätische Wohlfahrtsverband—DPWV), the Central Jewish Welfare Agency in Germany (Zentralwohlfahrtsstelle der Juden in Deutschland—ZWSJD), and the German Red Cross. After World War II, Chancellor Kondrad Adenauer, amenable to Christian churches' influence on German politics, tipped the balance to-

ward "association welfare." In 1961, just before his conservatives lost their absolute majority, they passed legislation that enabled the social welfare
nonprofits to regain their keystone role, especially the three biggest peak associations, Caritas, Diakonisches Werk, and AWO. They, the German Red Cross,
and the ZWSJD joined together in the Federal Working Committee of the Free
Welfare Agencies. Germany's Federal Administrative Court in Karlsruhe declared the subsidiarity principle to be constitutionally grounded in 1967
(Thränhardt 1983).

This "organized love of one's neighbor" suited a country characterized by
a decentralized state and a state-oriented civic society, with political parties a
major force in each (Bauer and Diessenbacher 1984). Germany rebuilt, prosperity widened, and society underwent atomization. These processes created
a sharpened demand for social services, and the nonprofit sector expanded
concomitantly with the welfare state. Its reliance on the nonprofits was heavy,
as, in turn, was those organizations' dependence on the public purse. By the
1980s, Caritas alone had more employees than Siemens, Germany's largest
private industrial employer (Groth and Müller-Gazurek 1983). The complex,
multidimensional nature of social policies defied attempts to describe them in
terms of a simplistic state-society opposition. Even specialists found it difficult
to navigate the system (Kowalski and Reiermann 1994).

The cozy world of social welfare provision came to cover immigrant-origin populations. Customized public services for them had neither the personnel nor the funding to fill all of the lacunae in general social agency offerings.
The advantages of delegating work with immigrants to the large nonprofits
were plain to federal officialdom. They performed a buffer and control function. They welcomed immigrants as a justification for further growth of the
social services sector and, in the beginning, took on their new tasks in an
unbureaucratic and voluntary manner.

When the arrangement became more formalized, it became necessary to
divvy up the immigrants. Brushing aside other possible classifications—such
as by alphabetical order, which is often the practice in German administrative
offices, or by year of immigration, socioprofessional status, gender, generation,
or policy area—federal and nonprofit officials decided to apportion immigrants according to predominant religious affiliation and, within that category,
by national background. The ethnoreligious division resembled the "Big
Three" nonprofits: Catholic, non-Catholic, non-Christian. Such a division of
labor among the largest social welfare associations was implemented without
any public discussion or legal codification. It was an outgrowth of the tradition of Catholic spiritual and social services for Italian and Polish foreign
workers that arose in the nineteenth century. The Roman Catholic Caritas
took over social work with Italians (1960), Spaniards (1961), Portuguese
(1962), and Catholic Yugoslavs (1962). In 1960, when Greek workers began to
be recruited, the welfare association of the Evangelical Lutheran Church,

Diakonisches Werk, volunteered to care for their welfare, as well as that of other Orthodox Christians (such as Serbs) and any Protestant immigrants. The secular, union-linked AWO agreed to work with immigrant workers from Turkey (1962), Tunisia (1965), and Morocco (1965). By express wish of the former Yugoslav government, AWO became "officially" responsible for its nationals' social welfare needs in Germany in 1969, although Caritas continued to handle Catholic Croats and Slovenes in practice. In fact, it set up institutions for Greeks and other immigrants that "belonged" to its colleagues. There were few links between the multiple structures that developed (Puskeppeleit 1989).

Despite official refusal to view guest workers as ethnic minorities, social welfare work nonetheless included strategies explicitly targeted toward them as such. The strong connection between ethnicity, culture, and confession reinforced a distinction that was in the process of losing much of its import in a secularizing Germany and that was not an organizing principle in the immigrants' homelands. Nor was it obvious at the time that Turks would come to represent the largest single national group in Germany. As a consequence, the financially weakest nonprofit, AWO, eventually became responsible for around half of the foreign workers from recruitment countries. The German Paritative Welfare Confederation—which in other policy areas grouped together alternative, unconventional organizations—was excluded from the arrangement (Stratman 1984).

In the 1960s, the demand was for technical counseling and job training for immigrant workers. Over time, "foreigners' work" expanded to form a complex component of family and youth policies. The Big Three nonprofits set up social counseling offices, and they linked together pastoral and syndicalist work with social work. They came to see themselves as lobbyists for immigrants and other poor people, petitioning federal-states and federal officials within the corporatist system. From the start there were discussions among the nonprofits, state agencies, trade unions, employers' organizations, churches, and local government associations. Funding came from the general federal budget, supplemented from the budgets for child and youth policies and by the states.

As pillars of the German establishment, Caritas, Diakonisches Werk, and AWO were party to the "instrumentalization of foreigners in the direction of the specific interests of the German organizational system" (Puskeppeleit and Thränhardt 1990, 168). The nonprofits established no participatory institutions for their immigrant charges and repeatedly refused to collaborate with immigrant associations. Given the large number of "customers," social work was of necessity reactive. It created a cliental relationship, a bond of dependency on social workers that was promoted by their political contacts and access to expert information. Individual casework reigned supreme. Immigrant-origin social workers lacked influence and respect. They could not apply for professional certification and thus remained completely reliant on their insecure positions with the social welfare nonprofits. As paterfamilias, each of them protected and spoke on behalf "its" deprived. Diakonisches Werk described itself explicitly as the "mouth of the dumb." The face on the other side of the coin was that of a stern, moralistic master trainer: as "helpless beings," immigrants required guidance (Puskeppeleit and Thränhardt 1990, 126).

This creation of client status gave rise to ethnic segmentation. Nationality-specific social work assumed a cultural homogeneity that ran up against very real cleavages within each national group. Watched over by German institutional gatekeepers, immigrants had little choice concerning which association they could turn to. Even a conservative Turk or Moroccan had no option but to be attended to by AWO, for example, just as agnostic or atheistic Italians, Portuguese, and Spaniards came under Caritas' wing. Immigrants represented a resource in the competition for political entrée and funding. Nonprofits won prestige and resources, yet in the process they grew dependent on the public trough and sacrificed their own autonomy. With no wish to challenge the system or underwrite broader social conflicts, they constituted a "cartel of silence" (Filsinger, Hamburger, and Neubert 1983).

German nonprofits, therefore, acted as controlling mechanisms and political breakwaters. They occupied virtually the entirety of the associational space, discouraging autonomous mobilization among immigrant-origin populations. To the Big Three the granting of autonomy to the immigrants' own associations meant endangering their own service monopoly. They habitually viewed such organizations as a barrier to successful social integration and as politically extreme—that is, Communist (see BDAG 1972). Regardless, immigrant associations increased in number and diversity as their communities became more deeply rooted in Germany. Left-wing labor movements, students, and trade unions opposed to homeland regimes were prominent in the beginning, followed by religious organizations. Much of this associational activity depended financially on homeland entities. Only in a handful of places did it receive official German support, and its legal status was unclear. Under the weight of the German institutional yoke, immigrants were being trained to structure themselves along ethnonational lines.

The same was true of policies to realize immigrants' political integration. Inured to corporatist decision making, German officials recognized the risk run by ignoring minority points of view. The Basic Law does not exclude nonnaturalized immigrants from political rights. Rather, theirs have been limited to those considered human rights—free association, expression, and petition—except when they include threats or a menace to public order or national security. German supreme court justices in Karlsruhe stood in the way of several federal-state governments' desire to extend local voting rights to resident non-EU foreigners. Hence, from the early 1970s consultative foreigners' auxiliary councils (Ausländerbeiräte) turned up in many cities and several states to facilitate immigrants' integration. Given the country's federal system, there has been variation in how these bodies have been organized, how their members have been selected, and how much latitude they have enjoyed.[5]

In the main, the mandates of these ersatz participatory structures evolved from furnishing officials with useful information about immigrants to speaking for them. A relic of earlier phases, representatives of trade unions, employers, social service agencies, the social welfare nonprofits, and other local institutions have sat on many of them—increasingly, in a nonvoting, consultative capacity. The advent of direct elections has lent more councils a broader and more immigrant makeup, but they have been no guarantee of a connection with the masses. In most places the absence of political party lists has restricted opportunities for meaningful influence. Without durable organizations standing behind council members, elected with an eye toward the policies and programs that they intend to advance, interest articulation and aggregation have rarely occurred (Hoffmann 1986).

Where they have been elected, immigrant-origin candidates have sometimes run as individuals. Far more often, the foreigners' councils have been organized along ethnonational lines in an implicit presumption of immigrants as homogeneous groups. Accordingly, the councils have created tensions between and within national groups and have impeded solidarity among them. Close German ties with official Turkish organizations and recognition of their associational emanations have stoked Turkish-Kurdish conflict (Uebel 1999). The diversification of immigrant-origin populations has made ensuring representation for smaller national groups a thornier challenge.

Since immigrants have realized they have no chance of protecting their well-being by voting in elections to fill the foreigners' councils, their participation rates, not surprisingly, have been low. They have been higher only where ethnic-based mobilization has gained salience and where ethnicity has become a resource. Frequently, in fact, council members have had to "self-ethnicize" in order to perform the functions they have been assigned. Such pigeonholing has resonated with host-society administrations, which, surprisingly, have chosen ethnicity as the way to organize the groups in question and confront the problems they are accused of posing. German officials have reacted with genuine surprise whenever council members have not divided along ethnonational lines (Puskeppeleit and Thränhardt 1990, 169). Like the schools, youth services, labor market, and legal system, the foreigners' auxiliary councils have done more to sustain than to reduce ethnic identities.

Welfare State Restructuring

Taken together, Germany's integration policies managed to produce a trend toward structural congruence, even as they lent meaning to ethnic divisions. As long as the German institutional system kept the lid on them, they were not visible. Economic crisis was threatening the status quo by the 1980s, however. Poverty was spreading and becoming linked with the presence of non-European immigrants. Cracks were showing in the system, and pent-up ethnic energies were able to assert themselves. Welfare state restructuring soon furthered those trends. Taking in decentralization, privatization, and delegation, and accompanied by notions of self-help and empowerment, the process released ethnicity from some of its institutional confines before the painful German unification brought matters to a head at the end of the 1980s.

The New Poverty

When that decade had dawned, foreign workers and their children still suffered from serious educational and training deficiencies, and they still lived in shoddier housing than their German coworkers. But all things considered, Germans patted themselves on the back for having avoided the immigration-related disconnection and conflict harrying their French and Belgian neighbors. Relatively speaking, structural indicators were inching toward congruency for the country's millions of immigrant residents.

However, the oil shocks of the mid and late 1970s had heralded an economic sea change that was throwing the postwar system into turmoil. Unemployment levels rose precipitously. The quasi-public Federal Labor Office (Bundesanstalt für Arbeit—BfA) in Nuremberg oversees German unemployment benefits. Its regional offices manage a variety of programs relating to education, training, and rehabilitation. The unemployed must register there in order to receive both types of benefits for those out of work: unemployment insurance (providing a set percentage of income, linked to previous employment and drawable for up to a year, and funded by employer and employee contributions) and unemployment assistance (providing less generous support, means-tested, and funded out of general federal tax revenues). Unlike the insurance, unemployment assistance is not limited in time, although the modest amount of support it affords frequently leaves recipients below the income poverty line (Schmitter Heisler 1992).

Nationals and some resident immigrants in that situation are eligible for social assistance. Although federal laws and policies have governed this safety net of last resort in Germany, local governments must finance and administer it. There are two types of assistance: help in special life situations (cash and in-kind aid to overcome particularly difficult situations, including illness and mental and physical disability) and help for life subsistence (cash to guarantee a minimum material existence). Subsistence is defined in connection with a basket of goods, part of the prerequisites for the life "worthy of a human being" that German social assistance law sets as the minimal social standard (Deutscher Caritasverband 1992).

By the mid-1980s, the growth in joblessness, together with cutbacks in unemployment benefits and the tightening of eligibility rules, was turning Germany into a "two-thirds" society. That share was comfortable—two-tenths floated just above the poverty line and one-tenth fell below it. The country appeared to be splitting into a prospering, high-tech South and a decaying, industrial North (Friedrichs, Häussermann, and Siebel 1986). Debates over the "new poverty" phenomenon echoed those over the urban underclass across the Atlantic (see Leibfried and Voges 1992).

Intense pressures were brought to bear on the social assistance system. Between 1973 and 1990, the number of people receiving help for life subsistence would more than triple to 2.3 million. Those receiving help in special life situations would grow by half to 1.5 million. The new poverty affected immigrant-origin populations disproportionately. Their lower incomes and shorter employment histories meant that they were less likely to receive unemployment insurance benefits, making them more dependent on social assistance. Secondary analyses of data drawn from the German Socio-Economic Panel suggested that non-German nationality increased the likelihood of going on the dole. In 1973 the share of the resident foreign population on help for life subsistence was 0.4 percent, far below that of German natives at 1.5 percent. Between then and 1990, the immigrant share rose to 12.7 percent, compared to 4.3 percent among those of German stock. A new population of the poor had materialized: families with many children and an unemployed family head, the long-term unemployed, single-person households, and those of non-German origin (Deutscher Caritasverband 1992).

Erstwhile guest workers, their families, and their dependents had access to the full array of social citizenship rights, including unemployment benefits, housing support, and social assistance.[6] German law stipulated that foreigners reliant on the latter could be deported, except those with a permanent residence permit. In practice, if non-EU immigrants drew social assistance for too long, authorities could invoke it as a reason not to renew their residency permit and thus lead eventually to their expulsion. Turks and North Africans were protected by the bilateral agreements that their homelands had signed with the EC.

Decentralization, Privatization, and Delegation

The 1980s proved wrenching for the poor, especially for immigrants, and for the German welfare state. Federal officials moved to overhaul it. Even though spending cuts drew the most attention, the impact on the organization and delivery of social services was more profound. Social-policy restructuring further weakened their social-control function, without reducing the role of ethnicity. The result was higher levels of political-cultural disconnection along ethnic lines.

In a slow struggle against entrenched interests, German governments had been chipping away at social spending for years. Rather than structural reform, the fight against unemployment in Germany proceeded first and foremost with piecemeal alterations in policies that had developed over the years by dint of a long, conflicted process of horse trading. The express aim of the reforms was not to strip welfare provisions to the bone but to scale back government social spending to a "reasonable" level. Unhappily, reductions in unemployment compensation and assistance only fueled demands for social assistance. By closing down a number of local social assistance offices, authorities generated higher demand for more costly home visits (see Olk and Otto 1989).

If such cutting could cause upset, the other side of welfare state restructuring—decentralization, privatization, and delegation—garnered widespread applause. Groups from the left to the right celebrated the transfer of new responsibilities to the local level and to the private and nonprofit sectors. In those moves supporters saw a means of allowing progressive cities to function as "counter-powers" to the central state (Social Democrats) or laboratories of grassroots democracy (the Greens), of implementing the subsidiarity principle (Christian Democrats), or of reducing federal spending (budget-conscious politicians of all stripes).

At one level the rearranging involved the introduction of market forces, pure and simple. Federal funds for socially supported housing decreased from the 1980s on, for example, while those allocated for rental allowances increased along with unemployment rates. A minor yet perceptible trend toward home ownership manifested itself. Left to the forces of the market, though, a significant segment of the immigrant-origin population was living more marginalized lives in Germany's big cities. Concentrations of poverty developed, characterized by old, substandard housing and an accumulation of social disadvantages. Coordinated social work and urban redevelopment had limited success in modulating such trends (see Cooke 1989).

Moves that lightened the load on federal coffers more often than not transferred it onto the backs of officials at other levels. Most seriously, the consequences of benefit cuts tended to fall to municipal governments in the form of heightened demand for social assistance. Because they did not have discretion over the amount of statutory entitlements, which were guaranteed by the federal-states, each German mark spent for social assistance was one not available for maintaining the streets or other local services. Municipal officials did exercise some leeway when it came to distributing one-off assistance (as with help in special life situations) and assuming rent payments, but those were far from their main expenditures.

Adding to the fragmentation aggravated by the decentralization of policy and the injection of market forces was the delegation of social policy formulation and implementation to the nonprofit sector. Given the traditional centrality of nonprofit associations in the German welfare state, what did delegation mean there? As far back as the late 1960s, people on the "new" left and the right, in the nonprofits and the budget offices, enthused over a vision of social policy that gave people more freedom of choice and a greater personal stake in their own well-being. With the big nonprofits' standard operating procedures coming under fire, the idea of substituting them with self-help organizations became a live option (von Kardoff 1989). Self-help became the stuff of dreams of grassroots democracy and responded to the allegedly demobilizing effects of the welfare state. Depending heavily on volunteer labor and monies deriving from lotteries and charitable giving, self-help also promised to deliver services more cheaply in a time of public belt-tightening (Kulbach and Wohlfahrt 1994).

The upshot was a full-blown crisis in social work circles by the early 1980s that upset the collaboration between German officialdom and the social welfare nonprofits in the area of immigrant integration. Traditionally heavy-handed methods were proving inadequate. Fewer and fewer immigrants were turning to the social welfare nonprofits for assistance, a conclusion borne out by opinion-polling data (see Ögelman 1999). Such estrangement forced the large associations to react. As early as 1980, Diakonisches Werk, its Greek client base dwindling, had preached that immigrants should be assigned to all available German social services. Quickly, the Big Three produced an array of conceptional proposals on how to modernize their social work and enhance their outreach to, among others, those of immigrant origin. They all came to the same basic conclusion: it was time to expend more energy actively defending marginalized people, which perforce would involve them in labor market, housing, and immigrant integration policies. When all was said and done, nationality-specific social services for foreigners had encouraged disconnection. Social work needed to be community action, encompassing the entire "life field" of immigrants and Germans alike.[7]

The new attitude had concrete policy implications. Immigrants would eventually gain the freedom to choose which welfare associations they could contact for assistance. Under the revamped approach the neighborhood became the spatial location where the development of new strategies and the preparation of immigrant-origin professionals took place. Pressures for problem-oriented work pushed out that organized along national-ethnic lines. Municipal and regional officials dispersed responsibility for immigrants to specific policy areas, with immigrant self-help organizations and initiative groups as frequent intermediaries. Holistic, community-based social work was seen as an "orchid" to nurture as long as there was money in the till (ISSAB 1989, 24). The old system had loosened its institutional grip, even if the nonprofits retained a position of honor within the German social welfare system.

There was in the end widespread verbal and material backing for a variety of self-help projects. These initiatives sometimes remained trapped on the edges of the system, but with all-around agreement on their value, they made inroads. Gradually, self-help developed into a sturdier pillar of German social policy. Dependence on public funding, however, did not diminish. Subsidies were available out of municipal budgets and the social security system. In addition to financial support, governments helped self-help through infrastructural support, in the guise of informational and contact centers. The relationship between self-help groups and political and administrative institutions depended on a number of contingent factors, such as the quality of communication, bureaucratic openness, strategic capacity, and the tightness of networks. To work productively with authorities, many self-help movements aped the social welfare nonprofits in forming local "umbrella" associations. In the process of joining policymaking, they thus risked becoming marked by the same top-heavy structuring. Strong associational life in Germany has always been close to the state and distinctly neocorporatist (Anheier et al. 1998). Often, when self-help made an appearance in municipal planning, it amounted to little more than a handy, self-serving label applied to a range of activities that had developed of their own accord.

When it did manage to have the emancipatory quality it was intended to, on the other hand, self-help had unintended outcomes. Authorities bestowing public subsidies had to decide which groups to assist or to stimulate, and their choices could produce competition, antagonisms, and open conflict between established social service providers and self-help groups. Immigrants' own associations came to look like the key to empowerment, important arenas within which to build social and political participation and the skills and self-confidence to fit into German society. These self-help groups were in the position to care for "their" national group. The cultural and recreational services they offered were the first to win official recognition and acceptance. Eventually, these associations started to substitute for more traditional forms of social assistance, absent a corresponding share in decision-making power. The outcome was an ungainly conglomeration of programs and projects, marked by aggravated ethnic fragmentation.

The Turkish associational spectrum, for example, ran the gamut from left-wing organizations of workers, to intellectuals, to nationalists and other right-wingers. Ideological, ethnic, and religious identities originated in the fatherland—home to some forty-seven distinct ethnic groups—and were then channeled through the German institutional matrix, which tried to "package" them into a smaller number of more manageable ethnic categories (compare Özcan 1989). The Turkish government moved to counter Kurdish separatism and, fiercely secular since the days of Atatürk, the spread of radical Islam. Anyone even calling for a dialogue between Kurds and Turkish authorities found him- or herself quickly pilloried by conservative Turkish media in Germany. The Turkish government's religious office, the Diyanet, joined consular officials in facilitating the formation of "acceptable" religious organizations across Germany. In the early 1980s, a new wave of political refugees and asylum seekers found their way from Turkey to Europe, among them party and trade union leaders of all political persuasions. German officialdom's de facto adoption of official Turkish policies toward minorities and opposition groups polarized their members and encouraged more extreme elements in them to come to the fore.

Homeland influence varied—and was allowed to vary, in line with German foreign policy commitments—across the national groups and fed organizational differences. Generally, it was difficult for immigrants to forget their status as nonnationals or their own ethnonational identity. For many, their homeland's membership in (or special relationship with) the EU put a spotlight on those divisions. Regional, religious, and ideological homeland institutions predominated within the Italian-origin community. Spaniards, for their part, rallied to defend their interests vis-à-vis the Spanish and German governments. Organizing around cleavages brought from Spain, they constructed dense networks of local associations that concentrated on cultural maintenance and mother tongue instruction. The same was true of Greeks, among whom even left-wing activists championed the so-called national schools, a position shared with conservative German officials. Smaller, newer non-European groups like the Moroccans and Tunisians rapidly forged associational networks that were tightly connected to consulates and homeland-based workers' and conservative nationalist movements.

Although those national groups mobilized most frequently at the local level, they experienced pressure to come together in broader organizations. As early as the 1970s and throughout the 1980s, German-style immigrant associational federations were forming. It was the only way to win legitimacy in the eyes of German officialdom and have a hope of exercising pressure on the German policymaking system. Less than successful attempts were made at multiethnic collaboration at the federal and federal-state levels.

In a range of policy areas linked to immigrant integration, officials latched onto ethnic-based tactics when trying to solve problems. In enforcing immigrants' social rights, the policymaking system employed ethnic markers to define who did and did not benefit from preferential treatment. The system thereby provided political entrepreneurs the perfect ethnic rallying points to fight on behalf of potential beneficiaries or losers. Also given a new war cry were far-right, nationalist political parties. For the first time since the days of the Grand Coalition between the Social and Christian Democrats twenty years before, right-wing extremists were showing up on the country's political radar screens. In the latter half of the 1980s, the Republicans and the German People's Union were making a breakthrough. In Bremen in 1987 and then in Baden-Württemberg, Bavaria, Berlin, Hamburg, Hesse, and Schleswig-Holstein, small, extreme-right parties flirted with and occasionally exceeded the 5 percent threshold necessary to win representation.

Unification

Then the arduous process of unification fanned the flames and forced alterations in social policymaking that, in turn, kindled more ethnic strife. Poverty had already taken on an ethnic cast, and the welfare states' control function had already started to slip when the two Germanys came together after forty years apart in 1989–1990. Ethnic conflict quickly grew into a major challenge. The years following the fall of the wall saw an upsurge in anti-immigrant violence and legislation that tightened up asylum laws and made it easier to deport unwanted foreigners. Policy decisions during the rush to unite Germany conspired to bring ethnicity even more to the fore and lent it decidedly negative connotations.

The federal government sought to limit immigration after unification. It pushed through a new law on aliens in 1990, which both stressed the principle of equal rights for immigrants and their free access to the welfare state and refined rules governing family reunification and settlement. Subsequent legal modifications in the early 1990s also facilitated naturalization, especially for immigrant-origin youths. Dual nationality was impossible in most instances, however, and adults not born in the country still had to wait fifteen years before applying for formal citizenship.

With its extremely liberal asylum law, an atonement for Nazi crimes, the "old" FRG was Europe's top recipient of would-be political refugees by a wide margin, processing more than three-quarters of the continental total. Anti-refugee sentiment escalated to dangerous levels with the new, postunification influx from the east. To lower tensions and to connect Germany's two parts, the federal government required all of the states old and new, to welcome a share of asylum seekers corresponding to the relative population of each. Thus roughly 20 percent of applicants were allotted to eastern Germany.

The policy was disastrous. Socially and institutionally, eastern Germany was unprepared for the tidal wave of problems that crashed down on it. The new federal-states had never had to deal with such a population.[8] Municipal governments faced the sudden and difficult challenge of developing social offices of a hitherto unknown type, finding and training appropriate personnel to staff them, administering policies completely new to them, and explaining the new benefits to dazed citizens. In addition to the asylum seekers, eastern Germany received one-fifth of the hundreds of thousands of "ethnic" Germans from what was once the Soviet bloc *(Aussiedler* and *Spätaussiedler)* who flowed into the country in the early 1990s. Thanks to the Basic Law (Article 116) and a 1953 law on refugees and expellees, those of German ancestry and those having lived in German territory within its 1937 borders could lay claim to the status of "statutory Germans." They were thus entitled to immigrate to the FRG, automatically receiving German nationality (while maintaining their former nationality) and significant cash and in-kind assistance. Jewish migrants from the former Soviet Union, moreover, usually entered Germany along its eastern frontier, further stretching the limits of local institutions (Bade 1994).

Immediately upon their arrival, asylum seekers in the east headed to five regionalized Central Processing Areas (*Zentrale Anlaufstellen*—ZAST), where they underwent initial processing before being sent out to communities. The fallout from such policies became glaringly apparent in the Lichtenhagen neighborhood on the outskirts of Rostock. Over a six-night period in August 1992, right-wing extremist youths clashed with riot police and attacked the overcrowded ZAST for the new federal-state of Mecklenburg-Vorpommern.

Key aspects of East German institutional life had evaporated virtually overnight. Unemployment, of course, was the most conspicuous sign of the former German Democratic Republic's problematical merger with the FRG. Police forces also fell to a tenth of their previous strength in many places and crime rose. Just as seriously, the social infrastructure, especially that for young people, crumbled when generous East German state subsidies disappeared. Security was gone. The strain on the western German institutions charged with absorbing the east became visible as well.

Hate crimes spread, targeting immigrants, homosexuals, Jews, and the disabled. The majority of these attacks, which had been occurring regularly since the early 1980s, took place in what had been West Germany. Assaults by skinheads on an Italian in Saarlouis and on two sub-Saharan Africans in Saarbrücken in autumn 1991 were just the most publicized of the many incidents there. A firebomb killed three Turkish workers in the western city of Mölln, near Hamburg, in November 1992. The next year, there was an even more murderous attack in Solingen. Clashes between Turks and Kurds gained in frequency and intensity in many western cities. In the former German Democratic Republic, where the increase in violence was more spectacular, the most unloved foreigners were the Turks, hardly any of whom lived there (Ireland 1997). Ethnic profiling was proving context dependent.

Germany's response was to tighten its asylum law in July 1993. After months of heated discussions, the major political parties reached an agreement to drop the guarantee of an individual vetting of asylum requests. Group identities won further value from the new focus on national origin. Applications from people arriving in Germany from other EU member states or "safe third countries" could be rejected without a court hearing. A simplified procedure was to deal with asylum requests from countries deemed "free of persecution." The federal government stripped the access to special status from central European ethnic Germans, since it determined that they came from countries where persecution could not exist. That same law set an annual ethnic German quota of 220,000, which in any case was never met after 1995. After they peaked at nearly 400,000 in 1990, the yearly numbers declined steadily to just more than 100,000. Benefits had gradually shrunk (Zuwanderungskommission 2001).

The ethnic tensions of the unification period, therefore, strengthened the forces unleashed by earlier changes in the prevailing institutional setup. Under attack, literally in some cases, immigrants fell back on—and were being assigned to—the ethnic identities that social policies and social work had culti-vated. Their structural position situation was affected, negatively for the most part, by policy decisions in the years following. A minority of immigrant-ori-gin residents managed to attain socioeconomic mobility and fit themselves into German social and political institutions. The bulk of them nursed their ethnic identities as political-cultural disconnection grew.

Immigrant Structural Integration

Immigrants' position in the labor and housing markets and the educational and vocational systems made few gains in the wake of unification. Almost 22 percent of immigrants in the old federal-states were unemployed in the mid-1990s, three times the native German rate (Norman 1998). From 1988 to 1993, the rate of immigrants drawing social assistance mushroomed to 184 out of every 1,000 immigrants, compared to only 62 out of every 1,000 Germans (Kanther 1996). Squeezed by ballooning deficits, federal officials continued to put the brakes on social spending.

A key factor in avoiding residential segregation, social housing was another victim of the times. Once the typical thirty-five-year mortgage was paid off on units that had received construction assistance, they were free to go onto the private market. As so much of socially supported housing was built between the late 1950s and early 1960s, a huge reduction in the supply of such units began to hit in the early 1990s. The postunification housing shortage and the government's withdrawal from the housing market had the potential of revers-ing the integrative accomplishments of past policies.

The rise and decline of the so-called secondary labor market also illus-trated the wrenching effects of the public sector's retreat. Federal labor legis-lation provided local authorities with the funds to place the unemployed in temporary positions through Work Creation Mechanisms (Arbeitsbeschaff-ungsmassnahmen—ABM) designed for those who risked long-term unem-ployment.[9] Under the make-work scheme, the local government would locate work, and the BfA would pay the wages. The majority of the jobs created were with municipal or other public or quasi-public organizations like social wel-fare agencies, foundations, and neighborhood associations. Organizations across the country became dangerously dependent on those positions. Their high price tag became a major sticking point in negotiations over the Solidar-ity Pact—the federal aid package for the east—in 1993. Financially strapped, the Bonn government decided to downsize the program. Mass demonstrations in spring 1993 did not force a reintroduction of the heavy subsidies, although a truncated version endured.

German unification created a trial and distraction for the social welfare nonprofits, too. Rebuilding the east siphoned off many of their resources and much of their attention. Caritas, Diakonisches Werk, AWO, the DPWV, and the Red Cross rushed in to replace the shattered East German welfare structure.

The unification treaty extended the subsidiarity principle to the new federal-states. After five years, the nonprofits had put some ten thousand institutions in place. The newfound responsibilities safeguarded the associations' position as the hub of the German welfare state, even as they stretched their resources and diverted them from immigrant-related concerns. Chafing against the paternalism of the two confessional nonprofits, several immigrant associations took advantage of the diversion and "defected" from them to align with the DPWV, which had emerged as a prime institutional buttress for immigrant self-help groups. Meanwhile, charges built that AWO had come under the domination of elements close to the Ankara government to such a degree that Kurdish, Islamist, pan-Turkish, and other "minority" activists could not profitably utilize it (Ögelman 1999).

Immigrant Political-Cultural Integration

These developments paralleled a drift away from congruence in the political and cultural realms. Thanks to the structuring of the German political and legal systems, autonomous immigrant interest articulation had become most likely in associations bringing together people of the same ethnonational background. Although modulated and filtered by the German institutional setup, policies and institutions in the immigrants' homelands also mattered and similarly fortified ethnic identities. The Turkish government's relaxation of bans on non-Turkish languages and minority associations, echoed by greater liberalism from its counterparts in North Africa, spurred identity politics among ethnic and religious subcultures (Faist 1998).

That said, entrenched German policymaking circles did not usually incorporate newer, less organized interests like those of immigrant-origin groups. Interactions between the social welfare nonprofits and local immigrant leaders in many places did not go beyond irregular, noninstitutionalized contacts. The BfA for a while even excluded immigrant associations from those eligible for ABM positions in the field of social work. Immigrants responded by retreating into ethnic shells, pulling back from the German institutional system. They directed themselves more to their own support systems and less to the services offered by Caritas, Diakonisches Werk, and AWO. In 1985 more than a quarter of Turks and a fifth of Italians had turned to them when they had personal problems. Ten years later, the shares had plummeted to 4.5 percent and 2.6 percent (Ögelman 1999). Also commonly taken as an indicator of disengagement was the sharp increase in homeland newspaper, radio, and television consumption among all immigrant-origin populations, even European ones. Since their use of German media was not declining inversely, the implications of that development were open to interpretation (Uebel 1999).

Less debatable was that the popularity of self-help and empowerment fueled pressures to differentiate. In the cities and neighborhoods where Germany's newly decentralized, privatized, and delegated social policies were deployed, their dissipating impact was evident. Internecine rivalry and tussles between immigrant associations and traditional welfare providers erupted as services were progressively converted to short-term project funding. The competition pitted ethnically and nonethnically organized projects against each other.

There were few indications of a connection between immigrant associational activity and a "ghettoized" existence. In fact, such involvement often correlated with stronger social networks and more effective problem-solving skills (Santel 2002). Immigrant associations, however, did follow a decidedly ethnic logic that ran counter to most German hopes: for example, only 11 percent of immigrant associations in North Rhine–Westphalia crossed national lines in 1999 (MASSKS 1999). By the 1990s, many of the immigrant associational federations were still operational, but they were weak and unstable. Largely the preserve of first-generation elites, formal organizations attracted the active participation of a small and declining minority of immigrants.

Such associations were failing to reach immigrant workers' children. They turned toward groups of similar ages and ethnic backgrounds as the forces of structural integration in Germany's urban centers languished. Disillusioned immigrant-origin youths shunned organizations and institutions that used to link their communities to German society and turned inward for protection. "When people realize that their efforts on behalf of this society no longer count," the federal commissioner for foreigners remarked, "then they quite naturally retreat back into their cocoons" (Schmalz-Jacobsen 1995, 28). Immigrant associations, dominated by the immigrant-worker generation, were failing to incorporate succeeding ones.

This phenomenon affected Turks and North Africans above all. Analysis of Marplan Institute surveys measuring immigrants' concerns and fears confirmed young non-Europeans' growing isolation. Among Turks this "self-ghettoization" generated support for the far-left Dev Sol movement, the nationalist Gray Wolves, and the Islamist Milli Görüs organization, among others outside the mainstream. Nationalism among groups that were minorities in Turkey, in particular the Alevites and Kurds, led to attacks against Turkish institutions on German soil.[10] Ethnic-based political parties sprang up, such as the Democratic Party of Germany, founded in 1995 by young Germans of Turkish extraction with ties to the government in Ankara. In cities across the country, other immigrant-origin young people were singing in rock bands of their predicament, caught between Germany and their parents' homeland. These "Kanak-Kids" contributed to a cultural flowering reminiscent of the Beur movement in France. Their unofficial spokesman, Feridun Zaimoglu, became known as the "Malcolm X of Germany's Turks" (see Zaimoglu 1995). Thomas Schwarz has drawn on a range of scholarly studies in laying out the potential for conflict among such immigrant-origin youths (Schwarz 1992).

The German institutional setup retained enough structuring power to hinder a true social movement or widespread rioting, but German authorities did not have the tools to fashion the sort of peak associations among Turkish, North African, and other minority populations with which they were used to dealing. They were stymied above all by Muslims' refusal to coalesce and adhere to an "appropriate" organizational configuration. The German system's back-door strengthening of ethnic and national identities fed rivalries with their roots in the Islamic world. Combined with the sheer diversity of thought among Muslims, they prevented the emergence of any organization capable of representing the entire faith.

German officials wanted just such an organization. The church-state relationship in the country is a matter for both the federal and federal-state governments. They must be neutral and equal in their treatment of all faiths, but the federal government pays officials of recognized faiths, subsidizes the upkeep and restoration of church buildings, and collects taxes in the name of each religious community that it then channels back to it. The system necessitates a representative council for each religion affected. Roman Catholicism, Protestantism, Orthodoxy, and Judaism have all won recognition as corporate bodies. Partly due to their own actions, German officials were less able to find or create an equivalent for Islam, compared to their Dutch and Belgian neighbors.

Muslims were simply too fragmented for concerted sociopolitical action. National communities reflected German labor recruitment agreements and refugee and asylum policies. Of the 2.7 million Muslims in Germany in 1995, three-quarters were Turks. But there were also almost 82,000 Moroccans, more than 26,000 Tunisians, and sizable numbers of Muslims from Afghanistan, Algeria, Bosnia Herzegovina, Iran, Iraq, Jordan, Lebanon, Pakistan, and Turkistan, not to mention the various minorities within Turkey. There were likewise some 100,000 German converts to Islam (Sen 1998).

Compounding national divisions was a secular-religious cleavage. Many Islamists opposed to the secular system in Turkey came to Germany in the 1970s and became influential. Their groups established Islamic cultural centers in Münster and Cologne in the early 1970s. An estimated 100,000 Turkish children had attended the Quranic courses offered by various religious groups by decade's end. Another religious group, represented by the (eventually banned) Islamist Welfare Party in Turkey, founded a national organization in Cologne in 1977 by pulling together some 250 local organizations with more than 25,000 members. The Turkish state's Diyanet responded in the early 1980s by establishing a union of religious establishments that followed Ankara's official secularist line. Although a latecomer, it quickly attracted over 60 percent of the mosque associations in Germany. Other such umbrella associations formed as well for radical and moderate Islamists, nationalists, Alevites, Muslim Kurds, students, and mystical sects. Multinational federations existed, but they were weak. Mosques serving the population of North African origin fell almost entirely under control of homeland governments, who watched anxiously as Algeria slid into civil war.

Radical Islam eventually replaced Kurdish terrorism as immigration's biggest perceived danger to Germany. Fears of Islamic parallel societies appeared misplaced (compare Heitmeyer, Schröder, and Müller 1997). The networks of Islamist cells that developed across the country never involved more than a miniscule minority of Germany's Muslims.[11] The German center-right nevertheless evinced a visceral rejection of radical Islam, and on the left, concern about human and especially women's rights under Islam was voiced. Authorities in Baden-Württemberg required an Afghan-origin teacher to remove her *hijab*—a headscarf worn by some Muslim women—in the classroom, deeming it both a "political symbol" and a "symbol of cultural isolation" (Sommer 1998). (The Federal Administrative Court would reverse the federal-state's decision late in 2003.) Many women from Turkey and North Africa had never worn a *hijab* in the homeland and were taken aback when Germans took their lack of one as evidence of the "progress" that resulted from living in a "modern" society (Kirbach 1999).

In the absence of a clear federal policy on mosques, the extent to which the religious practices of Muslims figured in urban planning depended on federal-state and city officials. Muslims maintained complicated, context-specific links with ethnic-specific and German associational networks. This was true even of associations linked to mosques, which found it impossible to offer educational and social welfare services to the Muslim population in isolation from other institutions. In the neighborhoods it was prosaic issues like the call to prayer, gender relations, and the ritual slaughtering of animals that caused the most conflict between Muslims and their fellow residents. Surveys suggested that religiosity was higher among older Muslims. Fewer younger people described themselves as religious, but among those who did, connections were stronger with more extreme forms of Islam (Sen 2002).

Muslim parents requested Islamic religious instruction for their children from the beginning of their settlement in Germany. North Rhine–Westphalia was the first to introduce such programs. They took place in the context of mother tongue instruction under the auspices of German school officials, who had responsibility for the curriculum. Bavaria, Hesse, Lower Saxony, and Rhineland-Palatinate adopted similar models. Teaching materials came straight from Turkey and were adapted by school authorities and Islamic associations. Hopes of introducing instruction in Arabic ran aground on Turkish complaints. In the late 1990s, officials in North Rhine–Westphalia determined that the diversification of that state's Muslim population dictated that such Islamic classes take place in German. Unresolved was the issue of where to find sufficient numbers of qualified, German-speaking teachers (Bukta 2000). A second model had teachers selected, paid, and sent for five-year tours

by the Turkish Ministry of Education and Diyanet. This approach was followed in Berlin, Bremen, Hamburg, Schleswig-Holstein, and Baden-
Württemberg. Participation, again, was voluntary and the instruction in
Turkish (Sen 1998). Everywhere, the training was not to indoctrinate but to
transmit knowledge about religious traditions, and it drew its legal basis from
an explicit provision in the Basic Law.

The effects of ethnic structuring, visible in the integration of the second
and subsequent immigrant generations and Muslims, continued to affect the
relationship between the German political system and immigrant-origin
populations overall. It was never clear which representatives, if any, could truly
speak on their behalf. The preeminent analyst of the foreigners' auxiliary
councils, Lutz Hoffmann, has argued that some of them became "little more
than a venue through which established homeland-oriented organizations"
could pursue their own "particularized goals" (Hoffmann 1997, 11). In a number of cities by the 1990s, Turks were occupying a disproportionate number of
seats on foreigners' auxiliary councils, increasingly dismissed as "Turkish
councils." Islamic lists soon came to outpoll the traditionally dominant left-
leaning ones among Turks and North Africans across Germany. At the same
time, turnout in elections to the councils was anemic. Opinion polls conducted among immigrant-origin populations suggested that few respondents,
regardless of national origin, were positively predisposed toward the bodies.
Only just over a third of Turks and just under a third of Italians in Germany
were even aware of their existence (Ögelman 1999).

The immigrant-origin population was also pulling back from other forms
of sociopolitical participation in Germany. Most notably, the share of union
members fell between 1980 and 1995 among Turkish men (from 58 percent to
31 percent) and Italian men (from 44 percent to 25 percent). Meanwhile, 26
percent of Turks were members of a homeland association or club, compared
to 14 percent who had joined a German one. For Italians, the national group
that should have been the best integrated, the corresponding figures were 22.2
percent in a German organization and 21.5 percent in an Italian one (Ögelman
1999).

As for expressed sympathy for German political parties, support among
residents of immigrant origin was strongest for the SPD and, to a lesser degree,
the Greens; many conservative Turks backed the Christian Democratic Party
(Christdemokratische Union—CDU). Only the CDU's Bavarian partner, the
Christian Social Union (Christlich Soziale Union—CSU), has snubbed
nonnational members, and all of the other major German parties set up
caucuslike organizations to link those of immigrant origin with native-stock
German members (ZfT 1994). Regardless, only 5.8 percent of Turks and 2.6
percent of Italians belonged to a political party of any kind in 1995; and for
82.6 percent of the former and 41.1 percent of the latter, that party was a

homeland movement. A Marplan Institute survey in 1999 indicated that only a barely measurable 0.4 percent of Turks, Spaniards, Italians, former Yugoslavs, and Greeks resident in western Germany belonged to a German political party (Santel 2002).

While the SPD and the CDU have each received support within immigrant-origin populations, neither has made more than timid moves to integrate those of non-European origin into their structures. They have made it easy for the Greens to don the mantle of inclusion in this respect. Already in 1987, a woman of Turkish extraction from Kreuzberg became the first such minority to enter a federal-state parliament—on the Alternative List. A decade later, immigrant-origin Green deputies were sitting in the parliaments of Berlin, Hamburg, North Rhine–Westphalia, and Hesse. The Greens' freestanding caucus for young people of immigrant origin, Immigrün, accounted for 10 percent of the party's federal parliamentary representation by 1999 (Seidel-Pielen 1999). All told, however, the ranks of elected immigrant-origin officials were thin, even for those with roots in Southern Europe. German institutions exercised a powerful social control function that shaped collective identities among those with or without a German passport and kept the latter contingent in a subordinate position within the German system. The relaxing of some of that control encouraged ethnic-based participation, of a type not always welcomed by host-society policymakers.

With its social insurance and assistance system Germany had crafted a security net for all, including nonnationals, which had contributed in an important way to social harmony. Hand in hand with other policies, the social welfare state suppressed conflicts and provided ballast for German society. Cutting it back and orienting it toward a more market-oriented strategy may well have saved employers money and heartened budgeteers. But those gains were purchased at the cost of weakening its social and political stabilizing functions. Social policy became fragmented and dispersed over a wide variety of public, semipublic, and private providers, and there was even less transparency than before. The policy shake-up impaired governments' ability to steer developments. The encouragement of self-help, aimed at unlocking groups' independent organizational potential, loosened the ties that bound them to the public sector and its management.

In a postunification context of rising crime rates, that weakened capacity came to epitomize a more serious loss of social control. Media reports and right-wing politicians associated "immigrant" with "delinquency." A blizzard of studies purported either to prove or to disprove that equation. The data were contradictory in many respects; yet while the number of Germans accused of crimes seemed to be holding steady, that of nonnationals rose dramatically. With controls in place on socioeconomic background, demographic structure, and types of crime, the figures narrowed dramatically. Traditional guest worker groups," said Ernst-Heinrich Ahlf, acting head of the Federal Crime Office, "are often even less prone to commit crimes than Germans" (quoted in Klonovsky 1994, 73).

Two groups were responsible for a majority of crimes committed by nonnationals: organized bands of foreign criminals operating in the FRG and immigrant youths whose integration into the host society had failed. Concerning the latter, immigrant-dominated youth gangs had sprung up in Germany in the first half of the 1980s. By the time unification occurred, they had multiplied and diversified. Roaming the streets of downtrodden urban neighborhoods, their members took part in robberies, murders, shakedowns, and angry confrontations with *Aussiedler* gangs, anti-immigrant skinheads, and the police. It was not just the tabloid press that began to speak ominously of the "Los Angeles syndrome" (Leggewie and Senocak 1993).

The vicious attacks against immigrants and refugees that rocked Germany in the years following unification galvanized youths of non-European origin. Within Germany's Turkish-origin community, the fight against racism lent unity, and talk of a "Turkish minority" was heard for the first time (Kastoryano 1996). The growing immigrant assertiveness could occasionally turn violent, as after the 1993 firebombing in Solingen. Groups of young people of Turkish background, joined by German supporters, rampaged through the streets for several nights, breaking shop windows and smashing parked cars.

Because it had taken a relatively long time for ethnic conflict to manifest itself in Germany, due to the effectiveness of structural integration policies and social control, policymakers were caught flat-footed. Some of them echoed former New York City Mayor Rudolph Giuliani in proclaiming "zero tolerance" for crime. Others campaigned for community policing and educational and recreational projects. Missing from most talk about security were the fears of the immigrant-origin population itself in the face of violence and crime.

The FRG anchored a general ban against racial discrimination in its legal system but not, as in many other countries, as a right, plain and simple. Following the same logic that prompted help for self-help, officials attributed anti-immigrant sentiment in part to the weak response of civil society. Popular outrage at acts of hatred built, and after every high-profile incident, hundreds of thousands of Germans took to the streets carrying anti-hate banners and candles. Broader, steady involvement was slower in coming. Public relations campaigns to raise popular awareness and to encourage bystanders to intervene became a cornerstone of the policy response in many federal-states and cities.

The Policy Response

Socioeconomic changes were producing a marginalized population, a segment of whose members grew more heavily dependent on the publicly maintained social infrastructure. The incomplete integration of immigrants, their ethnic and class diversification, the housing shortage, and the proliferation of the unemployed and those on social assistance were overwhelming the problem-solving capacity of the public and nonprofit sectors. Rising ethnic tensions, along with indications that immigrant-origin residents might be retreating into their ethnic shells, provoked a shift away from ethnic-specific tactics and toward problem-specific ones. The latter were organized by sector or administrative department, which worked against a unified battle against poverty more typical of France and Belgian Wallonia.

Social policy restructuring had meant different ways of conceptualizing service delivery. The demand for finely tuned, contextually appropriate social work escalated. The new goal was to diversify services and agents within the social welfare system, so as to match better the needs of a diverse population. In an era of tight funding, the only way to reassert social control was to marshal forces through network building at the street level. These measures encompassed formal and informal service providers and built bridges to self-help movements. Existing networks among friends and neighbors, voluntary associations, churches, schools and parents' committees, businesses, and meeting places created by the immigrants themselves afforded essential support and stability. At other times, though, networks could prevent mobility. Immigrant-origin youths, for example, could find themselves in counterproductive company, reacting in rebellion and crime. Ethnic identity could ossify into ethnic isolation if connections to the rest of society were absent.

The role of so-called ethnic businesses was uncertain. There were already 150,000 "foreign entrepreneurs" in Germany by the mid-1990s. They generated more than 200,000 jobs, almost a third filled by German nationals, and 41 billion marks in revenue in 1997. To cite just one noteworthy example, some 720 million Döner pita sandwiches were being consumed annually in Germany at immigrant-run restaurants, representing more spending than the McDonald's, Burger King, and Wienerwald chains combined (Özoguz 1999). For some commentators this entrepreneurial boom represented a sign of immigrants' advancing integration. The Center for Turkish Studies polled 1,600 Turkish enterprises and found that fully 81 percent of them met the formal requirements to train apprentices, although only 10 percent were doing so (Sen 1999). Pessimists, on the contrary, pointed to the limited opportunities and discrimination in the German labor market that compelled those of immigrant origin to strike out on their own.

Policies and institutions mold networks, meaning that the decentralization and delegation of the welfare state had an impact on immigrant communities' resources in this regard—on their "ethnic capital," in other words (see Borjas 1999). The official objective in Germany was to accentuate the steadying aspects of immigrant networks, fitting them into local and national German ones. Inclusiveness, it was hoped, could prevent the substitution of particularistic (that is, ethnic) resources for universal ones. Whether network building actually managed to compensate for lost social control depended on the success of the intercultural opening in social services. German policymakers borrowed the principle from the Netherlands, along with their techniques (regularly, in turn, borrowed from the United States and the United Kingdom) in the areas of education, professional training, and conflict resolution (see Schröter 1997).

One way to harness the energies inherent in ethnic identities was by adding to the ranks of immigrant-origin personnel in public services. Those tailored for immigrants were too often second class in terms of staff qualifications and skills. Much was made of their separate but unequal status, with some critics even speaking of "social work apartheid" (Gaitanides 1998, 59). More minorities had to be hired, German officials broadly concluded, and German-stock workers had to undergo specialized training. That task fell largely under the purview of subnational policymakers. In some federal-states and cities, there was an uptick in the number of immigrant-origin social workers, educators, and legal and nurses' aides. Yet in others, as well as overall in Germany, the results disappointed.

Open to nonnationals were the minority of public-sector positions that did not come under the civil servants' statute. Given their pivotal function in assuring social control, police forces were of central concern. Only German nationals can perform high-level administrative functions, make arrests, and search cars and houses, even if federal-states can make exceptions if they identify an urgent administrative necessity. In the mid-1990s, only 100 out of 230,000 people employed by police departments in Germany were foreigners (Stein 1998). Hoping to remedy that situation and anticipating participants' eventual naturalization, Baden-Württemberg, Bremen, Schleswig-Holstein, and Bavaria decided to admit immigrant-origin youths into midlevel civil service training programs in the mid-1990s.

By the end of the decade, Germany presented a very mixed picture. The creativity, goodwill, and determination to build a multiethnic society that characterized some localities were absent in others. Policy variation across Germany had only widened under welfare state restructuring.

Nor did far-right parties present a unified picture of strength. They did not pose a significant political threat to their mainstream counterparts nationally, but they did gain between 8 and 10 percent of the vote in elections in Baden-Württemberg as the 1990s drew to a close. From the mid-1980s on, their average vote shares in Bavaria, Berlin, Bremen, Hamburg, and Schleswig-Holstein had surpassed the national average of around 3 percent and occasionally came close to clearing the 5 percent hurdle to win representation. Elsewhere, they fared miserably, as in North Rhine–Westphalia, where they failed to win even 1 percent of the vote in 1998. That same year, the German People's Union garnered nearly 13 percent in state elections in Saxony-Anhalt (Karapin 1998).

While indicators of structural integration displayed equally significant regional and local divergences, the overall trend line did not always encourage optimism. Dr. Faruk Sen, director of Essen's Center for Turkish Studies, pointed out that 14 percent of Germany's Turks had purchased their home by the late 1990s, evidence of their intention to stay in Germany. Housing segregation remained less intense than elsewhere in continental Europe, where levels were highest in Belgium, followed by the Netherlands (see Musterd and Ostendorf 1998). Over the decade in Germany, however, levels of residential concentration and segregation of immigrant-origin populations had grown, markedly for Turks and North Africans. According to the EU, the unemployment gap between immigrants and Germans had widened from 0.7 percent in 1979 to 8.5 percent in 1998. General knowledge of the German language had not improved. Immigrant-origin students continued to be severely underrepresented at the higher levels of the educational system. They even received part of the blame for the country's poor ranking in 2001 by the Program for International Student Assessment. The newest immigrants suffered from higher rates of poverty than native-stock populations, and longer-term immigrants exhibited rates that were not much better (Hanesch 2001).

That said, Germany was undergoing potentially substantial positive changes. Naturalization had become easier for the children of guest workers in 1990, 1993, and 1994. After passionate political wrangling, the new SPD-led federal governing coalition managed to update German nationality laws. Latching onto a longstanding proposal from the liberal Free Democrats, the SPD cut a compromise that allowed the children of immigrants to hold both German and their parents' nationality at age sixteen, when one parent had lived in the country for at least eight years and had obtained a "stable" residency permit (unlimited or permanent). They had to decide on one nationality by age twenty-three. Eligible young people had to have lived for at least eight years in the country and to have attended German schools for at least six years. Dual status would be tolerated only when it was impossible to renounce the nationality of the homeland. Residency requirements were shortened, and the entire procedure was streamlined. Although the associated fees actually went up, the acquisition of German nationality was no longer blocked to an applicant who had received unemployment or social assistance (Münz and Ulrich 1999). While such reforms may seem paltry compared to developments in the Netherlands and Belgium, access to nationality in Germany was now flowing from a territorial principle and not simply from the veins.

Formal citizenship laws have been only part of the story. At least as important has been their implementation. A number of decisions regarding immigration and naturalization were up to local and state officials, which explained why naturalization rates fluctuated according to federal-state, city, and national background (normally being higher for Europeans). Nonnationals convicted of a crime were prevented from entertaining any possibility of obtaining a German passport. The new legislation yielded higher naturalization rates, but they ran behind governmental expectations.

By 1999, more than two-thirds of Germany's immigrants had lived in the country for more than ten years and 15 percent for more than twenty years. Many former guest workers were becoming grandparents. Every ninth baby born in Germany was Afro-German, Turko-German, or Polish-German, although use of those hyphenated labels could provoke angst. "Just as in America, it is identity that will be fought over, no longer a second or third passport," one journalist warned (A. Böhm 1999, 13). His prediction was borne out in spring 2002. After a prolonged period of political bickering and controversy, a new immigration law passed whose express intention was to authorize firms in the information technologies, construction, and health care industries to call on skilled immigrant labor when desired. It also marked the first time that German legislation recognized that the country had become a land of immigration. The 2002 law was thrown out by the supreme court in Karlsruhe that December on procedural grounds.

German policymakers' growing acceptance of a permanent immigrant-origin presence still contrasted with their discomfort with the ethnic identities that their policies had helped to create, however unintentionally. By the turn of the century, some public figures were openly fretting over "ongoing ghettoization, rising criminality, and burgeoning fundamentalism" (Margolina 1998). Concerns were raised over gender and class relations within immigrant-origin communities, the anti-Semitic rantings found in many Turkish- and Arabic-language publications, and the sometimes violent internecine divisions that rent immigrant-origin populations. Sporadic eruptions of anti-immigrant activity marred Germany's all-important international image and hurt business interests.

There was general agreement that there had not been enough emphasis on the duties that accompanied the rights accruing to permanent residents in Germany. Cultural identity, even in a multicultural society, had its limits: everyone had to respect universal human rights as developed by and within European civilization. If ethnic identities could promote integration over the long haul, as some scholars contended, they could only do so if a clear transition to the labor market and eventual political incorporation were possible and if guarantees of equal treatment were in place. It followed, then, that instead of a separate system to intervene on immigrants' behalf, the need was for concepts that took them into consideration, dealing with them separately at first, perhaps, but then integrating them into a more global social planning vision. It was less a matter of opposing targeted and general measures than of ensuring that the former permitted efficient access to the latter. Rather than true liberal neutrality, the vision was thus closer to a liberal multicultural one. People from other countries and cultures could retain their cultural identity if they wished. They had to respect fundamental principles like the equality of men and women and the freedom of expression, though, as well as master the German language.

Popular arguments have stressed the mobilizing effects that racism, welfare chauvinism, and in-born ethnic proclivities had on immigrant-origin populations. Changes in the organization and implementation of social policies would seem to have had a stronger impact in Germany. This finding jibes with interpretations that have attributed renewed minority political action in the United States to attacks against social programs in the 1980s and 1990s and in Australia to moves away from ethnic-based welfare delivery, both of which allegedly provoked a reversal of earlier co-optation (Erie 1987; Jupp and Kabala 1993). Similarly, the German welfare state's restructuring had major consequences for Germany's minority populations. Their self-appointed leaders obtained logistical, financial, and moral support from officials to take charge of "their" communities.

Self-help contributed to political-cultural disconnection and to conflict. What emerged were groups and movements that reflected the opportunities and confines of the political and institutional context. Nationality-based restrictions and a stringent naturalization regime conspired to keep those of immigrant origin out of public-sector employment. Such exclusion curbed their political incorporation and prevented the erection of an American-style ethnoracial management "regime" (compare Reed 1995). Changes in that direction, coming after decades of demobilizing nonprofit tutelage, generated friction and intergroup and interethnic discord. Immigrant influence and political incorporation remained limited. Subsequently, officials strove to bring about congruence with policies that blended self-help with social control. They aimed to encourage and harness the energies of immigrant-origin groups and other elements in civil society while preserving social harmony—and, critics charged, the primacy of German culture.

To verify the causal impact of policies and welfare state restructuring, it is imperative to move to local analysis. With social policy shifting down to that level, already significant subnational variation in Germany grew more pronounced. Cities offer opportunities to appraise the relative force of institutional, ethnic, and other factors. Beyond such theoretical concerns, immigration scholarship should not neglect to consider just how diverse working-class families have interacted in the neighborhoods in which they live and struggle side by side. It is to those issues that the following chapter turns.

3   # GERMAN CITIES AND
CITY-STATES
Facing Diversity in Diverse Ways

The decentralization, privatization, and delegation of German social policy detailed in the preceding chapter rooted immigrant integration processes in the country's urban neighborhoods. There, residents of native and immigrant backgrounds lived and built a multicultural reality on a daily basis (see Zaptçioglu 1998). Noisy immigrant-origin children playing in an apartment building courtyard, a discotheque's refusal to allow admittance to those children's older brothers and sisters, automobile insurance companies' discrimination against nonnationals, reservations about Muslim burial practices and religious celebrations—such sticking points were at the center of the integration challenge.

Local governments operated in a context of external constraints and limited resources. They were legally bound to implement federal and *Land* policies and had to operate within the ethnically defined naturalization regime. Integration depended in no small measure on economic and labor market conditions over which city officials had limited control. Within the corsets of national and state laws, funding cuts, and market forces, however, local officials did have some room for policy maneuver, and it only widened with welfare state restructuring. The question is how they exploited that margin and with what impact on immigrant integration and ethnic relations. In a country frequently accused of requiring immigrants to assimilate (liberal nationalism), local responses ranged from general policies to fight poverty and marginalization (liberal neutrality), to provisional policies targeting immigrants and specific ethnic groups (liberal multiculturalism), and even to policies that ensconced immigrant-origin cultures in the public realm (cultural pluralism).

After examining the position of local governments in the German policy-making system, this chapter will compare approaches to immigrant integration in four large cities. Under the microscope here, Berlin, Bremen, Essen, and Nuremberg gained fame for their policy activism with respect to immigrant-origin populations. Their experiences after World War II—and more specifically, after the oil shocks of the 1970s—were not identical, and their policy responses had disparate effects on ethnic identity formation and conflict. Not only do those four cases allow for comparative analysis of the impact of welfare state restructuring on cities exhibiting key similarities in their immigration history and ethnic makeup. They also make it possible to test the limits of local action.

The Local Burden

The tasks of administering many German laws and policies have been divided between federal, state, and local institutions. The federal-states define the execution of most social policies, overseeing their administrative framework, but they provide only a few social services directly—in prisons, state-owned medical and psychiatric hospitals, and similar institutions. Outside of the military, the federal role has been limited to research, planning, coordination, funding, and setting the legal parameters for social services. All told, local governments implement some 80 percent of all state and federal policies.[1] In their own right municipalities are in charge of schools and other educational facilities (but not education policy, a federal-state responsibility), urban planning and zoning, fire protection, streets, sanitation, tax collection, health care, and some aspects of housing policy. Their discretionary responsibilities include the maintenance of cultural institutions and recreational services. Critically, city social offices administer and finance the social assistance program. Municipal governments are explicitly charged in Article 28 of the Basic Law with managing the affairs of the local community, which includes the living conditions of their "resident population"—not "nationals." Local-level social policy has been expected to buy off challenges to the system, while taking necessary care to keep costs from undermining it (Breckner and Schmals 1989). Always easier said than done, that task grew nearly unworkable when cities became the sites most wracked by the crisis that hit Germany's vertically organized society.

Local-level immigrant integration policies originally amounted to subsidizing the activities of the social welfare nonprofits, with the federal and federal-state governments bearing a significant share of the expenses. It was the 1970s before the immigrant-origin population became more settled, more family oriented, and more visible in local housing markets and school systems. German cities experienced relatively modest levels of segregation, owing in part to federal regulations covering the labor and housing markets, the social security system, and other aspects of the country's overlapping federal structure. When those federal policies were altered, market forces were less restricted and fed a trend toward greater differentiation. Social and economic ills began to accumulate in certain regions, cities, and neighborhoods.

Long-term unemployment shunted the challenges brought by postindustrialization from federal authorities onto municipal ones. There was a statistically significant, strengthening relationship between high unemployment and high social assistance rates at the local level. The major component of communal social policy, social assistance accounted for sharp spikes in local government expenditures and interlevel political infighting. Cities formerly dominated by heavy industry, such as Essen and Nuremberg, were the most affected, as was the maritime two-city-state of Bremen. The city-state of Berlin, heavily subsidized by Bonn, had higher rates of social assistance along with lower rates of unemployment. To varying degrees, German federal-states ensured income to municipal governments through systems of revenue sharing. Only to a limited degree could municipalities raise their own funds (Jaedicke et al. 1991).

German cities were caught between fiscal shortfalls and increased social demands. Federal policymakers were devolving authority downward and adjusting their funding for social services just as demand for them was spiraling upward. New federalism, German style, widened disparities in benefits and social coverage.[2] Local officials had to explore previously underutilized opportunities to reduce the social assistance rolls and were compelled to cut services and infrastructural maintenance. Unavoidably, the fiscal squeeze affected the nonprofits' immigrant counseling networks. On average, they had one staff member for every three thousand potential clients, but the ratio swelled to one for every ten thousand for AWO in many localities (Hinz-Rommel 1998, 37).

Describing the 1980s as a "lost decade" for immigrant integration (Bade 1993, 446) neglects the initiatives taken in a range of German cities. For reasons of economic and social stability, it dawned on many German municipalities that they needed to utilize the abilities of their immigrant-origin residents. The costs of nonintegration, both material (tax revenues, social security contributions, police budgets) and nonmaterial (social order), were all too apparent (Loeffelholz and Thränhardt 1996). Whether ethnic relations degenerated largely depended on the inventiveness, dedication, and cohesiveness of local-level policymakers. Alongside their rapport with the social welfare nonprofits, those factors differed from city to city. To assess them and their impact on immigrant integration in Germany's urban centers, it is imperative to examine local-level policies. The federal level guaranteed that they initially lay stress on immigrants' structural position in the labor and housing markets and in the educational and vocational training systems. Eventually, the "foreigners problem" engulfed the cultural and political realms, too. The rest of this chapter compares the integration policy responses in Essen, Nuremberg, Bremen, and Berlin.

Essen: Liberal Neutrality along the Ruhr

While transforming itself from a center of heavy industry into an administrative hub, Essen was truer than the other case cities to the traditional tenets of German social democracy and to liberal neutrality in immigrant integration. Liberal multiculturalism was long confined to the educational sphere. The social welfare nonprofits retained their privileged role in immigrant integration, dropping only under duress their emphasis on immigrants' national background and loosening their grip enough to allow for some self-help mobilization. Such lukewarm support made for relatively weak, fragmented immigrant associations. Their frailty, in turn, hampered city officials' concerted attempts to turn the foreigners' auxiliary council into the prime venue for immigrant political integration and participation.

A Progressive Record

Essen's modern history began when in 1811 it became home to Krupp Works and, with it, immigrant labor from Poland. Supplying the Reich with tanks, artillery, cruisers, and U-boats, the gigantic Krupp complex employed a labor force of 277,000 by 1944, among them more than 55,000 forced foreign workers (Schneider 1991). After the war, factories and workers flowed into Essen from the Soviet-occupied eastern zone. The city's location in the middle of the Ruhr Valley (Ruhrgebiet), the regional railroad and canal networks, and the pool of highly skilled workers attracted small- and medium-sized manufacturers of consumer goods yet only modest numbers of immigrant workers.

Long a force in local politics, the SPD achieved a majority in municipal elections in 1956 and eight years later won that status for good—through the 1990s, at any rate. Local trade unions followed a similar trajectory: growth up through the 1970s and slow erosion by the 1980s. The left's power center was in northern Essen, where many immigrant-origin residents lived. The city's reputation for according them "liberal treatment" was a source of pride for civic leaders (Meys and Sen 1986, 7). The Ruhrgebiet was one of the few German areas in which melting-pot notions became current. Anti-immigrant themes never figured prominently in political party discourse in North Rhine–Westphalia's politics. The Catholic and Lutheran churches set the moral tone, in sync with and not in opposition to the Social Democratic, working-class culture so characteristic of the region (Thränhardt 1994).

Crisis and Response

That tolerant track record, not to mention the SPD's own staying power, received a severe test during the industrial restructuring of the 1970s and 1980s.

Rationalization and factory closings forced enormous job losses, affecting firms of all sizes. Unemployment translated into less tax revenue and more spending on social assistance. Cases increased between 1980 and 1995 by 86.4 percent among the native-stock German population (AESSW 1997b, 69). Immigrant workers were hit even harder, especially Turks, Portuguese, and smaller non-European groups like the Moroccans. By the end of 1981, 13.8 percent of immigrants were unemployed in Essen, compared to 8.1 percent of German workers, and the gap was widening. From a 1976 baseline of 100, youth unemployment among those of non-German nationality had reached the mark of 1,006 by 1982. The number of immigrants drawing social assistance would shoot up a stunning 3,374.9 percent between 1980 and 1995. That upsurge would leave almost a quarter of them on the dole, far higher than the 5.5 percent rate among native-stock Germans (MAGS/LDVS 1982, 138; AESSW 1997a, 83).

In the middle of the "largest crisis-ridden industrial conglomeration in Europe," Essen had to adapt or die (Neef 1992, 211). To slow the rise in social costs, it cut services for marginal groups. Saving became the order of the day, and at one point the city even looked into selling its grave sites (Gutenberger 1993). It established technology parks and refurbished industrial land, expanded leisure and cultural facilities, and developed new owner-occupied housing estates. At the same time, it economized on administrative expenses through cutbacks in city workers, fee increases, and the closure of "nonessential" public facilities.

By the early 1990s, Essen stood among the most important service and administrative centers in the Federal Republic (Kosok 1991). One testament to the city's successful conversion was a smaller immigrant-origin population than in neighboring cities like Cologne and Duisburg: in 1982 immigrants made up 5.9 percent of Essen's population, compared to a statewide average of 8.5 percent (Stadt Essen 1984a, 108). Two-thirds of the resident nonnationals had originally come as guest workers from countries with which Germany had signed labor importation agreements. Well over a quarter were Turks, followed by Yugoslavs. By the mid-1980s, family members were reuniting with their immigrant relatives in Essen, and refugees from such countries as Sri Lanka, Afghanistan, and Bosnia joined them. By 1995 some four thousand Lebanese, many of them Kurds, called Essen home, making them the third-largest immigrant group. The number of Moroccans had actually fallen over the preceding decade due to factory layoffs (AESSW 1997a, 4).

Immigrants' Structural Integration

In the early 1980s, the local government undertook a thorough study of Essen's immigrant-origin population. By 1984 it had set out its goals and strategies in an "action program" for structural and political-cultural integration, even while acknowledging its limited jurisdiction over many aspects of the agenda

(Stadt Essen 1984a, 1984b). The city's major concern was that immigrants and their families, although modest in number, were concentrated in particular neighborhoods. In fact, 83 percent of all immigrants lived in the densely populated northern core of Essen and the neighborhoods just north and west of it, near the larger factories. Some areas were home primarily to one national group, while others had a more multiethnic cast. The local SPD, nervous about such residential clustering, vowed to take advantage of its positive effects in terms of solidarity and ethnic capital (SPD-Ratsfraktion Essen 1986).

As elsewhere in Germany, one could not speak in Essen of an immigrant underclass or ghetto formation, but immigrant-origin residents did belong to those segments of the society that suffered most from socioeconomic disadvantage. Their housing units had fewer rooms and less square footage and were older and more poorly outfitted. This situation represented a barrier to successful structural integration, since adequate housing was a prerequisite for obtaining a permanent residency permit and bringing family members into Germany (KRG 1983). City officials had the municipal housing authority buy and fix up dilapidated housing, try to spread out immigrant families across neighborhoods, intercede with owners of large apartment buildings, and make infrastructural improvements.

When all was said and done, the municipality could do little to counteract the economic and social forces that were pushing immigrants into particular areas of the city. If anything, by diverting funds into economic development, it almost certainly fed them. While there was some centrifugal movement away from the core, the bulk of immigrants stayed in the same central and near-northwest areas: Katernberg, Westviertel, Stadtkern, Vogelheim, and Nordviertel were all among the top five concentration neighborhoods in 1983 (all over 12 percent) and would still be in 1995 (all over 17 percent). In some housing blocks there were concentrations of up to 80 percent (AESSW 1997a, 6).

With immigrant-origin families supplanting single immigrant workers, the overall immigrant economic participation rate fell and began to dovetail with that of the German-stock population. Most immigrants in Essen worked as mechanics and in cleaning services, hotels, and restaurants, and in construction, textiles, and other heavy industry. Generally speaking, Turks and North Africans were most heavily present in the latter three sectors. Even those immigrants with vocational training worked in lower-paying and lower-status jobs (MAGS/LDVS 1992). Still, there was growth in the ranks of the self-employed. There were around five hundred immigrants in that category in 1983, including seventy professionals, and around nine hundred by 1987. No hard figures were available for years after then, but the upward trend was unmistakable, one that local officials hoped would produce the middle class on which they pinned their hopes for integration (AESSW 1997a, 49–50).

Essen officials were careful always to highlight the fiscal and other economic contributions made by the immigrant-origin population, arguing that its incorporation into the labor market passed before all else: without it integration policy would be "little else but a charade" (Stadt Essen 1984a, 51). The underlying logic was decidedly social democratic, centered on individual rights and working-class identity. That bias did not stop the municipality from embracing the work of the big nonprofit social welfare organizations, which, of course, cultivated ethnoreligious identities. Up through the early 1980s, it had been largely up to Caritas, Diakonisches Werk, and, above all, the social democratic AWO to deal with immigrants. City hall had seen no need to set up independent social services for them.

Alongside more functionally organized municipal, federal-state, and federal services, the nonprofits were one-stop shops. By the 1980s, they were overwhelmed. Their casework approach was having trouble with the more complex problems and populations confronting them. Over half of staff time was being taken up by translation tasks, and the rest with "putting out fires" (Stadt Essen 1984b, 114). Social workers involved with non-Europeans found their caseloads mounting once again (see table 3.1). Compelled to shift some of its attention to the Arabic-speaking Muslims arriving in greater numbers, AWO reduced the number of counseling hours it offered to the Turkish-origin population.

The city government cut back its own funding in the 1980s, including that expended on ethnic German newcomers, and battled with the federal-state over how to pay for refugee services. Yet in the end, Essen reconfigured its social policies instead of dismantling them. Over the medium term, introducing multilingual staff members while slightly reducing employment levels globally seemed the only financially feasible way to handle the situation. In 1992 the link between social welfare nonprofits and immigrants of specific national backgrounds was lifted in practice.[3]

The nonprofits began to anchor their work in the city's poorer neighborhoods, attaching their offices to a specific piece of urban turf and assigning their workers to handle the entire immigrant-origin population there. The concept of culturally attuned, neighborhood-oriented social work had been a target of experimentation in Essen since the end of the 1970s. A pilot project was launched in the early 1980s in Katernberg and Beisen, neighborhoods with a high concentration of non-EC residents. The initiatives that resulted included block parties, casino nights, football clubs, oral history projects,

TABLE 3.1

Number of Immigrants per Social Worker in Essen

Nationality	1972	1982	1992
Turks	6,979	3,763	4,923
Italians	4,967	2,944	2,721

Sources: MAGS/LDVS (1982, 140), MAGS/LDVS (1992, 122).

antiracist public relations campaigns, new playgrounds, and mobile counseling centers (ISSAB 1989).

The Katernberg-Beisen experiment was taken as a lesson for Essen. Project assessments concluded that coordinated efforts and neighborhood solidarity could substitute for "dangerous" ethnic identities without adding to costs. Even though no exact means were available to evaluate program performance, official Essen claimed that life in the two targeted neighborhoods had improved markedly. Networks had begun to stitch together. On the other hand, the absolute number of those involved remained modest. Discussing issues had often initially heightened tensions. City hall was of critical importance: institutional actions kept more spontaneous ones from drying up when energies ebbed. It took time to build trust, organizers learned, making it imperative for initiatives to produce concrete betterment in neighborhood life (Hauptamt Essen 1992).

Integration was conceived in the 1980s as a step-by-step, participatory process by which Germans and immigrants learned to coexist peacefully, rendering their different, heterogeneous cultural norms, values, and "living-together styles" compatible. Not surprisingly, policies geared toward the education, professional training, and recreational activities of immigrant-origin youngsters became a priority. They followed the same logic as social policies and social work in general. The large nonprofits, the Christian ones above all, played a critical role. An oddity in Essen was that confessional schools accounted for a relatively large share (fully a third) of all such institutions locally. Churches and their affiliated nonprofits provided 79 percent of the spaces in Essen's kindergartens for immigrant-origin children in the early 1980s. Those organizations were likewise heavily implicated in primary and secondary education, job training, continuing education, and extracurricular offerings (Stadt Essen 1984b, 223–41).

Confessional schools held little appeal for Muslim parents. The social welfare nonprofits' heavy involvement encouraged a "segregated" school landscape that left a number of public schools in central Essen with very high concentrations of non-European pupils. In response, the city, the Big Three nonprofits, and immigrant associations began to combine their forces, and they bore fruit: in most areas with a high concentration of immigrant-origin children, spots in kindergartens were at a premium; but availability was brought to levels significantly above average in certain targeted areas, such as Essen's northwest. By contrast, the city's largely immigrant-free southwest faced chronic shortages (AESSW 1997a, 102–7).

North Rhine–Westphalia considered the successful completion of required education both essential for the integration of immigrant-origin children and useful in the event of their "return" migration. In Essen SPD officials supported preparatory and remedial classes for Turkish- and Arabic-speaking students, specialized counseling, instruction in the immigrants' mother tongues, strategies to stimulate immigrant parental involvement, the hiring of immigrant-origin teachers and mentors, and what in the United States would be called head-start classes. Given the "diktat of empty coffers," creativity was required (SPD-Ratsfraktion Essen 1986).

Criminality was not associated specifically with immigrant origin. Although more likely to be male and less well off, conditions that typically correlated with criminal involvement, arrested immigrant youths had a lower conviction rate than their native-German counterparts. Both cohorts were guilty of the same types of generally minor offenses. Rates were rising among youths of all national backgrounds, but Essen registered fewer violent crimes than other large German cities (Stadt Essen 1984b, 15).

The city was calm, yet fear of ethnic conflict was ever present. Essen officials had started to mouth a self-help philosophy in the early 1980s. They were not truly converted to it until later that decade and then with a clear eye toward integrating self-help projects into more traditional social work. To tap into but also channel self-help potential, the city instigated the Information Center for Self-Help Groups, Initiatives, and Projects in 1992, with support from the Krupp Foundation and the BfA. "This culture of active self-help and self-initiative is a good thing," said Lord Mayor Annette Jäger (SPD), sounding supportive but less than passionate (Werkstatt 1993, 1). She and the rest of Essen officialdom were more enthusiastic when such developments occurred safely implanted within more familiar networks. With the weight of social policy shifted to the neighborhoods, it was possible to "embed empowerment" where the people affected by marginalization lived their lives and where the nonprofits and other institutions could maintain control.

Immigrants' Political-Cultural Integration

A similar desire drove Essen's policies in the area of political-cultural integration.[4] At first, this dimension took a backseat to general structural integration policies geared toward all working-class residents. As self-help mobilization grew, however, so did the city's desire to keep it from threatening the prevailing social democratic system. As in social work, Essen channeled its immigrant-origin residents' political energies into institutions that kept their ethnic and national identities within tight confines.

The city government would have liked to add immigrants to the working-class electorate that kept the SPD in power. Blocked by federal institutions from doing so, it actively encouraged them to apply for German citizenship. Traditionally, the largest number of the applicants for German nationality in Essen came from Poland, Romania, and former Yugoslavia, and most were foreigners of German stock. The number of naturalizations would grow from 276 in 1985 to 2,412 in 1996—fully 1,170 of them Turks. The city acknowledged, however, that "naturalization does not protect one against discrimination or eliminate the need to ensure ethnic minorities in the city some form of interest representation" (AESSW 1997a, 185).

Essen had taken the lead in Germany in involving immigrants in politics. Instituted in 1975, borough councils—covering several neighborhoods—held question-and-answer sessions in which they responded to written queries submitted by any resident. In certain instances comments were allowed at municipal council committee meetings, and nonnationals were free to speak. Like many cities, Essen held an annual "Week of the Foreign Co-Citizen," featuring political speeches, food, and folk dancing.

The fulcrum of immigrant political involvement in Essen was the foreigners' auxiliary council (Ausländerbeirat), one of Germany's oldest, which took the form of a commission attached to the city council. First meeting in 1975, the council's membership included both immigrants and Germans appointed by the city council on the recommendation of German organizations active in the field—namely, the social welfare nonprofits and the trade unions. Spurred by the local SPD, the city enlarged the council in 1982, codifying a requirement to consult it in certain instances, determining that immigrant associations would henceforth appoint its non-German members, and instituting training programs in parliamentary procedure. Step by step, the foreigners' council grew more representative. Even so, a tight connection was made between its immigrant members and their national background. Each national group was allotted a number of seats in accordance with its share of the immigrant population.

From its initial focus on children, the foreigners' council gradually took in the whole range of difficulties confronted by Essen's foreign-born inhabitants. It successfully lobbied the local government to draw up a mandate laying out its rights and responsibilities. Information dissemination and counseling became first-order tasks of the council. It produced video magazines, newsletters, a yearly report on the state of the immigrant-origin population, and occasional publications on other issues of importance. From a separate line in the municipal budget, it distributed funds to immigrant associations (thirty thousand deutsche marks annually in the early 1980s), giving them official recognition through the "back door."

Essen's foreigners' council and its opinions were, by all accounts, taken seriously (Hoffmann 1986). It became part of the normal course of Essen politics to consult the council whenever an issue arose affecting immigrants. After much debate, the council was allowed to appoint so-called resident experts to important municipal committees. City hall welcomed what it saw as a tried-and-true interlocutor with its immigrant-origin residents. Close relationships had formed "not just because they sat together at meetings so often," the Lord Mayor argued in the mid-1980s, but because they were "sailing the same swells" (Meys 1986, 111). He opposed direct election of council members, which he feared would spell defeat for the Social Democratic Turks who were critical to his vision of a cross-ethnic progressive social movement. A few years later, though, his office bowed to pressure from the council for precisely such direct voting. The first election took place in 1987, the same year that the council came under the aegis of a newly constituted agency that oversaw social work with the immigrant-origin population. By 1992 each national group was guaranteed at least one seat on the foreigners' council. That year, eight Germans named by associations joined sixteen victorious nonnationals. The left-leaning Union of Essen Turks received almost half (44.3 percent) of the votes, followed by the DGB trade union (31.6 percent) and the Social Democrats (12.6 percent). Only the provision for "overhang mandates" ensured members for the Moroccans, Yugoslavs, and Portuguese.

Turnout in 1992 failed to reach even 21 percent. The council's reach was limited by its tight links to the local government. Lukewarm participation notwithstanding, the council's profile rose as issues facing local officialdom became more complex and finances tighter. Despite the budgetary constraints, members even began to receive an honorarium in recognition of their value to the municipal council. The maintenance of the language and culture of the homelands remained a focus. The council always requested the hiring of more translators and personnel familiar with each of the homelands. It compelled a neighborhood swimming pool to hold a women's-only day for Muslims, protested against ethnic discrimination by discos, and worked with Radio Essen to expand ethnic-specific programming. In certain instances it seemed to be calling for separate but equal treatment.

The Difficult 1990s

Essen witnessed ethnic conflict in the 1990s, but city hall's control held. There were several raucous demonstrations by Kurds, who accused the city and the foreigners' council of only ministering to Turkish interests. A peaceful festival against racism drew more than twenty thousand participants. There was little violence or anti-immigrant activity, however, which Essen's police chief attributed to the intense contacts his office had developed with the immigrant communities—above all local Turkish Social Democrats ("Polizeichef" 1993). Almost 80 percent of immigrants had the security of a permanent residency permit by 1995 (ASE 1996).

At least in key pockets, Essen had developed a strong multicultural civil society. German residents in the Beisen neighborhood organized a night watch over their "Turkish neighbors." More than forty institutions in the Altenessen neighborhood issued a multilingual brochure denouncing the attacks against immigrant-origin communities. In the Katernberg neighborhood residents collected money to run hundreds of ads in the local press voicing solidarity (Kassner 1993).

Essen's educational establishment had made real progress as well. The share of both immigrant- and German-stock students attending either a comprehensive or top-level secondary school had been raised higher than the state average. Higher numbers of immigrant children were successfully completing their education, even as officials admitted that they were not doing as well as their German peers. The city attributed the positive outcomes to close collaboration between local schools and the federal-state and to programs offered by the University of Essen, to which the city contributed 175,000 deutsche marks annually. Overall, the educational level in Essen was higher than in other cities in North Rhine–Westphalia (AESSW 1997a, 147–57).

Nevertheless, problem areas did remain. Overall, four times as many immigrant-origin students as German students left without secondary school certification. Lebanese students suffered the biggest disadvantages: almost half attended special schools for those with learning disabilities—but Turkish and Moroccan students were also twice as likely as their German peers to do so. When Essen school officials mentioned "problematic" immigrant groups by name, they were the ethnic Germans, Turks, and Arabic speakers (RAA/BIA 2001, 47). Immigrant-origin youths were far less likely to participate in events and programs at local youth centers, where fights occasionally broke out between them and their native-stock cronies. Evidence of positive trends could not mask the disparities that persisted or indications that ethnic "cocooning" was taking place (LAGA 2001, 33).

In the housing area municipal policies had brought improvements. Yet in the late 1990s, with neighborhood concentration proceeding apace, over a third of immigrants' units were classified as poorly equipped, compared to less than a tenth of Germans'. Immigrant property ownership also lagged. Local officials insisted that such splits correlated more with social disadvantage than ethnic background. While indicators for German-stock residents were superior on all counts, they, too, had their weaker elements. Local policymakers decided that even the best-intentioned targeted policies, those finely tailored to individual and personal needs included, ran into the constraints imposed by the stagnating labor market. Building on the changes already under way in social work, city officials inserted immigrant-oriented structural policies into broader ones that tackled blighted neighborhoods and unemployment (AESSW 1997b, 16).

On the political-cultural front, meanwhile, Essen stayed the course. The foreigners' auxiliary council retained its ethnic organizing principle and its role as the main instrument of integration along this dimension. In 1994, a new state ordinance governing municipalities made an elected foreigners' council compulsory for cities with more than five thousand inhabitants. That legislation disallowed Essen's "minority protection quota" for smaller national groups, requiring universal, open elections by secret ballot. Only immigrants, naturalized or not, could represent immigrants; any native-stock German members had to be nonvoting. Elections in 1995 and 1999 produced more diverse foreigners' councils in Essen. The latter year, the council gained its first immigrant president, a naturalized Lebanese, and included three women. Tensions and rivalries between the different lists were growing more pronounced, however. Council relations also cooled with the city government, controlled after 1995 by a traditionalist wing of the SPD that viewed immigrants primarily as components of the working class. The party had only 250 immigrant members (out of a total of 9,000), more than its competitors but not enough to exert any real force internally. The granting of local suffrage to EU immigrants, a quarter of Essen's nonnational population, further reduced the council's import. The relative euphoria of its early days gave way to indifference, suggested by a precipitous decline in participation rates: 20.7 percent in 1987, 19.6 percent in 1992, 20 percent in 1995, and a paltry 9.8 percent in 1999 (AESSW 1997a, 182–90).

Local ethnic relations were calm. Nevertheless, immigrants did appear to be retreating into their own fragmented associations, of which there were seventy-seven in Essen in 1995 representing some twenty-one countries of origin, including Turkey, naturally, and Morocco. Many immigrant-origin youths were "no longer finding their identity in German social life" but rather in their own groupings; some young Muslims, in "fundamentalist-oriented mosque associations," the city fretted. "We need to say clearly that this gives a push toward disintegration" (AESSW 1997b, 7). Qualms over disconnection combined with Social Democratic reservations about ethnic identities to curb official support for independent immigrant mobilization. Empowerment and self-help did not make the inroads in Essen that they did in social worker circles elsewhere.[5]

The Essen-based Center for Turkish Studies took the lead on several projects designed to encourage self-help among small businesses and in the housing area. The city government and the local AWO never got behind such initiatives with enthusiasm. Officials acknowledged the importance of immigrant self-help movements for cultural identity yet also saw in them a force for disintegration. Only the better-integrated individuals and groups worked with the foreigners' auxiliary council and received the funding that it doled out and the public "make-work" (ABM) positions in the city. Nonnationals were highly underrepresented in public services and in the nonprofit social welfare associations.

Essen had around twenty-four thousand Muslims in 1995. At most, 15 percent of them were active in local associations, among whose number figured eighteen mosque associations. A third of them were linked to the Diyanet in Cologne, close to the Turkish government, and several to Milli Görüs and the Turkish brotherhoods. Others served Alevites, Lebanese Kurds and Shiites, Bosnians, Muslim students, Moroccans, and Afghanis. Virtually the entire panoply of theologies was present in Essen. The city had a number of "courtyard" mosques, not even marked with a sign on the street. "Real" mosques, with minarets and domes, occasionally provoked complaints from neighbors. One Diyanet-backed mosque in the Katernberg neighborhood was firebombed in 1995, but that was a unique event (AESSW 1997b).

The municipality's clout kept Essen reasonably quiet. It did not stimulate enriching, spontaneous mobilization, however. When it adopted the concepts of networking and empowerment, it was in ways that incorporated them into the existing system so as to buttress and not alter it. There was a new emphasis on service coordination, responsiveness, flexibility, and the systematizing of "best practices." The federal-state, for its part, eventually adopted Essen's policy approach as an example that it encouraged other cities to emulate. Local officials took to stressing the importance of successfully integrated immigrants as a factor in making the city an attractive, cosmopolitan place for foreign direct investment and trade fairs (Stadt Essen 1999).

Political Change

The maintenance of Social Democratic control led the municipality to disregard needs not fitting within the traditional SPD vision. The resultant frustrations were not limited to immigrants: in September 1999, the SPD ceded control over Essen city hall to the CDU, losing both its city council majority and the city's first directly elected mayoral race. Local newspaper reports attributed the debacle to the arrogance and complacency of power. The SPD remained the strongest force in its traditional strongholds in the immigrant-rich near-north and northwestern core neighborhoods. But there, voter turnout had plummeted, ending in the lowest rate of participation in an Essen election since World War II, less than 50 percent. The ex-Communist Democratic Socialist Party and the far-right Republicans had both won a pair of seats.

Leaders of the new CDU-led governing coalition, collaborating with the SPD and Greens, took that modest accomplishment seriously. In his introductory speech the new Lord Mayor, Wolfgang Reiniger, spoke of the need for more citizen participation, self-initiative, and accountability. Invoking the celebrated "Essen consensus" and quoting both philosopher Michael Walzer (1997) and the head of the local Islamic Turkish cultural association, he stressed the importance of the city's legacy of tolerance: "With respect for and consciousness of each other, we can build peaceful coexistence and mutual trust by working together" (Reiniger 1999). The city soon introduced a new Intercultural Concept, which endorsed inventive programs in conflict resolution and education. Integration did not mean "one-way adaptation but an exchange and the development of new commonalities" (RAA/BIA 2001, 1, 47).

Ever worried about losing their hold over the ethnic mobilization that they themselves had encouraged, municipal officials coaxed into existence a would-be local umbrella immigrant association in 2000. The Essen Federation of Immigrant Associations brought together more than thirty member groups, most of them national and ethnic in their orientation. The city and the federation signed a cooperation agreement in 2002. Thereafter, all municipal funds in support of immigrant associational activities were to flow through the federation. The head of the foreigners' council, Muhammet Balaban, addressed the municipal council that year and congratulated the city for doubling the amount of money spent on work with immigrants—for lifelong learning, university research, and language instruction—in the face of a large budget deficit. The implementation of the new Intercultural Concept was nonetheless financed in part by reducing subsidies for security and administrative costs at two local homeless shelters (RAA/BIA 2002). In Essen the more things changed, the more they stayed the same.

Nuremberg: Embracing Multiculturalism

Unlike Essen, Nuremberg lies in a federal-state, Bavaria, that has not been known for its openness to immigrants. Also, whereas Essen's SPD retained its traditional outlook even while overseeing the city's transformation into a white-collar center, Nuremberg's Social Democrats warmed to liberal multiculturalism, self-help, and empowerment, even though their city stayed a blue-collar bastion. They eventually recoiled from the collective identities that their policies built up. Like their counterparts in the Ruhr Valley, they saw their longstanding political dominance evaporate before the 1990s drew to a close.

A Progressive Record

Nuremberg, home to Albrecht Dürer and other luminaries in the Middle Ages, was the site of mass Nazi rallies and the birthplace of anti-Semitic legislation in the 1930s. The city paid dearly for its associations with Adolf Hitler's regime: the "Metropolis of Franconia" was a major target of Allied bomber raids. Of course, its manufacturing base also made it a target. In the early twentieth century, Nuremberg had become a city of industry, where imported raw materials were converted into a wide range of iron and steel products. After World War II, the city found itself separated by the Iron Curtain from its traditional suppliers and markets to the east. Nevertheless, by the late 1940s, most of its prewar plant was back in production and little altered in structure. Nuremberg was on track to regaining its status as Bavaria's major industrial center, assisted by the development of highway and intercity rail systems, an airport, and the Rhine-Main Canal. It was only logical for the BfA to settle there in 1952.

With industry had come working-class political muscle. Returning to pre-Nazi tradition, the municipal council elections in 1946 left the SPD the strongest political party. Thereafter, it largely determined Nuremberg's postwar development. Known in Germany for toys and its eponymous sausages, Nuremberg was renowned in political circles for its innovative policies. As in

Essen, the policies included forward-looking responses to the city's immigrant-origin residents. Among big German cities Nuremberg had a moderate but growing immigrant population, rising from 1.9 percent of all inhabitants in 1960 to 7.2 percent in 1970. Typical of southern Germany, this foreign-born contingent was at first heavily Southern European, then younger, less male, and more Turkish as decades passed. The latter constituted a third of the immigrant population by 1981. Concurrently, smaller numbers of other non-European groups such as Moroccans were arriving in the city (Lux-Henseler 1997).

By the mid-1960s, Nuremberg was engaged in groundbreaking work with immigrants, notable for the attention paid to the political-cultural dimension of integration (Fröhlich 1993). The progressive outlook was all the more striking in light of the city's location in Bavaria. One of the few federal-states not to install a commissioner for foreigners, it limited benefits for immigrants more than other states. Perhaps out of necessity, local officials in Nuremberg grew highly inventive in their dealings with the immigrant residents for which they were legally responsible.

Crisis and Response

Starting in the 1970s, Nuremberg's economy shifted definitively toward services. Economic restructuring, international competition, and technological change wreaked havoc on the sectors that were its forte, the electromechanical and machine tool industries. The city matched industrial job losses with new positions in the service sector, although the share of working residents who were wage earners held steady. Not that the transition was painless: unemployment increased, reaching 8.3 percent by 1993. Poverty in the form of dependency on social assistance benefits climbed in tandem. Germany's highest percentage increase by far between 1980 and 1990 occurred in Nuremberg, where the number of people who had to resort to social assistance rose 415 percent (Ankowitsch 1993). Being an immigrant, Nuremberg's social office determined, correlated with more income poverty and poorer overall socioeconomic conditions than for native-stock Germans (see table 3.2). Influxes of ethnic Germans and asylum seekers only added to social outlays.

TABLE 3.2

Social Assistance Recipients in Nuremberg (All Sources)

Year	Number	Rate per 1,000	Immigrant Shares (%)
1987	39,657	83.5	27.1
1991	39,597	79.9	28.5
1993	43,132	86.3	34.2

Sources: Ankowitsch (1993, 17), ASFS (1997, 194).

Immigrants' Structural Integration

Neither the new poverty nor the immigrant presence was spread evenly across the city. Both were concentrated in neighborhoods near the urban core. Within the ring road encircling the inner city lived less than half of native-stock residents but more than two-thirds of immigrant-origin ones. In parts of some inner-city neighborhoods—Lorenzer Altstadt, Gostenhof, St. Johannis/Maxfeld, Südstadt, St. Leonard/Schweinau, Uhlandstrasse, Langwasser-Südost—the immigrant concentration could exceed 40 percent. Distribution of national groups within those neighborhoods was reasonably even. Only the Greek-origin population lived separately, on the western side of the core city in Gostenhof. Turks, North Africans, and Yugoslavs clustered a bit more on the south side (Gürtler 1985, appendix II-B).

The ongoing concentration of the immigrant-origin population, along with the puddling of social ills that accompanied it, upset the local government. Housing was especially worrisome. Nuremberg's stock had proved more difficult to revive than its industrial base after 1945. The availability and low price of suburban land had sparked an exodus of middle-class Germans from the city, which shrunk the tax base, made for inefficient use of existing infrastructure, and generated traffic and pollution problems. The flight was not halted until the 1980s. Competition for inexpensive housing in the city core then sharpened with urban renewal and most affected immigrants, asylum-seekers, ethnic Germans, people with large families, students, and the unemployed. The situation was "catastrophic" for non-Europeans and Greeks, stuck with overcrowded and poorly equipped units and paying unduly high rents (Karbach 1990, 443–44).

To reverse the situation, the municipal government intervened directly through its municipal housing authority and indirectly through zoning laws and infrastructural investments. The city brought to bear what pressure it could on private landlords guilty of rent gouging and failing to keep up their properties. It trumpeted initiatives that successfully brought immigrant and German families together, most conspicuously in the Gostenhof neighborhood. Since German households at the same socioeconomic level as immigrants lived in similarly concentrated and segregated conditions, Nuremberg officials decided that general improvement policies were most appropriate. Policies targeting disadvantaged groups like immigrants would nonetheless play a supplemental role (Gürtler 1985, appendix II-A).

From the mid-1970s on, undocumented immigration, inflows of asylum seekers, and family reunification lowered extremely high rates of immigrant economic activity. The vast majority of those employed were factory or construction workers or performed the lowest-level service jobs in hotels, restaurants, hospitals, nursing homes, and cleaning services. By 1992, though, over 6 percent of the active immigrant population would be self-employed. These small business owners would run half of all eating establishments in town (AKF 1994, 8–13).

Nuremberg had produced a series of immigration reports and studies in the 1970s. Their cumulative experience paved the way for the city government's development of a global plan. The Foreigner Program, introduced by the SPD and adopted by the city council in 1983, began unequivocally: "The city of Nuremberg considers the foreign families who live here to be co-citizens and does not consider their stay transitory." The goal was "equal rights and opportunities for foreign families," even while ensuring that they retained the "possibility of maintaining and nurturing their cultural identity" (Gürtler 1985, 2–3).

The program went on to detail fifty-seven interrelated projects, which defined immigrants as a separate target group, cut across functional lines and departments, and called for an operating budget of 2.6 million deutsche marks. Services for the general population were distinguished from "transitional" services specifically for immigrants. Equality of opportunity for all Nurembergers would be won through the cooperative labors of the local administration, trade unions, residents' associations, and the social welfare nonprofits—all of which had been consulted during the development of the program (Hanesch 1992). The major nonprofit organizations were as active in Nuremberg as in Essen. AWO had pride of place, given the city's working-class cast. But it was a Protestant stronghold, and the local branch of Diakonisches Werk had been founded in 1885. Caritas had followed twenty years later, as industrialization drew in Catholics from the Upper Palatinate and Upper Franconia. The nonprofit Big Three worked harmoniously with local SPD governments (Karbach 1990).

The city's financial troubles meant that it had to postpone investment in necessary building projects and close some public baths and schools. While layoffs of city personnel ranged from 10 to 50 percent across departments, those in the social policy area that worked with immigrants were kept at full strength or augmented. Even in hard economic times, Nuremberg did not make major cuts in spending on immigrant integration. Overall, the city's commitment to social institutions and activities doubled between 1980 and 1988 (ASFS 1997, 247).

In making integration their focal point, Nuremberg officials put themselves at loggerheads with their state-level counterparts. This opposition had its greatest ramifications in the field of education, largely under the purview of the federal-state. The Bavarian school system endeavored to keep immigrant students oriented toward the homeland. Nuremberg's Foreigner Program departed from that logic. Despite limitations on its influence, the city felt that it could effect improvements. As in Essen, equal access to day nurseries and kindergartens was seen as critically important to immigrant integration into the host society. In city-run establishments the concentration of immigrant children could be high. Taking into account state, private, and nonprofit institutions, however, their rates of attendance were far lower than for those of German stock. In response the program envisioned the introduction of more foreign-origin personnel wherever the immigrant concentration exceeded 30 percent (Gürtler 1985, 5).

The story was similar at higher educational levels. For every third primary or secondary student in Nuremberg, German was a second language in the mid-1980s. Sitting at the desks were students from twenty-two foreign countries. In 1984 twice as many of them left the educational system without having successfully completed secondary school as their German-stock peers. Nonnationals constituted 27 percent of public school pupils but only 5 percent of students in college preparatory high schools. Greeks, with their own primary-middle school, fared somewhat better (Kupfer-Schreiner 1992, 350).

City schools offered customized preparatory and remedial classes. To improve their rate of success, the program called for integrated home-stays and class trips, homework assistance, financial support for nonprofits active in the sector, training programs for immigrant-origin instructors and parents, voluntary afternoon German courses, and the mainstreaming of immigrant children into regular German classes (Regelklassen). Bilingual classes were abandoned. Instead, immigrant children's mother tongues would be recognized as their first required foreign language. Concomitant with that move was heavier stress on German language instruction (Gürtler 1985, appendix II-C, D).

Work with young immigrants was traditionally left to the social welfare nonprofits, which set up recreational, vocational, and counseling centers throughout the city. The municipal Youth Office cooperated extensively with them. Few local youth centers attracted a multiethnic clientele, but special sporting events, trips, dance parties, music classes, and programs for Turkish and other Muslim girls registered positive results. An equally complex palette of offerings was proffered in the area of professional training, where the Foreigner Program aimed to raise immigrant representation in municipal vocational schools and apprentice programs. As in other sectors, the local administration was proactive, organizing courses in conversational German and workshops tailored to specific interests, such as "sewing German" (see BSAS 1988).

Neighborhood-based associations made a critical contribution to such social work. A good example was DEGRIN, an initiative launched in 1977 by German and Greek volunteers and professional educators under the auspices of Diakonisches Werk. Formed to offer schoolchildren help with their homework, it expanded its mission to encompass a range of recreational projects, first in the Gostenhof neighborhood among Greeks and then across the city among all national groups. Out of spontaneous action there arose a stable organizational array that was a "fundamental component of the municipal social infrastructure," partially subsidized by the city of Nuremberg and the state of

Bavaria (BSAS 1988; see DEGRIN 1992). DEGRIN gave an impulse to "inter-cultural" (here meaning multicultural) education across Nuremberg. Peda-gogical strategies took root in many local schools that encouraged all children to strengthen their cultural identities and learn about each other's lifestyles. The pilot projects were forerunners of an eventual "Nuremberg Model," which gained a national reputation (Pommerin-Götze et al. 1992).

Feeding official optimism was the city's low crime rate—the lowest, in fact, among large German urban centers through the 1980s and 1990s (PIA 1997, 37). Local authorities felt confident enough to experiment with self-help and multiculturalism. Already by the mid-1980s, their focus was on neighbor-hood-level work and ethnic-based offerings, delivered by the nonprofits, im-migrant associations, and residents' initiatives and coordinated by the city. Since social costs were swelling, city officials had every reason to promote self-help organizing and network building. In an ideological sense, too, the local SPD and the nonprofits welcomed self-help. The commitment went deeper than in Essen, and AWO, Diakonisches Werk, and Caritas in Nuremberg adopted empowerment earlier and more enthusiastically (Sommer 1988).

Immigrant's Political-Cultural Integration

That outlook extended to the political and cultural realms. The immigrant naturalization rate was modest—a couple of hundred a year, primarily South-ern Europeans. Nuremberg's official position was that while that level was too low, naturalization was no solution in itself. Authorities were more concerned that nonnationals enjoy secure residential status. Almost half of all immigrants had lived in Nuremberg for more than eight years in the early 1970s, but only 1 percent had acquired an unlimited residency permit (Gürtler 1985, appen-dix II B4-6).

Until suffrage was broadened, the foreigners' auxiliary council was to be, as in Essen, immigrants' "connector" to the municipal council. In fact, only Troisdorf and Wiesbaden had set up a foreigners' council before Nuremberg in 1973. Spearheaded by Caritas and the Young Socialists, it was the country's first council directly elected by immigrants. From the start, it was evident that working relationships between its members and the social welfare nonprofits were very close. The latter appointed nonvoting observers, as did the ruling SPD. The setup looked cliental, and in hindsight the council's early leaders admitted that they allowed themselves to be manipulated. Immigrants, fur-thermore, were simplistically seen as national and ethnic representatives, which ignored the differences between those two identities. Candidates from each country of origin figured on a single slate, with one member elected per list. Dealings with homeland consulates were intimate and not infrequently controversial (see ASN 1993).

After the initial session in 1976, the local government introduced a new organizational setup without the council's input, pointing to a another trait:

hardly a legislative period passed without modifications to the council's charter and electoral system. In its mandate the foreigners' council was called on to advise the municipal council on all questions relating to immigrants, reflecting a traditional vision of the body as an information provider for German authorities (Fischer-Brühl 1981). For its part, however, the council felt free to critique the city government's Foreigner Program. It welcomed the initiative but advocated introducing paid immigrant-origin personnel into all social and cultural institutions. It constructed a data set on anti-immigrant activity, oversaw the annual "Foreigner Week" program and other seminars, and publicized services offered by local institutions. One consequence was spectacular growth in the number of those with permanent residency permits, from 1,221 in 1983 to 10,907 in 1989 (Llorens 1993, 30).

The council became more politically involved over the course of the 1980s. It intervened in specific cases, such as keeping German and immigrant tenants in one central neighborhood from being pushed out of their apartments by a large gentrification project in 1985 and convincing the social housing office to ban the frequent (legal) addendum "not for foreigners" from its listings in 1987 (Llorens 1993, 29). Collaboration was extensive with the large nonprofits' counseling services and the municipal departments of youth and schools.

At the end of the 1980s, pressure from the German trade unions led to foreigners' council elections being switched to a system of lists formed according to political and not ethnonational allegiances. The municipal council insisted on a minority protection clause: the six largest nationalities and the "Group of the Rest" had to have at least one elected member each; if the election did not produce such an outcome, there would be "overhang mandates" as in Essen. The first election under the new system in 1990 gave more than half of the thirty-five seats to the SPD and Green lists (ASN 1993).

Alongside a number of Southern European organizations, there were around twenty-five Turkish associations of all types in town and several Kurdish, Tunisian, Moroccan, and Berber ones. Only 10 to 15 percent of the immigrant-origin population belonged to such groupings, and only the Portuguese association could claim to be representative of its national group. Despite these organizations' limitations, they represented the only institutionalized "crystallization points" at which officials could reach at least part of the immigrant-origin population (AKF 1994, 41). Nuremberg's half dozen mosque associations were not eligible for outright support, but they did receive subsidies for their social and educational activities. Muslims had established seven mosques in the city, including an "official" Turkish one. They were not the objects of any particular popular or official concern, and they worked well with municipal agencies and other religious groups. The immigration of Catholics and Muslims, together with the postwar trend toward secularism, had left traditionally Protestant Nuremberg a balanced and tolerant place (PIA 1997, 27).

The sole point of real disharmony was religious instruction. Bavaria required three hours of it a week, and local schools offered Catholic and Protestant classes, with some of the former in Southern European languages. Muslim parents resisted teaching plans for Islam developed under the sponsorship of German educational authorities. Unfazed, the city called on homeland organizations to step in and help find a compromise acceptable to all parties (Kupfer-Schreiner 1992). Ethnonational identities were also central to city-sponsored work in neighborhood "culture shops," one of the most successful of which, in the Gostenhof neighborhood, had a Turkish teahouse and regularly brought in teams from AWO and Diakonisches Werk for Turkish and Kurdish counseling sessions (SKR 1992).

Interim measures to promote cultural understanding reflected the liberal multicultural perspective of the local government and nonprofits. It did not go unchallenged. True cultural pluralists—found in the ranks of the Greens yet also in the SPD—did not see ethnic identities as transitional. They warned against too much emphasis on equal opportunity, which would deny the enduring value of collective ethnic identities, and the adoption of "counter-productive, superficial, American-style anti-racism techniques" (Kalpaka 1992, 94). Traditional Social Democrats, on the other hand, felt uneasy with schemes to assist immigrants in maintaining ethnic identities even provisionally. So, too, did the CSU and the Republicans, albeit for dramatically different reasons. From 1990, the SPD led a coalition government with the Greens, and the Lord Mayor argued that "understanding does not mean that other cultures will necessarily be accepted in their entirety. Partnership encompasses disagreements" (Popp 1992, 58).

The Difficult 1990s

Perhaps getting more than its leader bargained for, Nuremberg experienced more political-cultural disconnection than Essen during the challenging 1990s. There were many expressions of solidarity for refugees and immigrants, and the impact of self-help and empowerment were evident. Thousands of demonstrators protested racist attacks and draconian federal legislation. The annual multicultural festival in the main marketplace took on a militant character. Organizers of a petition drive in favor of dual nationality garnered far more signatures far faster than they had dared hope ("Gleiche Rechte" 1993).

The city endured turbulence as well. In 1993 a band of Kurds occupied the local Kurdish cultural center to protest the federal government's ban against separatist movements accused of anti-Turkish violence. Although several protesters threatened self-immolation, the incident ended peacefully (Lindsiepe 1993). Afterward, though, local Turkish banks and travel agencies were bombed. Berber and Islamist associations noisily resisted control by left-wing Moroccan and Tunisian organizations. Police raided Kurdish, North African, and Chinese centers and restaurants, occasionally finding illegal arms and explosives ("Razzia" 1993). The four Republican municipal council members elected in 1990 sniped away from the far right, raising the specter of ethnic conflict and immigrant criminality. Their allegations notwithstanding, the trend was actually toward less immigrant wrongdoing. Tourists and foreign armed-service personnel were more likely to break the law than the resident immigrant population. However, its younger members were overrepresented among those arrested for violent crimes, drug offenses, and other violations associated with organized gangs. Nuremberg's police mounted interventions to defuse such activity (Polizeidirektion Nürnberg 1995).

While harassment of foreigners was common in next-door Erlangen, incidents were rare in Nuremberg. A former head of the foreigners' auxiliary council remarked that for two decades there had been no major incident, and virtually no organized right-wing extremists had turned up without being met with a broad wave of popular revulsion and official opposition (ASN 1993, 20). He and his colleagues drew a positive balance sheet of their relationship with the city. While they sympathized with its financial predicament in the 1990s, they feared that Nuremberg's wide-ranging integration policies were doomed for lack of adequate funding. "We in Nuremberg have exploited our margin of maneuver as much as possible," an SPD leader retorted. "Given the limits within which it has been forced to operate, Nuremberg has done well."[6] In difficult economic times, a solid foundation of services had been made available. The foreigners' council had its own budget by the early 1990s and was distributing public subsidies to immigrant associations and multicultural projects.

The turmoil of the period had left its mark, however. Contact between immigrant-origin and German residents shriveled to "reserved juxtapositioning," placid but superficial and subject to quick changes in times of tension (AKF 1994, 10). Hence, the city made an explicit political decision to shift from "foreigners policy" as such to strategic planning by functional area.[7] Immigrants' needs became part of the planning process in all municipal departments and institutions, which pledged to hire more immigrant-origin personnel. The city would assist immigrant associations and initiatives and encourage empowerment and self-help, with the social welfare nonprofits called on to fill a supervisory, "clearing-house" function. Only when indispensable— as for Turkish women and girls—would there be separate services. The municipality acknowledged that this tactic rendered it "practically impossible" to give exact figures on how much was spent by the city of Nuremberg on immigrant integration policies (AKF 1994, 14).

Earlier policies had made important strides, but the immigrants' structural integration was highly problematic. Immigrants comprised almost 30 percent of Nuremberg's unemployed by 1997, for example. They lived in relatively overcrowded conditions, albeit less than before, and fewer of them were able to secure public housing than Germans. Residential concentration had continued (ASFS 1999, 89). The municipal office of housing and urban renewal pointed out the advantages of such clustering in terms of comfort and security but did worry about trends toward "ghettoization" in Gostenhof and several south-side neighborhoods (Fichter 1998).

In terms of education and training, immigrant-origin students continued to lag behind their German-stock peers. They were less likely to find a seat in a kindergarten and more likely to take preparatory or remedial classes thereafter; it was more difficult for them to find an apprenticeship or employment after their schooling. Lagging at the top end of the German education system, they were nonetheless improving at the middle levels. Tellingly, a larger share of young Turks—long a policy target group—were obtaining a high school diploma than young Italians. Immigrants taken together were only half as likely as their German peers to do so. Another positive policy outcome was that immigrants in Nuremberg were not overrepresented in special education classes, a rarity in German cities (Schulämter Nürnbergs 1998). Studies were showing that German students in schools with high numbers of immigrants profited from the pedagogical techniques employed in multicultural classrooms. The state of Bavaria found the Nuremberg model so promising that it was expanded to include newer immigrant nationalities and refugees ("Türkisch als Abiturfach" 1993).

Similar complexity characterized the course adopted by the city's youth and culture "shops" as Nuremberg moved away from explicit multiculturalism and toward making sectorial services more attuned to immigrant-origin residents, singled out for street-level, results-oriented activities. Social work was shifting more insistently down to the neighborhoods. There, it became enmeshed in a crazy quilt of connections, friendships, and rivalries that took in immigrants and their associations, social movements, churches and mosques, nonprofits, and local administrators. Built up over decades, these networks meant that even immigrants with centrist or nationalist leanings enjoyed cordial relations with the SPD-controlled city hall.

Political Change

Nuremberg was undergoing a political makeover, however. Unemployment stuck at elevated levels as the city adjusted painfully to German unification and further economic change. A few years earlier than in Essen, the unthinkable happened: in 1996, the CSU won a plurality of seats (thirty-three out of seventy) on the municipal council; with representatives of two small centrist formations, it took control of the city. One of the center-right coalition's first moves affected the immigrant-origin population, which had grown to more than 17 percent of all residents by mid-decade. Roughly half were citizens of other EU member countries and thus able to vote in 1996. A pair of left-wing EU immigrants had won seats on the municipal council. The new government decided to reduce the size of the foreigners' auxiliary council in the name of "efficiency." To break the hold of left-leaning movements, elections would once again take place according to nationality. EU members would be nonvoting and appointed by the municipal council ("Ausländerbeirat kleiner" 1996; ASN 1997).

Leaders of the foreigners' council exploded in anger, triggering the cancellation of the annual multicultural festival that autumn. The money was used instead to organize discussions about the problems facing the council ("Wählen" 1996). Praising the cooperative stance of previous local governments, its president accused the new administration of trying to split immigrants and reduce their influence. There was an admission on the immigrant leadership's part that it had not always stayed in close enough contact with its base, which was painfully clear from the history of feeble participation in council elections: from a "high" of 18.6 percent in 1973 to a low of 10.5 percent in 1978. The introduction of political lists had produced an upward tick to 16.4 percent in 1990, but the CSU's tinkering would drive turnout back down to 12.6 percent in 1997 and 11.1 percent in 2003 (Llorens 1998; Stadt Nürnberg 2003).

The CSU called for "integration instead of parallel societies," attributed to multiculturalism and favored treatment for immigrants (O. Böhm 1999). But Lord Mayor Scholtz reiterated his party's longstanding support for the foreigners' council. Only budgetary and legal restrictions would limit the city's willingness to meet its requests (Scholz 1998). The neighborhood remained at the center of social policy and social work with immigrant-origin residents, with new projects co-financed by the federal and state governments and the EU focused especially on the city's south side. There were additional attempts to encourage young immigrants' self-organizations (Kreisjugendring Nürnberg-Stadt 2001). The foreigners' council drew up an inventory of Bavarian integration projects, which revealed that fully half of those launched in the large federal-state had started in Nuremberg (ASN 2000).

The March 2002 municipal elections ensured continuity. The CSU held onto its position as the strongest single political party in the municipal council and the principal in a center-right governing coalition. The far right had no more success than in 1996, electing two councilors. A bigger concern was voter participation, which sank to a postwar low of 55.3 percent. In a surprise, the mayor's race was won by the SPD's leader, who defeated the popular incumbent CSU mayor in a runoff. With bipartisanship the watchword, the municipal council's new Commission for Integration and Intercultural Offerings met for the first time that September and argued for the same distinction as in Essen between enriching "interculturality" and risky "multiculturalism." In short, it essentially endorsed the strange hybrid of the SPD's liberal multiculturalism and the CSU's liberal neutrality that had been in place since the mid-1990s (ASFS 2002). Echoing that balance, the Italian-born president of the foreigners' council argued that Nuremberg's social development could not come from either "forced Germanization" or "leftist-alternative do-gooderness" (Zelnhefer 2002). Rampant individualism and the ongoing balkanization of society into isolated subcultures required a response that stressed mutual encounters and dialogue. Immigrant-oriented cultural activities would blend in with others to showcase Nuremberg as a effervescent, cosmopolitan place whose dark history obliged it to carry the torch for tolerance (AKF 2003).

Up through the 1990s, Essen and Nuremberg had demonstrated the limits of local action and yet also the room for maneuver that German cities could exercise. Located in federal-states that, at least when it came to immigrants, represented the yin and yang of the German experience, both cities were able to develop consequential policies in the realms of housing, education and training, culture, and political participation. A host of common themes and strong points notwithstanding, local policies differed significantly. Essen stuck more to its traditional "assimilationist" Social Democratic approach. Nuremberg, in a less welcoming and more tight-fisted state, exhibited greater policy innovation. It brought in self-help more insistently and generated more ethnic associational effervescence and political-cultural disconnection. The far right won political representation, but immigration and Islam did not become major targets of political mobilization there or in Essen.

That said, neither city could truly defy the strictures of federal-state and federal legislation. Nor could they fight the powerful structural forces that were pushing immigrant-origin populations into certain neighborhoods—a trend whose effects were openly acknowledged as ambiguous. The SPD fell from its perch in both locales in the late 1990s, but immigrants were not among the major causes. Hard-pressed local officials in Essen and Nuremberg watched attentively—and not without some envy—their comrades in German city-states like Berlin and Bremen. Progressive positions on immigration there appeared to benefit from the greater autonomy that flowed from the fusion of municipality and federal-state.

In Germany's city-states further-reaching planning and decisional capacities coexist with susceptibility to both financial strains from a limited tax base and policy stasis from sheer institutional density. Bremen and Berlin bear witness to both the agony and the ecstasy of the city-state. Beacons of progressive immigrant politics, they both gained fame for their groundbreaking acceptance of self-help and empowerment and work on political-cultural integration. Their policies diverged in key respects, however. Bremen officials promoted self-help movements, even as they channeled them into a tight political setup that recalled Essen's in its emphasis on maintaining control. In Berlin, meanwhile, self-help came into its own under conservative-led administrations and never strayed far from the purely cultural realm. Neither Bremen nor Berlin was under firm SPD control after the late 1970s, and political volatility was matched in both by a relatively changeable and animated social scene, marked by more structural disconnection than Essen or Nuremberg but more political-cultural disconnection only in Berlin.

Bremen: Stimulating Self-Help and Solidarity

One of Germany's gateways to the world, Bremen has been a laboratory of social policy experimentation and, from the 1960s, an incubator of social movements. From the beginning, however, they were intended to strengthen the local administration, not to offer an autonomous alternative to it. Tight, overlapping institutional networks in the smallest German federal-state controlled and channeled political mobilization, producing peak associations even among immigrant-origin residents.

A Progressive Record

Bremen came to its worldly outlook through its status as a major port. Its harbor welcomed the bulk of Germany's cotton and tobacco imports in the colonial period. By the nineteenth century, the textile and shipbuilding industries developed. Bremen became a working-class mecca, and it pulled in many immigrants. For centuries, it had attracted workers and merchants from close-by Holland. Bremen's later industrialization would not have been possible without Eastern Europeans—Czechs, Poles, Russians, Bohemians, and Slovaks, as well as "internal immigrants" from Silesia and Posen (Poznan) (Knauf and Schröder 1993).[8]

After World War II, during which it was the site of several forced labor camps, Bremen and its sister city, Bremerhaven, fell under American occupation and then became the "two-city state." Rebuilding itself once again into a major center of maritime-related trade and industry, Bremen became linked in popular consciousness with coffee, bananas, and shipbuilding. Bremen also slowly regained its immigrant population. Under 2 percent of Bremen's population was foreign born in 1968, 6 percent in 1978, and just under 10 percent in 1988. Turkish passport holders comprised a large plurality of the immigrant population, followed by Yugoslavs and Southern Europeans. Progressively, they were being joined by workers and asylum seekers from North and sub-Saharan Africa and the Middle East (Plücker and Weber 1990).

In power since 1945, the SPD frequently enjoyed an absolute majority in the city-state. Bremen's state constitution established a clear division of labor and authority between the legislature (the state assembly) and the executive branch (the Senate). The majority in the former selected the latter, and the Senate, in turn, chose the mayor. The eighty members of the one-hundred-strong state assembly from Bremen City formed the municipal assembly. Vertical integration between city and state cemented SPD control. Cooperation between the public, private, and nonprofit sectors grew so close that they became known collectively as the "Bremen scene." City leaders were party to discussions, professional contacts, and lesson-drawing opportunities—but also to petty rivalries and internecine quarrels.

Crisis and Response

For a long time, Bremen reveled in its low unemployment rate and working-class solidarity. Prosperity was evaporating by the mid-1970s as the city-state stumbled from one crisis to another: shipbuilder bankruptcies, factory closures, industrial conversion, political scandals, and public indebtedness. In north German ports and coastal regions, the depression in the shipyards and related industries generated levels of unemployment and poverty similar to those in the worst hit areas of the Ruhr Valley (Kieselbach and Klink 1991).

The crisis spurred a search for alternatives. Bremen attracted a university, steelworks, high-technology defense contractors, and a Daimler-Benz aerospace plant that contributed to the European Space Agency and the Skylab program. It was the highly qualified laid-off shipyard workers who found employment in the new industries; the prospects for marginal workers were more miserable than ever. Immigrant unemployment rates were more than twice that of all workers, 15.4 percent by 1981 (Engel 1982, 32). Spending for social assistance was up over 28 percent between 1983 and 1986, then up over 25 percent between 1986 and 1989. Bremen's social assistance rates were the highest in the region and included mainly young people, single mothers, and immigrants (SJS 1991, 26–28).

Immigrants' Structural Integration

A shortage of appropriate housing also plagued Bremen's immigrant-origin population from the start. At first, the mostly single male workers were lodged on the same factory grounds where forced laborers and prisoners of war toiled during the Second World War. As immigration became a family affair, the private housing market grew in importance. Its tightness compelled municipal housing authorities to step in. They took over cheap hotels and pensions, converted military barracks into working-class housing units, and constructed densely populated, high-rise complexes in outlying northern and eastern areas (Panayotidis 1989). Nonnative residents tended to live there and in disadvantaged central neighborhoods with older, cheaper housing close by industrial areas.

As in other cities the trend was in the direction of spatial concentration. Bremen had no "quasi-ghettoes" like Berlin-Kreuzberg, Cologne-Kalk, or Frankfurt-Banhofsviertel, where immigrant concentrations could exceed 80 percent. By the early 1990s, the share ranged from over 39 percent in the sparsely populated industrial harbor (Industriehäfen) to none in upscale In den Wischen. Older core residential areas that had topped the list in the mid-1970s with concentrations over 15 percent—Ostertor, Lindenhof, Steintor—

retained many immigrants. Throughout the 1980s, however, the movement was toward more peripheral districts with large social housing developments—Tenever, Blockdiek, Grohn—with concentrations over 20 percent by the early 1990s. Those neighborhoods roughly corresponded to the ones scoring highest on the city-state's official index of social disadvantage, with Tenever coming to head the list.[9]

As the immigrant-origin population clustered, it grew more familial. The economic activity rate among Bremen's Turks fell from 72 percent in 1980 to 40 percent in 1986. Almost half of all immigrants were Turks, followed at a large distance by Poles, Yugoslavs, Iranians, Southern Europeans, and smaller numbers of Tunisians and Moroccans. Immigrants were disproportionately employed in lower-skilled jobs in shipbuilding, streetcar and airplane construction, metalworking, cleaning services, transportation, hospitals, textile manufacture, and fish processing (Bitter-Witz 1992). While many immigrants ran their own businesses in Bremen, authorities kept no separate statistics on them. They insisted that all entrepreneurs were treated the same.

Traditionally, social services in Bremen fell under state control and were tantamount to a Social Democratic fiefdom. The city-state was marked by intense collaboration between likeminded governments and nonprofits. Except when internal divisions impeded consensus at the top, concentrated decision-making enabled linkages between projects funded from different sources and operating across policy sectors, defying the departmental divisions typical in German bureaucracies. Encouraging experimentation was the diversity of the local trade union movement, a reflection of heavy industry's failure to dominate Bremen's political world. Neither were the Big Three nonprofit associations all-powerful, although the Social Democratic AWO and Protestant Diakonisches Werk were very active in this traditionally working-class, Lutheran part of Germany. The Catholic Caritas and a number of other "free carriers" were part of the kaleidoscope of social welfare institutions that, under forceful state guidance, offered a complex range of social services (Plücker and Weber 1990).

By 1978 the socioeconomic crisis had provoked a reassessment and reorganization of existing services and guiding principles. Far earlier and more intensely than in Essen or even Nuremberg, the "New Bremen Line" was bringing services down to the neighborhood level, championing self-help initiatives, and opening up cultural institutions to newer population groups. The term "empowerment" did not have currency, but the notion of having affected people help devise appropriate social work responses was already in operation (Kriebisch et al. 1978).

The following year a similar tack was taken toward immigrants, instigated by the lead-up to the federal Kühn Memorandum. In its 1979 "Integration Concept" the Bremen Senate argued that just as immigrants did not have to abandon the option of eventual return migration, they did not have to give up their cultural identities to fit into German society. "Germany has become a de facto country of immigration," the senator for labor stated flatly. Bremen explicitly rejected a cost-benefit calculus in its assessment of immigrants' value (SAB 1979).

As in the other cities, the younger immigrant-origin generations attracted policymakers' notice in Bremen from the outset. They adopted an educational policy that aimed to mainstream immigrant students as quickly as possible. Policies that took their special situation into temporary consideration were permissible, but only on a case-by-case basis. Permanently targeted programs would draw boundaries and legitimize discrimination and were thus unacceptable. Bremen proved receptive to new pedagogical methods. Intercultural education made fewer inroads than in Nuremberg but more than in Essen.

Educational authorities tried to spread out immigrant-origin children more evenly among local day nurseries and kindergartens, often setting a "threshold" (ranging from 20 to 40 percent) at which such policies kicked in. At the primary and secondary levels, Bremen underscored measures to incorporate immigrant-origin students into regular German classrooms: help with homework, bilingual instruction where appropriate, and, most fruitfully, native teachers who offered extra German classes with the assistance of immigrant-origin colleagues. Mother-tongue instruction also won a key position in Bremen schools. Students with an immigrant background trailed seriously at the top-rung schools, the *Gymnasien,* but steady advances were being registered at the middle level (see table 3.3).

The working-class state shone the spotlight on vocational training, with immigrants' involvement nowhere near proportionate to their numbers. Federal programs featured prominently in this sector, and collaboration was extensive with nonprofits of all types. Characteristically, Bremen was the only state in which the promotion of political and vocational training was not separated. This device ushered students into the integrated, SPD-dominated local institutional nexus.

Bremen's youth centers sought to complement educational and vocational initiatives on behalf of immigrant-origin young people. At the same time, several were closed so that resources could be tagged specifically for ethnic Ger-

TABLE 3.3

Secondary-School Qualifications in Bremen

	1978		1990	
Type of Qualification	Immigrants (%)	Germans (%)	Immigrants (%)	Turks (%)
None	25.1	8.2	18.6	15.1
Hauptschule (lowest)	50.8	29.1	26.7	20.3
Realschule (middle)	13.6	36.4	29.2	17.0

Sources: SAB (1979, 35), Plücker and Weber (1990, 7).

man *(Aussiedler)* youths. Tensions and rivalries between immigrant- and German-origin groups were not uncommon; nor were rivalries among youths of Turkish, Kurdish, Lebanese, Arab, and Berber backgrounds. In neighborhoods like Tenever, intercultural support groups and theatrical dramatizations attenuated such problems. Most effectual were projects that youths had initiated themselves (see Knaust and Linnemann 1984).

In retrospect, the head of Bremen's Institute for Turkish-German Cooperation would later acknowledge, the 1979 Integration Concept was "all in all very progressive compared to that in other federal-states" (La Grotta and Schmidt 1999, 18). In the late 1980s, the breakthrough of the far right tested such open-mindedness. In the 1987 legislative elections, Bremen was where the far right won representation in a German state parliament for the first time since the 1960s. Although it won only 3.4 percent of the total state vote and only 3 percent in Bremen City, the DVU/List D—an alliance of the German People's Union (Deutsche Volksunion—DVU), the Republicans, and several minuscule extremist movements—earned one seat. With 5.4 percent in economically reeling Bremerhaven, it had cleared the 5 percent threshold that applied separately for each of the two municipal voting constituencies.

The far right was a relatively minor presence, with only a couple dozen hangers-on prone to violence. Officials nonetheless took them seriously and pledged to keep careful tabs on antiforeigner and anti-Semitic acts (Senat Bremens 1989). Bremen's Social Democratic mayor forbade the new DVU deputy from having an office or even entering city hall. The Interior Minister equated the party with neo-Nazism, as he warned against simplistic "brown-and-white thinking." Trying to bait the ruling majority, far-right leaders pointed to war-torn Lebanon as an illustration of the dangers of multiculturalism and charged that immigrants were overburdening the schools and other institutions (Bremische Bürgerschaft 1991, 2316–449).

There were, admittedly, strains in the social counseling system. There was one AWO counselor for every five thousand Turks, far above the desired ratio of one for every three thousand. The organization could only avoid a deficit in 1991 because of the savings accruing from the long-term illnesses of several social workers. Both the clientele and the services provided were increasingly diverse, and the nonprofits' division of labor by ethnicity and religion came under scrutiny (Bitter-Witz 1992).

There were deep cuts in the police budget, even though Bremen had one of the highest crime rates in Germany. The downtown neighborhoods of Ostertor and Steintor were famous throughout the country as "The Hood" *(das Viertel),* an area of biker bars, gay clubs, cosmopolitan cafés, "Third World" stores, and other trappings of the alternative lifestyle. Accompanying the joie de vivre were prostitution and drugs. The neighborhood was ripe for infiltration by organized crime, some of it controlled by immigrants. Another hot spot was the Osterholz borough, which encompassed Tenever and its "Little Manhattan" housing projects. Plopped into fields on the eastern edge of the city-state next to the Hamburg-Hannover *Autobahn* in the 1970s, they were home to ten thousand people of fifty-three nationalities. Many undocumented immigrants and refugees hid out there, and interethnic conflicts broke out in their courtyards and stairwells (Bolesch 1994).

Bremen stimulated self-help groups but embedded them in the policy-making system. In Bremen they had a long tradition of working with the immigrant-origin population and of demanding and getting the ear of policy-makers. They were grouped together into the so-called Bremen Pot, their coherence matching that of the tight Social Democratic local administration that financed and shepherded them. Old-style trade unionists overcame their doubts about self-help, as did Greens their concern about co-optation and dependency (see Bremische Bürgerschaft 1987). Initial misgivings on the part of the social welfare nonprofits eventually gave way to rather ardent support. They actively advocated self-help and empowerment as ways to overcome social isolation and build solidarity.[10]

In October 1989, the Senate established the Central Office for the Integration of Immigrated Citizens to oversee all measures to foster integration and combat discrimination and racism. Unique in Germany, the Central Office received 800,000 deutsche marks a year from the city-state and the European Social Fund. Officials acknowledged but rebuffed criticisms that integration policy was becoming too much of a top-down affair (Zentralstelle 1992).

Immigrants' Political-Cultural Integration

Bremen's "overly organized state" made for a "complicated, labor-intensive decision-making process," according to a report issued by the city-state itself. Bremen's regulatory approach could be "provincial, structurally conservative, and dominated by networks of insiders" (Prigge 1998, 85). This arrangement, which minimized the far-right threat, likewise inhibited those forms of immigrant interest articulation that the local SPD feared it might not be able to control.

Perhaps not coincidentally, the naturalization procedure was a relatively slow, complicated procedure in Bremen, taking two years on average after the filing of an application, compared to six months in Berlin. Nor was Bremen as ready to rubberstamp double nationality, where permitted. Approval for naturalization applications remained limited: 167 of 258 requests were granted in 1988, and 267 of 678 in 1992. Citing the financial crunch and staff shortages, Bremen officials promised to try harder and to loosen cultural and linguistic requirements ("Die Einbürgerung" 1994).

They undertook intense efforts to secure local voting rights for resident immigrants. The state assembly approved such suffrage in June 1989, confirming earlier approval by the Senate, only to see the decision overturned by the Federal Administrative Court in Karlsruhe. While reiterating its support for immigrants' equal access to political participation and co-decision, the Senate acknowledged that insuperable legal hurdles precluded it. Ersatz structures like foreigners' auxiliary councils were dismissed for performing only consultative functions, even though Bremerhaven did establish such a council (Bremische Bürgerschaft 1991, 3012).

Alongside the workplace, the neighborhood emerged as the arena par excellence for promoting and channeling immigrant participation in Bremen City. In the early 1980s, the local administration had installed district councils *(Ortsbeiräte)*, which had no real power or specified areas of responsibility. In contrast to Berlin's and Essen's borough councils *(Bezirksämter)*, they were dependent on traditional structures and more involved in administering the city than in representing anyone's interests. To ensure control over immigrants, the state government had each district council establish an advisory Department of Foreigner Issues. Half of these bodies' staffs were resident immigrants, named by the membership on the recommendation of the political parties and in accordance with their ethnonational communities' size (Facklam and Sakuth 1984).

A less overtly paternalistic model prevailed in cultural policy. The city supported eight neighborhood "culture shops" and one cultural center. Officials did not meddle with the events staged in them, although they did watch carefully (see Kulturladen Gröpelingen 1992). More significant for immigrants was the subsidy program for their associations, which had started out modestly in the late 1970s. As the money spigot opened, local associational life responded. More than in most German cities, cooperation became the hallmark of interactions between the administration and immigrant associations. In a development unique in Germany, associations of different nationalities, organizational structures, and political leanings came together in a genuine peak association to lobby the Bremen Senate and other authorities. A product of the interethnic solidarity forged during the unsuccessful fight to keep the giant AG Weser shipyard from closing, the Umbrella Federation of Immigrant Cultural Associations in Bremen (Dachverband der Ausländer-Kulturvereine in Bremen—DAB) formed in October 1983. The DAB united twenty-four immigrant associations and initiatives, including Kurds, Turks, Moroccans, Tunisians, and refugees. The majority of member groups had a basis in a common ethnic or national background, yet others were organized along a multiethnic, gender, or thematic base.

Typical of first-generation associations, the DAB stressed maintenance of homeland cultures and international cultural festivals. As time passed, however, the rather different cultural and political preoccupations of the second and third immigrant generations, as well as their disinterest in structured associational life, rose to the forefront of concerns. The DAB's monthly magazine, *Stimme* (Voice), contained trenchant political commentary and analysis, along with sections devoted to cultural happenings, and was sold at kiosks across Bremen and Bremerhaven.

The DAB was celebrated by Bremen officialdom, which insinuated it into the work of local policymaking institutions, perhaps most significantly the Department for Subsidies in the Area of Foreigners Work. The DAB called for more empowerment, decrying the "patron-client" atmosphere in social welfare offices, and for more consultation of immigrants on issues affecting them. From its relatively privileged and subsidized position—receiving around 300,000 marks a year in the late 1980s—the DAB was unenthusiastic whenever the idea arose of instituting a foreigners' auxiliary council in Bremen City. Like other nonprofit organizations, the DAB relied heavily on the federal make-work program (ABM) and was strongly affected by its fluctuating fortunes.[11]

The DAB was a redoubt of traditional, left-wing workers of the first immigrant generation. Only gradually did it incorporate the concerns of religious Muslims. Mosques, the first of which was founded in 1974, did not create furor in the city-state. Several times in the 1980s, Bremen officials sought to compel the structuring of an overarching peak Muslim association along German (and DAB) lines. Ideological, theological, national, and ethnic divisions within the Muslim population doomed those efforts. Religious instruction was the major rub. The 1949 state constitution of Bremen, like those of the city-states of Hamburg and Berlin, codified nondenominational biblical instruction "on a general Christian basis." For decades, debate simmered over whether to amend that language to make it more religiously neutral or to replace it with ethics training (Bukta 2000).

The Difficult 1990s

After German unification, Bremen, in truth, had bigger problems than Muslims or immigrants. The new eastern federal-states endangered the financial equalization scheme *(Finanzausgleich)* that had barely allowed Bremen to keep its budgetary head above water. Crime, drugs, and financial distress posed major threats to SPD control over the two-city state, and the party's support dropped. Tricky negotiations following the 1992 legislative elections cobbled together a "traffic light coalition," an unlikely alliance of the "red" SPD, the "yellow" Free Democratic Party (Freie Demokratische Partei), and the Greens. The far right won five seats.

The new executive named Helga Trüpel (Greens) as senator for culture, foreigner integration, and youth services—another first for Germany. "We and the European continent are a country of immigration," she proclaimed, before quickly adding that she did not have enough resources (less than 2 percent of Bremen's global budget) to fulfill all wishes. Senator Trüpel acted as an ombudswoman, traveling on a rotating basis through Bremen's neighbor-hoods to meet with residents (the "Hot Seat") and inviting them to call her with their positive and negative multicultural experiences (the "Hot Line"). She and the senator for youth, social affairs, and health, Irmgart Gaertner (SPD), worked to increase citizenship applications from eligible immigrant-origin youths. Filling out the integration triumvirate was the commissioner for foreigners, Dagmar Lill (SPD).

Generally, the two-city state's response to threats of greater disconnection disappointed doomsayers on the far right. In terms of anti-immigrant vio-lence, Bremen sat at or near the bottom among German states. The worst in-cident was a 1992 home arson fire that, unlike in such cities as Hoyerswerda, elicited not applause from neighbors but solidarity with the victims. Bremen was the first state to inform nonnational crime victims that they could file for damages and, after three years' residency in Germany, enjoyed the right to equal compensation ("Entschädigung" 1994). The local administration vowed to hire more immigrant-origin personnel and to increase subsidies for immi-grant associations. Asylum, too, generated camaraderie as well as friction. With the city's indulgence, if not its blessing, several local churches sheltered Togolese and Kurdish asylum seekers in order to prevent their deportation (Iletmis and Heimannsberg 1993).

Only the Turkish-Kurdish fracas produced violent disturbances in Bremen's streets. Under the auspices of the DAB, members of the two groups had engaged in rare collaboration. From the Turkish perspective, however, the city-state was perhaps too accommodating to Kurds, several of whom were well-known DAB leaders. Up until the mid-1990s, Bremen and Hesse were the only federal-states wherein instruction in Kurdish dialects was offered. The first half of the decade saw both sides organizing protest marches, and there were riots and clashes with law enforcement officials. Turkish cultural centers and travel agencies were firebombed, and police raided Kurdish associational offices (see Hockert and Liebe-Harkort 1996, 338–63).

Tensions escalated after 1995, when the traffic light coalition burned out. The subsequent legislative election left Bremen governed by a Grand Coalition of the SPD and the CDU. None of the candidates of non-German origin run-ning on the lists of the SPD and the Greens won office. After the vote, Senator Helga Trüpel's position disappeared, folded into the Department of Women, Health, Youth, Social Affairs, and Environmental Protection. The new Senate made the commissioner for foreigners responsible for all aspects of immigrant affairs.

Of equal import, the new senator for internal affairs became autocratic Ralf Borttscheller of the CDU, which was trying to steal the far right's fire on immigration. Openly associating the drug trade and "abuse" of the asylum law with migration in general, he planned to institute draconian "Bavarian relationships" in his state (La Grotta 1999, 8). Naturalizations would nearly double between 1994 and 1997, with Turks undergoing more than half of them, but critics attributed the positive trend to adjustments in Turkish legislation that made dual nationality elusive (see Bremische Bürgerschaft 1999).

That ethnic relations were worsening was widely accepted. Where harmony once reigned, self-encapsulation was now evident. More immigrant-origin young people, in particular, were pulling back into their own social world—that is, when they were not coming to blows with each other, German youths, or the police. In Senator Borttscheller's eyes, the problem was that Bremen's "integrative capacity" had been "overwhelmed" by attempts to turn Germany into a multicultural country of immigration (Bremische Bürgerschaft 1995, 84). Muslims, above all, caused him misgivings. By the mid-1990s, they accounted for almost 4 percent of the resident population. The opening of the two-city state's first mosque with a dome and minaret in 1997 was a cause for celebration. At the city-sponsored "Islam Week" that July, one Muslim leader blended references to John F. Kennedy and Bremen's cherished past membership in the Hanseatic League, proclaiming, "Ich bin ein Hanseat" (SLHB 1998, 50). Such bonhomie was answered with mistrust. Senator Borttscheller spoke darkly to the national media of the danger of "Muslim parallel societies" and criticized the mosque in question, associated with the Islamist Milli Görüs movement, for "rejecting assimilation" ("Notizen" 1998a). A few months later, the senator banned a Kurdish association that had the backing of the SPD, the Greens, and the DAB, declaring it a front for separatist terrorists ("Notizen" 1998b).

Bremen had managed to reduce structural disconnection to some extent. Over the 1990s, little additional concentration of immigrant-origin minorities took place. In 1990 a third of immigrants had lived in the ten neighborhoods with their highest absolute numbers. By 1999 that share had slipped a couple of percentage points. Simultaneously, the socioeconomic gulf between neighborhoods with few and many immigrants had widened (Meng 2001, 16–20). The city-state inaugurated projects to chip away at ethnic-based housing discrimination—not illegal in Germany—and to improve the quality of life in Tenever's housing projects.

In education, too, Bremen authorities persevered. Right when one hundred teachers were receiving pink slips in the two-city state, the senator for education hired two additional Turkish teachers. Schools offered instruction in Kurdish, Arabic, and other mother tongues in their supplemental classes and, in a first for Germany, in some regular lesson plans (Özdamar 2000). And despite the continuing disparities that afflicted students of immigrant background, they were making advances, which was surprising in light of Bremen's monetary crisis. A fifth of young immigrants were dropping out of secondary school without a diploma, down from more than a third in 1980. They were increasingly overrepresented in special schools and languishing in the dual training system, but were more common in *Gymnasien*. An unusually high 80 percent of immigrant children were attending local kindergartens. In the middle ranks of the educational system, immigrants were present nearly to the same degree as in the local resident population. Meanwhile, German students' educational achievement was suffering a slight decline. The picture varied widely across neighborhoods, with outcomes more positive in those with *higher* residential immigrant concentrations (Meng 2001, 23–28).

In an exceedingly tight job market, sharpened competition and ethnic discrimination were hurting immigrants' chances of translating their educational gains into a better labor market position. There was a tendency toward socioprofessional segmentation along ethnic lines that acted as a significant barrier to immigrant social mobility (Lill 2001). The federal-state's economic difficulties had not ended, and immigrants were major victims. Icons of Bremen industry were closing, most painfully the Vulkan shipbuilding factory in 1996. Immigrant workers' unemployment rate, which had been 0.4 percent in 1970, reached 29 percent in 1999. They made up more than a quarter of recipients of social assistance. Simultaneously, a segment of the immigrant-origin population was achieving middle-class status. In 1993, only 0.3 percent of those training to work in Bremen public services were noncitizens; the share was 3 percent in 1999 (SAFGJS 2000).

Operating under the Integration Concept from the 1970s, when the guest-worker model retained much of its influence, Bremen had less and less money to deal with a more and more differentiated immigrant-origin population. Bremen contained nonnationals from 160 countries. A dozen nationalities had more than one thousand residents. Socioeconomic, generational, gender, and other divisions were increasingly pertinent. The DAB's struggles to incorporate groups with highly diverse perspectives pointed to how difficult it was becoming to balance peak-level management with self-help and empowerment (SLHB 1997, 15).

Senator Borttscheller's inflammatory rhetoric notwithstanding, funding for programs to foster integration escaped major cutbacks. As before, official Bremen avoided wherever possible policies that targeted only immigrants and favored general policies aimed at problems that were facing disadvantaged Germans and immigrants alike. Limited resources precluded grand programs. The stress was on small projects that could be bundled together at the neighborhood level to achieve the widest possible reach and impact. The neighborhood remained the locus of activities, even after the June 1999 legislative election brought policy evolution in other respects. The vote confirmed the Grand Coalition in power while reducing the far right's representation to one deputy. In Bremen City, it polled fewer votes even than the former East German Communists in the Democratic Socialist Party. Just as notably, a DAB activist, a woman of Kurdish origin, was elected on the SPD list. In the ensuing shuffling a more moderate Christian Democrat replaced Ralf Borttscheller as the senator for internal affairs.

Policy Change

That substitution heralded a modification in Bremen's view of integration in 2000. The focal point shifted decisively away from "compensating disadvantage" to nurturing self-reliance, creating equal opportunities, improving German language skills, and "not only guaranteeing rights but also delegating duties" (Breeger 2000). The Senate looked into requiring community service work from social assistance recipients. Politically, minority cultures were within their rights to pursue distinctive behaviors in the private, familial, cultural, and religious realms. The limits to this freedom were set by fundamental human rights, such as women's equality, and the constitution (ALB 2001). Intercultural programs would always be preferred to those focused on a single national or ethnic group (SAFGJS 2000, 8–14).

The new policy emphases did not represent an end to Bremen's distinctiveness. Officials praised the "thick Bremen migration net" of services and institutions to facilitate immigrant integration (ALB 2001). Despite all of the budget cuts and service reductions, elements of the old machine preserved their power. Their promise was evident after the terrorist attacks in the United States in September 2001. Bremen's "differentiated treatment" of Islam and "long history of intensive inter-religious dialogue" helped to avert the kind of anti-Muslim incidents that struck other European cities (ALB 2002). The city's Action Circle Islam drew national attention. Formed by Muslims of all nationalities and ideologies that autumn, it initiated projects to inform local residents about Islam and to voice positions on issues of common concern. In another illustration, local Tamils founded northern Germany's first Hindu temple in 2003, to wide-ranging approbation. By that same year, the municipality had managed to up the percentage of immigrants among enrollees in vocational training programs to 21.7 percent—from only 2.6 percent as late as 1999 (Röpke 2003).

All the same, economic and demographic developments jeopardized the system's capacity to rein in the empowered immigrant-origin residents and self-help groups whose energies it had stoked, harnessed, and directed. The challenge to the SPD's power was another goad to adjustment. Its leadership responded by espousing an explicitly liberal multicultural model that underlined more plainly the limits to ethnic mobilization that had always been implicit in its policy repertoire. In May 2003, the Social Democrats' strategy seemed to find vindication in legislative election results: voters saved the Grand Coalition, even as they demonstrated the personal popularity of the Lord Mayor, Henning Scherf. His SPD maintained its position (42 percent) in the face of the party's near collapse nationally and an upsurge of local Greens. The DVU elected a lone deputy, thanks as before to the federal-state's quirky electoral law and the party's popularity in parts of Bremerhaven. In Bremen City, meanwhile, its support was down to a trivial 1.4 percent from 2.5 percent in 1999.[12]

Berlin: Self-Help, Conservative Style

Like its fellow Protestant Hansa city to the north, Berlin has long been a center of cosmopolitan, working-class values. It, too, avoided incorporation into the area that surrounded it after World War II. Its experience as a divided city, with its western section an artificially propped outpost of capitalist democracy, nonetheless marked it as unique. Famous for vibrant social movements, some mobilizing immigrants, Berlin nurtured them through its early espousal of decentralized administration and the self-help philosophy.

A conservative government introduced those concepts, however, and it was as intent on saving money as on ensuring social actors' autonomy. "Cheaper" political-cultural integration trumped structural integration, except in the area of education policy. Subsequent coalition governments did not alter that course of action. Trying to separate politics from multiculturalism, Berlin's policy sorcerers appeared to lose control over their apprentices from time to time. After unification, the city-state's financial situation slid into Bremen-like direness. Officials recentralized services and reacted as their counterparts in Nuremberg had to far less upsetting manifestations of ethnic unrest: they imposed a functional approach that downplayed ethnic differences and made the immigrant-origin population an integral part of all local departmental and institutional mandates.

A Progressive Record

Although not a major port, Berlin has had an even more illustrious history of welcoming immigration than Bremen. French Huguenots, Bohemian Protestants, and African slaves were among the foreigners in Prussia in the seventeenth and eighteenth centuries. After 1871, the German Reich's foreign policy and its rapid industrialization cemented Berlin's status as a magnet for students, technicians, and workers from the Ottoman Empire, peasants from Eastern Europe, colonial subjects from Africa, and, after World War I, anticolonial activists and refugees from many regions, including many Jews from the post-czarist Soviet Union (see ASB 1992; M. Müller 1993; Runge 1993). No one used the term "multicultural" to describe the mix of peoples, but by the 1920s, Berlin was famous for its acceptance of a highly variegated nonnative population.

World War II meant exile or death for most of the foreigners. That catastrophe left few traces of Berlin's prewar diversity. By 1946, for instance, only seventy-nine Turks lived in what was left of Berlin. Later than other parts of West Germany, and thus at a time when Turkey and Yugoslavia were the nearest countries whose available surplus labor supply had not been tapped, Berlin eventually imported guest workers for its metalworking and textile industries. They numbered just under eighty thousand by the early 1970s. That figure may have seemed high in absolute numbers, but West Berlin was never a city with an unusually large portion of non-German residents. And East Berlin's foreign population of twenty thousand Cubans, Angolans, Mozambicans, North Koreans, Chinese, and Vietnamese amounted to a mere 1.6 percent of its residents (Pfleghar 1992).

Shorn of its eastern half, isolated in the middle of East Germany, West Berlin seamlessly blended municipal and federal-state governance. The city-state's postunification constitution, passed in a popular referendum in 1995, to a large extent extended the West's constitution of 1950. Berlin's legislature, the House of Representatives, elects the lord mayor, who then proposes the senators who, once approved by a majority of deputies, constitute the state executive. Underneath those central structures are the borough administrations, which have exercised greater authority and autonomy than Bremen's district councils. Neither municipalities nor public-law corporations, they have shared responsibility for policy implementation with the main administration. It, in turn, has divided along departmental lines, with each senator exercising considerable discretion. Coordination has proved problematic (Heinelt 1997).

Crisis and Response

Postwar Berlin was a politically artificial and highly subsidized island in a Communist sea. The federal government's lifeline spared West Berlin for decades the excruciating industrial restructuring that Essen, Nuremberg, and Bremen all endured. Not until the events of 1989–1990 had dried up the moat around them did Berliners face the harsh realities of globalizing markets.

Immigrant workers did receive a foretaste. Two-thirds of them were in unskilled or semiskilled positions in 1985, double the proportion among native-stock Germans. A similarly lopsided share—44 percent versus 25 percent—were in heavy manufacturing and thus more heavily hit by what layoffs did occur. Low-level service jobs could only partially offset those losses. Immigrant-origin youths suffered the most: in 1986 their unemployment rate in West Berlin surpassed 20 percent, three times as high as among their German peers and higher than among their parents. Structural unemployment and inadequate vocational training meant that they entered the labor market with little experience, competing against their elders and Germans (ASB 1991b).

Before reunification, West Berlin's artificially sustained industrial base had limited demand for imported labor. The settlement ban that the federal government introduced in 1974, which prevented non-Europeans from moving to areas where their percentage exceeded 12 percent, continued in West Berlin until 1990. It did not prevent family reunification but did keep the city-state's immigrant population under 14.5 percent before East and West came together. By then, almost two-thirds of Turkish Berliners had been born or raised in the city, and the percentage was even higher for Greeks and (soon-to-be) former Yugoslavs (ASB 1998, 31–32).

At first, employers provided housing for immigrant workers. Once family reunification began, they started to rent units on their own. They moved into older neighborhoods with cheaper housing, much of it in need of renovation. In terms of living space and private bathrooms, their units suffered in comparison to those occupied by native Germans. Immigrants from rural areas like Anatolia lived mostly in the city core. By 1973, fully 20 percent of the non-German population and 30 percent of Turks resided in Kreuzberg. The settlement ban restricted new moves there, as well as into the core Wedding and Tiergarten boroughs, and gentrification pushed immigrants into adjoining areas. The rental policy of the public housing corporations reinforced those trends and was scattering immigrant-origin families across the central city area (Kapphan 1995). For city planning purposes the concentration of immigrant-origin families appeared as a negative indicator in an neighborhood's social index (ASB 1991a).

Immigrants' Structural Integration

True to German form, West Berlin originally left the task of integrating immigrant workers and their families to the big nonprofit associations. Recalling Bremen and Nuremberg, AWO and Diakonisches Werk played key roles in the blue-collar, Protestant city-state. Already in 1971, however, West Berlin's Senate took up the issue of "foreigner integration," above all that of the second and third immigrant generations, and fashioned a planning team that included no immigrants. It produced a "needs-oriented" integration model that acknowledged Germany's status as a de facto immigration country and called for voluntary, long-range planning in each department concerned. In practice, the big nonprofits bore most of the burden of implementation.[13]

In 1981, the CDU took over city hall, ending the SPD's postwar dominance and joining forces with its erstwhile Free Democratic Party ally. Richard von Weizsäcker was lord mayor until 1984, when Eberhard Diepgen assumed the position that he would hold past the century's end. The structural marginalization of immigrant-origin residents was worsening, and the new coalition reexamined the entire relationship between general social services, experimental projects in the neighborhoods, immigrant associations, and the ethnic-based social work of the overwhelmed social welfare nonprofits. Turkish associational leaders decried the high ratio of Turks per social worker (4,278:1) in AWO (Puskeppeleit 1989, 14).

In 1985 the West Berlin Senate announced a new subsidiarity policy, which brought extensive funding for self-help groups, including those that were active in work with immigrants alongside the large nonprofits. Self-help services were more flexible and responsive, officials argued, and allowed for freer cultural expression. The original intention was for the government to provide only start-up costs. It was soon clear that many groups would never be able to pay their own way, and, ultimately, resources were provided for general operating costs, coordination, and personnel training. The administration did not commit to new personnel slots or open up decision-making processes. Unlike in Bremen, the groups and projects themselves were not permitted to help divvy up funds.

Almost a decade earlier than in Nuremberg, West Berlin was moving away from the existing ethnoreligiously delineated division of labor under nonprofit stewardship and toward a functional division among city-state departments. Decentralized efforts in the neighborhoods were key to the new line of attack, which started with pilot projects that built on an experiment in Wedding in the late 1970s. The idea was to move away from separate immigrant policies and to imbue all agencies with intercultural openness and savvy. Another motivation was to ensure the institutional future of existing providers: the nonprofits' work was being supplemented, not supplanted (Döcker 1992).

The city-state expressed a desire to reduce central tutelage. In reality, the administration confirmed and broadened the scope of its authority. In 1981 West Berlin had installed a commissioner for foreigners, Barbara John (CDU), who would still be in office when the third millennium began. Like her fellow commissioners for the disabled, addiction problems, and psychiatry, she had a mandate to monitor her charges, assess all policies affecting them, sensitize Senate departments and public opinion to their needs, and oversee the Senate commission that handled immigrant policies. Commissioner John's staff grew to twice the size of that at the Federal Commission for Foreigners in Bonn. She disposed of funds to support self-help groups active in immigrant integration. In her role as something akin to a court-appointed lawyer, she regularly took unpopular positions that did not challenge the system but forced it to be more inclusive and evenhanded (Boos-Nünning and Schwarz 1991).

The senator for health and social affairs that supervised both John's office and public social assistance programs did not coordinate well with other departments. Moreover, indirectly incorporating ethnic organizations did not lighten the weight of West Berlin's bureaucracy. Relations of dependence reduced organizational autonomy on both sides. The nonprofit associations' paternalism gave way to the paternalism of local policymaking structures, guided by their own interests—at least in the eyes of unhappy associations, churches, and trade unions (Grottian, Kotz, and Lütke 1986). Turkish and North African associations that had struggled to move out from under AWO's wings found themselves in the smothering embrace of the state (Effinger 1985, 74). Providers and projects began to compete against each other for the city-state's largesse. Ethnic divisions widened, organizational finances grew wobbly, and violence broke out.

West Berlin, a haven for rebellious youth, knew to take seriously the federal government's warnings about the ticking second-immigrant-generation time bomb. Apprehension spawned a range of programs that addressed all educational levels in the early 1980s. They were heterogeneous and not well coordinated, hampered by the entrenched, ethnic-based involvement of the social welfare nonprofits. The city-state accepted targeted schemes to deal with unique problems, but otherwise it imposed generalist, intercultural youth work (Schwarz 1992). In stark contrast with Bavaria, West Berlin's school system aimed from an early date for the full integration of immigrant workers' progeny: the German system predominated, and homeland language instruction was voluntary. The city-state started at the borough level. The aforementioned experiment with integrated social services in Wedding, for example, involved plans to mainstream immigrant-origin students and phase out "ghettoizing" specialized classes for them.

By applying and generalizing the lessons learned in its boroughs, West Berlin put together a policy response in the 1980s, even as it cut its budgets. Prized were quick, nonbureaucratic tactics designed to address a very rapidly changing set of problems and to bring about an intercultural opening of local services (ABW 1992). Despite its jerry-built quality, West Berlin's plan to better the lot of immigrant-origin youths widened the scope of interventions and recorded some successes in advancing their structural integration. Over half of the more than 100 million deutsche marks designated in the state budget for immigrant integration at decade's end flowed into the educational arena. The Senate took pride at having boosted parental involvement: it had initiated one of the two Turkish parents' organizations active in the city-state. Immigrant-origin children were overrepresented in West Berlin's kindergartens, a situation that the Senate applauded, since it meant early acclimatization to the German educational system. Positive trends likewise included falling percentages of immigrant-origin youths who left secondary school without certification—from 39 percent in 1981 to 30 percent in 1987—and rising percentages who attended a *Gymnasium*—from 14 percent to 23 percent. There were variations according to nationality, and among Greeks attendance at that highest level of schooling was almost as high as among German students. Also between 1981 and 1987 the percentage of job training positions occupied by immigrants doubled, to 9.4 percent, placing West Berlin first among the federal-states. There remained much room for improvement, the Senate acknowledged. Particularly vexing to officials was a drift toward ethnic and religious revival, evident even among better-educated youths (ASB 1991b).

Immigrants displayed the higher levels of criminality that typified lower-income groups in Berlin. Whenever they fell away from their tightly disciplined families, immigrant-origin youths got more involved in drugs and crime. As in other German cities, the hip-hop music and dance scene, dominated by non-European adolescents, was the benign manifestation of generational and ethnic tensions in West Berlin. The city-state also had an escalating problem with gangs, however. The earliest ones appeared in the mid-1980s to offer their members self-protection and autonomy. They were at first solely male and largely Turkish but gradually took in female members and youths of other national backgrounds. Clashing with young ethnic-German migrants and right-wing skinheads, they were rooted in particular neighborhoods.

In West Berlin young men were exempt from the military draft, and the city acted like a magnet for radicals and countercultural social movements. While they resisted attempts by anarchists and others to co-opt them, some immigrant gang members did take part in rioting in the Kreuzberg neighborhood on May Day 1987, occasioned by opposition to the federal census and the end of rent control on older housing units. An unexpectedly weak response from the forces of order—in the city with Europe's highest per-capita police presence—emboldened protesters. Over several days, they burned cars, smashed shop windows, and looted (Prey 1989). Immigrant involvement was spontaneous. Yet a couple of years later, just as run-ins with skinheads were declining, bona fide gang wars erupted. In 1989, a "peace treaty" was signed, and one of the most notorious bands, the Schöneberg Barbarians, converted itself into a youth center. The gang scene calmed down markedly thereafter, although many youngsters of immigrant origin were disconnected from West Berlin society (Greve and Çinar 1998).

Immigrants' Political-Cultural Integration

Despite all of that tumult, under its CDU-led administration West Berlin was earning a reputation for ingenuity in its dealings with immigrants in the political-cultural realm. It made immigrants' stay in the state as legally secure as possible, and a high share of the immigrant-origin population had permanent residency permits. It was the only state that allowed underage children to stay if their parents returned to their homelands. Additionally, four times as many immigrants were naturalized in West Berlin than in any other German city in the late 1980s. In 1958 the Interior Department had taken over responsibility for naturalizations from the police force and quickly adopted a very lenient position. Over the years, naturalization fees dropped significantly. The city-state grew more accepting of multiple nationalities, particularly for children who received most of their schooling in Germany. Formal citizenship was viewed by the Senate as a means of reducing barriers and tensions between West Berliners of different backgrounds (Rittstieg 1992).

When the Federal Administrative Court nixed local voting rights for immigrants, West Berlin focused on consultative bodies and immigrant associational activity. Most boroughs had their own commissioner for foreigners. In addition, most had an appointed, immigrant-led foreigners' auxiliary council, with the right to issue opinions on topics relevant to social relations in the neighborhoods. The councils could appoint nonnationals as "citizen deputies," envoys to local administrative departments (ABW 1992).

Overseeing the borough foreigners' councils, West Berlin's commissioner for foreigners pushed hard for the creation of umbrella immigrant associations that would serve her need for credible social partners. Regrettably for her, the immigrants' organizations mirrored the ideological divisions and social stratification within their communities. The Turkish "microsociety" alone produced more than one hundred associations (Wilpert 1991). Smaller arrays emerged from groups with roots in other countries, including Morocco, Tunisia, and other Arab countries. Distinct, loose associational networks gradually formed out of the worker, conservative-nationalist, and Islamist movements. Two major Turkish federations gelled, one more conservative and Islamic in orientation and the other close to the social democratic and trade union movements. Commissioner John's office backed the leftist federation, but it was unable to gain primacy (Blaschke 1987).

Regional identities rooted in the homeland were slowly giving way to neighborhood identities in West Berlin, and German activists trained in social work were handing the reins of leadership to immigrants. The city-state was happy to shift more responsibility for integration policy to the "clients" themselves. Once highly politicized associations metamorphosed into de facto social welfare providers. Their shaky finances meant that public subsidies were essential—more than 610,000 deutsche marks by 1984 (AB/SGSF 1985, 35). Islamic organizations were not eligible to receive public funds, and West Berlin's policy toward them was one of benign neglect. In 1988, Berlin contained more than thirty mosques and two Muslim cemeteries, one of them more than two centuries old. Islamic religious instruction was tolerated, but it was the responsibility of the religious communities themselves. The Milli Görüs movement was even allowed to establish Germany's first Islamic school in 1989.[14]

The Difficult 1990s

Berlin did not face a true challenge until after the wall dividing it had fallen in 1989. Unification brought transformations in the immigrant condition in both the western and eastern sections of the city. Emerging intact, West Berlin's center-led approach, which played up political-cultural integration more than the structural dimension, was extended to the east and generated more ethnic mobilization than in the other German case cities.

Whereas solidarity and subsidiarity were the West German watchwords, East Germany had developed expansive, centralized social policies. Yet East Berlin's small non-German population of contract laborers and students had been the subject of only spotty, sporadic social and cultural work, most often in dissident church circles. Immigrant voting rights, the product of East Germany's short-lived transition between state socialism and absorption into the Federal Republic, disappeared by the time unification was complete in fall 1990. Nonnationals elected to seats in borough parliaments in Hellersdorf,

Hohenschönhausen, Pankow, and Weissensee that May could not run again. Immigrant-origin candidates with German citizenship could and did, mostly in the western boroughs and on the Green and Alternative lists. Several figured on those of the SPD and CDU as well (Ireland 1997).

Not long after unification, Eberhard Diepgen was back at the head of a Grand Coalition and had to deal with the difficult 1990s. The end of Berlin's "island" status brought the end of its artificial life support. Half of the West Berlin government had been financed by federal aid. Those subsidies dried up as capital was diverted to rebuild eastern Germany. Industries began leaving in the same direction, and unemployment rates climbed, affecting immigrant workers most severely. By 1994, 22.3 percent would be out of work, compared to 13.3 percent overall (ASB 1998, 51). Social assistance rates climbed steadily, in consequence, with immigrants, children, and residents of Kreuzberg, Neukölln, and Wedding boroughs hit most severely. The financial crunch led to cuts in funding for social assistance, programs to help ease the unemployed back into the labor market, and child benefits (SLBE 1998). As the decade wore on, the immigrants were showing signs of continuing disconnection. By 2000, just more than a third of immigrant workers would be unemployed, twice the overall Berlin rate. Almost 40 percent of Berlin's immigrants met the Organization for Economic Cooperation and Development's definition of poverty, as opposed to 9.4 percent of native-stock Germans. Over 17 percent of the immigrant population was on social assistance, compared to only 5.4 percent of all residents (SGSV 2002, 100–102).

A perceptible number of immigrants were achieving socioeconomic mobility. Those who were not—still a clear majority—were undergoing processes equally manifest among poor native-stock Germans: poverty among the elderly, low educational and training levels among youths, and a reinforcement of disadvantage across generations. Obstacles specific to immigrants—language and cultural difficulties, discrimination—only worsened the situation. Berlin officials worried about the "ethnicization" of "socioeconomic segments," in other words, a hardening of the association between ethnic origin and socioeconomic disadvantage that could lead to a culture of poverty and anti-immigrant hostility (SGSV 2002, 108).

Further taxing authorities' capacity to respond, Berlin's immigrant population was diversifying. In 1997, 13 percent of Berlin's residents were immigrants. They hailed from 184 countries, just one less than the United Nations' 185 members. Turks constituted less than a third of the nonnationals, down from almost 45 percent in 1985, but still 36.1 percent in the West (compared to only 5.5 percent in the East). The Arabic-speaking population was fast growing, led by Palestinians and Lebanese. Building itself into Germany's capital, Berlin pulled in large numbers of construction workers from Morocco ("Ausländer in Berlin" 1997).

As Berlin inched toward its new status, exploding rents drove immigrants and other poor residents out of gentrifying boroughs like Kreuzberg, once tucked away behind a bend in the Berlin Wall and suddenly at the center of postunification activity. The emerging immigrant-origin middle class was beginning to move out of blighted inner-city neighborhoods, and immigrant concentrations grew in the more comfortable parts of the city and those outlying areas where refugee centers had been established (ASB 1998). There may have been a general trend toward declining segregation—a more even spread across the western section of the city-state—but the immigrant presence intensified overall as native-stock Berliners moved in droves to newly accessible suburbs in the federal-state of Brandenburg. Neighborhoods with higher-than-average immigrant concentrations scored lowest on the city-state's social index, indication of a movement in the direction of income homogenization. The housing situation improved with lesser segregation, but overcrowding still plagued the immigrant-origin population. Local housing corporations doubled their efforts to set aside units from the private market. Rental policy was adjusted to facilitate integration (SGSV 2002).

Earlier advances in narrowing the success rates of immigrant- and German-stock students in Berlin's schools were maintained in regular education, for the most part. The percentage of immigrant students without secondary-level certification fell to a record low of 23.2 percent in 1996, down from 35 percent in 1984 (in West Berlin). Among Germans the percentage was 9.7 in 1996, and the differential had held fairly steady. The percentage of students who successfully navigated a *Gymnasium,* passing their final examination *(Abitur),* and who were of Turkish origin had risen from 1.8 percent in 1984 to 10.3 percent a decade later. Immigrants were still relatively numerous among those with no secondary-school diploma or job-training certification and were relatively scarce among those who successfully completed the highest educational levels. Even at the high and low extremes, however, they were making headway, and in the middle ranges they had eliminated or narrowed the gap with their German peers (ASB 1998, 9).

The quota regulation that had limited the numbers of immigrant students in mixed regular classes was being abolished. Events had already passed that restriction by in several neighborhoods, however. In sections of Kreuzberg and Wedding, there were schools whose student bodies were more than 60 percent immigrant, two-thirds of them Turks; in a few classrooms the teacher was the only German present (ASB 1998, 8). Ominously, the share of non-Germans in special schools rose from .5 percent in the early 1970s to 40 percent by the late 1990s—when immigrants constituted less than 20 percent of the total student population (Greve and Çinar 1998, 44).

The tale was similar with respect to vocational training, where sharpened competition from better qualified applicants from eastern Germany and budget cuts in the mid-1990s had produced lower rates of immigrant participation. Nonnationals filled only 6 percent of training positions in 1996, down from more than 13 percent in 1990 (ASB 1998, 55). Immigrant-origin minorities were underrepresented in federally funded programs to fight unemployment and to find work for recipients of social assistance. Hurting the professional chances of immigrant-origin youths were poor German language skills, which prevented access to many job training and apprenticeship opportunities. In that area, at any rate, financing increased dramatically, up 160 percent between 1995 and 1999. Classes were designed for students but also for their mothers and teachers. Demand for German courses still seriously outstripped supply (BMI 2002; SGSV 2002).

Berlin was most active in the political-cultural realm, as usual, and its methods sparked more ethnic-based identity formation and activity. The office of Commissioner for Foreigners Barbara John was the nucleus of the integration policy world. Some CDU loyalists felt that she pushed her mandate too far. The Greens and many immigrant groups criticized her for caring more about individual cases than about wider policies and for assuming the primordial importance of ethnic identities (Doering 1996). She lobbied the federal government for a nondiscrimination law, despite the opposition of the Turkish-origin commissioner for foreigners of the Tiergarten district, who argued that such legislation "would create an ethnic orientation among part of the population and encourage racist reactions among others" ("Discussion" 1992, 145–46). Thanks in part to John's pressure, the 1995 Berlin constitution forbade all discrimination based on gender, race, language, national background, religion, political views, or sexual orientation (art. 10, par. 2).

Berlin maintained and celebrated its status as the federal-state with the highest naturalization rates. It granted 25 to 30 percent of all naturalizations in the Federal Republic, indicative of a sustained, targeted public information campaign. In 1991 Turks represented only 18 percent of those naturalized, but by 1998 that share had risen to 42 percent. Numbers were expected to rise after reforms of Germany's citizenship law. Applicants for formal citizenship would thereafter have spent less time in the country and would be expected to pass a German language test. Berlin's shortcomings in that area loomed critical. Officials scrambled to muster a riposte (BMI 2002).

Almost three-quarters of Turks had unlimited and permanent residency permits, and they and other immigrants were active in all mainstream German political parties. A handful of people of immigrant origin served in the Berlin legislature and borough councils in Kreuzberg, Schöneberg, Charlottenburg, and Wedding. Early in the 1990s, the city-state established a Foreigners Parliament, comprising more than one hundred appointed delegates selected on the basis of ethnonational background.

There was a gulf opening between that integrated immigrant elite and a disaffected mass base. Commissioner John commissioned a survey in 1994 in which 70 percent of the immigrant respondents said that no association represented their interests. Dominated by a tight clutch of activists, the estab-

lished, subsidized immigrant associations had entered into a dependent relationship with the city-state administration and had separated themselves from
their constituency. It was not spatial segregation, budget cutting, or a worsening structural situation that was generating political-cultural disconnection.
Rather, official reinforcement of cultural difference and their maintenance of
a paternalistic attitude toward their immigrant-origin charges pushed the bulk
of them into either resignation or confrontation.

Apart from the youth gangs, the ethnic revival was not so much militant as
it was defensive. Self-help movements declined and were in a sense replaced by
ethnic businesses. They numbered more than 16,000 by the mid-1990s, with
more than 2,200 in the former East Berlin, and employed more than 45,000
people. Trade (30 percent), construction (26 percent), and gastronomy (over
20 percent) accounted for most of this activity (ASB 1998, 7). Small entrepreneurs rarely had the time or inclination to engage in traditional associational
activity. The changing structure of migration also worked against it. Undocumented immigrants and refugees had limited opportunities to organize, and
the newer, smaller national groups lacked the stability and critical mass needed
to build up durable organizations.[15]

The Muslim population was becoming even more diverse than before, too.
Since Berlin's law on religious instruction spoke of "confessions," it was possible to argue for approval not of courses in Islam but in the Sunnite, Shiite,
and other traditions. Frightened by visions of fragmentation, the Senate's Department of Schools began talking with representatives of the Christian
churches about making religious instruction a public and not a denominational responsibility, making it an elective within the normal curriculum. General, nondenominational ethics classes would round out the options and ensure equal treatment. The city-state appealed a court decision that allowed a
local Islamic association to oversee instruction for Muslims, concerned that
fundamental constitutional rights (freedom of expression and the equality of
the sexes) might not be protected (Leicht 2001). To limit the reach of the
mosque associations, officials struggled to identify appropriate social welfare
providers for Muslims (see ASB 1998, 18).

Many of Berlin's immigrant-origin residents seemed to be turning inward,
toward their own informal social networks. Berlin's Senate called on the social
welfare nonprofits to open their ranks more completely to immigrants and
pull them in. Generally, local members of the DPWV exerted itself more than
the Big Three in devising innovative avant-garde intercultural projects, especially in its work with youths and senior citizens. Kreuzberg was cited as the
neighborhood where such beneficial network building had gone the furthest.
Eastern Berlin, too, was proving willing and able to profit from federal and
European funding designed to build up social infrastructure (BMI 2002, 68).

The Senate hoped that funding immigrant associations would stabilize
them, build up their competence and confidence, and enable them to make

real contributions to the intercultural opening process. As it was, they were still training their gaze principally toward the homelands and presented an uneven, disjointed organizational picture that jibed poorly with the vision of Berlin policymakers. They bemoaned immigrants' failure to organize into one or two major associations that could speak for their members, lobby, and usefully channel public funding and logistical support. The Senate warned about the danger to immigrant integration posed by dual nationality, which threatened to create "national minorities within the Federal Republic" and thereby "lay dynamite under the unity of the nation" (SIB 1999, 7).

The city-state took pains neither to dramatize nor to downplay criminal behavior on the part of immigrants. Berlin had a relatively high crime rate, and nonnationals were heavily implicated. As elsewhere, when they screened for social and structural factors and screened out organized crime, officials discovered that resident immigrants were, if anything, less prone to criminal involvement than those of native German stock. Kurdish separatists were very active in Berlin, as were far-left Turkish groups. Despite the sound and fury, only 1.3 percent of the immigrant-origin population was involved in extremist movements ("Ausländer-Extremismus" 1996). The city-state itself, like the other three local German cases, ranked low in terms of violent offenses against immigrants and asylum seekers. Analogies to Los Angeles notwithstanding, Berlin was not ripe for widespread interethnic rioting. To be safe, Commissioner of Foreigners John came up with a host of antiracism measures, many of which featured conflict resolution, cultural awareness, and mediation techniques imported from the United States. Projects ranged from recreational centers to street workers to a "rockmobile"—a minibus fully equipped with musical equipment and specially trained music teachers. John's office also engaged in individual arbitration to reduce prejudice between neighbors and people in schools, discotheques, public and private housing, and the workplace. In keeping with its predilection for policies in "softer" cultural sectors, furthermore, Berlin highlighted sports far more insistently than other cities as a venue in which to bring immigrants and native-stock Berliners together. Federal German officials touted the eclectic "Berlin strategy" for fighting discrimination and violence at EU meetings (ASB 1998, 15–16)

Policy Change

Well-intentioned and creative though they were, Berlin's immigrant integration policies were scattershot and, as noted, favored ethnic-based political-cultural aspects over structural ones. They thereby set in motion forces that they did not have the resources to dictate. Instead of structuring immigrant associations, Berlin provided enough assistance to encourage ethnic identity formation and interethnic competition—right at the time when anti-immigrant forces were targeting certain ethnic groups and forcing their defensive reaction. In 1998, Commissioner John's budget for approximately thirty-five

Turkish federations and individual associations was 1.5 million deutsche marks. That figure may have sounded significant, yet it amounted to only 10 marks per Turkish resident. Spending for education, job training, and housing continued to grow. Global financial support for the "artistic and socio-cultural" activities of immigrant associations declined by some 20 percent between 1996 and 2000, however, as did monies channeled through the district councils for the same purposes (BMI 2002, 36–39). Compounded by the drastic personnel cuts necessitated by the city-state's financial crisis, such tightening inhibited a full-scale drive to anchor the mobilizational potential of self-help initiatives and empowerment in networks that were pivotal to revamped social policies. Instead, Berlin stressed the coexistence of cultures and tried to do more with less.

In practice, it was small, street-level action that counted. Activities that raised cultural awareness and tackled prosaic concerns in a sprawling, variegated urban landscape took center stage. Commissioner John continued to orchestrate events on the immigrants' behalf. Eventually, an immigrant ombudsperson was instituted to facilitate interactions between the government and the immigrant-origin population. Aware of charges that its policies had lacked coherence, the CDU-led administration planned to introduce intercultural practices aimed specifically at facilitating integration into every corner of the local administration, a tack—it was believed—that would ultimately prove far more useful than the piecemeal projects that had predominated. In light of the city's dire financial situation, however, the raft of projects that the Berlin Senate hoped to compile in this respect would have to be "cost neutral" (BMI 2002).

There was a substantial public relations dimension to immigrant integration policy in Berlin. More than in the other case cities, even Essen, officials in Berlin portrayed the immigrants' colorful, diverse presence as a real contribution to the city-state's competitive position in the international economy. Ethnic businesses, especially restaurants, became an accepted indicator of the city's multinational, "fun" character. The commission for foreigners authorized a series of vignettes of the immigrant communities that had come to form the contemporary "world metropolis" of Berlin. There were regular telephone surveys of German-stock and Turkish residents, whose responses suggested that, give or take a hiccup, backing for integration was strengthening among the former (ASB 2001) and that feelings of well-being in Berlin were deepening among the latter (see table 3.4). The city-state was confident that its policies would prevent the development of parallel societies in Berlin (SSJS 2001).

The city-state's line of attack underwent only minor rectification after the 2001 Berlin election, won by a resurgent SPD (30.9 percent), which subsequently formed a controversial "red-red" coalition with the ex-Communist

TABLE 3.4

Turks in Berlin (Survey of +1,000 Turkish Residents over Eighteen)

	Very Well/ Good (%)	Well/ Good (%)	Not Well/ Good (%)	Unsure (%)
"Do you feel well in Berlin?"				
1993	28	48	24	
1999	22	58	20	1
2001	29	53	18	
2001 (<30 years old)	33	52	15	
"How does your future look?"				
1993	6	33	52	9
1999	5	52	36	7
2001	9	48	38	5
Interviewer assessment of respondent's German language skills				
1993	49	25	26	
1999	48	21	31	
2001	52	25	23	

Source: ASB (2002, 2–3, 7, 16).

Democratic Socialist Party (19.6 percent). Klaus Wowereit of the SPD became the mayor. In their coalition statement the two parties declared their support for the ongoing intercultural opening of city-state services, full exploitation of any leeway in federal immigration laws, equal opportunity for immigrant "clients" as a cross-sectoral policy goal, the implementation of EU policies on equality of treatment, the fight against racism and discrimination, faster and simpler naturalization procedures, and a concerted fight against the sexual trafficking of women and children (SPD Berlin 2001). Butting up against the age limit for public service, Barbara John stepped down as commissioner for foreigners in June 2003. Her replacement, Günter Piening, was named commissioner for integration and migration. A sociologist and journalist close to the Greens who had served since 1996 in the same position in the new federal-state of Sachsen-Anhalt, he held views that appeared to diverge from Barbara John's only in that they were turned more insistently eastward. Commissioner Piening oversaw the implementation of the Berlin Senate's decision in 2003 to establish a Federal-State Council for Integration and Migration. Sitting alongside seventeen representatives from the Berlin government and associational scene were six members "elected" by officially recognized immigrant organizations. The city-state maintained its benevolent tutelage (SGSV 2003).

Conclusion

A comparison of structural and political-cultural integration policies in Essen, Nuremberg, Bremen, and Berlin from the mid-1970s to the start of the twenty-first century yields several key lessons. The evidence suggests that institutional restructuring set off by unemployment, immigration, and welfare state evolution mattered more than cultural factors in determining the state of local ethnic relations. Structural disconnection escalated, then reversed slightly over the 1990s. During that initial period, policies to foster political-cultural integration generated ethnic tensions and sporadic violence when they emphasized cultural identities and fused with the social welfare nonprofits' ethnic-based logic in the absence of effective public-sector control.

The structural and political-cultural integration indices employed in each locality indicated definite, if still insufficient, progress over the focus period taken as a whole. Never more than modest, spending levels on immigrant integration policies held steady in the face of severe budgetary constraints. The same was true of social policies in a broader sense, notwithstanding those reductions that did occur. Hit by the fallout of economic restructuring and the burdens dumped on them by the federal government, the four German cities rose to the challenge. The best efforts of municipal and city-state policymakers managed to keep the trend line in education, vocational training, and housing quality from dipping. In all four cities young people of immigrant origin made only limited advances in the labor market and in the political and cultural realms. If improvements in their lot could sometimes appear glacially slow, enough advances were made to defuse revolt. Essen, Nuremberg, Bremen, and Berlin were relatively tranquil, if gritty places.

In spite of some bettering of housing conditions, local officials were unable to prevent residential concentration. It was an open question whether the spatial clustering of immigrant-origin populations contributed to disconnection and conflict. A complex phenomenon, it has been a perennial subject of debate in urban research circles since the days of the Chicago School. Was concentration a barrier to integration or its incubator? No clear answer emerges from this study. Since levels of disconnection fluctuated, while the movement toward concentration was steady, no strong relationship seems to hold.

The four German cities showcased here had accepted their multiethnic reality by the late 1990s, in spite of fears over its divisive aspects. Authorities struggled to reconcile their responsibilities for the well-being of the entire local resident population with the demands of the constituencies voting them into and out of office. Each municipality explicitly criticized the federal government's refusal to acknowledge that the country had become a country of immigration and called for local-level immigrant suffrage.

Those local governments had several integration-related priorities in common. For example, behind the overwhelming majority of programs for immigrant-origin students everywhere was the intention of educating German- and immigrant-stock youngsters together as soon as possible. Intercultural education grew from an exotic notion into a mantra, put into practice with varying degrees of success, and accompanied by a growing insistence on the German language as a lingua franca. There was likewise a common movement toward small-scale, neighborhood-level social work that was targeted and group specific only when it had to be. Even coordination was decentralized: instead of overarching social engineering, planning dimensions were introduced into the social administration itself and into relationships between all implicated institutions and actors, defined in terms of concrete, geographically rooted interventions. The goal was to provide interactive projects that would link local agencies and consolidate local actions, harnessing a city's associational energies and containing crime.

In general, each municipality sustained privileged relations with the large social welfare nonprofits—Caritas, Diakonisches Werk, and AWO. They lost ground everywhere, even so, giving way to a broader range of associational actors but also to functionally delineated city services. "Administration" ceded to corporate-style "management." The impact of budgetary restraint from the late 1970s was ambivalent. On the one hand, cities were less excited about financing new associational initiatives, especially those that represented new demands with little legitimacy. On the other hand, cities tried to use the new movements as multipliers, encouraging self-help in order to circumvent fiscal constraints.

In social work circles, too, agreement gradually built that the field's existing methodologies—case work, group work, and community work—had to be blended and transcended to produce a flexible response toward social problems. The popularity of self-help groups and notions of empowerment faced social workers with a twofold challenge: they were confronted with an atypical conception of social work, putting in doubt the relevance of established ways of doing things, and also had to deal with new competitors for available monies. The growing complexity of immigrant-origin populations and the diversification of their needs and demands caused the contradictions between administrative logic and associational desires to rise to the surface.

Policy responses were far from identical. How the process played out depended on the ways in which the kaleidoscope of local institutions, services, and associations lined up and interacted. Sometimes a resilient web of personal connections, friendships, and rivalries took shape. Underplayed in the literature, which has focused overwhelmingly on conflictual and cultural aspects of the immigrant experience in Germany, this more constructive side of the story bears telling. Policy decisions had real consequences, even if local officials often felt as though they were "shoveling snow in Alaska" (John 1995, 5).

Although Berlin, Bremen, Essen, and Nuremberg had been bastions of the

SPD, local conditions and particularities produced significant political variance, which, in turn, yielded distinctive policies for immigrant-origin residents. Social Democrats did not come through the trying postboom decades
in the same shape in the four cities. Their discrete experiences led them to react in distinctive ways to such concepts as self-help, empowerment, and multiculturalism. Ethnic tensions did not flare to the same heights in each locality. Structural and—despite higher rates of naturalization—political-cultural
disconnection reached its highest levels in Berlin, where gentrification actually
reduced segregation (if not concentration) over the three decades at issue.
Apparent were the disconnective by-products of self-help and social policy
decentralization as they occurred under the auspices of the Christian Democrats, who coupled self-help with a concentration on cultural identities.
Bremen demonstrated that top-down direction was not always incompatible
with the stimulation of collective identities and empowerment. Such energies
were harnessed and channeled effectively there, at least until the money and
political will played out. Crime and drugs grew into more prominent causes of
anxiety and objects of policy in each of those two city-states than in Essen and
Nuremberg, whereas the far right posed a greater political threat in Bremen
and Nuremberg than in Berlin and, especially, Essen. Officials in that Ruhr
Valley city tinkered with traditional Social Democratic policy in their predilection for the foreigners' auxiliary council and accepted the Big Three
nonprofits' ethnic-based approach. They retained their basic assimilationist
assumptions and their control, though, even as a modest move toward congruence in structural integration continued to temper conflict. Their counterparts
in Nuremberg switched more definitively away from ethnicity and toward
functional services operating on intercultural principles when self-help and
empowerment appeared to breed political-cultural disconnection. Then, the
Christian Social Union took over and tried to reduce that side of integration
to a celebration of culture and folklore.

Developments were modulated by the ways in which welfare state restructuring proceeded in the four localities. Even in cities with so much in common, structural and political-cultural integration policies varied from the
start, and their sequences and trajectories reflected differing local emphases.
They clearly marked the integration processes of immigrants of all generations
from Turkey and Morocco, to whom particular attention has been paid.

Even in the pioneering cities that have figured here so far, the sums
expended to further immigrant integration were never vast. Local officials
found it impossible to resist broader structural forces that were generating
structural unemployment and spatial concentration. They had to operate
within a legal framework set at the federal and (in the cases of Essen and
Nuremberg) federal-state levels and accept the responsibilities defaulting onto
them. The next chapter adds to the mix several neighboring cases to which

progressive German officials sometimes longingly looked for ideas: the Netherlands and Belgium, where the legal and policy parameters were, by and large, more expansive and where financial outlays in the area of immigrant integration were larger (see Zuwanderungskommission 2001).

4 THE NETHERLANDS

Pillars, Pragmatism, and
Welfare State Restructuring

As the twenty-first century began, German ethnic relations owed more to so-cial policy restructuring and related integration policies than to immigrants' ethnic backgrounds and cultures. Instead of climbing in linear fashion, ethnic tensions fluctuated over time and location. They were not always high. Gen-erally, in fact, they were lower than might have been expected, given the enor-mity of the challenges associated with immigration and the ferocity of the anti-immigrant reaction.

Belying their reputation for passivity in this area, federal, federal-state, and local governments actively sought to facilitate immigrant integration, even if they were not willing or able to dispense large sums of money. The compari-son of four German cities has suggested the range of progressive policy re-sponses. Where structural integration was the focal point and municipal con-trol was maintained, as in Essen, ethnic conflict remained rather minimal. In the absence of official sponsorship for self-help movements and empower-ment in social work, however, immigrants started to detach themselves from local institutions. In Bremen structural integration policies were accompanied by others in the political-cultural realm both to unlock immigrants' potential and then to exploit their dynamism. The outcome was somewhat more con-flict but also a peak immigrant association that corresponded to German expectations and fit with the German policymaking process. In Nuremberg the stimulation of self-help and acceptance of empowerment occurred without as much initial concern over control. When policies produced ethnic-based fric-tion, the local government swung from ethnically targeted programs toward responsive yet functionally divided services that minimized ethnic demarcation. Berlin, finally, was one city where political-cultural integration received more emphasis than structural integration. There was much ethnic effervescence—some of it creative, some of it destructive. Boundaries between ethnic groups took on greater meaning and visibility.

The German national and local cases thus suggest that the relationship between structural and political-cultural integration policies has important implications for ethnic relations, in the context of welfare state restructuring. The Netherlands represents the ideal case to probe that relationship. As opposed to their counterparts at the federal level and in many federal-states and cities in Germany, who focused in the beginning almost exclusively on structural integration, the Dutch policymakers responsible for immigrants only slowly came to converge on measures along that dimension. Political-cultural integration was the initial focal point. Up through the early years of the new millennium, Dutch policies—linked to a different process of welfare state restructuring and different attitudes toward self-help and empowerment—initially produced less structural congruence, but more political-cultural congruence, among immigrants than in Germany. The result was ethnic-based mobilization that Dutch policymakers understood and welcomed, at least until it took on forms that they had not expected and spawned disruptions.

A Latecomer to Immigration

Owing to its traditional status as a commercial and trading power, the Netherlands has had a history of contacts with the Muslim world. It was the Ottoman Turks, after all, who gave the Dutch their first tulips, a plant native to central Asia, in the 1500s. When it came to population movements, however, the Dutch were far more likely to leave than to welcome immigrants. Early on, the Netherlands, unlike Germany, acquired and held onto colonies in Asia (Indonesia), South America (Surinam), and the Caribbean (the Dutch West Indies and Aruba). Lack of industrial development back home made for a minuscule presence there of people from those areas of the world.

After World War II, the Netherlands did receive two groups of immigrants from Indonesia following its independence in 1949: the Indo-Dutch, those of mixed Dutch and Indonesian ancestry who were treated as expatriates, and the Moluccans, former native members of the Dutch colonial army who were considered temporary residents in the Netherlands. The Indo-Dutch became the beneficiaries of housing and employment programs designed to facilitate their integration into Dutch society. The Moluccans were subject to a "segregationist" policy, housed in isolated hut camps and entirely dependent on social assistance (van Amersfoort 1982).

The Netherlands came relatively late to the imported-labor recruiting game, since it had little heavy industry or coal mining. The consequence was fewer foreign residents overall but more non-Europeans than many places in

Europe: Turks came to make up over a quarter of those of immigrant origin, and Moroccans, more than a fifth. West Indians, Arubans, and others from impoverished rural areas and overcrowded cities around the Mediterranean Sea rounded out the nonindigenous population. The country's overall immigrant presence may have appeared slight—less than 5 percent—but it was highly concentrated. Fully 60 percent of it was found in North Holland and South Holland, two provinces that were home to just over a third of the Dutch-stock population. Most immigrants moved into the Randstad ("ring city") comprised by Amsterdam, Rotterdam, The Hague, and Utrecht (Tesser, van Dugteren, and Merens 1996). Thanks to liberal naturalization laws, furthermore, the immigrant-origin population always loomed larger in Holland's urban centers than national statistics might suggest. Turkish and Moroccan adults worked primarily in heavy industry and construction (80 percent in 1979, 75 percent in 1985), which was true of only a much smaller share of the Dutch-stock population (a third in 1975, just over a quarter in 1985). Employed Turks and Moroccans were more likely to be unskilled or semiskilled manual workers than their Dutch, Surinamese, West Indian, Aruban, and Moluccan counterparts (Delcroix 1992).

Dutch Policy Evolution

The Dutch demonstrated more pragmatism and policy coherence than their German neighbors. Dutch authorities would first institute a policy and then make it the subject of scientific analysis. Time and again, commissioned studies cast doubts on policies, convincing officials to change them. In the consensus-driven Dutch "chatting culture," every policy issue would be discussed thoroughly. No sincerely presented point of view would be dismissed out of hand (Mahnig 1995).

Even before they had clearly defined a bundle of policies toward immigrants, Dutch officials were responding to the givens of postwar migration. "Guest workers," mostly Southern Europeans in the early 1960s, were first in the care of Catholic nonprofit groups, which received increasing levels of public support: from 40 percent in 1964 to 100 percent in 1975. When large numbers of non-Christians began to arrive later in the decade, the renamed Foundations for Assistance to Foreign Workers lost their denominational character and became targeted at guest workers in general.[1] An extensive subsystem of public, semipublic, and nonprofit organizations developed to deal with the housing and welfare needs of the non-Dutch population. These partnerships were more intricate than in Germany. Nonprofits were more varied and unruly, shepherded by tax exemptions and other indirect incentives. The essentially etatist Dutch context notwithstanding, they were often the only means of allowing the government to escape making decisions that could produce unrest in a plural society (Gidron, Kramer, and Salamon 1992).

This logic underpinned the "pillarization" system that the Dutch had institutionalized in the nineteenth century to manage their own diversity. In Gøsta Esping-Andersen's typology of social welfare states (1991), the Netherlands stands as a corporatist welfare state like Germany and Belgium, marked by a relatively high minimum benefit level and an active labor market policy. It wavers "between Bismarck and Beveridge," with conflicts hidden by a centralized institutional framework and consociational bargaining (Cox 1993, 203). Cultural decentralization found its clearest expression in the 1917 agreement between Catholics, Calvinists, and secular forces. That pact put private and public schools on equal footing and represented a concession on the part of socialists in return for universal male suffrage.

Based on vertical interest groups in all spheres of public life, this arrangement required cooperation among different confessional and secular groups (Lijphart 1975). The major cultural communities—Christian Reformed, Catholic, and Liberal/Humanist—had their own trade unions, political parties, schools, social work agencies, and broadcasting associations. Many tasks that public authorities carried out elsewhere "were put in the hands of para- or quasi-governmental institutions in the Netherlands" (Toonen 1996, 615). Pillarization was more complex than it appeared from the outside, with significant regional differences and local variations. Consensus had to be won continuously. Differentiated and fragmented, the system nonetheless facilitated social and political integration.

Political-Cultural Integration

Perhaps not surprisingly, Dutch officials turned to their pillars when immigration appeared to threaten that integration by the late 1970s. The Dutch parliament officially dropped the rotation system in 1972. The oil crisis of 1973 led to a halt in new labor recruitment but wound up encouraging further emigration from its even harder hit colonies in the Caribbean and South America. The Netherlands made no move to prevent family reunification, and newly immigrated women and children enjoyed free access to the labor market. No explicit integration policies had materialized.

As immigrant-origin communities developed, scuffles broke out between some of their members and native-stock youths in Rotterdam's diversifying Afrikaander neighborhood in 1972 and in its suburb of Schiedam in 1976. During the same period, some supporters of an independent Moluccan Republic resorted to terrorism across the country, occupying schools and city halls, hijacking a train, and causing the deaths of eight people (Meinhardt 1989). Political mobilization against migrants was also emerging: in the early 1970s, the Netherlands People's Union and, after 1980, the Center Party (*Centrumpartij*) picked up strength. The Center Party won a seat in the national parliament's Lower Chamber in 1982 (which it would later lose and

then regain) and would do reasonably well the next couple of years in a special election in Almere and in neighborhood council elections in Rotterdam
(Entzinger 1984).

The state responded by embracing an ethnic outlook on political-cultural
integration. Pillarization meant that the Netherlands had significant sunk
costs in cultural identity and was prepared to conceptualize residents of immigrant origin as ethnic minorities. The independent Scientific Council for Government Policy acknowledged that many immigrants were going to stay in the
Netherlands and that the country had to learn how to cope (WRR 1979). In
1983, the government presented a new ethnic minorities policy. It applied to
Surinamese, West Indians and Arubans, Moluccans, Southern Europeans,
former and remaining Yugoslavs, North Africans, Turks, travelers, and Sinti
and Roma.[2]

Fearful of the formation of "foreigner colonies" if those minorities shut
themselves up in their own organizations, the government sought their collective "emancipation" over two or three generations (MBZ 1983). The new
policies required that all public service institutions in the country be accessible
to immigrants and acquire the expert knowledge to help them. A new institutional division of labor became necessary. Municipal officials gained
responsibility for spatial planning, building regulations, public order, the
implementation and subsidization of social work with immigrants, and the establishment of houses of worship. Most large cities appointed a member of the
municipal executive to oversee local policy on ethnic minorities.

There was a corresponding decentralization of social welfare programs,
with most of the duties and monies that used to redound to national institutions rerouted to municipal authorities after 1985. It was decided to maintain
multiple levels of responsibility—local for the ongoing work and provincial
and/or national for financial support and general management. That setup
made it possible to adjust policies on the ground while effecting a modicum of
standardization. On the other hand, such a multilevel approach made consensus building cumbersome (Hetzel-Burghardt and Schirmer 1990).

Social work underwent changes as well. The professionalization of immigrant counseling services, ongoing since the mid-1960s, had resulted in the
founding of seventeen specialized Foundations for Foreign Workers and associated welfare associations. These nonprofit organizations, which did not have
the legal status that their German counterparts enjoyed, provided "categorical"
(or targeted) social counseling. Another difference with Germany was that
staff members in this area were almost all of native stock, and a majority
served on a volunteer basis.

In the early 1980s, the foundations were disbanded, and their advising and
assistance functions passed to general welfare associations. Later in the decade,
parallel to the decentralization of social policies, it became official policy to
"decategoricalize" social work. National officials identified the lack of ad-

equately trained immigrant cadres as a major stumbling block. Linguistic and methodological difficulties could be serious. The veiled, distant stance adopted by social welfare counselors failed to resonate with minority groups, who expected a more personal relationship based on trust and comprehensive treatment of their problems. General social welfare personnel evinced little enthusiasm for work with immigrants, since they meant for them more work and an uncompensated widening of their basic mission and responsibilities. In response, agencies added extra positions for immigrant-origin staff members, and the national government earmarked funds for training programs (Lutz 1992).

As the Netherlands' immigrant-origin minorities settled in during the 1970s, they founded associations. Dutch officials cited the subsidiarity principle as justification for encouraging them; they received subsidies and were urged to participate in social welfare work. Even Communist-oriented groups obtained state funds. The homeland was the immigrants' focus at first. Religious, regional, and other cleavages retained their force, varying with intensity and mobilizational force across provinces and localities. Although their starting assumption had been that helping immigrants maintain their homeland cultures would facilitate their expected eventual return to their homelands, Dutch authorities were uncomfortable with the associational disorder, above all the absence of any hierarchy. Hence, they began to fashion organizations that were intended to speak for immigrant-origin minorities in official circles. From 1981, national-level advisory councils for Surinamese and West Indians and then Turks, Moroccans, and Tunisians took shape. These bodies collaborated in the National Advisory and Consultative Structure (Landelijke Adviesen Overlegstructuur). They were not very representative and often refused even to acknowledge minority perspectives. Kurds and Alevites found no hearing from the Turkish council, for instance, and neither did opponents of the regime in Rabat from its Moroccan counterpart (Can and Can-Engin 1997).

Immigrants were brought into social welfare employment, and service agencies added offerings for the immigrant-origin population. Projects were designed to create a "snowball effect," training organizers and offering seed grants at all levels. Migrants from the (by then) former Dutch colonies received the most attention early on. Southern Europeans, Turks, North Africans, and others were steadily putting down roots in the Netherlands, too, however. The overwhelming majority of immigrants—over 80 percent by 1989—had obtained permanent residency permits (Meinhardt 1989). Negative reactions to social policy reorganization and cuts spurred national authorities to lay even greater stress on self-help.

Furthermore, naturalization, a process handled by the national government through provincial offices and already far easier than in Germany, was further facilitated. The naturalization rate reached well over 5 percent annually in the late 1980s (Voogt 1994). Dutch officials welcomed that progress but argued that it did not in and of itself equal integration. In Rotterdam in 1979 and in Amsterdam in 1981, municipal councils authorized resident non-nationals to participate in local elections with no restrictions, and they voted mainly for the established parties. That positive experience led to a constitutional change in 1985 that codified the practice nationally for immigrants having lived at least five years in a given city. Although turnout differed by ethnic background and locality, immigrants participated in lower numbers than native-stock Dutch, and critics charged that they did not have the strong position within local political parties that would permit them to push through their demands.[3]

That said, immigrants did gain a foothold in public decision making that their counterparts in Germany lacked. Extensive immigrant political rights in the Netherlands meant that formal citizenship lost the central importance that it had in German debates. The Dutch ethnic minorities conception was based on social, economic, cultural, and religious characteristics and not on nationality or legal status. The end goal was a cohesive yet pluralistic society comprised of ethnically bounded but nested groups (Heijs 1995).

Islamic movements were part of the mix and not a source of worry. The Netherlands had long had contact with Islam through trading and in its colonies. The difficult history of Catholic emancipation and the country's earlier experience adapting to humanist beliefs and Jewish practices helped clear the way for Islam. The first "true" mosque, complete with dome and minarets, opened in Almelo in 1975. Dutch officials entered into serious dialogue with Islamic organizations in the 1980s, because of their rising profile but also in the belief that they could help implement the minorities policy.

The financial relationship between the Dutch state and the churches—the so-called silver chords—had drawn criticism since the end of World War II. State recognition of religions was de facto and not de jure, as in Belgium, yet it brought a number of benefits. In 1983, a long process of self-examination ended in the state's adoption—after consultation with representatives of Christian denominations, Hindus, Muslims, and humanists—of an agreement to move toward true separation from religion. The national government would no longer fund the construction of houses of worship. Even so, local governments received authority to disperse subsidies for social and cultural work, including that performed by mosque associations (Landman 1992).

Although the old social networks were partially intact, the Dutch themselves were abandoning their pillars. Ironically, then, there was open discussion about establishing a Muslim one. Dutch officialdom fueled the emergence of the corresponding institutions and networks. The government introduced subsidies for prayer rooms, sanctioned and regulated the ritual slaughtering of animals, initiated the Islamic Broadcasting Foundation, put imams on equal legal footing with other spiritual leaders, and likened the Muslim call to prayer to the ringing of Christian church bells (Shadid and Van Koningsveld 1997).

The process had both advantages and disadvantages for Muslims. They had equal rights when it came to time off for Friday mosque attendance and access to military and prison chaplains. Then again, the inclusion of religious-cultural instruction in the public school curriculum made it more difficult to open up separate Islamic schools. Plus, by handing out subsidies, authorities expected to have an influence on their behavior and activities. Even more than the Germans, the Dutch emphasized social and political dialogue. Despite opposition from both the Dutch far right and left-leaning immigrant groups, Islamic associations were brought into the National Advisory and Consultative Structure.

To Dutch officials' chagrin, the Islamic associations whose growth they had stimulated withstood enticements to construct a unified Dutch Islam. There was no basis for such an organization, which ran against officials' own ethnonational structuring. Surinamese Muslims and, later, Hindus, were the first to mobilize and to coordinate local initiatives on the national level. Turks and Moroccans lacked the means and organizational capacity to follow suit. Their mobilization was more limited and anchored in local realities, and internal conflicts aggravated by the arrival of imams from the homelands led to the founding of separate, nationality-based organizations (see Werkgroep Waardenburg 1983). All sorts of Islamic groups were active in the country, from mystical brotherhoods to local manifestations of worldwide movements.

Structural Integration

Compared to its neighbors, the Netherlands experienced noticeably more harmonious social relations during the 1980s, a period of economic stagnation and labor-market contraction. Trouble was brewing, however. Policymakers had underplayed structural integration, which meant that even the moderate advances recorded in labor markets, housing, schools, and vocational training in Germany were missing in the Netherlands. Its political-cultural integration policies, resting as they did on ethnic identities, stimulated the drawing of new battle lines, even as they accelerated immigrant political inclusion.

By the late 1980s, it was clear that minorities' social and economic marginalization had deepened. The Netherlands' cultural line of attack had prevailed over a German-style focus on such structural phenomena. The Dutch ethnic minorities policy, financed to the tune of some six hundred million guilders yearly between 1984 and 1988, had dealt rather incidentally with the labor market and spatial concentration. Unemployment rates had soared to 27 percent among Surinamese, 42 percent among Moroccans, and 44 percent among Turks in 1987—compared to 13 percent among those of Dutch stock (Penninx and Groenendijk 1989). A stubbornly high number of immigrants who had lived in the country for decades did not speak Dutch (Engbersen, Hemerijck, and Bakker 1994).

Disparities between native- and immigrant-stock educational performance remained wide overall, to the detriment of Moroccan youths above all. Their dropout and truancy rates were the highest, and they occupied the lowest echelons of the Dutch education system. Young Turks were not much better off. In 1991, 78 percent of Moroccan-origin youths and 72 percent of their Turkish-origin peers in the Netherlands had completed only primary education. For other non-European ethnic minorities, such as Surinamese and West Indians, the proportion was around half (Roelandt and Veenman 1994).[4]

Social housing in the Netherlands was governed by a sophisticated system of government intervention, involving national funding, municipal policymaking discretion, and intermediate implementing organizations like the nonprofit housing corporations. Since 1901, the latter had had the status of "authorized institutions": they were to work for the public good and submit to public sector regulation, in return for financial sponsorship and a preferential position in the design and development of public-sector housing. Conscious efforts were made to achieve ethnically mixed patterns of construction. In the accommodations that the 750 housing corporations and the municipal governments themselves allocated, the position of immigrant workers and their families improved markedly (van Kempen and Priemus 2001). They continued to experience severe difficulties in the private market.

On the whole, moreover, the clustering of immigrants in certain urban neighborhoods was proceeding apace. Anxiety mounted that the spatial concentration of ethnic minorities and other socially marginalized groups would weaken social cohesion. In the four biggest cities in 1986, one-tenth of neighborhoods had a minority share in excess of 30 percent. By the mid-1990s, one-quarter would. Concentrations grew even higher in those older areas where they were already significant. Joining them were neighborhoods of immediate postwar construction, just out from the city cores. There were also areas with sizable housing projects. Officials devised a segregation index that indicated how many nonnative people would have to move out of a neighborhood in order to achieve demographic balance. Policies failed to have a positive impact on such indices over the course of the 1980s in the ring city conurbation (TWCM 1995).

More so than in Germany, there was a general assumption in the Dutch literature that the concentration and segregation of immigrant-origin populations was a bad, even dangerous phenomenon. Despite the passage of national legislation to ensure a fairer distribution of urban housing, as well as housing corporations' attempts to "spread" immigrants more evenly, policy moved inexorably toward conformity with the rules of the market. Rent subsidies supplanted brick-and-mortar construction subsidies. Privatization reduced the presence of the housing corporations from a high of 42 percent to just over a third by the early 1990s. They did not become true market players but rather typically Dutch hybrids that maintained their public mandate while they gained private goals as well. Suburbanization, meanwhile, left more affordable housing available in older central and near-central neighborhoods (Tesser and van Praag 1996).

Along the political-cultural dimension, Dutch integration policy had consequences that led to both congruence and disconnection. Overall, there was a pronounced surge in immigrant and ethnic mobilization during the 1980s. Turkish, Moroccan, Surinamese, Moluccan, West Indian, and Cape Verdean football clubs, mosques, temples, women's groups, and student associations sprang up alongside the older, political, homeland-oriented organizations. Evidence of a budding, pluralistic civil society in some observers' eyes, they looked to others like chaos and manufactured "problem categories" and "minorities." The ethnic-based organizing stimulated by Dutch officialdom had "perverse" effects, it was charged, leading to "un-Dutch" fragmentation and divisiveness (Rath 1991).

Before the close of the decade, officials moved away from supporting organizations and initiatives that cultivated ethnic identity and solidarity within minority groups big and small. The ethnic minorities policy was scaled back in favor of combating deprivation in neighborhoods that suffered from an accretion of socioeconomic ills. Equal access became the ultimate goal, attainable by ensuring a secure legal status for immigrant-origin minorities and by opening public institutions to them. Only when necessary would officials undertake specially targeted measures. Southern Europeans, it was agreed, had done well enough to be phased out as targets of such programs (Lindo 1994). Policies no longer referred to "ethnic minorities" but to "*allochtonen*"—disadvantaged people of nonnative origin.

The Difficult 1990s

In a broader sense the Dutch welfare state was evolving. In 1990 Christian Democratic Prime Minister Ruud Lubbers moved to cure "Dutch disease" (skyrocketing social costs and stagnating economic growth) by introducing incentives for flexibility in the labor market (in other words, part-time, temporary, and contract employment), training schemes, and a new round of social welfare restructuring. An emphasis on human capital enhancement and a calculus of rewards and penalties were the hallmarks of what became known as the "new Dutch model." Before long, growth rates rose and unemployment fell. Domestic and foreign critics spoke of a shell game, where the jobless slipped from unemployment to the disability rolls (Visser and Hemerijck 1997). The Netherlands was still spending more on social benefits and subsidies than any other European country, 54 percent of gross domestic product in 1992.

The national government tried to mask the cutbacks that did occur with a grander celebration of self-help, empowerment, and decentralization. Paternalistic reliance on social assistance was repudiated. Social services were to build bridges to the entire assortment of ethnic-based associations that had cropped up. For some immigrant-origin residents, moreover, emancipation would mean release from precisely those identities and freedom to embrace new ones. Social counseling services were called on to become more relevant to and involved with labor market policies.

Whether in response to the possibilities offered by minority social networks or out of desperation at a labor market in which they faced discrimination, ethnic entrepreneurs multiplied from 9,400 in 1986 to 19,000 in 1992, including some 1,900 Turks and almost 900 Moroccans (Kloosterman, van der Leun, and Rath 1997, 65–66). Although concerns were voiced in certain quarters that this "independent entrepreneurship" fed segregation, the phenomenon was more widely welcomed as a sign that minorities could preserve their culture and identity and achieve economic success. Besides those who established their own businesses, those of the first immigrant generation who managed socioeconomic mobility usually did so as employees of the welfare state. There they performed "ethnic functions" reminiscent of the African American experience (Böcker 1994a). The Dutch equivalent of Germany's ABM makework scheme, the so-called Melkert jobs provided tens of thousands of public service positions to the long-term unemployed—many of them immigrants—in neighborhood social services (Rath 1995).

The new round of welfare policy decentralization really added up to both stretching and recentering: national institutions devolved part of their authority downward; but the scope of social services widened territorially as once-municipal institutions developed a neighborhood-level presence and gained responsibility for an entire region or province. Under their tutelage, immigrant associations and other voluntary organizations took on a more extensive role in service delivery. Powerful government intervention and the pursuit of vibrant market conditions, two contradictory Dutch ambitions, would be reconciled through strong horizontal and vertical networking across sociopolitical institutions and levels of governance.

The Netherlands would loosen direct top-down control and replace it with "caring" and a "needs-oriented" social work that geared itself more to satisfying its "consumers." The focus shifted from filling in service deficits to activating immigrants' potential and stimulating their involvement. The empowerment principle was making deeper inroads than in Germany (Noelle 1996). Individual casework ceded to broader approaches, which all fell under the rubric of "development work": holistic approaches that linked together all interested local and neighborhood groups with administrative and political institutions (Geelen, van Unen, and Walraven 1994). Lobbying for immigrants in the political arena was rendered problematic by the fact that the various actors and agencies working with immigrants got their funding from a bewildering range of sources.

In the meantime, to serve their charges and to guarantee their own survival, social agencies, nonprofits, and immigrant associations alike had to engage in the competitive hunt for grant funding—the "project carrousel"—which encouraged them to "problematize" their clientele (van der Zwaard 1998, 35). Subsidies constituted an essential font of funding, but dependence on them led to a loss of autonomy and a delinking from the rank and file. Much of the money provided was "soft" and had little potential to influence the broader social context. Political and fiscal pressures to cut services coincided with a boom in short-term projects that targeted specific social subgroups.

Education, as a generator of human capital, was another focal point of the new integration policy. Earlier concerns about preparing immigrant children for an eventual return to their "homelands" faded. The Ministry of Education spearheaded initiatives to expand instruction in Dutch as a second language and to involve parents of all ethnic backgrounds in their children's schools. Both immigrant-origin students and those of Dutch stock were obliged to take intercultural instruction designed to prepare them for harmonious life in a multicultural society. A general consensus had built around the importance of having everyone master Dutch, but there were disagreements about teaching immigrant languages and cultures. Policies ended up reflecting the autonomy that Dutch schools had traditionally exercised in developing curricula (Lucassen and Penninx 1994).

As in Germany, the 1990s brought new policy challenges and another disconnective blip. In the Netherlands, where integration had always been viewed first and foremost through a political-cultural lens, Islam was the pretext for controversy in the wake of the first Gulf War and the Salman Rushdie affair. In September 1991, the leader of the liberal-right People's Party for Freedom and Democracy (Volkspartij voor Vrijheid en Democratie—VVD) and eventual EU commissioner Frits Bolkestein asserted that elements of the Islamic belief system ran counter to liberal Western values (Bolkestein 1997). The country was not free from racist outbursts, and officials alternated between accommodation and alarm (see van Thijn 2000). The Ministry of Home Affairs met with the National Islamic Council, established by a broad gamut of Islamic associations, but it soon split in two. The ministry also made unsuccessful attempts to encourage secular and Islamic North African associations to collaborate. The weakness of national-level Muslim organizing reflected the lack of cooperation between Turks and Moroccans and the legacy of policy-inspired internal divisions within each community (De Mas and Penninx 1994).

As before, Dutch policies went under the microscope. Consequently, the Netherlands moved a bit closer to French-style neo-republican, liberal-neutral conceptions that aimed for individual structural integration and purported to ignore ethnicity. In 1992 the government's Commission on Non-Indigenous Students issued a report, *Cedars in the Garden,* in which it called for a more nuanced strategy to combat disadvantage and to facilitate social integration

(CALO 1992). Out of this analysis grew a Citizenship Program constructed around municipal-level contracts. In 1996, the Integration Policy for Newcomers pushed the notion further. The government decided to require new immigrants to learn Dutch and set up local Offices for the Reception of Newcomers to implement the program. In fact, proficiency in Dutch became the gold standard of immigrant integration (Bakas and Dost 1995).

Behind the new assimilationist bent was an intention to avoid the "calcification" of ethnic difference, and the United States was taken as an example of how it could become dangerously politicized (see TWCM 1995). Conversely, the American experience with diversity management in the workplace received its share of positive attention in the Netherlands (see Rooijendijk and Somme 2000). Such policy responses came under fire for being superficial and "one-size-fits-all": they would not work for an immigrant-origin population that was increasingly diverse and differentiated by ethnicity, occupational category, gender, and generation (Dashort and van der Werf 1995).

In the context of a perspective on citizenship that strove to balance reciprocal rights and responsibilities, officials retorted, it was up to immigrant associations to do the calibrating. Self-help and empowerment lost none of their force. They would drive bottom-up mobilization, which would determine the appropriate means to achieve the objectives of integration and congruence. The change was from cultural maintenance to partnership and collaborative actions that aimed for equal access, and immigrants were no longer to be talked *about* but *with*. The local and neighborhood levels took on paramount importance, as policies were to be more finely tuned, transparent, and flexible.

Local-level policymakers had considerable room for maneuver. Education, social housing, and social policies that the national level had originally overseen were further decentralized and bundled together into a Big Cities Policy (Grote Steden Beleid—GSB), for which a coordinating minister was appointed in 1998. It encompassed all policies directed toward the most marginalized groups in society and the most vulnerable areas in the country's largest cities. The GSB did not seek to apply standard national solutions but rather to "cultivate the fruits of local-level community work" (Sackmann 2001, 93). To access GSB funds, however, each eligible city had to submit a detailed long-term plan of action and a budget to national authorities. Cooperation and contact were to be intensive among inhabitants, public institutions, housing corporations, and local employers. The new prominence of structural integration was visible in the emphasis on economic development and employment. Ultimate success would hinge on the progress of the second and third immigrant generations. Policies geared toward specific groups might be needed temporarily, it was admitted. They were not an end in and of themselves and could not be allowed to stigmatize the affected population. They had to fit within broader actions to fight disadvantage and marginalization and to vouchsafe harmony and solidarity.

The reorganization of the Dutch welfare state had contributed to the dilution of its social control function. Sounding like their German neighbors, the Dutch expressed worries that poorer neighborhoods in their major urban conglomerations might come to resemble France's suburbs or even America's inner cities (Crul 2000). The emerging nexus of youth gang violence, the drug trade, and petty crime—known as "the circuit"—grew into an obsession. In the mid-1990s, one out of three Moroccans and one out of four Turks between ages twelve and eighteen had been taken to police headquarters at least once because of criminal activities (usually theft, altercations, or vandalism). Joining them was only one out of ten of their native-Dutch cohorts. Fully half of those in Dutch prisons were of non-Dutch backgrounds (Can and Can-Engin 1997). Dutch police officials traveled to Los Angeles to learn how to deal with knifings and shootings. There were calls for more police in the streets and less leniency in the courts.

National officials and the welfare state preserved enough of their influence, all the same, that preventative measures were just as likely to find a sympathetic hearing. There were proposals for more recreational facilities, youth centers, and programs to combat drug and alcohol abuse, as well as to strengthen social solidarity and citizens' feelings of responsibility for the welfare of their own community. Dutch officials spoke of broad, durable "compensation" policies that would tackle the negative social fallout of spatial concentration (Wuertz 1994). As before, Dutch institutions managed to prevent the eruption of widespread social disorder.

Control was offset by more political-cultural openness. A legal reform enabled several groups of immigrants—most notably, Turks, Moroccans, and Iranians—to obtain Dutch nationality without surrendering their original passport. Almost one-third of Turkish and Moroccan residents had dual nationality by the mid-1990s. Naturalizations rose to the point that the nonnational share of the total Dutch population actually fell. Dutch governments labored as well to devise more consistent and efficient asylum procedures, the fuel for much of the German far right's fire. Its Dutch fellow travelers managed to win only two municipal council seats in 1998, losing its six seats in the national parliament.

Candidates of immigrant origin, for their part, won 1 percent of all council seats in the 1998 local elections. Half of the winners were of Turkish origin, and a quarter were Surinamese. Eighteen percent were women. In the national parliament 9 deputies out of 150 were of immigrant origin at the end of the decade. By a wide margin immigrant minorities' participation rates trailed those of native-stock Dutch—among whom the immigration issue seemed to have minimal impact on the choice of a political party. Parties of the left remained the primary beneficiaries of the local immigrant vote, although, as time passed, it reflected the diverse population from which it emitted (Irwin and van Holsteyn 1997).

By the end of the 1990s, Dutch integration policies were conforming to their familiar pattern: a greater degree of political-cultural congruence coexisted with residential concentration, high unemployment, and far from stellar performance in the areas of housing, education, and training. The spatial segregation of immigrant-origin people in the Netherlands was broadly comparable to that in Belgium and Britain but higher than that in Germany. Unemployment was also higher than in Germany. In 1995, a third of economically active Turks and Moroccans were out of work, compared to 7 percent of native-stock Dutch. The immigrant-origin population still lived in worse housing. As for education, there had been steady improvement among the second immigrant generation, whose members were staying longer in school. The 1990s even witnessed noteworthy increases in the number of Turks and Moroccans attending higher education. Women accounted for a disproportionate share of those scholastic gains. Yet the advances were not keeping up with those registered by their Dutch peers. According to one government-commissioned study, immigrant-origin minorities would represent almost two-thirds of residents with the lowest level of education and skills by 2015 (Marinelli 1999, 178–79). The "ethnicization" of social disadvantage continued.

There was room for improvement on all fronts in the Netherlands, but more progress had been made in cultural and political integration than in sectors that related to immigrants' socioeconomic position. Guided more by pragmatism than by principle, the Dutch spent more money than the Germans on stimulating immigrant associational mobilization, and they were quicker to bind it to Dutch society when disconnection developed. By implicating the immigrant-origin population—especially its organizations and leaders—in projects aimed at securing stable social relations, policymakers kept them at the bargaining table and out of the streets. When polled, Turks and Moroccans evinced a deep desire to live, work, socialize, and attend school with mixed populations of both immigrant and Dutch origin (see NCB 1995).

In shining the spotlight squarely on ethnic identities, however, Dutch officials had drawn attention to them. When structural integration faltered, persistent disconnection in that area became attached to ethnicity. Subsequent policy changes were not able to remove that association, and there was more noise in the Netherlands than in Germany over non-European cultural practices and Islam (Sunier 1996). Its positions on sexual and family relations were hotly debated. International events and the overblown pronouncements of several "media imams" stoked passions as the new century began. In summer 2001, a Moroccan imam in Rotterdam, Khalil el-Moumni, condemned homosexuals as "worse than dogs" and was taken to court on charges of discrimination. The terrorist attacks against the United States that fall tested Dutch tolerance, although by avoiding the worst excesses of intolerance in the aftermath of the attacks, the Netherlands seemed to bear out the general efficacy of the policies implemented by the government to "practice diversity" (SAMS Den Haag 2002b, 4). After September 11, another imam—with the unlikely name of Abdullah Haselhoef—appeared repeatedly in the Dutch media to speak on behalf of the country's Muslims. In October, he proclaimed that homosexuals deserved the death penalty, provided that at least four eyewitnesses could attest to the act of sodomy.[5]

The ensuing firestorm served as the backdrop for the mercurial rise of Pim Fortuyn. A provocative newspaper columnist writer, politician, wealthy entrepreneur, and erstwhile Marxist-leaning sociology professor and talk show host, he had become widely known in his hometown, Rotterdam, for his campaigns for improving public services and providing residents with more security. Fortuyn was also openly and proudly gay, and he came to argue that Muslim culture could not coexist with Dutch permissiveness. He gravitated toward the Livable Netherlands *(Leefbaar Nederlands)* movement. Such oppositional social movements had existed for years in major Dutch cities and comprised loose collections of citizens worried about the health care system, immigration, and crime. They were to the right of the political mainstream, but they were not viewed as an extremist challenge to the prevailing order. The events of September 11, 2001, gave them a fillip, and Fortuyn became their standard-bearer.

His subversive positions struck a chord. Ignoring the Dutch tradition of cultural pluralism, he argued that a "modern society places an emphasis on individual responsibility, whereas Islam places an emphasis on collective responsibility" (Hooper 2002). Ignoring the silver chords, he asserted that "we have separation of church and state. The laws of this country are not subject to the Quran" (Lang 2002). Ignoring police statistics, he maintained that "Moroccan boys never steal from other Moroccans, have you noticed that?" (Hooper 2002). At the same time, he admitted to having slept with many Moroccan men over the years.[6]

In February 2002, Fortuyn was removed as leader of the Livable Netherlands movement when, in an interview with the newspaper *De Volkskrant*, he suggested abolishing Article 1 of the Dutch constitution, which forbade discrimination, and referred to Islam as a "backward culture." He founded Livable Rotterdam and in March shocked the city's political world by winning a plurality of 36 percent and sixteen council seats in a city that had been in firm control of the Labor Party (Partij van de Arbeid—PvdA) since 1947. For the national legislative elections that May, he formed the List Pim Fortuyn (LPF). It stood for a drastic reduction in bureaucracy, better public services, a clampdown on crime, the repayment of much of the country's contribution to the European Union, the slashing of disability and sickness benefits, a freeze on spending on health and education, a "zero Muslim immigration" policy, cuts in the overall number of new immigrants allowed into the Netherlands, and more successful integration of the resident immigrant population. Fortuyn seemed on his way to a strong finish when he was assassinated by a Dutch animal rights activist. In his absence the List won some 1.3 million votes and 26 seats out of 150 in the lower house of the Dutch parliament.[7]

Despite his anti-Islamic comments, Fortuyn was not anti-immigrant in the same way as France's Jean-Marie Le Pen or Austria's Jörg Haider. He did not advocate the repatriation of immigrants from the Netherlands, nor did he suggest that they be discriminated against in the area of social welfare rights. He claimed to argue not against immigrants but against further immigration into the country. Those already in the Netherlands could stay, but they needed to make an effort to integrate. To obtain a permanent residence permit, a foreigner should have lived for a long time in the country, have acquired knowledge of the Dutch language, and have compiled no criminal record. The LPF won support from some ethnic minorities, few of them practicing Muslims. One of Fortuyn's closest associates was of Cape Verdean origin, and one of the LPF members elected to parliament was a young woman of Turkish descent (Stroobants 2002).

After the election, the LPF took control over four key portfolios: immigration, health, education, economy, and transportation, as well as five of the fourteen secretary of state posts in the national administration. The new secretary of state for emancipation (and elected LPF member of parliament) was Philomena Bijlhout, a native of Surinam. The coalition agreement between the Christian Democrats, Liberals, and the List foresaw a host of restrictions in the area of immigration. New immigrants would be required to take an "integration course." (If they passed, half of the associated costs would be refunded.) Conditions for family reunification were to be tightened up, along with the asylum law, and steps would be taken to ensure that a higher number of rejected applicants were repatriated. The new minister of foreigners and the interior, Hilbrand Nawijn (LPF), intended to end subsidies for projects that only benefited immigrant-origin residents. He failed to rally support for his plan to strip Dutch nationality from naturalized Moroccan youths convicted of serious crimes. Infighting and lack of political experience eventually doomed the coalition by fall 2002. In the General Election of January 2003, the LPF lost eighteen of its twenty-six seats, in part because the mainstream parties of both the left and the right had conceded to many of its positions. Several of the policies that the List advocated had taken effect. For instance, in September 2002, seven Turkish imams became the first to attend a new mandatory integration course for all non-Western religious leaders arriving in the Netherlands after the first of that year.

The Pim Fortuyn phenomenon worked against attempts to reduce ethnic discord. By the same token, it motivated more immigrants to take advantage of the channels of political participation that were available to them. After

1998, immigrant political participation increased slightly for all national groups, and minority voters were beginning to exert an influence on candidates' placement on party lists. Then, Pim Fortuyn came along to provoke immigrant-origin residents further. By 2002, there were 305 local councilors belonging to ethnic minorities, up from 150 four years prior. A survey carried out by the Public Institute on Politics indicated that 54 percent of these councilors were of Turkish origin, followed by Surinamese and Moroccans ("Higher Number" 2002).

Their gains, of course, were taking place at the same local level out of which Pim Fortuyn burst, eventually to throw into question the Netherlands' reputation for tolerance. The restructuring of the Dutch welfare state had transferred much of the burden associated with the presence of immigrant-origin populations downward to the cities and neighborhoods where they lived. No less than in Germany, local officials had no choice but to take up the yoke in the Netherlands. There could sometimes be a vivid contrast between national-level ideological squabbles and practical policymaking at the local level.

Many functions of the Dutch welfare state, then, devolved down to the municipal level starting in the 1970s. The reasons resembled those put forward elsewhere in Europe—namely, a mixture of grassroots democratizing and central administration buck-passing. Dutch cities, like others, picked up more responsibilities than resources.[8] Relatively speaking, officials there were in a better financial, legal, and political position to experiment than their German counterparts. Having a nonnational component to their electorate, in conjunction with a substantial naturalized one, gave them every motivation to see to immigrant concerns. If anything, however, national-level tutelage loomed larger than in Germany, given the tight central control over funding that characterized even decentralized Dutch social policy. Local officials did not have to worry about paying for a swelling social assistance program. If they devised immigrant integration policies that went above and beyond the standard package, they were only responsible for a tenth of the costs. But those projects had to meet with national approval, and they were not permitted to stray too far from national guidelines. Municipal governments in the Netherlands have very little taxable income of their own, with more than three-quarters of their financial resources deriving from the central state (Van Kempen and Priemus 2001).

Rotterdam and The Hague, the two cities in Holland figuring in this study, bear witness to the steady top-down direction that the Dutch state wielded. The general policy trajectory described above for the country overall was visible in each. Even so, the cities won praise for their tolerance and proactive policies, which diverged from the national pattern in certain key respects. Most critically, Rotterdam resisted the pull away from ethnic-based strategies in the late 1980s and experienced an above-average level of ethnic conflict in the

TABLE 4.1
Non-Dutch Citizens by Nationality and City
(In Percentage of Total Nonnational Population, 1997)

	Rotterdam	The Hague
Turks	28.6	22.6
Moroccans	25.5	23.6
All Nonnationals	10.7	10.8

Source: COS (1998b, 162–64).

1990s. The Hague, on the other hand, erred on the side of structural integration policies, taking the edge off ethnic identities while striving to channel their vitality. In each city Turks and Moroccans constituted comparably large immigrant groups (see table 4.1), and their relationship with local institutions and other immigrant-origin groups differed appreciably.

Rotterdam: Celebrating Diversity

A major world port, occupied Rotterdam was almost entirely destroyed by British bombers late in World War II. The city that reemerged was quirky and vibrant, if far from a conventionally beautiful place. The mainstream left, the Labor Party (PvdA), set its political tone but did not dictate it. Rotterdam's colorful, progressive associational life reflected warmer acceptance than elsewhere of private actors' independent initiative (SZWG Rotterdam 1997). It was the case city in this study that embraced self-help and empowerment the most wholeheartedly and that enacted the widest arrangement of policy initiatives—a hodgepodge of programs and projects. Its integration policies encouraged congruence in the political-cultural realm. In the presence of serious structural disconnection, they instigated ethnic tensions in the process.

Crisis and Progressive Response

In the late nineteenth century, laborers flowed from rural Zeeland and Brabant into areas near Rotterdam's port to accommodate its industrial and commercial growth. Colonial and former colonial subjects from Indonesia, the Dutch Antilles, and Surinam followed in their footsteps in the decades after 1945. They, in turn, were eventually joined by Turkish and Moroccan immigrant workers. When economic troubles hit local industries in the early 1970s, the neighborhoods in which immigrants had settled started to deteriorate. Many native Dutch residents left, and older housing units were sold at high prices to investors, who then turned them into pensions. The result was severe overcrowding, which together with linguistic difficulties and cultural differences led to social tensions. In 1972 and again in 1976, Rotterdam and its near environs experienced rioting, the likes of which the Netherlands had rarely seen.

The local Social Democratic administration downplayed the ethnic dimension of the conflicts and put the accent on exploitative landlords (Buijs 1998).

In 1980 officials adopted a "deconcentration" policy, which aimed to integrate housing and distribute the immigrant-origin population more evenly across the city. With complaints pouring in from local nonprofit associations and immigrants, national authorities forbade implementation of the policy on the grounds that it was discriminatory. Thereafter, Rotterdam's neighborhoods grew more diverse ethnically and more homogeneous socioeconomically. By the late 1980s, "white flight" had left the two central districts with the highest immigrant concentrations, Delfshaven and Feijenoord, with higher levels of segregation. They also had the highest rates of unemployment, crime, and social assistance dependence (de Jong 1996).

Rotterdam was learning how difficult it was for a local government to affect such broad structural trends. In response, the city introduced many of the social policies that would eventually be enacted in other Dutch cities and in Germany. After the rioting in the 1970s, the city had established a Migrant Office. It produced the first municipal document to deal explicitly with immigrant integration (Gemeente Rotterdam 1978). The focus was on according equal opportunities to "cultural minorities" and on reversing their marginalization. The means were a loose assortment of policies in the areas of education, vocational training, and recreation that were implemented at the district and neighborhood levels. The participation of target groups' own organizations was the linchpin of these strategies, emblematic of Rotterdam's early embrace of the empowerment philosophy (see de Jong 1986).

Immigrants' Political-Cultural Integration

Rotterdam anticipated the national ethnic minorities policy and took the lead in fashioning policies to advance immigrants' integration in the political and cultural spheres. Having been the first city to allow resident nonnationals to vote in municipal council elections in 1979, Rotterdam authorized a Turkish Islamic party to run candidates for the district *(stadsdeel)* council in 1984. It won no seats, but its 43 percent share of the Turkish vote was enough to spur the local Christian Democratic Party (Christen Democratisch Appèl—CDA) to make overtures to the community's many conservative members. Its labors bore fruit, with surveys soon showing that the CDA was the preferred party among Turks by a wide margin (Doomernik 1995). On the other hand, a municipality-sponsored drive in the early 1980s to devise a representative consultative council for nonindigenous residents fell to grief. The effective structuring of associational development was a long time in coming.

Rotterdam's early experience with Islam was a case in point. The story was one of evolution from reluctance to deal with religious organizations and ad-hoc, reactive policymaking to the erection of a relatively inclusive, coherent regulatory structure. In the 1970s, the municipality had few contacts with

Rotterdam's Muslim associations, which was in keeping with its hands-off attitude toward all local religious institutions. Policymakers, seeing Islam as monolithic and uniformly problematic, long barred the formal establishment of mosques. Municipal officials had to contend with the side effects of the ongoing decentralization of social welfare programs for ethnic minorities, however, and gradually incurred responsibility from the central state for distributing subsidies to local voluntary groups. The city agreed to attribute small sums to mosque associations for their social and cultural activities geared toward integration, even though Christian churches were no longer eligible for such support. The goal was to reduce political-cultural disconnection, facilitate Muslims' emancipation, and break the "monopoly position" of left-wing homeland organizations. By 1981 there were thirteen mosques in the city. Their rapid expansion, along with the heightened struggle between Muslim and secular associations, compelled officials to formulate a more integrative policy. "Like falling dominoes," local institutions found themselves forced to reconsider their positions and adapt to the Islamic presence (Rath et al. 1996, 177).

Rotterdam became the first Dutch city to deal with mosques—and Hindu temples—in a forthright, systematic manner. Its policymakers hoped to position mosque associations as key "social partners" and encouraged them to merge their scattered, makeshift religious centers into a few larger, well-maintained ones on major thoroughfares. The immigrant-origin communities themselves hardly represented a model of unanimity. Ideological, theological, and national divisions all rendered collaboration problematic. Secular, progressive immigrants organized a federation but declined to welcome Islamic associations (Gemeente Rotterdam 1983). In 1988 the city established a Mosque Project Office and the Associational Platform of Islamic Organizations in the Rijnmond (Stichting Platform Islamitische Organisaties Rijnmond—SPIOR). The only organization of its kind in the Netherlands, the SPIOR was an appointed advisory body representing twenty-one member associations, with no official ties to any homeland government or organization. Its mission was to facilitate cross-cultural dialogue and to oversee a long-term antidiscrimination and integration program. Its basic annual municipal subsidy grew more than sixfold between 1989 and 1995 to 326,000 guilders. As important, officials made sure that the SPIOR was included in local policy networks.

The incorporation of Islamic instruction into local curricula posed few problems. The setting up of separate Quranic schools was a thornier issue. Two such institutions opened their doors in the late 1980s. Requests to establish additional ones met with municipal stonewalling. Fear that they might pose a threat to public education and social harmony was pregnant. The minutes of municipal council debates on Islamic schools through the early 1990s contained occasional references to "ghetto schools" and "apartheid."

Rotterdam, in the end, decided to treat Muslims like any other ethnic minority. The municipality downplayed strictly religious aspects and emphasized cultural ones, and Islamic organizations, like their Catholic and Reformed predecessors, built on a history of government-initiated partnership. Decentralization of the Dutch policy system meant that local institutions and circumstances affected outcomes to a greater degree than before. As Jan Rath and his colleagues (1996) have shown in their comparison between "open" Rotterdam and "closed" Utrecht, even in cities with similar immigrant-origin populations and run by the same political party—in their case the PvdA—local networks produced contrasting Islamic associational profiles and relationships between Muslims and municipal officials. Often, indirect policies affected Muslims' organizational space more than direct policies dealing with religious denominations per se.

Immigrants' Structural Integration

By the end of the 1980s, Rotterdam's pioneering reputation was safe. Less clear was whether its policies had achieved the desired results. A city report in 1991 found that the immigrant-origin population was too frequently seen in terms of "groups dependent on assistance" (Gemeente Rotterdam 1992). Recoiling at deepening residential segregation and the disconnective consequences of their version of multiculturalism, Rotterdam officials reevaluated their position. National integration policies were being blended into more general ones to fight social marginalization. When Rotterdam introduced its own general policy in 1991, the municipal council felt that in certain cases it would not be enough. For that reason, they put forward a "facet policy": the various sectors comprising Rotterdam's policymaking system would assess the situation and, in light of overarching guidelines, decide if specific, targeted interventions were needed. Yearly reports in which policy responses had to be matched to a set of common objectives and evaluation indicators would serve as a controlling and coordinating instrument. The spotlight fell on activities that stimulated the mobilization, integration, and participation of marginalized groups. National Dutch policy shifted decidedly toward the areas of youth, labor, antidiscrimination, and communications. In Rotterdam that change was more muted, as officials and immigrant leaders alike argued for an intensification of explicit integration and diversity policies (SAMS Rotterdam 1999).

In terms of structural integration, the trend in Rotterdam was undeniably toward disconnection in the early 1990s. The nonindigenous population had grown by over a third between 1988 and 1993. It had diversified, leaving the city with Europe's second largest Cape Verdean community, for example (Strooij 1997). People of immigrant origin would represent a fifth of the city in 1991 and a quarter by 1996.

After The Hague, Rotterdam had the country's highest levels of residential segregation (Tesser and van Praag 1996). Five districts in or ringing the city core had ethnic minority concentrations superior to a quarter, with Delf-shaven (48.1 percent) and Feijenoord (40. 3 percent) still at the top. Turkish and Moroccan nationals comprised more than 20 percent of Delfshaven's residents (12 percent and 8.3 percent) and 22 percent of Feijenoord's (15.8 percent and 6.2 percent) (COS 1994, 85–91).

The districts with high immigrant concentrations contained Rotterdam's least desirable housing and much of its social housing stock. As in all four German case cities, housing conditions had improved, for Turks and Moroccans included, but they remained inadequate. As in Berlin there was movement into somewhat newer neighborhoods surrounding traditional concentration areas. Between a quarter and a third of residents in these areas were on general royal (national) social assistance, over half on royal assistance to the unemployed, and another 5 to 8 percent on added municipal assistance, which the national government subsidized heavily. Delfshaven and Feijenoord, consisting entirely of immigrant concentration neighborhoods, ranked the highest on indices of social disadvantage (COS 1995, 24–31; 1998b, 179).

Unemployment rates reached 40 to 50 percent. The labor market situation of West Indians and Arubans, while trailing behind that of native-stock workers, had improved over the course of the 1980s. Turks and Moroccans did not experience quite the same lift; but when they could find jobs, they were no longer as restricted as they had been to the very lowest rungs of the industrial and service-sector employment ladder. Local labor market policies concentrated on equal access. There were initiatives to promote nonindigenous small businesses, which would account for about a third of local business start-ups by the late 1990s (BDR 1998).

In the educational area, too, the record was mixed. Ethnic minority children were on their way to comprising just under half of all local students by 1995. Moroccans stood at a lower level than other groups in the city and lower even than their compatriots in most other Dutch cities. Turkish women faced similar hurdles, but the situation for Turkish men was notably stronger. All immigrant-origin groups had made advances into the higher levels of education. Their rates of completion had not kept pace, though, and many of them ended up with no more than primary-school qualification. The gap between native- and immigrant-stock pupils widened right after compulsory education (RSJBR 1997a). Although the municipal government had only limited control over Rotterdam schools, which came under the auspices of education officials, it formulated a comprehensive municipal policy to fight educational disadvantage within the context of its youth policy.

The Difficult 1990s

In 1997 a municipal advisory committee concluded that the overall state of immigrant integration in the city was insufficient. It was able to refer to detailed statistical information gleaned by the Minority Monitor, a statistical collection service unique in the country. The data suggested that outcomes of local policies over the preceding twenty years had been neither "good" nor "bad," but "variable." Much was left to be done for certain groups, even though general services had put in a positive performance. They had to be adapted. The big question became one of determining where to put the accents so as to achieve equal opportunity for all "Rotterdam citizens," without allowing specific policies to degenerate into separate and unequal treatment (BDR 1998, 8).

Rotterdam's version of the national GSB involved a bundling of neighborhood-level policies. The district governments were to carry out most of the work and were charged with collaborating with immigrant and other ethnic associations whenever possible in the formulation, development, and implementation of policies. The local government had already engaged in projects in disadvantaged districts like Delfshaven and Feijenoord. The GSB embraced and expanded on those initiatives, and the Rotterdam experience lent much to the new national policy.

The municipality doled out the funds, provided by the national government, that enabled this process to proceed. In Rotterdam, talk of general policies in particular districts and neighborhoods never took on the explicitly territorial basis seen in France or French-speaking Belgium. From an early date the main idea was to bring policy closer to the diverse residents affected by it, not to gloss over group differences. Target group policies—referred to as "specific arrangements" in the Rotterdam context—were viewed as secondary but entirely acceptable. When Rotterdam adjusted its general antipoverty policy in the late 1990s, the specific needs of immigrant-origin groups won recognition and attention, even if the development was not always openly acknowledged as such.

A need to build up "multicultural competence," which resembled empowerment in social work, was identified. Engaging residents in decision making was reconfirmed as a way to make social problems concrete and to address them productively. Self-help would boost self-awareness and have an "emancipatory" effect. Coordinated action at the submunicipal level would nourish social networks and lead to the realization of a "complete" city (Berger et al. 2001). Networks would provide the sinews to harness the energies released and to prevent fragmentation. Therefore, the city studied how to encourage their development and how to integrate immigrants' networks into those of other residents. Pilot projects tested the waters in neighborhoods across the city, and the municipality followed their progress carefully. The most promising initiatives figured in municipal best practices reports and received subsidies. They included highly specific, microlevel policies, such as closing a noisy courtyard ball field, replacing burned-out lightbulbs in corridors and entryways, installing playgrounds, and instituting more flexible hours in local day cares.

Other programs cast their net more widely. They counseled nonindigenous Rotterdammers on how to navigate the nonprofit associational world and lobbied "white" institutions and services to diversify both their staff and their "customer" base (CSV 1999). City officials committed themselves to increasing the nonindigenous presence in the municipal administration. "Allochtons," women, and the physically and mentally challenged all constituted priority groups for the "pluri-form" personnel policy of the Rotterdam municipality. Their numbers in municipal agencies only slowly neared their share of the resident population: 9.1 percent (versus 23 percent) in 1995 (GAO 1996, 7).

Immigrant political participation became a priority. In the 1994 municipal elections, Rotterdam and Amsterdam had had the lowest participation rates among nonnationals of the five largest Dutch cities. Seeing in immigrant suffrage a means of producing political-cultural congruence, Rotterdam authorities committed themselves to improving turnout. A major informational campaign ensued, with "meet-the-nonindigenous-candidate" sessions, campaign jingles, posters, flyers, television broadcasts, and counseling services. Immigrant associations took an active part. By 1998 Rotterdam had eight immigrant and immigrant-origin municipal councilors (out of forty-five); another four dozen were district councilors. Turnout, which actually dipped overall from 57 percent in 1994 to 48 percent in 1998, did rise in those neighborhoods and among those groups that had been specifically targeted, Turks and Moroccans. Such improvements were not seen in other cities (see table 4.2). Turkish voter participation continued to outpace that of other ethnic minorities, owing to the presence of a larger number of Turkish-origin candidates or perhaps greater levels of social capital (Fennema and Tillie 2000). In any event, the number of elected minority political representatives had grown along with participation rates. The far right, too, was achieving moderate suc-

TABLE 4.2

Immigrant Political Participation in Rotterdam and Amsterdam, 1994 and 1998

| | Nonnational Voter Turnout by City (%) | | | |
| | Rotterdam | | Amsterdam | |
Nationality	1994	1998	1994	1998
Turkish	28	42	67	39
Moroccan	24	33	49	23
Surinamese	24	25	30	21
Cape Verdeans	34	33	—	—
Nonnationals	57	48	57	46
Immigrant-Origin Councilors/Total	2/45	8/45	11/45	8/45

Source: Coronel (1998, 22–24).

cess in district council elections, winning twenty-five seats in 1998, a third of them in Delfshaven and Feijenoord (Dominguez, Groeneveld, and Kruisbergen 2002).

Immigrants' political-cultural integration fell well short of congruence, and social networks were not robust enough to channel and contain fully the ethnic-based identities and tensions that Rotterdam's policies had helped to set in motion. The confirmation came in open political confrontations between Turks and Kurds in the late 1990s. Secular Turks and North Africans likewise took to the streets to demonstrate against Islamic fundamentalism, occasioning clashes. A public-school principal told Muslim parents that if they did not like the way he was dealing with their children, "then go start your own school"; fifty of them called for a separate secondary-level Islamic school, a demand to which the municipality capitulated (BDR 1998). Homeland languages also returned as a major issue.

The central government, meanwhile, had added another layer of government, the city-province of Rijnmond. Larger and less urban that Rotterdam proper, the new region reduced the political weight and clout of immigrant-origin people, since they did not exercise suffrage at that level. Rotterdam officials were uncomfortable with the watering down of immigrants' political rights and the absence of a viable interlocutor to speak on their behalf. By 1999 the municipal Social and Work Affairs Department had hatched the Municipal Advisory Council on the Multicultural City (Stedelijke Adviesraad Multiculturele Stad—SAMS), an appointed body of fifteen immigrant- and native-stock members that was modeled on a similar organization in The Hague. The SAMS monitored ethnic relations in the city and issued consultative opinions on all issues of relevance to immigrant-origin groups.[9]

Several peak immigrant associations had also formed. Alongside the one for Muslims (SPIOR), there were loose umbrella organizations grouping Moroccans, left-leaning immigrant workers of various national backgrounds, Surinamese, Cape Verdeans, and West Indians and Arubans. All told, Rotterdam had more than two hundred immigrant associations by 1999. The less informal and transient of them enjoyed a fairly institutionalized relationship with the district-level governments, at the very least in order to look after the dissemination of subsidies. City hall itself, so solicitous of ethnic communities and their social networks in the abstract, had only ad hoc and sporadic contacts with their organizations. Collaboration tended to occur when a specific issue or crisis called for it—for example, after the 1999 Turkish earthquake. Although immigrant associations had input into the formulation of policies that affected their constituents, they were largely ignored when it came to policy implementation. They sometimes complained about serving only as "decoration." The local government's financial largesse went to sustain activities that advanced its objectives of integration, crime prevention, and participation. If they wanted the money, immigrant associations had to tailor their agendas accordingly. Given their lack of experience and their voluntary nature, they found it necessary to work closely with professional and thus more powerful social welfare institutions in order to carry out their projects. The link between the more established immigrant leadership and the mass base could be extremely tenuous under such conditions. The SAMS warned about the dangers of social isolation and disconnection posed by the cleft between "regular" associations and smaller, weaker, and less visible forms of organization (Das and Arslan 2000).

While unwilling to admit that they had little bearing on structural disconnection, Rotterdam officials kept shifting their gaze back to political-cultural integration. Under national government supervision, they developed a Newcomers' Integration Project. Rotterdam was unique in that it developed an integrated package of "newcomer activities" for both immigrants and asylum seekers. It included the SAMS and the SPIOR, which were to provide "welcoming" and orientation services and assist in setting up the Dutch language courses that were central to the program (Oostindie 1997).

In 1998 the "Many-Colored City" (Veelkleurige Stad—VKS) project made its debut, settling within the parameters of the facet policy and thereby the GSB. Underlying it was a determination that ethnic minorities were too passive. The manager of Rotterdam's VKS campaign was the director of a firm that trained immigrants for administrative and managerial positions. Not surprisingly, she stressed the need for people "to take responsibility for themselves." The city's policies to date, she argued, revolved too much around "little figures" *(cijfertjes)*. She wanted to experiment with "change agents," highly placed managers who worked "to effect interculturality" in all types of organizations (van der Molen 1998). Embedded within the VKS project was "Rotterdam DiverCity," a collection of efforts aimed at four "talent groups"— allochtons, women, the disabled, and young people—that were designed to encourage ethnic small businesses, cultural events, and immigrant-origin residents' own initiatives to contribute to Rotterdam society (VKS 2002). Clearly, city officials persisted in adhering to notions of cultural pluralism, but its meaning and content had changed. Increasingly, they had decided to limit it with references to a more liberal multicultural model and neo-republican notions of citizenship.

The Challenges of a New Millennium

The immigrant-origin populations' structural position reduced authorities' choice in the matter. Segregation had declined but stayed above average in Rotterdam, particularly for Turks and Moroccans (see table 4.3). Residential concentration had intensified, as urban renewal in disadvantaged neighborhoods on the south side of the city pushed poor, immigrant-origin residents into equally poverty-stricken adjoining areas.

Minor improvements in the structural integration of immigrant-origin

TABLE 4.3

Segregation in the Largest Dutch Cities

| | Ethnic Minority | | |
	Turks	Moroccans	All Ethnic Minorities
Amsterdam			
1980	30.0		
1995	40.7	39.1	31.7
1998	42.3	41.2	33.1
Rotterdam			
1980	46.5		
1995	51.7	46.8	43.0
1998	49.9	44.2	40.8
The Hague			
1980	55.5		
1995	54.6	49.9	43.1
1998	53.0	48.6	41.8

Share of population category needing to move to obtain citywide distribution equivalent to that of the rest of the population. Maximum value = 100.

Sources: Tesser and van Praag (1996, 60–62), Bolt and van Kempen (2000).

minorities had been registered. Major discrepancies remained: such residents were three times more likely to be unemployed than those of native stock, and the share of long-time unemployed and part-time employed was also more substantial. A segment of the immigrant-origin population, predominantly young and as likely as not female, had been able to achieve upward social and economic mobility. The bulk of the non-European population lagged. Positive developments in vocational training and personal income growth benefited Turks, Moroccans, and West Indians far less than others. Save for Southern Europeans, immigrant-origin families were more than twice as likely to have household incomes classified as low, although the second generation was in a stronger position than the first. Dependency on social welfare benefits was harder to break than for native-stock residents overall, although again rates were lower among those under thirty-nine years old (Dominguez, Groeneveld, and Kruisbergen 2002, 141–45).

In education Turks and Moroccans were the farthest behind, despite some glimmers of hope. At the end of the 1990s, the municipality's annual report on public schools announced that "black" (immigrant-rich) schools were performing better than many had suspected and that several even did better than many "white" ones. Small-scale projects had proved more likely to produce desired changes than grand schemes. Education was an area of structural integration that the city's political-cultural policies had been able to influence positively ("Zwarte scholen" 1999). Thereafter, progress inched along at the elementary school level, due in part to backsliding among West Indian and native-stock pupils. In secondary schools first-generation Turkish and Moroccan immigrants once again represented the most problematic groups.

Irrespective of the advances that they were making, the Moroccan and, to a slightly lesser degree, Turkish minorities had become associated with social problems in the city. City officials took pains to stress that it was an oversimplification and a distortion to make a facile distinction between "native" and "foreign" young people. It was no secret, however, that young Moroccans turned to crime more than their Dutch- and Turkish-stock peers (Eddaoudi 1998). Their criminal activity caused concern even among Moroccan parents, who set greater store by coercive social control than the native Dutch (Akinbingöl et al. 1996). Municipal officials took trips to Morocco's major cities in an attempt to understand the homeland culture.

Threats to public order and public safety had been named by 73 percent of Rotterdammers as the city's top problem in 1973. That share fell to 59 percent in 1998, after the municipality had instituted an "integrated security policy" that blended preventative and repressive measures. The pervasive impact of North American conflict resolution programs was evident in the use of such neologisms as the adjective *outreachend* in official reports (RSJBR 1997a, 26). The injection of millions of guilders made it possible to put more uniformed police on the streets, hire long-term unemployed as auxiliary security guards, open new playgrounds, and improve lighting in public places. The infamous "coffee shops," purveyors of soft drugs and hothouses of criminal activity, were refedined as youth centers and made subject to their regulatory regime.

While the city expressed its pleasure with the positive outcomes of its security policies (see RSJBR 1997b), there was ample evidence that concern over crime was widespread and climbing again by decade's end. Immigrant-origin youths were more likely to be crime suspects, with Turks less implicated than Moroccans and those of West Indian, Aruban, (former) Yugoslav, and Somali background. More than Turks and Moroccans, West Indians and Arubans were overrepresented among those in prison. There was actually a trend toward the convergence of the crime rate of minorities and that of young people overall, even without controlling for demographic and other background characteristics. Much of the general perception of declining social control was owing to the behavior of Dutch-stock youths (Dominguez, Groeneveld, and Kruisbergen 2002). The looting and trashing of much of Rotterdam's downtown after the local football team's victory in the Dutch national league championship match in 1999 stood as a case in point.

Non-European youths, especially Moroccans and Turks, received most of the blame. Together, they served to incriminate Islam, blamed for fostering values that worked against integration. According to the SPIOR, only around

10 percent of Rotterdam's Muslims were active in a mosque. Regardless, the city had treated religious minorities like other ethnic groups and always assumed the importance of such collective identities. Rotterdam officials commissioned several surveys of Turkish, Moroccan, and Dutch young people. The major finding was the gradual emergence of an individualized, tolerant, pluralistic Islam "made in Holland." It constituted a key source of identity for most of the interviewees. More education and contact with Dutch students correlated with less conformity and subcultural isolation. Muslim girls, irrespective of any head covering they chose to wear, exhibited stronger feelings of self-worth and more satisfactory educational achievement than their male counterparts (Phalet 2000). Moroccan girls displayed levels of emancipation comparable to those of their Dutch-stock peers. Younger immigrant-origin minorities displayed less traditional attitudes than their parents, except among Turkish boys, whose attitudes toward male-female relationships diverged dramatically from those of the native Dutch. Turkish- and Moroccan-origin youths were more conformist than their Dutch counterparts (Dominguez, Groeneveld, and Kruisbergen 2002, 145–46).

No mention was made of the contribution that Islam could make to local values through its sense of community, hospitality, and respect for the elderly. This omission was striking in light of the heated debate over a perceived loss of "good manners" in the city. A significant minority of native Dutch respondents (25 percent) referred to Islam as "violent" and "dangerous," even as a similar share of Muslims rejected European culture (Phalet 2000, 20).

It was in this ethnoreligiously charged atmosphere that the Pim Fortuyn juggernaut was launched. The Livable Rotterdam (Leefbaar Rotterdam— LR) movement was founded by a schoolteacher, who invited local celebrity Pim Fortuyn to head its lists of candidates in the March 2002 election. His puckish nationalism gained him many followers, and he won a stunning victory. The LR took 34.7 percent of the vote and sixteen municipal council seats. The PvdA (22.4 percent, eleven seats) and CDA (12 percent, five seats) elected their lowest number of councilors since the war; the Liberals of the VVD (18.1 percent, four seats) did not do much better. The Labor Party performed most strongly in areas suffering from social disadvantage and containing the highest shares of immigrant-origin residents. The LR had done best in the wealthier, "white-flight" areas on the city's periphery without many minorities. Nevertheless, it was the top vote getter in fifty-three of Rotterdam's sixty-seven neighborhoods. It won in several areas of immigrant concentration, but ecological analysis offered no discernible connection. Nor was there a clear transferal of earlier support for far-right political parties and support for LR. (At their apogee in 1994, the anti-immigrant Center Party and Center Democrats had only won six seats in Rotterdam's municipal council.) At the district level, only in Delfshaven was the PvdA the strongest party; everywhere else,

LR finished in first place. At just over 55 percent, voter turnout had been 5.5 percent higher in 2002 than in 1998 (Linders, van Rhee, and van Lith 2002, 10–22).

After the election, a governing alliance of LR, the CDA, and the VVD was formed, with the mayor from the latter party. In their agreement, the coalition partners stressed "quality of life" issues like crime, traffic, public transportation, and public spaces. There was no specific mention of immigrants or ethnic minorities in discussions of those concerns. "Insecurity, excessive immigration, dissatisfaction, and unrest have loosened social ties in the city," the coalition pact went on to affirm, however. Then, more unexpectedly: "Difference (pluralism, multiculturalism, diversity) is a given and that also means differences in services. Immigration has not only brought Rotterdam a wealth of problems but surely also a great number of possibilities for the future. Rotterdam, as a pluralist metropolitan society, must lay the accent on living together." The Dutch language, laws, rules, and undefined social values and norms were described as the prerequisites for that harmonious condition. "Vital associations of Rotterdammers" were to be implicated in the solution of social problems, "such as, for example, Turkish, West Indian, and Moroccan organizations with language classes and in the fight against educational difficulties" (Leefbaar Rotterdam 2002, 1).

If in practice the influence of LR did not appear to push the local government too far away from its ethnic-based, inclusive stance, it had served to galvanize the city's immigrant-origin population. The debate over Pim Fortuyn's anti-Islam comments—on account of which the SPIOR and a national-level Moroccan association filed suit against him—heightened Muslims' political involvement. Almost 40 percent of Moroccans voted in 2002, most of them backing the six Moroccan-origin candidates found on two party lists. Spurred on by the presence of fourteen Turkish-origin candidates spread out over six party lists, almost 55 percent of Turks went to the polls. By contrast, less than a third of other ethnic minorities voted. Moroccans and Turks without Dutch nationality voted more than those with it. While gender played a role that varied by group, there was little intergenerational variation evident among nonnational and naturalized immigrant voters (van Rhee 2002). As their structural integration stagnated, the steady drift toward political congruence in Rotterdam seemed destined to bring further ethnic turbulence.

Ethnic identities remained the touchstone of Rotterdam's policy mix. Especially when dealing with immigrant-origin women, for instance, the SAMS stressed the need for services more attuned to ethnic-specific needs. Feelings of trust and belonging within "one's own" ethnic group were deemed a crucial precondition for emancipation. Categorical policies were sometimes necessary to fight exclusion and to compensate for groups' different starting positions in the emancipation process (SAMS Rotterdam 2001). After the 2002 elections, the SAMS advocated taking the "worthy elements from different cultures" as the starting point from which to build up the multicultural city, strengthen the social bonds between residents, and reverse the unrest that fed movements like LR. It was willing to admit that there were examples outside the Netherlands of where policies addressed too insistently to ethnic groups generated discord (SAMS Rotterdam 2002). Such concerns were behind the proposal for a "City Podium," bringing authorities and residents together in public to discuss tough issues, and the "Day of Dialogue," organized in October 2002 to build bridges across ethnic and religious boundaries (SAMS Rotterdam 2003).

The Hague: Balancing Structural and Political-Cultural Integration

Just a short commuter train ride north of Rotterdam, its fellow South Holland metropolis, The Hague followed a policy trajectory that was distinctively Dutch in key respects. Given its status as the Netherlands' political capital, the city would probably have been hard pressed to deviate too much from national policy guidelines. What's more, the left did not dominate the city's political life as much as in Rotterdam. The political setup was closer to the national norm: the Social Democratic PvdA was the strongest single party, but the Christian Democrats (CDA) and the Liberals (VVD) were each just about as powerful. The alternative Democrats 66 (*Democraten 66*) put in a respectable electoral showing, too. Compromise was indispensable.

In spite of those features, Hague officials adopted a policy course as distinctive as that of their colleagues in Rotterdam. Whereas their neighbors had concentrated on political-cultural integration more than national policy dictated, in The Hague it was structural integration policy that ended up receiving more attention. Targeted policies were accepted as necessary whenever general policies failed to provide adequate offerings. But the city never opted for a comprehensive target-group policy in the sense of a packet of housing, legal, labor, and social welfare policies for groups of the same ethnoreligious background. Services were established for particular groups in particular areas within the context of overall integration policy. The Hague thereby developed an approach that diverged rather significantly from those of both the national government and Rotterdam. The Hague's struggle to advance structural integration was marginally more successful. In combination with political-cultural integration policies that learned to avoid ethnic structuring, it managed to edge toward congruence along both dimensions while avoiding overt ethnic conflict.

Crisis and Progressive Response

An administrative center, not a port city, The Hague did not share Rotterdam's colorful proletarian past. It developed a substantial industrial base, all the same, and with it a comparable presence of immigrant-origin residents. By 1995, almost 11 percent of the resident population would be nonnationals, and almost 20 percent of immigrant origin (AVEB 1998). Its members exhibited the same characteristics as elsewhere in the country: high unemployment (33 percent, as opposed to 23 percent overall)—far worse for Turkish- and Moroccan-origin youths (40 and 45 percent), who suffered from low levels of academic and professional achievement (Delcroix 1992, 160–61).

From the start of large-scale migration in the 1950s, immigrant-origin residents were concentrated in the worst housing of the city—that is, in the nineteenth-century private stock surrounding the inner city. Only the least attractive and cheapest units in the social housing market, located in adjoining neighborhoods that dated from the immediate postwar period, took in any sizable numbers of immigrants. The neighborhoods where most of them lived—Zeeheldenkwartier, Stationsbuurt, Schildersbuurt, Transvaalkwartier, Groente en Fruitmarkt, and Binckhorst—lay in the central boroughs of Centrum and Laak. In 1966 a fire broke out in a pension for Mediterranean guest workers on the Orangeplein near the city center. It took one life and drew painful attention to the problems that existed. It was during this period that The Hague developed its penchant for early, preventative policy responses and for structured consultation in the formulation of major and minor policies dealing with its immigrant-origin residents. In the early years, local policy responses had been as ad hoc as at the national level.

Immigrants' Structural Integration

The late 1970s and early 1980s witnessed a struggle between the national government and those of the Netherlands' largest cities, which wanted to be able to tailor integration and other social policies to local conditions. Even before decentralization was decided upon, The Hague moved on its own. With a nervous eye on evidence of disconnection down the road in Rotterdam, the city defined a certain number of target groups in 1982. It adopted a "two-track" policy: parity between general and categorical policies. The Hague decided of its own accord to shift its emphasis from social welfare to education, housing, and the labor market. It thereby took a policy path that departed from those of the national government and other large Dutch cities. Modest moves toward policy decentralization were making such differences of emphasis more sustainable. In 1983, responsibility and the corresponding funding for first-line, street-level social work with Surinamese and Dutch West Indians was transferred from the national to the local governments; eventually, second-line institutional work with those groups, as well as with other minorities, followed suit. Whether in the employ of municipal agencies or nonprofit associations, social workers took their cue from city hall (BDH 2002).

In The Hague's initial policy cut, immigrants qua ethnic communities figured prominently. The Hague was less liable than elsewhere to equate ethnicity with country of origin. The national government's ethnic minorities policy was emerging, and it targeted former colonials and guest workers and their families. The Hague added in other disadvantaged groups, namely Chinese (many of them from Surinam) and Pakistanis, and considered the Kurds within the Turkish-origin population to be a group apart, too. Alongside ethnic-specific strategies were those that divided residents functionally and according to their gender and age.

Policy clusters, each with its own funding and focus, homed in on their difficulties. The problems of each group came sharply into focus, and through trial and error new plans of attack and policy instruments came to light. In collaboration with local immigrant associations, governments of The Hague introduced initiatives in the education and housing sectors aimed at nonindigenous residents. Eventually, funding flowed from the central administration, supplemented by local-level monies specially earmarked for integration programs. The Hague was contributing more than a million guilders a year on its own, even more by the mid-1980s (BDH 1998a).

By then, the drawbacks of categorical policies were visible. They frequently proved too narrowly defined and disjointed. General social service agencies found it too convenient to use them as a pretext for not changing their own procedures or tactics. By 1986 immigrants' retarded structural and political-cultural integration was arguing for more far-reaching projects. The Hague enacted a more coherent package of policies directed against disadvantage. It was no longer the target group that stood at the center but rather the problem in need of resolution, and everyone suffering from it was considered a suitable client. This approach called for a bundled set of offerings from a series of policy sectors—housing, education, social welfare, employment, and culture—all operating under a common administrative and financial framework. Under its rubric the various municipal departments were expected to take and implement their own initiatives.

Immigrants' Political-Cultural Integration

There was a decline in the influence of immigrant associations, which had formerly played a critical role in the formulation and implementation of target-group policies. They included initiatives to strengthen immigrants' identity as a prerequisite for their integration and emancipation. Affected populations were still to give their input, and a consultative council for immigrants served as their link to the new policies. The appointed delegates of nineteen associations sat next to Dutch trade union, religious, and associational representatives on the body, whose president was a member of a special municipal commission that oversaw all local integration work. This advisory board joined a similarly appointed consultative organization that represented the interests of (former) colonials from Surinam, the Dutch West Indies and Aruba, and Moluccans (Delcroix 1992).

These institutions had arisen from the desire of the local administration to know what their immigrant-origin residents wanted and expected from it, as well as from their frustrated hopes of identifying credible spokespeople among their number. The advisory councils' recommendations in the beginning were more the codification of previously reached compromises among all concerned parties than the product of independent assessments. Immigrant representatives grew frustrated by the dominance exercised by the municipality's liaisons. It became painfully apparent that the bodies' raison-d'être was to advise and opine but not to take an active part in decision making.

By the late 1980s, the diversification of both the immigrant-origin population and the local associational universe was weakening the established players' authority. Some of the new immigrant groups took public exception to the opinions emitted by the advisory councils. They had grown more bureaucratic, with ever more committees and work groups. City hall, for its part, found it more arduous to forge a consensus. The awarding of local suffrage to resident nonnationals in 1985, along with the heightened stress on structural disconnection, had altered the local integration policy dynamic. When the municipal government decided to concentrate on the fight against social and economic marginalization, it left advisory councils and the major immigrant associations less room for maneuver and political influence. More than their counterparts in other Dutch cities, not to mention in Germany, policymakers in The Hague resolved to speak to immigrants as individual residents and not only with their organizational leaders (BDH 1998b).

That is not to say that Hague officials were deaf to institutional needs. The presence of Islam, for example, was acknowledged and sanctioned. In 1980 the city set aside 200,000 guilders from national Interior Ministry funds for the purchase of a former synagogue, which was then converted into a mosque. The subsidy was later reduced to 175,000 guilders, the maximum allowed by national law (BDH 2002). In 1988 the city's first Hindu school opened, quickly followed by another and then a Muslim school as well (CWGSR 1998).

The Difficult 1990s

The central state, desperate for new ways to facilitate immigrant integration, tried to take advantage of The Hague's extensive experience and reputation for innovation. National officials introduced a pilot program for "newcomers" there and in Tilburg in the late 1980s that involved intensive Dutch courses and mentoring. In spite of their very real successes, the palette of policies introduced in The Hague did not seem up to the task by the start of the 1990s.

When defined as all residents who either themselves or one of whose parents had been born outside the Netherlands, the immigrant-origin population by mid-decade would easily top a third of The Hague's total (Boelhouwer 1997). Even as the structural situation of Turks and Moroccans deteriorated, an immigrant elite had emerged, comprised mainly of Surinamese and Moluccans. They were more easily able to access programs aimed at improving entry into the labor market, be they programs supporting ethnic businesses or those retraining laid-off unskilled laborers. The unemployment rate among immigrant-origin workers stuck at high levels, affecting Turks and Moroccans more than others. Their disproportionate presence in low-skill and low-wage sectors, together with their expanding presence among the long-term unemployed, was a source of official distress.

Residential concentration had deepened. The Centrum and Laak boroughs contained the districts with the highest concentrations of immigrant-origin residents, Schilderswijk (23 percent Turks, 17 percent Moroccans) and Transvaal (23 percent, 12 percent), which contained several neighborhoods that were almost half non-European. The kingdom recognized Schilderswijk and Transvaal, along with several adjacent districts, as "social problem accumulation areas" (Gramberg, Reverda, and Kleinegris 1992). In addition to high immigrant-origin concentrations, they also had the most families with numerous children and one breadwinner and the most unemployment. They were getting company, however, as The Hague's longtime partition into a disadvantaged nineteenth-century core and a richer adjoining ring gave way to a three-part division. An inner band of postwar neighborhoods, wedged between the center and the well-to-do neighborhoods along the North Sea dunes, witnessed the greatest accretion of social ills (DBZ Den Haag 1997).

More so than their counterparts in Rotterdam or the Netherlands in general, Hague officials were open to the possibility that residential concentration could be an opportunity as much as a problem. Although The Hague was the most segregated city in the Netherlands, spatial disconnection on the basis of ethnic origin was never the object of municipal policy (SAMS Den Haag 2002e). The official view was that the phenomenon had positive aspects in the form of social networks and arose from a voluntary decision to live together—in other words, "congregation." The availability of relatively affordable housing around the city center and immigrants' working-class status were held accountable for many of the spatial trends. Furthermore, having their community around them seemed to be more important to Turks and Moroccans than to native-stock Dutch (Kullberg 1996). Even in its most advantageous manifestation, however, such congregating could degenerate over time, due to white flight and the passing of elderly Dutch residents. In practice, neighborhoods with ethnic stores and mosques nurtured *gezelligheid*, the beloved Dutch version of cozy German *gemütlichkeit*, but could also breed problems associated with low-income, unemployed, and otherwise marginalized people.

The city's segregation index was falling, from 55.5 in 1980 to 43.1 in 1995 (see table 4.3). Simultaneously, differentials in income levels across neighborhoods were rising, from 19.1 in 1989 to 25.1 in 1995 (Boelhouwer 1997, 45–47). It was hard to tell whether spatial segregation was getting better or worse, in truth, since the picture looked different depending on whether one started at the level of the housing block, street, neighborhood, or district. There was only one district in The Hague that was less than one-tenth nonindigenous (Duindorp), and ethnic minorities were spreading out into next-door neighborhoods and across the city. The same pattern of distribution was visible in Berlin, Bremen, and Rotterdam, and to lesser degrees in Essen and Nuremberg.

In The Hague, at any rate, the municipality learned that the relationship between spatial concentration and segregation on the one hand and political-cultural and structural integration on the other was not a clear or direct one. The fight against segregation could even encourage disconnection more than reduce it (Roseman, Laux, and Thieme 1996). Integration policies were indispensable, therefore, but officials needed to think them through carefully. The entry of a far-right candidate onto the municipal council in March 1990 alerted them to the political risks that they were running. Four years later, the far right increased its representation threefold. The VVD became the strongest single party, followed closely by the PvdA, Democrats 66, and CDA. The municipality vowed to take full advantage of discretionary national-level integration programs, for which it had to cover only 10 percent of costs. It rejected proposals to institute affirmative action programs, which it feared would create tensions and rivalries between ethnic groups (Gemeente Den Haag 1995).

The Hague's "kaleidoscope" of integration policies underwent a slight turn once again (BDH 2002). The accent in The Hague's Multicultural City Plan between 1992 and 1997 fell on tackling structural disadvantage in education and vocational training, housing, and the labor market. The municipality was in some respects recommitting itself to the course it had followed in preceding years. It continued to strive to offer to its residents, no matter from where they came or what they looked like, the same rights and opportunities. That said, The Hague's "integrated integration package" was not color-blind. Officials acknowledged that differences in cultural background and life experience had great relevance in determining the most effective manner to deal with problems. General social services, provided they were sufficiently flexible in their methods and possessed the requisite expertise, would best meet the challenge. Targeted policies lost even more ground, except where seen as unavoidable. Thus there were actions on behalf of Turkish- and Moroccan-origin youths, especially those who fell in the cracks between programs for hardcore problem groups and regular educational and training programs (BDH 1998b, 28).

Integration policy melded with the fight against social disadvantage in general, which, in turn, fell in line with the national government's attempts to strengthen regional administrative capacity. (The Hague became part of the Haaglanden region in mid-decade.) Decentralization went forward, with central authorities maintaining their hold on the purse strings. Unlike in Germany, the transferal of responsibility was accompanied by a broadly corresponding increase in financial wherewithal. Municipal officials had to draw up plans and request the bounty; it was forthcoming as long as local strategies fit within general parameters. The Hague tied its integration policies to a systematic budgetary procedure that necessitated yearly assessments and constantly opened up possibilities for corrections or innovations as needed. Flexible leadership and close relationships with national officials—located, after all, only a few blocks away from city hall—proved their worth at critical moments. Close, intense national-local dialogue was the cornerstone of The Hague's method of integrating immigrants (BDH 2002).

The new tack made use of lessons gleaned from previous experience, as city officials worked toward a cohesive policy package to be implemented in the districts. Decentralized integration policies did not replace those at the municipal level but, rather, operated in tandem with them. Local policymakers tested out ideas with packages of neighborhood-, and even block-level work in the down-at-the-heels districts of Transvaal and Bouwlust (DWFM 1993). Schilderswijk's coordinated plan of action in 1995 won The Hague recognition and funding from the European Union. Municipal grants, many of them envisioned as seed money, were awarded through a competitive procedure. City hall took on the role of central manager, broker, and monitor. In 1996 it installed integration coordinators in each neighborhood, attached to a Deconcentration Department. Policies operating in the different sectors were linked together more tightly with respect to content, organization, and funding.

All told, the Multicultural City Plan pumped between six and eight million guilders annually into the drive to see The Hague warrant that label (BDH 1998b, 64). By the late 1990s, local policy was converging with the national GSB, shifting toward the fight against social marginalization in all its manifestations. Problems were to be solved in their social and territorial context. Targeted efforts, once more, were only appropriate to deal with narrowly defined, short-term challenges; The Hague's version of multiculturalism was decidedly liberal. The GSB in the Hague meant an integrated approach combining the infrastructural, social, and economic dimensions, each with a coordinator in the local administration. No new, overarching mandates were drawn up. It was up to each sector to provide its piece of the puzzle, fitting into the city's overall policy and budget.

The Challenges of a New Millennium

City officials freely acknowledged the difficulties inherent in evaluating the relationship between integration policy outputs and outcomes, as well as the unreliability of quantitative indicators of integration in the social welfare area. A decision was made, more consciously than in the other case cities, to evaluate policy outcomes by taking into consideration direct outlays, the internal and external factors that facilitated or impeded the effectual use of allotted funds, and their positive and negative multiplier effects (BDH 2002).

Within the context of such qualifications, the city saw evidence of positive developments during the latter half of 1990s. There had been undeniable improvements in the immigrant-origin population's position in the local labor market, not in the least with respect to ethnic small businesses, as well as overall measures of disadvantage. Benefiting from broader economic trends, unemployment among workers of non-Dutch stock, which was 16 percent in 1998, had fallen to 10 percent by 2002. The socioeconomic differences between residents of Dutch and non-Dutch stock were narrowing. There was talk of socioeconomic mobility (BDH 2000, 6).

Local officials were of the opinion that the city's housing-related troubles had ended more or less successfully. A municipal survey conducted in 1997 showed that immigrant-origin residents were less satisfied with their housing than their Dutch-stock neighbors. The discrepancy was not huge—7, compared to 7.5, on a 10-point scale (with 10 the best)—and there was no serious variance across neighborhoods or city districts (ABO 1997). Social housing corporations and local housing policy received credit for reducing discrimination and increasing the supply of cheap rental units. In a sop to the proprivatization fashion of the times, the city introduced an individual rent subsidy in the mid-1990s. The change left individuals face-to-face with the market. While retaining its dubious distinction as the Dutch urban area with the most housing segregation, The Hague had brought about the largest decline among large cities during the 1990s—even as the number of immigrant-origin minorities in the population had sharply increased (see table 4.3). Now, however, less restricted market forces began to yield knots of immigrants in rental housing that threatened once again to feed segregation.

Surveys of immigrant-origin residents painted a complicated picture that prevented officials from drawing any clear conclusions. Immigrant-origin residents enjoyed living next to their compatriots, with easy access to religious institutions and ethnic businesses. Still, immigrant minorities recognized the disadvantages that came from living relatively isolated from the rest of local society (see BDH 2002). As before, the municipality believed that where concentrations of "cultural groups" existed, they were primarily the consequence of history, income, unemployment, and free will, as well as the inability of some residents to take advantage of all possibilities open to them in the social rental sector. Officials maintained that irrespective of ethnic background, people were affected by the unequal distribution of housing, work, and other lifestyle characteristics, and those in similar circumstances found themselves bunched together in certain neighborhoods. There, prejudice could produce further clustering by block or building (see Boelhouwer 1997). But even when income, education, and length of residency were controlled, other observers retorted, Turks and Moroccans were least able to move out of poverty-stricken neighborhoods (Bolt 2001).

In the crucial educational area, immigrant-origin children's level of achievement was rising as the city spent more money on basic education and vocational training. "*Allochton*" and "problem" became less inextricably linked in local schools, and migrants were being seen as a group with great potential. Impressively, the final examination scores of Moroccan students at the intermediate levels were now actually higher on average than those of their native-stock peers. The *Kaas-Cous* project—a play on words on "couscous" and the Dutch word for cheese—was assisting them in the transition from school to work, involving elderly residents and leading figures from the local Moroccan community as mentors and "personal coaches" (BDH 1998b). It and similarly innovative projects fell under the umbrella of "The Leader" program for Turkish- and Moroccan-origin youths in Schilderswijk and Transvaal, into which extra Multicultural City funds poured (BDH 1998a). In the place of the officials who traveled from Rotterdam to Casablanca and Tangier, it was mostly young students from the Schilderswijk and Transvaal districts who journeyed from The Hague to Morocco, visiting the rural Berber areas from which many of the city's Moroccan nationals hailed (BDH 1997).

Social work in The Hague, which had traditionally followed the target-group strategy, underwent intensive review in the 1990s. It found its remit broadened far beyond casework and culturally grounded counseling to become part of a range of social policies implicated in immigrant integration. The advisability of adhering to empowerment principles was accepted without discussion. The municipality felt that if it consulted immigrant-origin residents when formulating general policies, they could be adjusted to deal with specific problems—thus reaping the positive effects of a categorical policy without the negative by-products. Experiments along those lines with West Indians, Arubans, and Kurds proved disappointing. The city concluded that it would take longer than expected to deliver adequate, "decategoricalized" services for such groups as a subset of general offerings (BDH 1998b, 49–50).

The city responded with pilot projects in two neighborhoods that introduced a competitive element into funding. Henceforth, the municipality would award additional subsidies beyond those that covered basic operating expenses only as a bonus for more inventive actions. It prized street-level, solution-driven tactics and private-public partnerships, as well as ethnic entrepreneurship and small business ownership. The city government, police, residents' organizations, immigrant associations (including those at the mosques), and all relevant social providers participated actively. Not the effort but the result was to be rewarded. Officials claimed to be answering social workers' calls for a financing scheme that spurred creativity even while ensuring sustainability (DBZ 1997).

Within the city administration, department heads were to be more conscious about putting meat on the bones of the official multicultural personnel policy. Budget cuts and staff layoffs rendered it difficult to undertake any large-scale changes, so, not surprisingly, a premium was put on organizational "bundling" and initiatives that promised to improve the functioning of existing public services. Few disputed that there were far too few Turkish- and Moroccan-origin social workers (Multiculturele Instelling 1997). The ongoing privatization of municipal services, which counteracted aspirations to diversify staff, included those involved in sanitation and the maintenance of public spaces, which had traditionally hired many people of non-Dutch stock. Even so, training and monitoring programs managed to make enough progress that in 1999, the municipality's work force was 16.1 percent minority, ahead of the 14 percent target set for the Haaglanden region. The Hague was doing better than Rotterdam, which was falling short of its comparable regional target of 13 percent (BDH 2002).

The finesse with which Hague officials mixed general and more nuanced policies, treating ethnic-specific deficiencies without drawing undue attention to them, was repeated in the political-cultural realm. Structural integration may have seemed to triumph over political-cultural integration in The Hague's policy programs. On the contrary, they tagged the social, political, and cultural participation of immigrant-origin residents as a priority, and self-help mobilization was a critical element. The local administration treated immigrant associations as an information transmission belt to and from their constituents. In 1994 the city appointed the SAMS, precursor of Rotterdam's body of the same name, to lend it guidance. The SAMS was the successor to the advisory councils for immigrants and (former) colonials. Headed by a naturalized immigrant, it was to serve as a think tank, independent monitor and evaluator of integration policies, and a contributor to discussions about how to live in a multicultural society. It gave advice whenever and on whatever topics it chose. Able to range in number from fifteen to twenty, the SAMS members were drawn by an ad hoc committee from a pool created by an open nomination process. (Two of its original members were of native-Dutch stock.) Similar bodies existed to provide advice and counsel on issues affecting women, people with disabilities, and homosexuals in The Hague (SAMS Den Haag 1998).

The SAMS agreed with the city that general services were preferable to categorical ones, but it felt that institutions targeted at immigrants had made valuable, frequently overlooked contributions to The Hague. They should not be cut off from municipal subsidies until mainstream agencies proved willing and able to serve as an adequate replacement. The SAMS recalled an old Dutch folk saying that warned against throwing out old shoes before obtaining new ones (SAMS Den Haag 1995).

Eager for reliable, representative collaborators, the local government did what it could to stimulate the grouping of immigrant organizations when it proved difficult to bring immigrants, particularly the smaller and newer groups, into existing associational life. Hague officials welcomed such structuring when it occurred on a district or neighborhood basis—for example, the Schilderswijk Multicultural Platform. But they expressed reservations when it proceeded on the basis of a common ethnicity or national background—as when fifty Moroccan groups formed the Moroccan Platform to lobby for their compatriots. Network building became the desired means to marry interest articulation with interest aggregation (BDH 2002).

The municipal government cited surveys showing growing support among both native-stock and "allochtonous" residents for equal participation in all aspects of local society as evidence that its integration policies were working (see SAMS Den Haag 2002c, 4). Broader than mere co-decision, participation was seen as going beyond involvement in formal administrative structures to encompass associational life, political parties, elder councils, and formal and informal forums for collaboration at all levels. A major problem for self-help associations was securing a place to meet. The city offered to retool a former administration building and to permit the use of school classrooms and other facilities after hours. Officials earmarked funds for groups that had not previously received support (or had lost it) but could demonstrate that their activities would facilitate integration. They also had to be willing to pool resources with more general organizations and, wherever possible, merge with them. A regulation in 1996 made it necessary for organizations to have at least fifty members each contributing at least fifty guilders per year in order to receive municipal subsidies. Unlike such cities as Berlin, The Hague did not set great store by sports clubs, and at least one Moroccan football club complained bitterly about not receiving funding (Multiculturele Instelling 1997). Associational activities had to jibe with the priorities set by local policymakers.[10] New associations materialized that hewed the desired municipal line.

The city saw self-organizations, both secular and religious, as the "glue" between the individual and the surrounding society (BDH 2000, 9). As before, Muslim associations were included among the binding agents. The 1990s brought intensified dialogue between the municipality and all immigrant faith-based organizations. Mosques and mandirs did not receive regular subsidies, because they were expressly religious organizations. Thus no "regular" support was forthcoming for the Islamic Associational Platform of The Hague, a loose local version of Rotterdam's SPIOR "social partner," because its goal was to sponsor Islamic practice. Nonetheless, when such organizations engaged in activities that increased participation and social development, they were eligible for tens of thousands of guilders worth of "incidental" subsidies. Religious instruction, conducted by Muslim and Hindu teachers, spread throughout local public schools; The Hague and Rotterdam were the only two Dutch cities where that was happening (CWGSR 1998). Islam was not a source of serious local conflict, although officials noted with unease the emergence of Islamist groups like the Turkish-Islamic Center, which Kurdish separatists tried to burn down twice.

Residents reported the most security-related anxiety in the same districts and neighborhoods that ranked highest on the municipality's indices of social disadvantage. There was a chasm on this score between the core districts with the largest immigrant-origin concentrations and the rest. Well over three-quarters of respondents in all neighborhoods told city pollsters that they felt some personal responsibility for the livability of their neighborhood (ABO 1997). According to the municipal "Quality of Life Monitor," immigrant-origin residents' concerns were dovetailing with those of Dutch-stock residents. Both groups named street litter the "number one nuisance" in The Hague and cited "too many non-indigenous residents" as number two. Immigrant-origin youths mentioned boredom as the major problem in their lives. A similar percentage of immigrant-origin (77 percent) as native-stock (82 percent) residents evinced little desire to move out of their neighborhood, which the same share (51 percent) of each considered a pleasant place to live. However, native-stock Dutch (78 percent) were significantly more likely than nonnationals and naturalized immigrants (58 percent) to feel unsafe there (Verdurmen, van Wensveen, and Oudijk 1997).[11]

Accessing monies set aside for "youth and security" projects under the GSB, the municipality instituted preventative activities. Moroccan youths remained a primary target. Local police admitted that they had a more negative view of them than of other national and ethnic groups (Multiculturele Instelling 1997, 4). Commissioned studies determined that their Turkish, Kurdish, and Somali peers warranted specific policies, too, as did immigrant-origin girls. Mentoring and accompanying youths' "life trajectories" were the preferred methods (BDH 1998b). City hall saw a steering role for itself in the process and launched training programs for staff members, mediators, and paraprofessionals. It recruited Moroccan fathers to patrol city streets near the central train station in a bid to reduce youth crime. A "fathers' center" in the Laak borough worked on the "personal development" of immigrant men. Concern over social cohesion was behind those endeavors, as well as a push for network building. Local authorities did not expect the process to be conflict free and, in true Dutch fashion, set great store in residents finding common ground from continually "talking to one another" (BDH 2000, 13).

The immigrant vote did not stir the municipality's ardor as much as in Rotterdam. Hague authorities were more focused on stimulating and steering immigrant associational participation. They made a blanket appeal for nonnationals to vote in municipal elections but did not undertake any organized mobilizational campaign. Overall immigrant turnout was virtually identical to that in Rotterdam: 57.6 percent in 1994 and only 48 percent four years later. In 1998, however, participation was significantly lower among Turks (36 percent) and Moroccans (23 percent). That year, 16 percent of Turks supported a Turkish party, Demir, but another 13 percent voted for the Turkish candidate of "Multicultural '98," a multiethnic political alliance. Ten percent of Surinamese and 8 percent of West Indian and Aruban voters supported it as well, perhaps reflecting The Hague's reluctance to highlight ethnic differences

(Tillie 1998, 86–87). Also that year, the far right disappeared from the municipal council, "replaced" by the environmentalists.

At the end of the 1990s, The Hague, like Rotterdam, had its share of problems. In several of its neighborhoods, despair and petty criminality made the
city seem like anything but a multicultural wonderland. Both structural and
political-cultural integration advanced, slowly but surely, and in neither realm
did ethnic identities receive much official encouragement. The new citizenship
policy, which became operational in 2001, was off to a quick start in orientat-
ing the newest immigrants toward life in the Netherlands; its success made it
possible to give "oldcomers" (already resident immigrants) due attention as
well, specifically in the area of Dutch language instruction. Significantly more
national and local funds were being funneled into programs to facilitate the
acquisition of Dutch language skills (MGSIB 2002).

The force of The Hague's approach rested with the high level of policy coordination and the tightly organized system of subsidy disbursement that was
linked to it. The various departmental and project budgets flowed from a
single central spigot and could be trained together at a target when necessary.
The amounts in question were comparable to those made available in
Rotterdam, most of them coming from the same national source, and far more
than local German officials had at their disposal. From around five million
guilders in 1980, the national government had steadily upped its funding of
integration-related projects in The Hague, as had the local government.
Officials at both levels awarded grants for pilot projects and policy responses
to unexpected developments. The SAMS questioned how useful such subsidies
"from on high" were in meeting policy goals, and it felt that the city's policy of
reimbursing associations instead of advancing them subsidies penalized
smaller and financially weaker groups. It did not cast any doubt on the local
administration's intentions.[12]

The mayor, Wim Deetman, spoke of his dream of an "undivided city, one
without marginalization, disadvantage, or discrimination." The means to that
end was a long-term process of emancipation, the "strengthening of the ties
between native-stock and non-indigenous residents, with equal opportunities
and possibilities for all" (BDH 1998b, 4–5). Hagenaars, no less than Rotterdammers, were accepting what their German colleagues had started to suspect:
a society with truly integrated immigrants would be a transformed society.
Host cultures and ways of life would not be the measure of all things.

Nevertheless, when officials emphasized the knowledge and values necessary for each resident to become a self-sufficient and actively engaged citizen,
they made Dutch language acquisition and acceptance of the "responsibilities
of citizenship" the heart of the matter. The Hague's integration policy for the
years 2002–2005 had a total budget of 7 million guilders, more than 2 million
of which were to be devoted to adult Dutch language instruction; another 2

million guilders were tagged for district-level work. The points of reference were to be emancipation, interculturalization, and diversity (SAMS Den Haag 2001b, 13–14). The city was committed to spending significant sums of "extra" money (around 10.5 million guilders) in order to reduce waiting lists for Dutch language courses and to work with immigrant associations to raise awareness of the new citizenship program (SAMS Den Haag 2002a, 4–5).

Local officials held open discussions on how the city could become a true home for people from over 162 national-ethnic backgrounds. Could there be unity in multiculturalism? Or did one culture always have to be dominant? Did a multicultural city have to be marked by insecurity? In the course of the debates, issues came up that were the source of sharp disagreements and misunderstandings in Rotterdam: gender relations in immigrant families, female circumcision, polygamy, and so on. Much work was done with immigrant women, especially Muslims. It became clear that a share of their social isolation was owing to their new environment. They cited language problems, fear, homesickness, and even medical problems (such as skin conditions caused by receiving less sunlight than was usual) as much as patriarchal family relations in explaining why they stayed at home so much more than they had in North Africa and Turkey (SAMS Den Haag 2002a, 7–8). The reasoned discourse over Islam was the product of policies that had systematically worked against the reification of ethnic and religious identities.

Perhaps for the same reason, The Hague resisted the Livable movement more than Rotterdam. In the 2002 local elections, the governing coalition held its ground, with neither the PvdA, VVD, or CDA suffering serious erosion. Livable Hague (Leefbaar Haag) only managed to win four seats—twice the score of their comrades up in Amsterdam but far less than next door in Rotterdam. With no clear program or well-known candidates, Livable Hague had taken pains to distinguish its positions from those of its "right-wing" opposite number in Rotterdam, but to no avail. In The Hague protest took the form of voter abstention, as only 44.4 percent of those eligible cast a ballot, the lowest rate in the country (Linders, van Rhee, and van Lith 2002). In the run-up to the election, the PvdA received warnings from political experts that it risked losing at least one council seat for not having included a Turkish-origin candidate on its slate. The tendency for Turks, more than other groups, to cast an "ethnic" vote was accepted and discussed as part of electoral strategizing. A Turk had offered to run but was rejected by the party's candidate commission, which worried about his leadership of the local Milli Görüs organization. "That's crazy," he retorted, "I am the head of a mosque association, but that does not mean that I do not accept the separation of church and state" (SAMS Den Haag 2001a, 4). In the end, the PvdA did lose two seats and its position as the largest local party. Its key position in the coalition that ran The Hague was unaffected.

The Hague had managed to balance immigrant integration policies in the structural and political-cultural areas in such a way as to avoid acute ethnic conflict. While striving to exploit the self-help mobilization that national policies unleashed, Hague officials made a conscious stab at undermining the ethnoreligious identity and boundary construction that they encouraged. Interethnic, generational, gender, and functional divisions crosscut overtly ethnic ones. Policymakers likewise accentuated structural integration and achieved enough of a move toward congruence along that dimension to prevent it from being attached to ethnicity and fueling conflict. Rotterdam officials took the opposite tack. They stuck with ethnic-based political-cultural policies even after they had been officially abandoned at the national level. They made largely unsuccessful attempts to avoid the spatial concentration and segregation of immigrants, whose effects on disconnection were ambiguous but neglected structural integration. Disconnection along that dimension linked up with stronger ethnic identities to yield a higher level of conflict in the city. Along the political-cultural dimension, immigrants were far from congruent with native-stock residents, but they were headed that way organizationally and with respect to political participation—farther in the two Dutch cities than in their four German counterparts and farther in more conflictual Rotterdam than in The Hague.

Within a more inclusive institutional and legal framework, national authorities in the Netherlands never really relinquished their power to orchestrate developments at the local level. They pumped far more money—with strings attached—into integration policies than their federal German counterparts. For that reason, The Hague proved more dynamic and peaceful than Bremen, which followed a similar policy mix but shouldered more severe financial burdens. Rotterdam, in turn, proved more congruent and peaceful than Berlin, even while nurturing Pim Fortuyn.

Even where political-cultural integration was prized more than the structural variety, the more systematic, better-funded policies in the Netherlands narrowed the structural integration gap with Germany, making up a share of its initial underperformance along that dimension even before improvements slowed in that neighboring country. Dutch policies generated more impressive numbers of naturalized immigrants and public-sector employees of nonnative backgrounds, not to mention a cohort of nonnational voters at the local level. Together, they could be seen as potentially influential stakeholders in integration policymaking (see Erie 1987). It would probably be an overstatement to call them anything akin to a regime of ethnic relations management (see Reed 1995).

The previous chapters have shown that institutional and policy differences can have a major impact on the nature of ethnic relations. Integration policies and the broader social welfare system of which they were a part differed organizationally and changed over time in Germany and the Netherlands, as in the four German and two Dutch cities serving as local case studies so far.

Policymakers were not always able to realize the outcomes that they pursued. What they did mattered, however, and the interplay of national and subnational levels of governance affected the formation of collective identities among immigrants, their ability to act on the rights that they enjoyed, and their interaction with host-society institutions. Welfare state restructuring seemed to entail a Europe-wide convergence on decentralization, privatization, and delegation to nonprofit associations and, with them, a liberal multicultural vision that considered institutional support for ethnic identities a necessary but provisional evil on the road to the ultimate good of equal treatment and opportunity for each individual member of society. Yet a closer look at the German and Dutch cases revealed the very real cross-national and local-level variation that existed and persisted.

The complex interplay between structural and political-cultural integration, national and local institutions and politics, and ethnic-based and other policies seemed to determine the nature of ethnic relations in Germany and the Netherlands. The influence of those factors should have been even more visible in Belgium, moreover, given the wider degree of institutional and policy variation that was possible there. The next chapter takes up the Belgian case, where federalism went much further than Germany and where integration policies ranged from Dutch-style cultural pluralism to pointedly French-style disregard for ethnic identities in the public sphere.

BELGIUM

Between Cultural Pluralism
and Liberal Neutrality

To understand the small but complicated country of Belgium, one must keep in mind that it comprises several separate nations: Dutch-speaking Flanders in the north, French-speaking Wallonia in the south, officially bilingual Brussels in between, and a tiny German-language region off to the east. Between the 1970s and the early 2000s, Belgium's integration policies grew more regionally variegated as its welfare state underwent decentralization far more definitively than its Dutch or German counterparts. Flanders and Wallonia followed distinctive paths—though, by the end of the period, their policies came together a bit as Flemish and Walloon policymakers learned from each other's and their neighbors' successes and mistakes.

Belgium responded to the evolution of the immigration challenge with policies that recalled those devised across its northern and southern frontiers in the Netherlands and France. Postwar Dutch and French integration policies represented the end points on the European continuum. The Dutch started with political-cultural integration and normally expended less time and energy on structural integration. Their pillars were in decline, but they leaned on them to experiment with cultural pluralism when dealing with immigrants, institutionalizing a role for ethnic identities in the public sphere. At times, they even toyed with a communitarian pluralist model and considered the erection of a Muslim pillar. In the end, they opted for an approach that replaced cultural pluralist elements with a liberal multiculturalism that foresaw the eventual phasing out of ethnically targeted policies.

French policymakers, meanwhile, situated themselves at the other extreme and long espoused liberal nationalism, which stressed the complete assimilation of immigrants. Since the Revolution, the Jacobin model has dominated France as a general paradigm. Under it, membership in the national community involves a voluntary commitment to the republic and its values. Ethnic, religious, linguistic, and other subcultural identities have been relegated strictly to the private sphere. Birth on French soil, rather than descent, has largely decided the granting of formal citizenship, and naturalization procedures have been intended to turn immigrants into French men and women. Once ensuring that frequently painful process were powerful agents of assimilation: the army, the French Communist Party, the trade unions, the church, and the centralized educational system. They all waned after World War II. Ad hoc labor and housing policies, the sheer magnitude of the population movements, and selective treatment of resident immigrant communities elevated ethnic-based identities that were often absent among arriving immigrants (Ireland 1994). Just as its social welfare policies were undergoing decentralization and delegation to nonprofit associations, France's assimilationist Jacobinism was refashioned to take account of the new ethnic diversity, swinging toward liberal neutrality. From time to time, policymakers even made a nod toward liberal multiculturalism. They continued to swear allegiance to egalitarian republicanism. Local authorities insisted on framing policies on a "territorial" (in other words, neighborhood) and not an ethnic base; nevertheless, they had no choice but to adapt to street-level ethnic realities (Ireland 1996, 2000).

French and Dutch integration policies had converged somewhat by the dawn of the twenty-first century. Movement in that direction was visible in Belgium, too. There, however, the Dutch ethnic minorities policy retained more of its force in Flanders, and Wallonia resisted even more firmly than in France policies that recognized ethnic boundaries and identities. The impact on immigrants' structural and political-cultural integration, as well as on ethnic relations in general, could be seen most clearly at the local level. The cities of Ghent (Flanders) and Liège (Wallonia) bear witness to the strength of institutional factors in determining how immigrants fit into Belgian society.

A History of Immigration

Belgium was the first area on the European continent to develop large-scale iron and steel industries in the nineteenth century. Wallonia pulled in labor from Flanders, neighboring countries, and Southern Europe, even while other Belgians headed to northern France or the United States for work. After World War II, few Belgians emigrated, but Italian and Spanish workers were drawn to the mines and factories of French-speaking Wallonia. Although it had possessions in central Africa, the ignoble Belgian imperial experience was short-lived and involved severe restrictions on emigration from the colonies. There was virtually none until the 1950s and thereafter only a small contingent of univer-

TABLE 5.1
Nonnational Share of Population in Belgium

	Flanders	Wallonia	Brussels	Belgium
Nonnationals/Total Population (%)				
1980	4.1	12.6	23.7	8.9
1990	4.4	13.2	29.8	9.6
1995	4.5	13.5	32.0	9.9
Nationalities/Total Nonnational Population in 1997 (%)				
North Africans	16.9	7.6	—	16.7
Turks	13.6	5.4	—	8.6
EU	53.9	77.5	—	60.6

Sources: van Peer and Lammertyn (1990, 10–12), NIS (1996), SERV (1998, 21).

sity students from independent Congo (Kinshasa) and a handful from Burundi and Rwanda. By the end of the 1990s, even after an influx of refugees and asylum seekers, there would be only fifteen thousand to twenty thousand Congolese and other Africans in Belgium (Martiniello and Kagné 1997).

A prospering Belgium began to recruit Moroccans and other North Africans in the 1960s. Conscious of the competition posed by its equally labor-hungry neighbors, the Ministry of Employment and Work went so far as to distribute a brochure in the Maghreb on "Living and Working in Belgium" (Attar 1994). Turkish immigration commenced a few years later, taking place in three stages: first into industrial Limburg Province and Charleroi, then into Luxembourg Province and Brabant Province (all in Wallonia) to work in the mines and in construction, and, finally, in the 1970s, into Liège and other big Walloon cities and Flanders for factory and low-level service-sector jobs. That historical experience made for a larger but more evenly distributed immigrant presence in Wallonia than Flanders (see table 5.1). Large-scale migration into Flanders was concentrated in major cities like Antwerp and Ghent. Brussels also had a long tradition of relatively high immigration, and the influx was very sizable after 1960. Those movements left more Turks in Flanders, more Moroccans in the Brussels region, and more Southern Europeans in Wallonia and Brussels (SERV 1998).

Belgian Policy Evolution

Belgium was a Johnny-come-lately *(nakomertje)* when it came to integration policy (Phalet and Kiekels 1998, 151). Until the late 1980s, national officials had rather limited objectives: controlling entry and settlement in the kingdom, regulating access to the labor market, and determining the conditions to be met for the acquisition of formal Belgian citizenship. In the immediate postwar period, the emphasis was on family migration, since Belgian authorities thought it would make for fewer problems of adaptation. At the same time, the welfare state took care to define immigrant workers as "foreign," so as to justify treating them differently than native-stock workers (Deslé 1996). Voluntary associations, both religious and secular, and trade unions came to immigrants' aid.

Belgium produced a pillarized welfare state. Highly complex, the social security and social assistance systems grew by accretion from the charitable actions of the Catholic Church, before being matched by Socialist and liberal networks. Policy implementation fell in large part to these vertically integrated organizations. Hence, trade unions administered unemployment benefits; mutual aid societies, the payment of sickness benefits. Public sector subsidies and private initiatives operated side by side in a number of areas. Like their Dutch counterparts, the pillars became structurally essential components of the Belgian welfare state, major employers and bases of political mobilization, marked by organizational concentration, hierarchy, and differentiation.

When immigrants began to arrive, charities bore most of the responsibility for their integration, supported "here and there" by social service agencies (van Peer and Lammertyn 1990, 34). In practice, it was up to nonprofit gatekeepers, especially Catholic institutions like *Caritas,* to assist immigrant workers and their families in trying to adjust to life in Belgium. Trade unions played an equally critical integrating role. Decentralized organizations in Belgium, their outlooks differed. From 1946 the Catholic unions were active in recruiting and incorporating Southern Europeans as national groups. It took the deaths of 136 Italian workers in a 1956 mining disaster at Marcinelle in Wallonia—which led Italy to abrogate its bilateral labor agreement with Belgium—before the Socialist unions showed real awareness.[1] The Liberal unions were even slower and more subdued in taking up the cause. Variations in responsiveness notwithstanding, all trade unions professed solidarity with immigrant workers by the late 1970s, defining them as an integral component of the Belgian working class. These "victims of global capitalism, in need of help from Belgian workers," deserved equal social, economic, and political rights (Deslé 1997, 16).

In 1948 the Belgian state had set up the Tripartite Commission on the Foreign Work Force within the Ministry of Employment and Social Security. Comprised of governmental, trade union, and employer delegates, it mainly gave advice on the numbers to be admitted. Replacing it in 1965, the larger Consultative Council on Immigration was to "create conditions permitting the integration and assimilation of the families of migrant workers into the Belgian community" (Blaise and Martens 1992, 9). That body included representatives of several central ministries, regional economic councils, and provinces with numerous immigrant residents.[2] Provincial services with the same mission sprang up during this period in several Walloon cities, the first ones in Liège in 1964. They were soon joined by local-level consultative commissions across Wallonia and in the Brussels region. To coordinate their efforts, the Liaison Committee for Immigrant Worker Organizations brought together trade union representatives and immigrant workers' own "international brother" movements. Its reach extended into Flanders in the late 1960s, when that region began to welcome imported labor.

Noticeable from an early date, then, was the Belgian propensity to lay more stress on representation and less on social and political dialogue than their Dutch cousins. Belgian activists long dominated the field of immigrant integration. Until 1984, nonnationals were not allowed to form their own nonprofit associations or receive public subsidies unless three-fifths of their members and contributors were Belgian nationals. Government funding domesticated labor and other social movements. In the social work sphere the fight against structural problems took a back seat to help for individuals and groups to escape poverty and fit into mainstream society.

The financing for pensions, unemployment insurance, workers' compensation, family allocations, health insurance, and vacation benefits came from employer and employee contributions and general federal taxation. When economic crisis hit in the mid-1970s, contributions and taxes were raised and benefits were cut for certain categories of workers. National and interprofessional negotiations between labor and employers began to break down, and decision-making by Brussels officials gradually occupied a more central position (SPF 2001). A guaranteed subsistence income was introduced, along with the right to public social assistance for those not able to participate in the labor market. As in the Netherlands, general taxation has covered the lion's share of charges for social assistance, which is administered at the local level. In each city a Public Center for Social Assistance processes applications and administers financial, in-kind, and counseling assistance, its work usually supplemented by local and provincial social service agencies. The centers can put beneficiaries to work in temporary positions in the public, nonprofit, or private spheres. While limitations on immigrants' access to benefits fell by the wayside over the years, the process was a lengthy one: the social welfare state that seems monolithic in the literature is actually a collection of many discrete policies. In principle, only Belgian nationals can take advantage of social assistance benefits. Several countries—including Turkey, Morocco, and Tunisia—signed bilateral agreements with Belgium and the European Community that secured equal treatment for their nationals.

Federalization

Like their German and Dutch neighbors, Belgium halted new immigration in 1974 and vowed to integrate its resident immigrant population. In 1981 the Moureaux Law finally established an administrative framework for immigrants and outlawed incitement to racial discrimination. Thereafter, Belgian policy went through a schizophrenic phase. Naturalization procedures for the second and third immigrant generations loosened up a bit, and programs to ameliorate language instruction and other educational opportunities for immigrants came into force (Leman 1991). Ironically, so-called dispersal policies made their appearance during the same period. The Gol Act of 1983 authorized restrictions (by royal decree) against the settlement of non-European immigrants in certain towns and districts. The government later extended this permission to 1995 for certain *communes* in Brussels. Spatial concentration, it was believed, led to marginalization and hostile reactions from native residents (see KCMB 1993).

The split Belgian personality manifested itself institutionally, linguistically, and regionally as well. A response to the economic and social upheaval of the period, federalization was in full swing by the late 1970s and deepened in the 1980s. Admissions and asylum policies, citizenship law, voting rights, and most social welfare policies remained under *federal* purview. Responsibility for "orientation" policy and employment issues became a charge of the *regions* (Wallonia and Flanders). At Flemish insistence, the social security system began to be regionalized as well. Education was the joint duty of the municipalities, the provinces, the central state, and the private (in effect, Catholic) school network. Having gained cultural autonomy in 1971, the *linguistic communities* (French, Dutch, and German speaking) took charge of educational curricula, day-to-day management, and financing, as well as cultural affairs in general. They soon subsidized local centers to upgrade the reception and inclusion of immigrants (Dutch) and institutions to assist in their assimilation (French). In the absence of clear-cut national policies, cities like Ghent and Liège took the initiative and became known for their proactive stance. Municipalities gained access to specially earmarked, supplemental funds to support their own initiatives.

The strengthening of "centrifugal forces" in the Belgian state fostered the "differentiated political construction of ethnic categories of immigrant origin in Wallonia and Flanders" (Martiniello 1995, 132), for each held a particular conception of the nation, with its own implications for immigrant integration and ethnic identities. In its own way, Belgian decision making was as pragmatic as that in the Netherlands. Nonetheless, because it was imperative to balance linguistic and regional cleavages in Belgium, new policy arrangements tended to be added on top of existing ones. The result was a baroque institutional and administrative system whose multiplicity of layers and actors made it challenging to create a coherent, overarching policy vision.[3]

Wallonia and the French Community

Walloon politics borrowed heavily from the French model of citizenship and national identity. In France, multiculturalism met resistance in the name of the republican model of individual assimilation. Historically, a type of Walloon ethnic nationalism existed alongside the French-style republican one.

But the political dominance of the notion of the nation-state inhibited discussion of such matters and helped "to impose a local version of assimilationism within the framework of a general strategy" to deal with hard economic times. The conception of a Walloon "community of destiny," a nation à la française, was a political construction that took on even more significance when the Walloon region was created during a period of economic decline (Martiniello 1995, 138–39).

In fact, that strategy went back much further. Flemings who arrived during the early days of Wallonia's industrialization had either returned home or melted in without a trace. Many politicians of Flemish descent were leaders in the modern Walloon socialist movement, and the Socialist Party (Parti Socialiste—PS) held onto its supremacy in the region. That history of assimilation, combined with the pervasiveness of Socialist rhetoric, explained the long neglect of the cultural and ethnic dimensions of immigration in postwar Wallonia. Academic and political discourse centered on social and economic issues; targeted policies for "ethnic minorities" were taboo. Walloon and French Community policymakers took immigrants into consideration as resident foreign members of the working class, destined for absorption. The Dutch notion of nonindigenous ethnic communities—*allochtonen*—was an alien one.

Indirect structural integration policies predominated. Initiatives that affected immigrants were embedded in broader social policies designed to eliminate inequities in employment, housing, health care, and marginalization in general. As early as 1976, the French Community had a budget for projects in the immigrant "milieu," even though no specific legislation was forthcoming. Engaging in emblematic wordplay, the Francophone head of the region of Brussels-Capital argued that multiculturalism was passive, with groups living in their own corners of a city without talking to one another. "Interculturalism," on the contrary, was an active, integrative, mutually enriching process that aimed for the "insertion" of immigrant-origin residents (Picque 1992, 127).

Encouragement of private ownership and maintenance of a very limited social rental sector marked national Belgian housing policies more than in Germany and the Netherlands. Subsidized mortgages and interest rates, grants, cheap land, and tax cuts were used to stimulate the construction and ownership of private, single-family dwellings. Although important aspects relating to taxation and private rental regulation stayed under federal supervision, housing fell under the authority of the regions, which handled social housing (including assistance and subsidies). Local governments bore responsibility for housing quality; local housing corporations, for the management of social housing. Wallonia mimicked the French model, focusing on schemes to assist the homeless and renters in substandard units. French-style Priority Intervention Zones (Zones d'Intervention Prioritaire—ZIP) became the centerpiece of urban and housing policy. Territorially defined, these zones were intended to fight disadvantage and not to steer energies toward any particular groups. Walloon housing policy was characterized by public interventions at all levels of government, which hardly favored coherence. In another echo of French developments, several Walloon cities sprouted large housing projects on their suburban fringes (Francq 1992).

The story was similarly Gallic in the area of education policy. In the French Community education officials laid the emphasis on three major points: intercultural exchanges, French language instruction, and attention to "hinge" moments in schooling (the transitions between levels). In contrast to Flanders, teachers from the immigrant populations (and not from the foreign consulates) brought their homeland languages and cultures into the Belgian curriculum and served as the bridge between them and Belgian pupils. These instructors spearheaded moves to expand offerings in the immigrants' mother tongues—such as Italian, Arabic, and Turkish—and to have them fill foreign-language requirements. French-style Priority Action Zones (Zones d'Action Prioritaire—ZAP), which included educational and vocational work, were introduced in the latter half of the 1980s. As in France, budgetary problems limited their reach, but the ZAP's territorial base typified the French Community's inclinations.

In the French Community no separate pass-or-fail figures were compiled for Belgian and nonnational pupils—a revealing indicator in and of itself. Taken as a whole, the French-language system had a high rate of students who repeated a year of school and fell behind according to other measures. Beyond the typically French disdain for ethnic-based social categories, the more even distribution of immigrants in Wallonia than in Flanders also contributed to the lower level of concern over their children's presence in the classroom. At the same time, it became undeniable that nonnationals were overrepresented in vocational education and underrepresented at the higher levels of general education. In 1985–1986, almost two-thirds of Belgians attended regular secondary schools, compared to just under half of nonnationals. As for special education, over a quarter of students enrolled in such programs at the secondary level were foreign nationals (Leman 1991, 144). The accent in the French Community was on better coordination of existing general youth-oriented policies across departments and layers of government and across the public and private sectors. Realization dawned only slowly that the fight against marginalization could not proceed without taking into consideration the specific cultural problems of the immigrant-origin populations.

Subsidies were given to immigrant associations in Wallonia, but they were weighted differently than in the Netherlands or Flanders. Most funding went not to ethnic associations but to Belgian-led groups that worked to build solidarity at the neighborhood level and reduce social marginalization (KCMB

1991). Consulates dominated the associational activity of newer groups like Moroccans and Turks. Continuing to reflect older patterns, Spanish and Italian organizations maintained their connections with Belgian and homeland Catholic and labor movements. Although institutional channeling nurtured homeland orientation longer in Belgium, the organizational panoply resembled that found in France. Officials preferred to see immigrants as representatives from other countries (Vandenbrande 1995).

That viewpoint helped to explain the emergence of advisory bodies for immigrants in Wallonia. They married the Belgian desire to identify immigrant representatives with their "international" status. The country's first consultative communal council for immigrants *(conseil communal consultatif des immigrés)* formed in Liège Province in 1968. Forerunners of Germany's foreigners' councils, they seated delegates elected by nonnationals along national lines. The experiment spread rapidly, and thirty-five councils were set up by 1976. They requested improved public services in neighborhoods with a high concentration of immigrant-origin residents and organized social and cultural activities (vacation camps, foreign-language libraries, and so on) (Blaise 1994).

A royal decree in 1979 created the Consultative Council for Immigrants in the French Community (Conseil Consultatif des Immigrés auprès de la Communauté Française—CCICF), which was up and running by 1981. It included representatives of the trade unions, employers organizations, provinces, the French Community, and the regions of Wallonia and Brussels-Capital. It suffered from an absence of sustained contact with public authorities and insufficient institutional and logistical infrastructure. In 1987, the CCICF became the Consultative Council for Populations of Foreign Origin (Conseil Consultatif pour les Populations d'Origine Ètrangère—CCPOE) and added delegates from associations representing Walloon municipalities and immigrants themselves. The new council announced that it was embarking on a search for a coordinated strategy to integrate young immigrants, embedded in general policies fighting social marginalization. Regional branches popped up in the provinces of Liège, Namur, Hainaut, and Brussels-Capital to ensure that they fit local realities. The Walloon region's battle against socioeconomic disadvantage grouped policies together into cohesive social plans, which were supposed to permit enriching interchanges, limit sterile competition between agencies, and, ultimately, oversee the harmonious cohabitation of all local communities. Financial support flowed through regional foundations, their names an indication of the perceived imperative to facilitate the integration of the immigrant-origin population without openly acknowledging any ethnic-based particularities of its component groups: the Stimulation Fund for Immigrant Policy and the Fund to Lead Specific Local Actions to Fight against Social Exclusion and for Security (see Leclercq 1998). The CCPOE was still condemning federal and Flemish use of the term "ethnic minorities" in 1991, as it did not "capture the reality of the immigrants' experience and situation" (Blaise and Martens 1992, 60).

Flanders and the Dutch Community

Despite living in what was the more economically dynamic and politically powerful region of Belgium by the 1980s, Flemings had traditionally seen themselves as an oppressed minority culture within the country, which made them sympathetic to ethnic-based policies. Moreover, in heavily Catholic Flanders, notions of charity and subsidiarity combined with the influence of the Dutch to the north to produce acceptance of a pluralistic model in which cultural—in the form of ethnic—identities were deemed worthy of public patronage. Political-cultural integration policies were important in their own right and were considered a boon to incorporation into the labor market.

The Dutch Community organized the Flemish Oversight Committee for Migration Development in 1977 to coordinate activities. It eventually espoused a targeted, multicultural model reminiscent of the one being tried out in the Netherlands. That lesson-drawing would become codified when the Flemish Center for the Integration of Migrants replaced the committee in 1990. In addition to a policy coordination and logistical support role, its ambitious mission included the formation of immigrant-origin leadership, and immigrant representatives qua ethnic associational leaders constituted one-third of its general assembly and administrative council. In the Netherlands there was a Surinamese, Antillean, and Moluccan elite with some familiarity with the system; in Belgium, as in Germany, such people had to be recruited and trained. Funding came from the official Flemish Fund for the Integration of the Disadvantaged, with 60 percent of the money funneled to the largest cities (Blaise and Martens 1992).

In 1982 the executive body for the region of Flanders established the Flemish High Council for Migrants.[4] With one-third of its members of foreign origin, it made a host of policy suggestions, few of them heeded. Even so, earlier than in French-speaking Belgium, the council inspired the establishment of regional and local integration centers. That initiative could entail either adding services within the public administration or setting up a subsidized nonprofit association. The centers, overseen by a body in Brussels, carried out a whole range of activities, from information sessions, sensitivity programs, and cultural exchanges to counseling, cultural events, and language courses in Dutch, Arabic, and Turkish. The regional centers coordinated and assessed the more concrete local-level efforts, which included shoring up immigrants' self-help movements and raising public awareness of "Flanders' multicultural society" (Hermans 1994). Cultural pluralism and local initiative were part of the landscape in a way that was unheard of in Wallonia but endemic in the Netherlands.

Such variety was in keeping with an official "deconcentration" strategy in education, celebrating local autonomy, teaching about Dutch-Belgian and immigrant cultures, and trying to keep the percentage of immigrant-origin pupils at a "manageable" level in every school. There was an official consensus in the Dutch Community that once a certain threshold was reached—usually assumed to be between 20 and 25 percent—"white" parents would pull their students from schools. A segregated school landscape would be the result. In 1986–1987, just under 10 percent of Belgian pupils in Flemish primary education had to repeat a year of school; just under a third of their nonnational peers did—and 6.5 percent of them, twice. Only half of immigrant-origin students moved on to secondary education. The primary objective of the Dutch Community's educational policy became to apply a strategy of spreading out immigrant-origin students, teaching the Dutch language, and allowing for instruction in the mother tongue and culture. The overall attitude was encapsulated in an illuminating label: "Mutual Encounter Education." Officials did not shy away from designating ethnic-based target groups (Leman 1991, 141–50).

In other policy sectors, too, the Dutch Community and Flanders were toeing the line followed in the Netherlands. In housing, for example, there was a powerful role for nonprofit housing corporations, and growing reliance on the private sector led to more residential concentration over the years. Flemish regional authorities pushed for policies intended for those at risk in the labor market—namely, women, people with disabilities, and those of immigrant origin. Flemish officials made some cautious moves toward affirmative action, still anathema in Wallonia.

Integration centers in the Dutch Community awarded subsidies to sociocultural centers for immigrant integration, something that the French Community was just beginning to contemplate. Likewise, Flanders instituted ethnic sensitivity training programs for civil servants, the police and gendarmes, antiterrorist brigades, educators, and job trainers at all levels well before Wallonia. Social service agencies worked with immigrants directly, not by means of immigrant associations, which were weak, unrepresentative, and too laden with political and religious connections to the homelands. Strengthening such groups became an explicit goal in Flanders. Before long, a full-fledged, regionwide cultural policy was extending financial assistance to autonomous, "democratic," ethnic-based immigrant associations. Local integration centers had already been doing so for years. Ethnic-based immigrant associations, some geared toward Belgium and others toward the homelands, came under pressure to adapt to the "Flemish model" of interest-group organization (Vandenbrande 1995).

Policymakers did not deny that they were engaged in social engineering. There was a general understanding that the "immigration problem" could be boiled down to the consequences of the sudden confrontation between cultures. The average Fleming—the fabled "Jan with his cap"—could not come to grips with the phenomenon on his own (Deslé 1993, 65). The amazing array of "little policies" *(beleidjes)* was designed to help him deal with the social and political dimension of immigration. Habitually, they involved categorical measures directed toward immigrants as ethnic groups.

The Difficult 1990s

Over time, the seeming contradictions between ethnic-based and general policies in French and Dutch Belgium gave way to attempts to distill the positive aspects from both and to develop a more balanced policy mix. Walloon policymakers arrived at the conclusion that general policies to effect structural integration, abetted by work in the political-cultural realm that likewise downplayed ethnicity, had to be given more nuance. In Flanders, meanwhile, ethnic-based approaches to political-cultural integration were not leading to structural congruence. Proximity rendered it easier to draw mutual lessons. But the added regional and cultural dimensions also made the process more complicated and, with respect to the institutional tinkering required, more costly.

Structural and political-cultural disconnection characterized both parts of the country as the 1990s commenced. Unemployment, inadequate housing, and educational deficiencies continued to plague immigrant-origin populations. With its largely blood-based nationality law and refusal to grant immigrants voting rights, Belgium resembled Germany in its failure to address adequately that dimension of integration, notwithstanding its earlier and more extensive institution of consultative municipal councils. Spatial concentration was again an intermediary, double-edged factor, feeding Belgian policymakers' fears and contributing to the construction of ethnic communities. It proceeded inexorably in the country's large urban centers, where more than half of those of immigrant origin resided. In several cities a relatively high number of unoccupied units owned by speculators compelled local officials to introduce new taxes, which only aggravated the forces that were closing immigrant and other disadvantaged families out of the local market. No true ghettoes formed. Segregation stuck at levels comparable to or slightly higher than those in the Netherlands (Bougarel 1992).

In Flanders, as in the Netherlands in general and in Rotterdam in particular, celebration of ethnic identities and cultures had drawn attention to them and battle lines around them. The extreme-nationalist Flemish Bloc (Vlaams Blok—VB) made political hay out of ethnic tensions. Its breakthrough in local elections in 1988 owed much to its strategy of playing on fears of Arabs and Muslim immigrants. In Wallonia and Brussels, several small and fragmented fellow travelers of the VB appeared. But there, urban violence gave the real wake-up call. Gallic policies that had concentrated on general labor market, housing, and education policies had yielded a Gallic (sub)urban crisis. Unemployment had risen among immigrant-origin youths and was affecting almost half of Moroccan and Turkish boys and even more girls (Leman 1994, 72). Nor was there significant compensation for structural disadvantage in cultural and political policies. After years of tension, several Brussels neighborhoods erupted into riots pitting police against non-European youths in 1991. Again as in France, Islamic references were prominent in the reproaches they leveled at Belgian society. The unrest spread to Walloon cities. It was not explicitly ethnic, even though it involved young people of Moroccan origin far more than their Southern European or Turkish cohorts (Rea 1996).

There were signs that a counterculture was emerging. It manifested itself in an unstructured, anarchic fashion, as in the "hip hop" movement that permitted immigrant-origin youths to express their malaise and bitterness and to find their niche (Lapiower 1997). Others turned to *raï,* with its closer links to the dialects and concerns of the Maghreb. There were instances where the assertion of identity took on a more structured form, where it "more or less followed the broad lines laid down by the integration model put forward by official Belgian policy." There were also youth associations that rejected that "paternalistic" model, which they accused of requiring radical assimilation (Hermans 1995, 12). Second-generation organizations were not numerous, as most of their constituency refused the "young immigrants" label and opted to work within Belgian youth movements, if at all. Good-natured French social movements like SOS-Racisme produced but a fainter echo in Wallonia and Brussels. Preoccupied with homeland culture, first-generation associations had only a weak hold on immigrant-origin youths (see Deschamps and Pauwels 1992).

Premier Wilfried Martens, heading up his eighth government in the late 1980s, created a national advisory institution, the Royal Commission for Immigrant Policy, to assist the government in formulating coherent policies. It published a series of three reports and a number of briefer ones in which it denounced the government's "inertia" and called for "reciprocal acceptance" on the part of Belgians and the immigrant-origin population. Globally, it found, immigration was not overwhelming the country. Integration indicators contradicted themselves. For example, studies of Turkish-origin youths in Wallonia suggested that the younger age cohorts (under twenty-six years old) were fitting into the host society and naturalizing at higher rates, but their older siblings were retreating into their own ethnic-specific groupings. Muslim religious practice was becoming generalized among young people and, as it happened, coincided with improvements in French language proficiency. More young Turks were earning their secondary-school diploma. Only a minority attended school beyond the compulsory grades, however, and certification levels had actually fallen. While immigrants' housing had generally improved, it was well behind native-stock Belgians' in size, comfort, and conveniences. Concentration trends were visible at the local level, even if one could not speak of true residential segregation (KCMB 1989, 1990).

In its first major report in 1989, the Royal Commission provided its definition of integration: assimilation where "public order" demanded it (that is, conformity with the penal and civil codes), the promotion of "social insertion," and respect in other areas for cultural diversity as a mutually enriching exchange. In tandem with that political-cultural agenda was the structural betterment of immigrant minorities in the labor and housing markets and in the educational and job training systems. In this grab bag of policy aims were elements of both the French republican and class-based socialist interpretations of integration typical of Wallonia and the more ethnic-based ones found in Dutch-speaking Flanders. Later, the Royal Commission would add that there were "some fundamental principles" that existed in other societies but could not fit into Belgian society: it judged female circumcision, marital repudiation, and truancy as unacceptable (KCMB 1993).

In line with the Royal Commission's advice, the federal legislature moved to promote the requisite reforms. Discussions opened over how to standardize the system of subsidies to autonomous immigrant associations and how to encourage the development of typically Belgian national or regional federations. Immigrant associations had to become a useful "discussion partner" for authorities (KCMB 1990, 28). A pitched national debate opened over whether Belgium should follow the Netherlands and grant local-level suffrage to resident nonnationals.

In the early 1990s, the country grew more inclusive. Unemployed immigrants who refused to participate in French or Dutch language courses were penalized, but so were their Belgian opposite numbers who refused to enroll in professional training seminars. The counterpart to the heightened focus on learning French and Dutch was growing acceptance of Arabic or Turkish as a fourth language in Belgian schools, after the former two and English. The distinction between "great" and "ordinary" naturalization (the latter making a person eligible to vote but not to run for legislative office) disappeared, as did the legal import of being "Belgian by birth" (Ouali 1994). While reforms in citizenship law after 1984 preserved its general slant toward *jus sanguinis,* they made the process more consistent and transparent. Moreover, Belgium did not normally require immigrants to give up their prior nationality when acquiring formal Belgian citizenship (Es-Saida 1994).

The political integration of nonnationals was a lower priority, though. They did not receive local-level voting rights. The consultative communal councils atrophied. Apart from several token candidacies in the 1988 local elections and the 1991 parliamentary elections, naturalized Belgians of immigrant origin did not start to run for elected office in significant numbers until after the citizenship reforms of the early 1990s. In areas of immigrant residential concentration, such as the Saint-Josse district in Brussels, immigrant-origin voters were developing into a political force. Their candidates had some success in races for municipal councils in 1994, including candidates of Moroccan origin who ran in districts in Flanders with few of "their" compatriots. By contrast, it was in Wallonia, with its far smaller Turkish-origin population, that the first councilor from that national group won a seat that year. Most naturalized immigrant candidates ran on the lists of the PS, ecologists, the Stalinist Belgian Workers' Party, and, to a lesser extent, the Christian democratic parties.

In both Wallonia and Flanders, policymakers were well aware of the differences in the two regions' integration policies. The advantages and drawbacks of the "French" and "Dutch" models were the subject of spirited discussions. During the 1990s, there was a narrowing of the gap between the two Belgian nations' policies. Instructive in this regard was the case of Brussels, where French and Dutch speakers lived cheek by jowl and where there was thus of necessity a balance of sorts between policies once regional institutions came into being. Brussels also demonstrated, unfortunately, that in the Belgian context such reforms tended to yield institutional complexity, higher costs, and the risk of duplicating efforts (see Vandenbrande 1995).

The Flemish/Dutch executive and legislature both reacted positively to the recommendations of the Royal Commission. The Dutch Community was realizing, as was the Netherlands, that group-specific policies could fuel tendencies toward social balkanization and ethnic conflict. What would later strike some observers as Flanders' "halfhearted acceptance of categorical integration policy" (Phalet and Kiekels 1998, 160), was in fact an outcome of the conscious broadening of its tack beyond ethnic-based policies in the political-cultural realm. Slowly, general policies, more of them striving for structural congruence than before, took shape. Flemish policymakers declared their advocacy of policies *à la wallonne* that fought social injustice and exclusion and guaranteed equal opportunity more generally. Marginalization was seen as a process that affected individuals who belonged to a number of different groups (HRV 1992).

The old policies were not abandoned as much as they were added to, in classic Belgian fashion. In 1998 the Flemish parliament accepted a decree-law on ethnic minorities that aimed at the stimulation of resident immigrants' and refugees' emancipation and participation, the admission and reception of newcomers, the humane treatment of the undocumented, and the strengthening of the social and administrative preconditions for successful structural and political-cultural integration policies. In every area they were to be inclusive of all city residents, formulated with their input, and clearly explained to the populace. Flanking measures would promote peaceful social relations and, where necessary, services for specific target groups, including ethnic-based offerings. With the latter destined to be reduced to an absolute minimum, general policies had to do a better job of reaching ethnic minorities. They would thereby gain a multicultural character (SID 2001).

The French Community and Wallonia, in the interim, had been discovering that general policies against structural disconnection might not be enough by themselves. By the early 1990s, the Walloons were learning that immigrant origin and ethnicity acted as markers of social marginalization that did not fade when global policies were put in place to fight poverty and exclusion. France was learning the same lessons. There, policy was still laying the stress on equality but had begun to embody "justified discrimination," even if rooting it in a specific physical context. The "ethnic management" of social housing was an open secret (De Rudder and Poiret 1999).

After the 1991 elections, policies changed in French Belgium, too. Lingering references to the immigrants' specific needs had fallen by the wayside in favor of the fight against "social exclusion," a semantic change intended to take away any impression that they were receiving special treatment or favors. Poverty was an individual problem to be fought with actions that opened up opportunities for each person to participate equally in all aspects of Belgian society. On the ground, however, policies grew much more sensitive to ethnic differences and to the cultural dimensions of immigrant integration. A series of projects showcased collaboration among immigrant parents of various ethnic backgrounds, schools, and French Community education officials, for example, and courses in Moroccan, Turkish, and Portuguese cultures were fitted into the regular curriculum (KCMB 1993).

As for politics, the ruling Socialist Party persisted in its view that it and the Belgian labor movement were the proper vector for immigrants' participation. In 1994, responsibility for immigrant integration policies was transferred from the French Community to the Walloon region. Trade unions joined with employers' organizations to create a new commission that brought together the social partners, voluntary associations, and the integration centers. Its twenty-four voting members included several appointed representatives of the immigrant population (Thyré 1998).

The Walloon government issued a decree in 1996 in which it explicitly distanced itself from the French integration model and defended a liberal multicultural vision that endorsed the temporary, instrumental use of ethnic-based policies. In the new Regional Integration Centers that took shape in Charleroi, La Louvière, Liège, Mons, Namur, and Verviers, the concept of affirmative action, previously far more pronounced in Flanders, began to appear in official reports. Its justification was the weakening of traditional integration machines like the schools and the trade unions, along with the perceived benefits of adding a "differentialist" element into what had been purely "universal" measures. The change was evident two years later in a French Community council decree in 1998 that aimed at assuring all students an equal opportunity for "social emancipation" by means of "positive discrimination" (Bortolini 1999, 47–48). To ensure good working relations with local associations, immigrant and otherwise, the integration centers each set up a Council of Participation. The centers formed a federation to champion "transversal and concerted action" against social exclusion (CEOOR 2002, 10).

While Flanders had implemented affirmative action programs years before Wallonia began to consider them seriously, the electoral advances registered by the far right had since caused Flemish officials to tread very carefully around such concepts. In both regions the goal was not only to forbid intentional discrimination but also to promote and encourage initiatives aimed at halting the reproduction of social discrimination. All the same, affirmative action was not understood as preferential treatment that would change norms or supplant a commitment to guaranteeing equal access to all aspects of social and economic life for those of immigrant origin. The Walloons in particular distanced themselves from what they considered an Anglo-Saxon vision of the concept (Liebermann 1996).

Islam and Insecurity

In Belgium, Islam was a bigger issue than in Germany and the Netherlands at the national level. Except for a couple thousand North African miners who spilled over the French border into Wallonia in the 1920s and were largely ignored, Belgium had not had the Netherlands' historical experience with Islam. Aping the Dutch, the Belgians talked about setting up a Muslim pillar along the lines of the Catholic/Flemish and Social Democratic/Walloon institutional networks of associations and services. Like other immigrant groups, Islam did not have strong organizations in Belgium, however, nor had a common faith superseded national and ethnic differences. The regionalized settlement patterns of Turks and Moroccans had aggravated them, as had direct integration policies, particularly in Flanders.

Belgium guaranteed freedom of religion and the separation of church and state. Still, in the belief that religions served social and moral purposes and promoted general well-being, it also had a system of formal recognition of faiths that opened the door to many financial advantages: the payment of religious officials' salaries and pensions; grants for the purchase and upkeep of religious venues, including utilities and supplies; tax concessions; and exemption from postal charges. Religious education in public schools received full state funding, and such instruction had to be organized if any parent so requested. Once the state "recognized" a religion, a commission (instituted by law or royal decree) managed its material resources and served as a liaison body with the authorities. Six faiths won official recognition: Catholicism, Protestantism, Anglicanism, Judaism, Orthodoxy, and, in 1974, Islam.

The problem was that for a religion to activate its status and access the attendant benefits, it was required to set up a representative executive body. Several attempts by various groups and Belgian governments to comply failed miserably. In December 1998, elections were finally held to a fifty-one-member assembly, with seats allotted to "national colleges" of Turks, Moroccans, and converts—heedless of the diversity of Muslims in terms generation, gender, and ideology.[5] That body, in turn, selected eleven representatives to sit on the Chief Body of the Faith. In 1999 it received a budget of five million Belgian francs to perform its narrowly defined duties in the areas of religious education, counseling in prisons, and advising on issues affecting the Muslim population (Panafit 2000). While official recognition of Islam came about at the federal level, unlike other faiths it was to be organized at the provincial and local levels.

While institutional gridlock ruled at the top, local authorities had been free to determine the location of mosques by means of building permits and safety regulations. Belgium permitted private schools, and they were eligible for state funding if they met certain basic criteria. The big stumbling block for Muslims was that organizers themselves were responsible for finding a suitable building. The country's only school based on Islamic principles opened in 1989, the al-Ghazali school, founded in Brussels with help from a Saudi Arabian religious movement (Renaerts 1997). The country contained almost four hundred mosques by the late 1990s, two-thirds of them run by Moroccans. The Ankara government's religious office, the Diyanet, oversaw two-thirds of the Turkish mosques; the Islamist Milli Görüs movement oversaw most of the remaining third. Mosques proliferated in Belgian urban centers, precisely where secularization was reducing the number of practicing Catholics. Surveys of Turks and Moroccans indicated that a majority were loyal to "mainstream Islam," with smaller, equally sized groups adhering to "secular" and "fundamental" forms. Secularism had spread to a larger degree among Moroccans than Turks (Lesthaeghe 2000).

Local issues were becoming more salient in Belgium, part of a general trend toward decentralization. There was a shifting of responsibilities onto the municipalities, who were free to add to policies flowing down from other levels. Municipal governments were cast as the intermediaries in a national dialogue about education and youth social work. Nor was Belgium's system of social security assistance to asylum seekers and refugees centralized. Each municipality's Public Center for Social Assistance was responsible for providing welfare services to the destitute and to asylum seekers whose applications had been declared admissible. In principle, the federal government reimbursed funds spent on asylum seekers, but larger cities that sheltered larger contingents of those populations were frequently shortchanged.

Debates over undocumented immigrants and refugees, Islamic education and mosques, and Muslim youths drew the spotlight to the myriad social problems that plagued Belgium's large cities: criminality, poverty, crime, poor public services, urban decay, the accumulation of ills in certain neighborhoods, and the widening gulf between rich and poor. The Royal Commission worked closely with the charitable King Baudouin Foundation and the federal Incentive Fund, which had been created from national lottery funds in 1991 to support immigrant integration projects. Three-quarters of allocated grants wound up going to the five largest Belgian cities—Brussels, Antwerp, Ghent, Liège, and Charleroi—for well-defined projects and for limited periods of time (KCMB 1993).

Following a parallel line of reasoning was the Royal Commission's successor, the Center for Equal Opportunity and the Fight against Racism. The center strove to inject promising elements of the policy mix in the Netherlands and France into Belgium in order to reduce the risks of conflict posed by structural and political-cultural disconnection. Established by law in 1993, the center was under the prime minister's aegis but autonomous. It administered the Incentive Fund and focused on the prevention of delinquency and social marginalization among youths, the encouragement of intercultural activities, support for educational projects, and actions to enhance youth employment and popular understanding of Islam.

The center acted as a lobbying and public relations unit for the immigrant-origin communities. It was par for the course in Belgium, where each group had its champion to argue its cause, before a compromise coalesced that was more or less acceptable to all and more or less reflected the strengths of the stakeholders. The center's director, Johan Leman, complained that the same federal government that spent three hundred million Belgian francs to spur integration spent more than three billion on security and repression programs (Bortolini 1996). Those were the primary charges of the federal Foreigners Office, whose autonomy he likewise criticized. From 1992, the minister of the interior entered into formal agreements with local authorities and awarded grants to support crime-fighting programs. These security contracts were all customized; the one constant seemed to be the increase in the number of enforcement personnel and social workers that they ensured (Blaise 1995).

Whereas first-generation immigrant workers, particularly Southern Europeans, had settled into Belgian society in a relatively quiet, if segregated manner, the children of non-European immigrants were at the intersection of deep worries about crime and Islam. Flanders' economic strength was attracting more immigrants, above all Moroccans and Turks, and Brussels remained a prime destination as well. The growth of the far right marked the political landscape there. In stagnating Wallonia, by contrast, extremists were weak, but it faced sporadic urban unrest. In fact, both regions were becoming familiar with that dysfunctional form of immigrant participation. There was a fresh outbreak of riots in Molenbeek in the Brussels metropolitan area in April 1995 and again in a number of neighborhoods in Brussels, Liège, and outside Antwerp in November 1997. Although Belgium had no real youth gangs, less organized crime "webs" were active in many cities and involved young people of North African and, increasingly, Turkish origin.

Belgium's policymakers did not stop responding gamely to such challenges. Federal officials inched toward allowing third-country nationals into civil service employment, as the Flemish government had already done. For non-European Union immigrants the work permit system was being softened and simplified. Nationality law moved closer to *jus soli* through modifications after the mid-1990s. A change in 2000 made it easier for immigrants to acquire formal citizenship by a simple declaration after five years with an unrestricted permit (obtainable after five years continuous residency) and through the regular naturalization process after three years of living in the country (two years for refugees). Naturalization remained free of charge, and an expressed willingness to integrate was dropped as a prerequisite. The country had thus developed some of the most liberal legislation in Europe, even though restrictive interpretations on the part of federal administrators occasionally blocked their implementation. The issue of voting rights for non-EU citizens resurfaced periodically in Belgium, partly owing to the delay in granting voting rights to EU citizens caused by Flemish fears that they would tip the balance toward French-speaking forces (Bortolini 1997; "Belgium" 2002).

Exactly such stalemates were becoming the norm. As the institutional complexity of the country hamstrung officials, political clans were free to step into the breach and assure a share of the spoils for their clients. In the niches of this patron-client system, criminals found themselves relatively free to operate (Lesage 1998). Even in such areas as land use regulations and zoning laws, clientelism, nepotism, and a considerable amount of outright corruption had been a factor in weakening moves to prevent or at least slow spatial segregation. It was a pedophilia scandal that brutally awakened Belgians to what had happened to their political system. Early in 1997, the discovery of the sexually molested corpse of a nine-year-old Moroccan girl, Loubna Ben Aïssa, reminded them of the immigrant communities suffering from its pathologies as well. Prime Minister Jean-Luc Dehaene gave a speech after her funeral that triggered renewed debate over immigration, Islam, and the political rights of immigrants.

Whether the policymaking apparatus was up to the task of implementing any decisions was an open question. Evidence was accumulating that revamped policies in Flanders and Wallonia had been having positive effects on immigrants' structural and political-cultural integration. Yet Islamic practices, chiefly the practice of repudiation of wives, grew into major bones of contention. In the Brussels commune of Schaerbeek, three nights of violence erupted in May 2002 after the killing of a Moroccan couple by their Belgian neighbor. Upset at police handling of the matter, both before and after the shooting, Moroccan-origin youths from across the region took to the streets. More riots broke out in Antwerp that November and December, after a Moroccan Islamic teacher was murdered by a neighbor. In that city the Lebanese-Belgian founder of the Arab European League, Abou Jahjah, won a following among immigrant-origin youths after authorities prevented his association from carrying out street patrols to monitor police behavior. Jahjah, dubbed the Arab Malcolm X by the Belgian press, rejected the notion of integration and vowed to expand his radical civil rights group into the Netherlands ("Authorities' Mishandling" 2003).

The already shaky six-party governing "rainbow coalition" of Flemish and Walloon Liberals, Socialists, and ecologists threatened to fall several times when disputes flared over immigrant integration policies. Nevertheless, the Belgian legislative elections of May 2003 strengthened the Liberals and Social-ists in both regions. Together, they won almost two-thirds of the 150 seats in the Belgian federal parliament. While the Greens suffered major losses, the Flemish Bloc gained three seats (to eighteen) with its 18 percent of the vote. In the Walloon city of Charleroi, the anti-immigrant National Front registered an unheard-of 12 percent. On the other hand, seven candidates of immigrant origin were directly elected, up from only one in 1999. Most of the candidates (five) were from the electoral lists of the Flemish Socialists and their moder-ate Flemish regionalist allies in the new "Spirit" movement. An Islamic party, mainly comprised of naturalized Belgians, scored up to 2.5 percent in certain cantons in the Brussels region. Allied with the Communists, Abou Jahjah's Arab European League received only minimal backing. At the federal level, clearly, Belgian politics had lost few of its incongruities ("New Belgian Parlia-ment" 2003).

From the 1970s on, meanwhile, municipalities picked up weighty respon-sibilities for their immigrant-origin populations. In trying to bring about their integration, the major players were the linguistic communities and, later, the regions. It took a while before local officials were fully implicated in the definition and resolution of social problems, and their role was enfeebled by the slow emergence of coordinating policies at higher levels of governance. As municipalities mobilized to execute their mandates, they applied for funding from regional, community, and federal governments, as well as from the EU and the various Belgian foundations. A range of nonprofit, public, and pri-vate-sector institutions were engaged in the country's cities. In the resulting whirl, it was not always possible to determine how many resources local officials were expending in their work to integrate their immigrant-origin populations.

Elections to municipal councils occur every six years in the country's 589 localities, with the number of councilors varying with the size of the popula-tion. Presiding over the councils is the mayor, appointed by the monarch on the recommendation of the federal interior ministry. The council selects the heads of the various departments that complete the executive. The social assistance system is comparable in its workings to the German one, in that local-level authorities are required to organize and implement it. As noted, though, the federal government covers most costs of the program, as in the

Netherlands.[6] Local governments have permission to act in the interest of their residents. They are under the jurisdiction of their region, however, and enmeshed in an intricate web of federal, regional, community, and provincial institutional linkages, not always leaving as much latitude as might exist on paper.

In the sections that follow, the policy trajectories in two key cities in French-speaking and Dutch-speaking Belgium—Liège in the Province of Liège and Ghent in the Province of East Flanders—show that variation was possible in the country but highly dependent on regional and community supervision and subventions. Liège cleaved to a liberal national vision that derived its potency from the Walloon blend of French-style republicanism, Belgian consensualism, and social democratic discomfort with ethnic identities. The city concerned itself far more with structural integration than political-cultural integration. Officials submerged measures dealing with both dimensions within general social policies for all residents that proved of limited efficacy. Ghent, in contrast, crept toward the Dutch-style Flemish ethnic minorities policy, focused on political-cultural integration. Belgium was stingier than the Netherlands in extending political rights and formal citizenship to nonnationals, however. The structuring of ethnic identities redounded to the detriment of immigrant-origin residents as they became associated with structural disconnections and exploited by the far right to make its most impressive advances among the eight case cities in this study. The limitations of the policies implemented in the 1970s and 1980s led officials in Liège and Ghent to borrow from each other's playbooks in the 1990s. In Liège neighborhood-based policies allowed for surreptitious consideration of ethnic specificities, while in Ghent the participatory aspects of political-cultural integration were highlighted in a strategy that aimed to mix it and structural integration more or less equally.

Liège: Trying to Ignore Ethnic Difference

Seat of a powerful bishopric in the Middle Ages, Liège became the hub of the coal mining and iron and steel industries during Wallonia's industrialization in the latter half of the nineteenth century. It fell on very hard times with the restructuring of those industries after the 1960s. By the 1990s, it was vaunting its return as a center of services, billing itself as Europe's third largest river port and the crossroads of its highway and high-speed rail systems.

On the surface, Liège looked like the archetype of urban Walloon politics: a citadel of the Socialist Party, run by a good-old-boys network of battle-scarred trade unionists set in the French assimilationist tradition in their attitudes toward immigrant workers. A large kernel of truth notwithstanding, Liège proved a much more complicated case. It mingled PS assimilationism with elements of the Belgian consensual model.

Postwar Immigration and Crisis

Not by chance had Liège become a partner city of Rotterdam's, for it was hard to think of cities in either country more closely associated with the mainstream political left. Essen, Germany, might have been an even better choice. Like the SPD there, the PS in Liège was an "old-style" social democratic party not taken to multicultural notions. It dominated postwar Liégeois politics, emerging every six years from municipal elections in a governing coalition: in 1971, as a junior partner with the Liberal Reformist Party (Parti Réformateur Libéral—PRL); in 1977, as the lead partner with the PRL; in 1982, with the ecologists (Écologistes Confédérés pour l'Organisation de Luttes Originales—Écolos); and in 1988, with the Christian Social Party (Parti Social Chrétien—PSC). Intraparty politics within the PS was often the most important game in town. Mirroring the clout of the PS and the PSC in the city was that of the socialist trade union and the progressive Christian Labor Movement (Mouvement Ouvrier Chrétien—MOC).

Like the other progressive case cities, Liège had a long immigration history. The first migrants to the city were farmers from the Ardennes, followed by Flemish and then eastern and southern European workers recruited to work in the mines and the metals industry. At the start of the twentieth century, the district of Liège counted around thirty thousand immigrants, predominantly Russians, Poles, and Italians (CEW 1960). After the Second World War, there was severe labor demand in the coal mines, which was aggravated by the wholesale refusal of Belgian workers to return to them. Belgium first requisitioned German prisoners of war, who were succeeded by Italians, Poles, and Hungarians. The number of immigrants in the district of Liège nearly doubled between 1947 and 1965. That year, the immigrant population represented 16.5 percent of the total population, compared to 11.2 percent in the province and 6.5 percent in Belgium as a whole. The migratory fluxes altered after 1965, with many Moroccans and Turks arriving, some of them from France and Germany and others from the Brussels-Capital region. In the wake of the new immigration stoppage of 1973–1974, family reunification, refugees, and students (many of them sub-Saharan Africans) accounted for much of the growth by the 1980s. Almost 20 percent of Liège's residents were immigrants then (Martiniello and Kagné 1997).

Liège was broken down into twenty-one "administrative entities," and immigrant concentrations varied significantly across them. The city was remarkable for the large share of its immigrant (nonnational) population who lived in social housing: almost 21 percent in Liège Province in 1970, placing it second after coal-mining Limburg Province and above the average for Wallonia (18.8 percent), not to mention Flanders (6.5 percent). Many of the social housing units in Liège were, as in France, in high-rise projects in peripheral

TABLE 5.2
Immigrants and Private Housing in Belgium, 1970 and 1981 (%)

	Belgian Share		Moroccan Share		Turkish Share	
	1970	1981	1970	1981	1970	1981
	57.2	63.0	2.5	11.3	2.2	15.2
Flanders		66.3		11.7		15.3
Wallonia		64.0		14.2		15.8
Brussels		31.0		8.0		10.3

Source: KCMB (1989,140–42).

districts like Droixhe (KCMB 1989). Over time, the thrust of Belgian policy was apparent in a marked increase in rates of private home ownership (see table 5.2).

In 1970 two-thirds of Liège's immigrants were blue-collar workers, and 3.7 percent were unemployed. The industries that had long employed most immigrant and native-stock workers underwent serious downsizing and shaking-up after the late 1960s. The unemployment rate among immigrants would rise to 20 percent by the early 1990s, and the portion of them who labored in factories and mines would fall by more than a third, to just over 40 percent (Martiniello and Kagné 1997, 11–12). Low-level service jobs, such as sanitary services, were employing more of them as time passed and manufacturing declined. Wallonia was the only region where the economic activity rate for immigrants ran higher than for Belgian nationals, but Liège also had among the highest shares of its inhabitants living on full income support (Manço 1998).

In 1988, the immigrant population of Liège was 43 percent Italian, 15 percent Moroccan, 11 percent Spanish, and 6 percent Turkish. The city was proving less and less attractive to EU immigrants and to Belgians. In October 1989, however, concern over asylum seekers compelled the municipal council to pass unanimously legislation that limited the influx of immigrants into Liège. The law, which sought permission from the federal government to follow a practice still authorized in parts of Brussels, made no distinctions between nationalities. The move jumpstarted the development of a broader integration policy (KCMB 1989, 83–87).

Integration Policy Responses

Until the 1990s, there was no explicit immigrant integration policy in the French Community, Liège included. Social welfare in the city was the bailiwick of Municipal Social Services, which operated along generalist lines. It worked with all residents, associations, and institutions on an individual, case-by-case basis, indifferent to nationality, age, gender, or the type of social problem from which clients were suffering. Part of the local administration, the agency collaborated with the local Public Center for Social Assistance (Centre Public d'Aide Sociale—CPAS). Legally autonomous, the CPAS implemented federal and state social policies for "problem" populations like immigrants under the guidance of the municipal council, whose majority and opposition members elected its fifteen board members. When the Walloon Ministry of Employment and Labor had supported the creation in Liège of a Provincial Immigration and Welcoming Services Center (Services Provinciaux d'Immigration et d'Accueil—SPIA) in the mid-1960s, its original aim had been to increase the number of immigrant workers and to assimilate them into local society. Eventually integrated into the provincial administration and outfitted with a more progressive mandate, the SPIA grouped together regional trade union federations, sports and cultural associations, and homeland organizations. In Wallonia the message was that residents of native and immigrant stock were "equal in their misfortune," subject to "social policy centering exclusively on exclusion and marginalization" (Modolo 1997).

Liège appeared to lend its indirect structural integration policies a political-cultural aspect with the Consultative Immigrant Council of Liège (Conseil Consultatif Communal des Immigrés de Liège—CCCIlg). After a 1964 recommendation from the Council of Europe in Strasbourg, such councils had sprouted up as vehicles for immigrant involvement in local decision making. In consensual Belgium it was always important to solicit the views of all concerned parties. As mentioned above, the first such councils appeared in the Province of Liège in the late 1960s. In the city of Liège, the SPIA, trade unions, and several municipal departments entered into discussions with eighty local immigrant associations. In 1973 voting was held by nationality to elect forty-one members to the CCCIlg, divvied up according to the size of each group in the local population. Italians traditionally predominated in Liège, and their associations long purported to speak for the entire immigrant-origin population. Their working-class and Catholic-worker leanings fit well with the outlook of the Socialists running city hall. Just the same, it was a lawyer of Congolese origin, long established in Liège, who presided over the body as its first president.

Liège depicted the CCCIlg as a representative body organized by country rather than ethnicity. Its actions suited a conception that was avowedly "intercultural"—not to be confused with multicultural in Liège. City officials always referred to "foreign persons" or "persons of foreign origin." That insistence on the alien aspect of immigrant-origin residents was in keeping with the traditional PS and trade union model of welcoming members of "brother" labor movements outside Belgium into their ranks with no ethnic-based intermediation. Immigrants represented either an integral part of the host society working class or a temporary international presence (see CEOOR 2002, 9). For its part, the CCCIlg defined itself as the "working joint" between the local administration, of which it was an emanation, and the local associational world. Criticisms that immigration organizations were not legitimate interlocutors, since their leaders were normally unelected, were dismissed. The CCCIlg was to intervene with authorities on behalf of immigrants—never immigrant communities—and reconcile the two sides. It was empowered to issue opinions and make recommendations.

The municipal council was nervous that, despite its best efforts, it might have inadvertently given a fillip to ethnic-based identity development by organizing the body along national lines. It changed the method of electing CCCIlg members in the mid-1980s to a more typically Walloon system that favored multiethnic, ideological lists. The 1984 elections produced a council with fifty-one members who belonged to five different political families. The ideological flavoring of its executive bureau reflected the changing partners of the PS in the city at large, notably in picking up members close to the Écolos. By the end of the 1980s, immigration had become a more contentious issue in Belgium. Fierce disputes over immigrant voting rights had seemingly sapped the consultative immigrant councils of much of their momentum and relevance across the country. Only five were functioning in the country, one of them the Liège council. Their usefulness was a topic of policy and academic deliberation (Groupe de Sociologie Wallonne 1994).

The Difficult 1990s

Liège did not experience unrest of the same scale as in the Brussels area, but the early 1990s brought evidence of both structural and political-cultural disconnection. Immigrants were clustered in several inner-city and suburban neighborhoods, where they seriously trailed native-stock Liégeois in the labor and housing markets and schools. Improvements on all fronts had been relatively modest. Statistics were harder to come by than elsewhere, as city, provincial, and regional officials usually declined to separate out and publicly enumerate immigrant-origin residents in their policies, plans, and assessments.

In a trickle, targeted policies for immigrants entered into the policy mix. The Royal Commission and the King Baudouin Foundation made the city a prime object of their medley of joint actions. In 1991 five social housing complexes belonging to a local housing authority were renovated, with the units then rented out to immigrant-origin families. Young immigrant apprentices completed a good share of the work. In the months that followed, strings of colored lights were distributed to residents for use during neighborhood festivals. The troubled neighborhood of Droixhe, meanwhile, acquired a cultural center run by local youths in collaboration with representatives of the city government. A seminar, "A Bridge to Professional Training," helped to prepare young people of immigrant (mainly Turkish) background for local training programs. At the initiative of the CCCIlg, a project came on line to familiarize young immigrants with computer technology. A campaign was mounted to raise consciousness about racist graffiti and its consequences (KCMB 1993).

The steady decentralization of responsibilities over the course of the 1980s had left regional integration services like the SPIA the fulcrum of activities for and by immigrants. It became the SIA in 1985, when the "Provincial" part of its name was dropped, even as it was absorbed into the provincial administration. When the immigrant workers' children experienced greater disconnection, new impetus was given to such work. The structural and political-cultural aspects of integration were seen as separate but related. "Social insertion" was the goal as far as the first was concerned, entailing a fight against discrimination and racism and programs to encourage French language mastery. The second aspect drew corollary initiatives that espoused intercultural education and cultural expression geared toward both the homelands and the immigrant condition in Liège.

The SIA would eventually take a back seat to Liège's quasi-public regional integration center, decreed by the Walloon legislature in 1996. At the close of 1997, after two years of acrimonious negotiations between local authorities and voluntary associations, the Regional Center for the Integration of Foreign or Foreign-Origin People in Liège (Centre Régional d'Intégration des Personnes Étrangères ou d'Origine Étrangère à Liège—CRIPEL) was founded. The last of the centers to be established, it won nonprofit status in June 1998. It maintained close relations with the provincial government, the city, and six other municipalities and public social service centers in the metropolitan area. The Walloon region provided a modest annual operating budget of 750,000 Belgian francs, and support was also forthcoming from the federal government and the European Social Fund (Parmentier 1999).

Earlier policies had received funding on a limited, annual, or even one-off basis, which had prevented the development of long-term projects and the diffusion of best practices. The CRIPEL was designed to concentrate precisely on those two challenges. Such regional centers rested on six-year, renewable contracts, and the local projects that they sustained could run initially for as long as three years. Their work was to complement European initiatives and embrace the richness of the homeland cultures, even while seeing to it that the fundamental rules and democratic principles on which Belgian society rested were followed and protected (Villan 1996).

The CRIPEL's founding and subsequent operation was made more difficult by the political cleavages rending local associational life. Italian control had declined along with its share of local residents. Its legendary fragmentation had been overcome to a degree by the Memoria Committee, which grouped the principal Italian associations in the city to organize cultural events and colloquia on the immigrant experience and immigrant integration. By the late 1990s, there were also hundreds of non-European associations engaged in all manner of activities. Turks and Moroccans (and other North Africans) founded a range of political, religious, ethnic-based, sports, cultural, and regional organizations. Some were informal collections of a handful of people, while others had an organizational structure and their own facilities (Blommaert and Martiniello 1996). Early on, Moroccan and Turkish associations in Liège tended to fall into two camps: conservative movements under homeland governmental control, and secular, leftist homeland movements. Over the decades, their gaze grew bifocal, considering homeland and local issues. Mosques and Islamic associations multiplied, too, and they alternatively struggled to build a public image for Islam (for example, the al-Itissam mosque), keep their religion firmly in the private sphere (the al-Mouahidin mosque), or maintain close ties to consular authorities (the al-Iman mosque). Unlike their secular opposite numbers, Islamic associations had only occasional entree into policymaking circles. For all that, Islam was not a source of local turmoil. Liège was the first major Belgian city to allow Muslim cemeteries on its territory (Bousetta 2000). By the turn of the new century, the municipality would be organizing celebrations to mark the end of the holy month of Ramadan, seeing it as an occasion to acquaint residents with their Muslim neighbors and their religion (CBE 2001).

Egged on by the CRIPEL, Liège's non-Islamic immigrant associations began to structure themselves into three large multiethnic groupings in the late 1990s. Concerto pulled together more than thirty associations close to the PS and the Socialist trade union. D'ici et d'Ailleurs (From Here and There) gathered more than forty associations linked to the PSC and the Christian Labor Movement. The Union of Independent Associations, finally, united more than thirty nonpartisan, centrist associations (Martiniello and Kagné 1997).

A regional integration center like the CRIPEL was designed to be a second-line institution that collaborated with first-line ones—agencies, associations, and social workers active in the area of welcoming and overseeing the social, professional, and cultural integration of groups of immigrant origin. The spread and enlargement of French-style ZAPs in Liège marked the replacement of traditional sectoral social and pedagogical work with more coordinated and "territorialized" services. They crossed departmental lines to tackle problems that were seen as affecting a physical territory in its entirety and fitting better within a societal logic than an ethnic one (Barras, Nisolle, and Pourtois 1998).

More slowly than in Flanders, new left emancipatory notions were seeping into the ranks of social workers. Many of them were arguing that within the ZAP it was necessary to break with the "assistance" mentality of the past. Meeting the challenge of integration, they maintained, required the stimulation of identities that would allow disadvantaged people to take stock of their own experiences and abilities—those connected with their homeland cultures included in the mix—in the context of integrative projects oriented toward the host society. There was an urgent need for more street-level immigrant "animators." The task for Belgian social service providers was to energize and generalize the mobilization and solidarity that characterized certain immigrant-origin communities. Such a complex mission called for more continuity and more coordination between first-line and general social services (Manço 1998).

The CRIPEL was required to achieve parity between Belgians and immigrants on its management team, administration, and general assembly. Hence, the former body numbered six members from Concerto, five from D'ici et d'Ailleurs, and three from the Union of Independent Associations, alongside public officials and representatives of the three local ZAPs. Unlike the members of CCCIlg, those on the CRIPEL's representative council were appointed by the respective institutions. The "spontaneous" participation of interested parties was welcomed on an individual basis (Gosseau 1998). The whole institution was no less an exercise in top-down decision making, which drew the ire of many local immigrant activists and social workers. Defenders argued that the representative council, often referred to mistakenly as a parliament, was really more the "lungs" of the regional center: it was through its activities and advice that the CRIPEL's viability would be assured (Targosz 1998).

As for the CCCIlg, it remained in existence but ceased operations in 1991. The Maastricht Treaty's requirement that EU member countries institute local-level suffrage for all EU citizens sparked upset in Belgium. In Liège the mayor promised to reconfigure the CCCIlg, which threatened to become a "communal ghetto," and turn it into a true participatory organ for non-European immigrants in the city. Other local officials argued that the CCCIlg had never really worked and that immigrant leaders participated more meaningfully in local politics as advisers without any official legitimacy. Unlike Brussels or Ghent, Liège had no immigrant-origin elected officials. The Hôtel de Ville gave more play to the Consultative Communal Council for Solidarity between Liège and the "Third World" than to the CCCIlg. Local officials' focus on development projects in Liège's "sister" city of Lubumbashi, Congo, received the moral and financial support of the new federal secretary of state for codevelopment (see Ville de Liège 2002).

The municipality encouraged immigrant youths to naturalize, seeing it as a sign of successful integration. In Wallonia the objective of achieving professional insertion, stressed by city policymakers, compelled a disproportionately large number of Moroccans to acquire Belgian nationality: almost 12 percent of the total number. Youths of Southern European origin, Italians especially, were not as willing to naturalize as might have been expected. Only around a third became Belgian nationals. Regardless of their national origin, young people in the most marginalized social and professional situations were the least likely to apply for formal Belgian citizenship (Ouali 1998, 6).

Ethnicity on the Sly

In 1995 the local administration opened an Intercultural Relations Service—the first of its kind in Belgium—under the Department of Youth, Sports, and Metropolitan Housing. The service labored to open dialogue and build networks between inhabitants and the municipality, to strengthen services in the most disadvantaged neighborhoods, and "to improve relations among Liégeois of all nationalities." It tried to "amplify" initiatives proposed and undertaken by immigrant associations, holding competitions among projects for financial wherewithal and launching pilot projects in various neighborhoods and institutions (such as hospitals and schools) on diversity management, conflict resolution, and mediation (Ahkim 1998). Ostensibly targeted were not immigrants but all city residents as individuals. The republican model held sway. The goal was to make intercultural issues the subject of a community debate in Liège, establishing a beachhead so that they would not be swept away by current events or otherwise ignored. When journalists or politicians sought an interlocutor with the immigrant-origin communities, the municipality directed them to the intercultural service. The new mandate was transversal, meaning that all municipal departments were to adapt their offerings accordingly. The service waged its "peaceful war" independently of social services.[7]

When all was said and done, the Intercultural Relations Service could not help but take an angle of attack that was cultural to some extent. Ethnic identities were winning grudging acceptance. Standing at the center of the urban renewal policies that dominated Liège's concerns were "neighborhoods in difficulty." That geographical basis was a mask for cultural projects with immigrants, and they necessitated differentiated strategies. Part of the very definition of a deprived neighborhood, after all, was having a resident population that was more than 5 percent Turkish and Moroccan. Accordingly, the areas with the most non-Europeans were also the ones attracting the most urban policy attention (Ville de Liège 2002).

It was imperative not to duplicate efforts and reinvent the wheel, typically Belgian foibles whose effects were being aggravated by social spending cuts. Confusion resulted from the growing number of budgetary sources, different institutional charges and selection criteria, the multiplicity of partners and actors, and the weakness of oversight organizations. As always in Liège, the interpersonal dynamic was critical. The city and province had a conflictual relationship, for instance. The PS was in control at both levels but in coalition with different parties: as of 1994, in the city with the Christian Democrats of the PSC; in the province with the liberals of the PRL. Within the Walloon region, Liège and Charleroi, the two biggest cities, insisted on receiving the same largesse from above. The son of the Congolese man who had presided over the CCCIlg for fifteen years was made alderman of the Intercultural Relations Service. Tensions between it and the local housing authority helped to explain why relatively little was accomplished in that area.

The municipal elections of 1994 that had yielded a majority composed of the PS and the PSC gave representation for the first time to the far right. In Wallonia, anti-immigrant forces had congealed into two small political parties, Agir (Act) and the National Front. Between them they elected four municipal councilors in the city. Immediately upon their entry into the local legislative body, however, Liège became the first Belgian city to adopt a charter on the fight against racism that championed the participation of "people of all origins at all levels of local life" (Conseil Communal 1995). The political storm over the far right calmed thereafter.

The immigrant population of Liège was settling in and diversifying. In 1998, 17.6 percent of the city's inhabitants were nonnationals, 38 percent of them from outside of the EU. Over 40 percent of the immigrants were Italians, followed by Moroccans (14.6 percent), Spaniards (8.9 percent), Turks (7.6 percent), French (6.9 percent), and Congolese (3.3 percent). All told, members of over 130 ethnic groups lived in Liège. Four districts, each part of a ZAP, had concentrations that were well above the citywide average: Glain (40 percent), Droixhe (36 percent), Saint-Léonard (30 percent), and Sainte-Marguerite (28 percent). Droixhe was the only district whose non-EU immigrant population was larger than that from elsewhere in Europe (Martiniello and Kagné 1997).

As in France, the undocumented (sans-papiers) dominated the immigration agenda at the end of the 1990s. They occupied university buildings, demanding amnesty and better treatment for people in their predicament. Their actions generated sympathy, even as they accentuated concerns over security. Run-ins between immigrant-origin youths and local police occurred with alarming frequency. Young Liégeois were also borrowing from perceived American reality, referring to their neighborhoods as "Chicago" and "Los Angeles." Poverty, violence, drug dependency, physical deterioration, and environmental degradation plagued the infamous housing towers of Droixhe. Unemployment and dependence on social assistance stayed as high as ever—that is, when they did not go up. In such downtrodden neighborhoods, Belgians and immigrants were in competition for the same overtaxed public social services. The neighborhoods were not ghettoes, given the incredible ethnic diversity present. What was missing was socioeconomic heterogeneity. People with very different lifestyles and behavioral patterns were coexisting: an elderly population annoyed and frightened by the massive presence of young people, very poor Belgians getting along only with difficulty, and an assortment of ethnic communities often in conflict amongst themselves (Vanderkam 1997).

Nationally, the Ministry of the Interior had become the largest single source of employment increase in the public sector. Locally, there was a political imperative to "look tough" to impede the far right and to receive the security contracts that unlocked regional and federal subsidies, which were being tied to the fight against crime and drugs. Institutional adaptation to the pluralist reality of the Walloon region posed a major challenge for policymakers, who had to respond to burgeoning, interconnected demands relating to social cohesion, economic and cultural development, demographic issues, and urban crime. All too frequently, Liégeois officials argued, behind a conflict that was quickly labeled "ethnocultural" hid a situation similar to that affecting a native-stock family. To direct immigrants automatically toward homeland "specialists" was to push them back to their cultural roots without trying to understand them, their hopes, and their desires: "The people brought here by immigration are confronted with forces of exclusion and segregation the same as any disadvantaged person," ran the official line. "Their ethnic origin only reinforces these phenomena" (Targosz 1999, 4). Therefore, an overly strict application of republican laws, one that failed to take into account the cultural dimension, could actually harden ethnic boundaries, feed encapsulation, and block dialogue.

It was in that backhanded way that ethnicity entered into Liégeois policy. Even in the heart of Socialist Wallonia, local officials grew more willing to admit that cultural and ethnic conflicts did exist and, in less explicit fashion, to respond accordingly. They took to celebrating the "rich associational tapestry" in Liège, which they hailed as an "intersection of cultures" and thereby an attractive destination for tourism and trade fairs (ERI 2002). The Intercultural Relations Service distributed a catalog of local "intercultural actors" to public institutions across the city, including the neighborhood police stations and youth centers. Some 245 different organizations were listed, including the CCCIlg and ranging from the African Christian Moms of Liège to an artists' group called the Zone. The service launched a project to develop fresh arguments against racism and to construct an "intercultural village" in collaboration with the city's intercultural associations and under the rubric of an annual world music festival. Immigrant associations were active as well in the "Intercultural Fortnight," two weeks of festivities, seminars, cultural expositions, and so on. The municipal council provided modest subsidies to support such harmless activities. It targeted immigrant-rich neighborhoods for programs to encourage the integration of Turkish and Moroccan girls through sports (CBE 2001).

Tacitly, ethnic identities were built in as factors in land use planning, urban redevelopment, and decentralized social services. Diversity, it was agreed, was valuable. It was crucial to avoid the "ghettoization" of neighborhoods. Respect for differences and the promotion of exchanges would reinforce social cohesion. They were indispensable to a flourishing urban center, even though it was up to immigrants to adapt to the "mentalities and particularities" of the city (Ville de Liège 2002). Diversity was described in terms of "the young and the less young, the disadvantaged and the favored, those born in Liège and those who have decided to install themselves here and adopt the city or to be adopted by it." If managed correctly, this variety would help everyone to integrate into society and produce solidarity within a context of mutual respect among "all citizens of the city" (Ville de Liège 2000).

The municipal council election in 2000 confirmed the Socialist-led coalition in power. With twenty seats out of forty-nine, the PS was able to run the city in tandem with the PSC (ten seats).[8] The Liberals (eleven seats) and Écolos (eight seats) formed the opposition. The top vote-getter in the election, Willy Demeyer of the PS, was named mayor. One PS councilor, Fouad Chamas, had come to Belgium from Lebanon in 1975. The president of the CCCIlg was a naturalized Italian who had run in the bottom half of the PS list and had failed to win election. As the new century began, Liège seemed destined to stick with its by and large general, territorial, neighborhood-based structural policies. Its nods to ethnic identities and to the political-cultural dimension of integration were not gratuitous. But as in Essen, Germany, the traditionally minded trade unionists and Socialists who ran the city were loath to abandon totally their hope of turning immigrants into labor activists and voters. Political-cultural congruence was restricted by federal policies in each instance. Residential concentration was lower and, according to available indicators, structural integration higher in the German city. While there was not much more ethnic conflict in Liège, the marginalization and dispossession of immigrant-origin residents was more significant.

Ghent: Recognizing "Ethnic Cultural Minorities"

If Liège could be considered the textbook case of Walloon responses to immigration, then Ghent presented the Flemish experience equally starkly. Once one of the most powerful cities in northwestern Europe, Ghent was a center of luxury linen production in the High Middle Ages. In the nineteenth century, it grew into a major textile-manufacturing city, the "Manchester of the Lowlands." As such, it attracted thousands of workers from rural areas of Flanders and beyond, gaining in the process a strong Socialist and Christian trade union tradition (Deslé 1996). Ghent's cosmopolitan image was cemented when it organized the World Exposition of 1913, just before World War I and its aftermath ushered in a period of stagnation. Only when the high-tech industry turned Flanders into the wealthier half of Belgium after the 1970s would Ghent regain some of its earlier luster.

Postwar Immigration and Crisis

It had never lost its progressive, consensual policymaking approach. Ghent was proud of its reputation as a forward-looking place. The Socialist Party (Socialistische Partij—SP) exhibited noteworthy strength, but Flanders was not Wallonia. Multiparty coalition governments were the rule, and Catholic religious values motivated activists in most local political movements. Likewise typically Flemish, Ghent was relatively late in receiving immigrant workers in important numbers. Only by the late 1970s did the Turkish and Moroccan presence gain much notice. By then, they were already concentrated residentially in certain districts marked by an accumulation of social ills. The private housing market was problematic for immigrants from Turkey and North Africa, and several social housing corporations resisted renting to them. When the Flemish regional executive body in 1990 listed cities and districts that suffered from significant disadvantage, basing the assessment largely on the share of both residents on social assistance and non-European immigrants, several Ghent districts scored high (APD 1993). There was a subsequent rise in social tensions. Ghent—of the eight case cities in this study, the one with the lowest overall immigrant share—was the one wherein the far right presented the greatest political menace.

Integration Policy Responses

With immigrants initially lacking many of the prerequisites for active participation in local society, a network of specialized, Belgian-run organizations presented themselves as the defenders of their interests in Ghent. Later than in the Netherlands, but earlier than in Liège, social workers in Ghent began to embrace notions of emancipation and empowerment, even if the weight and complexity of the Belgian institutional system tended to thwart their implementation. Whereas rivalry characterized the city-region relationship in Liège, Ghent officialdom jumped whenever the Flemish/Dutch Community government tandem issued a directive (KCMB 1989, 108).

Despite their modest numbers overall, immigrants' structural position in Ghent, as in Essen, did not differ significantly from their status in case cities with larger shares. Because postwar migration reached Flanders comparatively late and was of comparatively moderate proportions, the city's policymakers had at first taken little notice of it. Immigrants' position in the areas of employment, housing, educational, and vocational training was deteriorating compared to that of native-stock residents. Their political and cultural integration attracted no more municipal attention than their integration along the structural dimension.

The Difficult 1990s

Ghent officialdom, like its neighbors in cities such as Antwerp and Genk, woke up to the trends toward disconnection in 1991. Municipal elections that year sounded the alarm. Mounting a campaign that rested in part on upset at the inflow of Muslim immigrants and asylum seekers, the Flemish Bloc won a Ghent council seat, and its strength seemed to be building. In provincial elections in East Flanders, it also performed well in the city (Haelsterman and

Abramowicz 1997). At the time, only 8 percent of Ghent's 230,000 residents were nonnationals. Adding in naturalized immigrants and refugees, the percentage rose to 10 at most. Three-quarters of them were from Turkey and Morocco, but there were also many Europeans. Altogether, people of more than 130 nationalities lived in the city (VFIK 1995).

In 1991, not coincidentally, Ghent established a Municipal Migrants Center (Stedelijk Migrantencentrum—SMC). Its mission was to ensure immigrants an equal place in Ghent society—socially, economically, culturally, institutionally, and politically. Integration was defined as immigrants' adaptation to their new environment, from the starting point of respect for the ethnocultural identity of each component group. They were all to be incorporated into Ghent society on the basis of solidarity and equity; they, in turn, were to respect existing laws and not threaten public order. The SMC counseled all Ghent residents on issues related to their legal status and rights, referring them to the appropriate office or institution. Across the boards, general services had to assume their responsibilities toward marginalized populations like immigrants. Specific provisions for them had to be created and sustained where necessary: "However much we may believe that general policies should be put in place to serve all population groups," municipal officials reasoned, "targeted offerings are sometimes the only solution at hand" (SID 1999b, 4).

Ghent, in short, was adopting an ethnic minorities policy that smacked of cultural pluralism, just as the Netherlands was tacking away from it and toward liberal multiculturalism. The SMC's social department put a team of translators, counselors, and legal assistants at the disposal of the immigrant-origin population. A training and sensitization cell tried to raise awareness of immigrants and their contributions and to provoke positive changes in mentality among the general public. The SMC trumpeted the opportunities and new possibilities that the presence of "different cultures" offered to Ghent, and it and regional authorities viewed its workshops on the immigrants' and refugees' homelands as valuable contributions to mutual respect and integration (Vlaams Parlement 2002). The SMC had an antidiscrimination department, created as a joint project with the Center for Equal Opportunities and against Racism in Brussels, and programs to aid immigrant-origin women, youths, job seekers, and adults seeking knowledge of Dutch or other continuing education. In principal these initiatives targeted those groups in general, with the idea being to facilitate access for immigrant-origin residents. Relations were close with the municipal departments active in the areas of welfare, education, culture, and recreation. The SMC's documentation center, with its collection of works in Turkish and Arabic, was available to all, as were its culinary classes. By 1997 it had a full-time, paid staff member, no small matter in light of tight budgets (de Regge 1997).

Political-Cultural Integration

The SMC acted in the name of the municipality in offering administrative, logistical, financial, and in-kind support for local immigrant and other associations. The city saw in them the appropriate vehicles by which to foster cultural development and participatory potential among the immigrant-origin population. Consultation was a tried-and-true element of Belgian policy-making. Regional officials insisted that the center have an advisory board and that at least a third of its members be immigrants who through their "knowledge, position, and/or experience in a local association" could make a "real contribution" to its work (van den Brande and Martens 1998). In consequence, the Municipal Integration Council (Stedelijke Integratieraad—IR) was set up in 1993 with an annual budget of 100,000 Belgian francs. Like the CRIPEL in Liège, the IR and the SMC were public-sector services charged with fulfilling a mandate laid down by the municipal administration and dependent on the recognition and subsidies that it tendered. They were second-line institutions whose express goal was to coordinate those engaged in first-line work (SID 1999a, 8–22).

True consultation required viable, representative interlocutors. Policy-makers turned toward activating self-sufficiency and what they considered suitable associational activity on the part of target-group populations. Overall outcomes were disappointing, although some advances were made among immigrant women. In the absence of a dominating, controlling political force, immigrant associations did not undergo even Liège-style or Essen-style (and certainly not Bremen-style) structuring into the desired peak organizations. Immigrant associational life in Ghent was fragmented and marked by internecine squabbling. The IR's twenty-eight members attended meetings only intermittently. In between, little was accomplished; the work was unremunerated, after all. Linguistic problems were not uncommon. Belgians who worked with immigrants lobbied the municipality for directly elected ethnic minority representatives as a way to make participation more extensive and meaningful.[9]

The SMC fronted the drive to transform an abandoned office building into a meeting place run by and for local associations and residents. "The Central" opened its doors in 1994, with its ambition to safeguard immigrants' right to their own cultural identity by facilitating their expression through the fine and performance arts. The center also provided help with grant applications to foundations and funding agencies. The Kom-Pas Center for Non-Indigenous Newcomers, meanwhile, provided Dutch language instruction, counseling, job training, and a "client tracking" system for new residents, especially Turks and North Africans. The Flemish government eventually took it up as a model for reception policy in the region (Kom-Pas 2002b).

Ghent was home to the Provincial Minority Services Office for East

Flanders. It also harbored four neighborhood integration centers, run by nonprofits or district authorities, and they entered into formal cooperation agreements with the SMC. In the late 1990s, they came under the municipal umbrella. There was a push for closer coordination and cooperation between the municipal center, the provincial office, private actors (real estate agents, landlords, employers, discotheque owners, and the like), and nonprofit organizations, under the guidance of Johan Leman's center in Brussels. In a departure from its hierarchical pyramid model, the municipality installed temporary internal matrix groups to troubleshoot and to monitor functioning, organization, and coordination. Once a working group had emerged to link general social services, the SMC, Kom-Pas, and the agency running Dutch language programs, the matrix would dissolve (SID 1999a).

Islam did not unduly upset municipal officials in Ghent. There were a number of Muslim associations in town. Active throughout Flanders since 1978 in defense of Islamic teachers, the Association for the Education and Emancipation of Muslims was the only Muslim association present locally that transcended monoethnic and monodenominational membership. By the late 1990s, Ghent had six Turkish mosques (half of them under Diyanet control), three Moroccan ones, and two for Pakistanis and sub-Saharan Africans. Most of the Turkish institutions dated from the mid-1980s, when the government in Ankara sent imams to Europe in an attempt to check surging Islamist movements, led by dissidents from organizations banned back home. Ghent officials offered the Turkish government's imams contracts to organize Islamic instruction in public schools. Ghent's Moroccan community, meanwhile, was smaller than its Turkish counterpart and more traditional and closed in on itself, at least among the first immigrant generation. There were fewer mosques, restaurants, and stores geared toward serving Moroccans' specific needs. Still, Ghent was the only Flemish city in which Moroccan youths organized their own mosque, El-Markaz et-Tarbawi (The Education Center), in part reflecting greater receptivity on the part of local officials than in Antwerp or Brussels (Laytouss 1999).

It was concern that the far right could make political hay out of fears of Muslims that drove Ghent officials to act. In December 1997, the Ghent municipal executive confirmed a disciplinary action against a Muslim pupil for wearing a headscarf, justifying its position by referring to the constitutional principle of state neutrality in religion. The sore points tended not to be related to religious practices, however. The nationalist Turkish Gray Wolves had a small local presence, for example, and Kurds and Turks engaged in verbal sparring.[10] Also, immigrants from North Africa and Turkey washed their floor rugs and dried them in the sun, and some of their Flemish-stock neighbors complained when they covered courtyards and sidewalks. The municipality organized a collective washing area to prevent the issue from degenerating into real conflict. The SMC's annual reports even tracked the volume of wool washed, using it as a performance indicator. In a self-evaluation it admitted that no serious attempts had been made to give the activity a more positive spin, to see it as the expression of a different culture and thus as an enrichment (SID 1999a, 40–41).

The Structural Integration Afterthought

Ghent's integration policy response centered on political-cultural aspects. It enlivened ethnic identities and drew notice, both positive and negative, to them. Structural integration was not ignored, yet it was not of equal importance at first and suffered for it. The overwhelming majority of immigrant-origin Ghent residents were blue-collar workers, most of them in low-wage jobs in horticulture, textiles, and other industries, as well as in hotels and tourism. The unemployment rate in Ghent normally exceeded the Flemish average, above all with respect to youths and the nonindigenous. Immigrant-origin workers represented a growing percentage of the local unemployed population—from 6 percent in 1993 to 12.2 percent in 1998 in Flanders—although it fell far short of nonnationals' 21.7 percent share in Liège that latter year (de Regge 2002, 60). With immigrants responsible for demographic rejuvenation and Flemings for aging, tensions between the young and the elderly became almost automatically tensions between people of immigrant and Flemish origin. Turkish youths had fewer problems overall than their Moroccan peers (Steunpunt WAV 1999).

Spatially, Ghent was resembling Holland more than Wallonia. Three-quarters of the immigrant-origin population lived in a belt of neighborhoods with nineteenth-century-worker housing that arched just north of the historic city center—St.-Amandsberg, Rabot, Muide, Brugse Poort, Ledeberg, Gentbrugge, Heusden-Zolder—lower-lying areas that had historically been prone to flooding from the rivers Scheldt and Leie (Vanneste 1985). In modern times, immigrants were concentrated where social disadvantages like poor housing and environmental problems were the most serious. Lower costs had drawn and discrimination had pushed them there, the city felt. Compared to Liège, Ghent employed a social housing strategy that relied more heavily on private markets. Combined with the effects of chain migration, they encouraged the residential concentration of immigrants from the same countries or regions. While the municipality saw their clustering as a possible source of security and opportunities, it felt that neighborhoods with an accumulation of social disadvantages could limit possibilities for congruence (SID 1999a).

By 1998–1999, over half of immigrant-origin children would be behind by more than a year in compulsory education, compared to less than one-fifth of native Belgians. The situation for both cohorts had deteriorated since 1990–1991 (see tables 5.3 and 5.4). The number of concentration schools in Ghent was growing steadily. They gained a negative reputation among parents of all backgrounds, even while receiving extra funds to organize customized lan-

TABLE 5.3

Ghent Nonnational Pupils behind in School (%)

	1990–1991	1998–1999
Belgian nationals	16.9	18.3
±2 years behind	1.4	1.5
Nonnationals	49.4	54.6
±2 years behind	12.1	13.5

TABLE 5.4

Allochton Target-Group Students by Level, 2001–2002

(% of Total)

	Basic Education	Secondary Education
Flemish Community	13	9
Municipal	27	23
Catholic	15	4
Provincial	—	22
Total	19	8

Target-group students are those officially defined as having a maternal grandmother without Belgian or Dutch nationality and a mother with an education not past age of eighteen.

Source: de Regge (2002, 47–53).

guage instruction and counseling services. Dutch-language courses were over-subscribed, but otherwise, lifelong-learning classes failed to attract a large number of immigrant-origin enrollees (SID 1999b).

Belgians ran the organizations that had the strongest impact on immigrant-origin residents, most notably the important social welfare institutions. Municipal officials hoped to harness the nonprofit sector and its mobilizational capabilities. They leaned on the nonprofits to hire more immigrant-origin personnel, but budgetary restrictions rendered that difficult. Nonnationals could fill only temporary slots. As in Liège and Essen, then, but unlike in the Dutch and the other German case cities, empowerment and self-help had a hard time breaking out of social worker circles and into the policymaking realm. Integrated neighborhood action based on district-level social development plans was a goal, but it was liable to go missing in the plethora of other objectives. True territorialization, along Liégeois lines, did not take place.

Later than in the Netherlands, authorities in Ghent shifted toward a blend of structural and political-cultural policies. The Flemings did not give up on the ethnic minorities approach as readily as their Dutch neighbors. In 1998 the Flemish parliament passed a decree-law, fully operational in 2000, that sought to bring changes both in form and substance to the area of immigrant integration policy in Ghent. It broadened the definition of the target groups. The new policy went even further than next door in the Netherlands and described the population arising from migration as "ethnic-cultural minorities," even if the more general Dutch term "nonindigenous people" *(allochtonen)* cropped up in common parlance. Ethnic minorities were those who, whether of Belgian nationality or not, had at least one parent or grandparent born outside the country and who found themselves disadvantaged on account of their ethnic background, ancestry, skin color, or socioeconomic position. These people usually had roots in a country outside of the EU, but Iberians, Italians, and Greeks were added for historical reasons. The word "background" ensured that naturalized immigrants and their children would be included, along with the refugees, asylum seekers, travelers, and undocumented immigrants and refugees.

There was newly reinvigorated insistence by regional authorities that their municipal counterparts take the lead in formulating a policy plan for ethnic-cultural minorities. It was incumbent on local governments to adapt Flemish policy to local conditions and apply for recognition and funding. In response, Ghent changed the Migrants Center's name to the Municipal Integration Services (Stedelijke Integratiedienst—SID) in 1998. There followed a series of pilot projects that, officials hoped, would give concrete form to the inclusive policies adopted in various sectors. Money for the SID came from the regular city budget, the Flemish Regional Integration Center, the region, and federal security contracts. None of those sources involved the same rules, stipulations on use of funds, or mandates to be met. Strategic planning became obligatory before and during the course of all subsidized programs. Grants covered infrastructure, start-up costs, operations, and personnel. Hundreds of thousands of Belgian francs were pegged to each aspect, with detailed guidelines covering what they were to be spent on and when.[11]

Ghent's policies were organized into nineteen thematic "core results areas" tagged for focused treatment and accompanied by a raft of operational indicators and benchmarks to enable ongoing quantitative evaluation. The priority was placed on neighborhood-level action. A delicate balance had to be struck between diversity management and minority self-awareness and self-assurance. Target groups would play an active part in decision making. It would thus be necessary to engage in structural interventions and encourage their empowerment. The new policies were promoted as a "radical means of ensuring equality of opportunity for all residents of Ghent." Rights were not unidirectional, the SID hastened to add, and everyone was obliged to obey the laws of the land (Kom-Pas 2002b).

Following the Flemish lead, Ghent was preaching a vision of an "active welfare state." It called on residents to accept responsibility for their own lives and well-being. If they were not able to do so, the city, region, and federal government would provide assistance, removing the barriers to their full participation in society. Local officials vowed to incorporate targeted policies "as much as possible" into more general, neighborhood-based ones fighting social disadvantage. The growing diversification of ethnonational backgrounds and legal situations complicated all such efforts. There was, in the final analysis, far more willingness than in Wallonia, Germany, and, from the early 1990s on, the Netherlands to accept that cultural and linguistic differences would render categorical policies durable in certain areas. At the same time, the diversity that existed within each minority group—in terms of gender, ancestry, age, and sexual orientation—would be taken into account (Stad Gent 2001).

The SID depended on an alderwoman from the Socialist Party, making it vulnerable in the event that the Flemish Bloc upped its vote totals. That was precisely what happened in the 2000 municipal election. As before, that vote left the city led by a Socialist mayor and his party—with fourteen seats, including one held by a man of Turkish origin—in an alliance with the Flemish Liberals and Democrats and a small "Flemish-alternative" formation. The Christian Democrats and environmentalists were in the opposition, unwilling to work with the VB, which had become the second-largest political party in the city, with eleven seats.

After the election, the SID stayed in place, its mandate essentially unchanged. In the coalition agreement for 2001–2006, however, there was more emphasis on security, Dutch-language training, and the fight against social marginalization and spatial segregation (Stad Gent 2001). More social housing would be constructed, and an explicit "spreading" policy would inhibit "ghetto formation." Even more than before, local authorities stressed the need to coordinate activities in the city and to avoid duplication of efforts. No less than in Liège, this imperative explained in part the top-down nature of local relations with immigrant-origin residents and the reluctance to implement a full-bore policy of self-help. From "exclusive complementarity" between the integration service (SID) and the integration center (IR), the former became the "director," fleshing out the local policy response, and the latter became the "actor," charged with providing an independent running critique and assessment. The "band shell" was provided by the regional Flemish administration (de Regge 2002, 7–8).

There were other actors in the nascent network as well, each with specific roles to play in the context of the policy plan. Prominent here was the Intercultural Network of Ghent (Intercultureel Netwerk Gent—ING). The 1998 Flemish law on a "renewed" minorities policy put in motion a process that led to the founding of the ING as Ghent's official integration center and the absorption into it of the city's four preexisting integration centers. The ING was to complement the SID and the local branch of the provincial integration center. Together, they would target ethnic-cultural minorities along three tracks: emancipation (the fight against social disadvantage and barriers to full participation in local society), admissions (initial intake and processing for freshly arrived individuals, irrespective of their residency status), and reception and orientation (measures to facilitate the integration of newcomers by means of intensive Dutch language instruction and social orientation programs) (Kom-Pas 2002a). Dutch language immersion and other intensive instruction were critical in all three areas. The city admitted that it hoped to require Dutch classes for newcomers and perhaps "oldcomers" as soon as it could provide a "full and free set of offerings." Demand for courses in Dutch as a second language increased by a third between the 1998–1999 and 1999–2000 school years (de Regge 2002, 24, 54).

Ghent's integration policy plan for 2003–2005 included objective data covering the ten areas for which the municipal administration had some responsibility: housing, education, continuing (adult) education, the labor market, welfare, health, culture, sports and recreation, recognized faith communities, and security. The SID, ten years old and with sixty staff members in six locations across the city when the new plan was approved in 2002, was to devote more attention to structural integration than before. It observed that residents of immigrant origin were still far more likely than native-stock Gentenars to be out of work, unemployed for more than a year, underemployed, or in part-time employment. From just over 12 percent of the active population seeking work in 1998, they comprised 28 percent in 2001—more than in Liège. Ghent, too, was worse off than most of Flanders with its rate of a bit under 13 percent (compared to 7 percent). There was wide variation within the immigrant-origin workforce. Turks and Moroccans were still at the bottom of the employment ladder and represented fully 54 percent of the nonindigenous unemployed. A study commissioned by Ghent officials found that discrimination hurt ethnic minorities' chances when applying for a job in 40 percent of cases. The city also blamed their weak contacts with Belgian social networks as a cause, not a consequence, of unemployment (SID 2002, sec. 5.2).

Unfortunately, to be eligible for special make-work programs, one had to have been out of work for at least two years. In the meantime, the local government had introduced a host of initiatives to enhance immigrants' chances in a labor market that, it conceded, was for the moment "closed." Like the other cities, Ghent celebrated the growth in ethnic small businesses, which numbered around 1,150 in 2001. It organized training classes for would-be entrepreneurs. At the neighborhood level, groups of likeminded native- and immigrant-stock businesspeople had begun to form associations (de Regge 2002, 64).

There were other signs that the immigrant-origin population was undergoing differentiation and that socioeconomic inequalities were widening. The clientele of the Ghent Housing Foundation had evolved from almost exclusively Turks in 1978 to a much more heterogeneous mixture by 1999, only one-fifth Turkish and almost one-half from some forty other nationalities. Fully a third were Belgians, a fifth of them of immigrant origin. The city noted that whenever it compared the housing conditions of native-stock and immigrant-stock residents, Turks and Moroccans were found to be living in the poorest neighborhoods, overrepresented in the lowest levels of the rental sector and underrepresented in single-family housing. Yet whereas 49 percent of native Belgians had purchased their home, most of them in the primary sector, nearly 56 percent of Turks had, albeit mostly in the residual and middle-range sectors (SID 2002, sec. 2.1). Social housing corporations struggled to meet ethnic minorities' demands for larger units near their compatriots, although they had received a mandate from the local and regional administrations to steer clear of aggravating residential concentration. Public social rental offices leased private apartments, which they then renovated and rented out to qualified applicants (AWB 2000).

There was a connection between immigrants' housing difficulties and high unemployment rates and their low levels of educational achievement and Dutch language skills. The gap between ethnic minority and native-stock youths was narrower and immigrant concentrations greater at the secondary level than the primary level—taken as evidence that the pains taken by the local government to create more diverse schools citywide, to mentor and guide immigrant-origin pupils through the system, and to involve minority parents were having an effect at the start of the pipeline. Excitedly, municipal officials pointed to a study conducted by Professor Jan Van Damme from the Catholic University of Louvain, who found in 2000 that immigrant-origin students who spoke no Dutch at home actually made faster progress in secondary schools than their native-stock peers who started at the same level in middle schools (de Regge 2002, 51).

There were no strong signs of a regime of ethnic relations management or an ethnic minority voting bloc. Less than 2 percent of the local administration's staff members were ethnic-cultural minorities in 2001. The numbers were increasing but barely higher than in the 1990s. Not very plentiful, naturalizations were nonetheless multiplying, particularly among the young. The city, which was not forthcoming with hard data, said simply that it found room for improvement. Factors beyond its control—federal legislation and procedures, the Dutch language qualifying exam—limited what local authorities could accomplish (de Regge 2002, 66–70).

As a result, the integration plan that was approved in 2002 devoted considerable analysis to the issues of nonnationals' cultural and political participation, defined as equal representation. The city confessed that it had few statistics on that involvement at its disposal. Officials' operating assumption was that it was rather low. Of the more than 450 local voluntary associations, just over a hundred were immigrant-origin organizations. About half of those were recognized by the municipal government, and around a fifth received a "basic" subsidy of just under a thousand dollars. In Flanders half of the 800 local immigrant associations were grouped into fourteen regional federations, two of which were headquartered in Ghent: the Federation of Progressive Turks (Federatie van Vooruitstrevende Turkse—FVT) and the Federation of Self-Organizations in Flanders (Federatie van Zelforganisaties in Vlaanderen—FZOVL), formed by Turks, Slovaks, and sub-Saharan Africans. In 2001 Flemish legislation toughened up the screening process by which such federations received subsidies. Almost as consistently as in The Hague, officials in Ghent recognized that ethnic differences rooted in the homeland could influence cultural and political expression and requirements in the host society. They cited Berbers in Morocco, Kurds in Turkey, and Roma in Slovakia as cases in point. They took pains to distinguish between data collected on the basis of ethnicity and national origin.[12]

Islam was receiving due attention and important support. Although there was no municipal record of individual religious preferences, Ghent had between fifteen thousand and eighteen thousand residents from primarily Muslim countries in 2002. By then, seven of the city's mosques, five Turkish and two Moroccan, had applied for official status once Islam had won federal-level recognition as a faith community. If their application proved successful, the federal Ministry of Justice would pay for their imams' salaries, and the city would cover costs associated with the mosques and their operations. The Province of East Flanders would be expected to contribute to their upkeep. It was clear that fewer mosques would be recognized than already existed, making it imperative that the municipality engage the Muslim communities and their rather informal associations in a dialogue. For the annual Muslim feasts in 2000, the city awarded over a million Belgian francs for the rental of a slaughterhouse, butchers' salaries, and disposal and cleaning costs. Local agreement was proving elusive on Muslim burials in public cemeteries. Ghent schools had not dealt systematically with Muslim students and their needs, and they failed to make allowances for prayer times or holidays, including Ramadan. The municipality did pay seventeen teachers to offer Islamic instruction in local schools (SID 2002, sec. 12).

Much municipal effort went into coaxing the "Forum" into existence in 2000. It was a loose federation of immigrant associations, within which immigrant-origin representatives could discuss issues of concern with the local administration. The leadership of the two existing local immigrant associational federations, the FVT and the FZOVL, were key players in the Forum. It was eventually complemented by a sounding board that, in true consociational fashion, pulled in a smaller network of individuals with key roles who met periodically to reflect on the situation of ethnic-cultural minorities and mediated between them and the local administration (SID 2001).

Officials pledged to see to it that ethnic-cultural minorities' organizations took full part in policymaking. The Flemish Community had criticized the city for failing to spell out a clear, step-by-step process by which it intended to reach that goal. Nothing spoke more eloquently of the distance that Ghent had to go before it achieved that objective than a tally of ethnic-cultural minorities' membership in thematic municipal advisory councils, like the Forum, which represented the most valuable means available to immigrants of exerting influence on local policies: the eleven such councils contained only twenty-one minority representatives—every single one of them in the Forum.

Immigrant associational leaders and city hall alike fretted over their failure to reach into the ranks of immigrant-origin youths, and special municipal subsidies were extended for projects to reverse the trend (Stad Gent 2001). Concern over crime was a primary impetus. As in the late 1990s, the Security Monitor indicated that in 2001 most Ghent residents felt threatened only seldom or never as they went about their daily lives. However, the number of those who did sometimes or often worry about their safety had increased. Turks expressed sharper fears than native-stock Belgians, worrying most about threats to their person and drug-related crime, while the latter group's concerns centered mostly on crimes against property. At the neighborhood level there was little difference between the responses of native-stock and ethnic-cultural minority residents. Young Moroccan men were a source of particular concern among all groups, including those of Moroccan origin. However, ethnic background, gender, age, and socioeconomic level all played a role in determining whether or not members of a particular group were more or less likely to commit a particular type of crime. Overall, the picture was too complex and complicated to allow for easy generalizations.

In 1999 national Minister of Justice Marc Verwilghen commissioned a Dutch scholar to assess the relationship between youths of immigrant origin and criminality in four Belgian cities, including Ghent and Liège. There was little cross-city variation, but the findings confirmed that there were discrepancies across ethnic groups—defined in the study according to country of origin—and gender. Girls of Turkish and Moroccan background were significantly less likely than those of other national groups (including Belgians) to engage in criminal activity; their male counterparts, however, were more likely. Each nationality had its own "specialty": Moroccans, disproportionately implicated in most types of crime, were particularly likely to be charged with theft and other "economic" crimes; Turks were more often charged with crimes involving violence and threats to public order; and South Americans and Belgians were most responsible for the drug trade. Ghent officials concluded that institutional racism and socioeconomic disadvantage, while certainly major factors in hindering immigrant integration, were unlikely culprits when it came to crime. Did Asian and Turkish youths really face less discrimination than their more crime-prone Moroccan peers? Why would young, white Eastern Europeans be more likely to commit crimes than Congolese youths? Turks' unemployment rates were higher than Moroccans', on average, and the socioeconomic position of immigrant-origin girls was certainly no better than that of boys (de Regge 2002, 91–92). Ghent, more than the other case cities, remained convinced that ethnic cultures were the crux of the immigrant integration conundrum.

Conclusion

The national and local Belgian cases, to conclude, widen significantly the range of integration policy responses under consideration in this study. Like their counterparts in Germany and the Netherlands, Belgian authorities were unable to stem the steady shift toward the spatial concentration of immigrant-origin and other disadvantaged populations in certain neighborhoods. They could not erase discrepancies between those of native and immigrant stock in housing, education, and training, either, although limited progress was registered on those fronts. Local officials struggled within a complicated set of federal and regional institutional corsets.

Officials in Liège tried to develop strategies to advance structural integration but buried them within comprehensive general policies targeted toward certain neighborhoods. They achieved only modest gains and in the process contributed to what could only be called geographical stigmatizing: policies delineated boundaries not around ethnic groups but around underprivileged sections of the city. Political-cultural integration was defined in individual and class-based terms, and ethnicity was dealt with in terms of international worker solidarity. When structural disconnection persisted, policies were retooled. They began to take ethnic identities into consideration, somewhat furtively.

Officials in Ghent, like the Dutch, led with policies to advance political-cultural integration that were based precisely on ethnic identities. When they began to generate tensions along those lines, structural integration gained prominence, and policies' ethnic aspects were downplayed. As in Liège, however, change proved halfhearted. Ethnic cultures retained their central position in Ghent's efforts to solve the integration challenge. The rapprochement between multicultural Flanders and republican Wallonia was very much a work in progress.

Ethnic tensions never exceeded modest levels in either Belgian city, including Ghent. There, the nationalist Flemish Bloc may have tried to exploit them, but the neighborhoods stayed calm. In the May 2003 legislative elections, the VB actually lost votes in Ghent (Deloy 2003). Troubles in Liège's housing projects were more likely to take the form of anomic, multiethnic protests of the dispossessed than distinctively ethnic movements. In their attempts to forge some measure of coherence out of all the programs, policies, and mandates emitting from their various institutional partners and masters, local officials in Belgium wound up squelching bottom-up empowerment. Structural disconnection was comparable yet not reversing in as many areas as in the Dutch cities. Political-cultural disconnection was greater than in Rotterdam and The Hague, where more political rights and more meaningful channels of consultative participation produced more ethnic-based pressure from below. Except perhaps for Essen, German cities, too, experienced higher levels of ethnic-based mobilization from below than Liège and levels similar to or even higher than Ghent. Structural integration presented a more complicated, variegated picture, but German policymakers in the four case cities could point to more specific instances in which their efforts had produced moves toward congruence.

6   CONCLUSION

The Defining Role of Policies and Institutions

Ethnic tensions have not always and everywhere wracked European societies. The integration of Europe's immigrants, it should be clear by now, is a broad, multifaceted, dynamic process that has affected the "hosts" as much, if not more, than the former "guests." Integration is not an endpoint or the outcome of any discrete policy. Nor have policies designed to bring about immigrant integration necessarily gone missing or fallen short. Countries have varied in the extent to which they have developed direct and indirect integration policies and in their emphases, content, bases, and impact. Those institutional and policy differences have mattered.

Cultural Drawbacks

The three national and eight city cases examined in this study offer up evidence that contradicts widely held cultural explanations for the ethnic conflict rightly or wrongly associated with the presence of immigrants. Specific ethnic traits could not be responsible for the shape of social relations in the cases considered. The range of bases on which immigrants organized was wide, with ethnicity, national origin, immigrant status, religion, gender, and generation serving as meaningful lines of division depending on the institutional context. Ethnic groups mobilized in ways that resembled those adopted by others in the same city more than those of the same group in another city. Groups that clashed in some cities—Turks and Kurds, Moroccan Arabs and Berbers—collaborated in others. Associational fragmentation would be the rule in one place; peak immigrant associations would form in another. The Turks who were seen as difficult in German cities were viewed as relatively unproblematic in their Dutch and Belgian equivalents. Nor did youths of the same ethnic background who were involved in criminal behavior engage to the same degree or in the same criminal "specialties" across the cases.

Ethnic identities were strengthened by the spatial concentration of immigrants, which intensified in Belgium, Germany, and the Netherlands. This trend, too, was the result of conscious national-level choice to give freer rein to market forces in the housing and urban policy areas. Local-level policies intended to avoid such clustering were outgunned. Certain European neighborhoods witnessed the accumulation of social disadvantages like unemployment and dependence on social assistance, and immigrants and immigrant-origin residents suffered disproportionately from them. While Berlin, Essen, Rotterdam, and The Hague witnessed higher immigrant concentrations in most neighborhoods, citywide segregation indices actually declined, due to ethnic spreading into areas adjacent to a gentrifying city core. No less than in the other cities, however, concentration acted more as an intermediary factor than as a cause. It was not easy to tell whether the phenomenon was good or bad for immigrant integration or social relations overall. Did it isolate immigrants from society at large or provide them a safe harbor within which to stitch their own networks of mutual assistance? That question sparked serious study and debate in all three countries. Immigrant concentration neighborhoods were feared in some places but ignored or welcomed in others.

Even cities with moderate immigrant and immigrant-origin populations contained areas with extremely high concentrations. Yet they did not come close to producing acute crisis or sustained violence. Sporadic Turkish-Kurdish clashes and gang activity in the German cities, intermittent rioting in Belgium, and spikes in petty crime in Bremen, Berlin, Rotterdam, and Liège notwithstanding, the streets remained calm. The gains of anti-immigrant political parties were not substantial, except in Ghent and Rotterdam. There, ethnic conflict did not register particularly high scores, and local governments upheld policy programs that blended cultural pluralism and liberal multiculturalism in the face of political pressures. Since the trend toward concentration was constant, whereas ethnic tensions ebbed and flowed, residential settlement patterns seem like an unlikely candidate to explain ethnic conflict in any event.

Everywhere, those of immigrant stock, and certainly non-European Union residents such as Turks and Moroccans, faced discrimination and were in an undeniably disadvantaged position. Nevertheless, in a number of neighborhoods marked by a buildup of social problems, something resembling a multicultural society was materializing. It may have seemed that Dutch cities had gone farther down that path. Dutch governments at all levels poured more money into policies that were intended to further immigrant integration:

nearly impossible to quantify, given the array of departments and agencies implicated, interviewed Dutch officials named figures that were significantly higher than in Belgium and that ranged from ten to fifteen times the spending levels in Germany.

Nevertheless, at least until its employment picture began to darken seriously in the late 1990s, Germany in several respects produced greater structural congruence than either the Netherlands or Belgium. With the possible exception of The Hague, overall immigrant unemployment was as high if not higher in the early 2000s than in the late 1970s in each of the cases. Eurostat's comparative employment data are controversial, but, taken broadly, they indicate that the gap between nonnationals' and nationals' joblessness rates had not narrowed at the national level (see table 6.1). Then again, there were improvements in immigrants' vocational training picture. The number of small ethnic businesses was on the rise. Even though the picture could be muddled, and statistics could be found to back almost any conclusion, there was no consistent decline in immigrants' housing or educational situation either, aside from a stagnating situation in Liège. Structural integration policies had not brought congruence, but they had not suffered wholesale malfunction. Speaking very generally, the trend line was mildly positive in Belgium, Germany, and the Netherlands. The relative strength of Dutch funding streams yielded results. But German policymakers had paid more attention for a longer time to immigrants' position in the labor and housing markets and the educational and vocational training systems; hence, immigration remained largely off the national political agenda until unification at the end of the 1980s. Whatever the host country, when specific ethnic or age groups were targeted for particular policy attention, occasionally dramatic improvements were evident. Examples here were the betterment of Turks' naturalization rates across the Ger-

TABLE 6.1

Percentage of Unemployed Nationals and Nonnationals, 1985–2000

	1985	1990	1996	2000
Belgium				
nationals	10.0	6.0	8.0	6.6
non-EU nationals	33.0	28.0	32.0	30.7
Germany				
nationals	6.0	4.0	8.0	8.0
non-EU nationals	13.0	8.0	18.0	15.5
The Netherlands				
nationals	10.0	7.0	6.0	2.7
non-EU nationals	33.0	35.0	26.0	10.1

Source: Münz (2000, 12), Muus (2001, 45), European Commission (2002, 210–11).

man cases and young Moroccans' position in Dutch schools, as well as the comparatively more impressive educational advances of young Turks compared to Italians in Nuremberg.

Regardless of their formal citizenship status, young people of immigrant origin, especially Moroccan and Turkish, lagged behind their native-stock counterparts in all of the case countries and cities. Their special disadvantages were often hidden in analyses within national statistics and rights, even in the disaggregated, relational indicators employed here. There were steady, if far from sufficient, improvements in the structural and educational position of the children and grandchildren of the immigrant workers in many of the cases. They suffered their most serious disconnection in high unemployment rates, limited access to vocational training programs, and weak involvement in associational and political opportunities. Berlin was the only case city in which the local administration managed to incorporate to some degree the movements of the younger immigrant generations, perhaps out fear that they might join forces with the radical youth groups active in the city-state. Rotterdam launched a concerted campaign to get out the immigrant youth vote, but the outcome was disappointing.

National and local officials alike routinely echoed Elmar Hönekopp of the Institut für Arbeitsmarkt- und Berufsforschung in Nuremberg in describing young immigrants' abysmal structural position and political-cultural disaffection as a "ticking time bomb" (Stallmayer and Heckel 2001). Some second- and third-generation immigrants turned inward into ethnic and religious "cocoons," closing themselves off within their own pseudo-traditional institutional world. Immigrant-origin youngsters' contacts with the host society sometimes boiled down to the police station and the social assistance office. Other youths appeared to opt for more destructive pursuits. Compared to their native-stock peers, immigrant-origin youths exhibited higher rates of delinquency. They suffered disproportionately from the classic precursors of criminality: poverty, racism, school failure, unemployment, drug addition, dysfunctional families, and male gender. What's more, there were any number of immigration laws that only nonnationals could break. When studies have corrected for such factors, as in one undertaken in Liège in the early 1990s (Junger-Tas, Terlouw, and Klein 1994), no clear relationship appears between ethnic origin and particular forms of criminality. At the national levels and in certain areas of Belgium, Germany, and the Netherlands, crime was a major concern and was chronically equated with youngsters of certain ethnic backgrounds. Despite moderately elevated rates in Berlin, Bremen, and Rotterdam, though, it did not attain distressing proportions in any of the case cities.

There were social welfare cutbacks in the three case countries, but spending on policies dealing with the integration of immigrants of all generations was maintained or even increased. Local officials in Germany were caught between escalating costs for social assistance programs, for which they were responsible, and those for integration projects. All the more impressive, therefore, was their refusal to scale back spending on policies affecting immigrant-origin populations. The same could be said of Ghent and Rotterdam, where political pressures rivaled financial exigency in tempting authorities, in vain, to scale back their policies on behalf of immigrant-origin residents. The widespread belief that the climate was a harsh one for measures to enrich social provision for the vulnerable was thus not always valid as far as immigrant-origin minorities were concerned. There was a willingness in certain contexts to address "newly recognized risks," if rarely enough money to carry efforts through fully (compare Pierson 2001). Whether that fiscal problem itself was a matter of choice or not was another question.

The Impact of Institutions and Policies

This study has argued that institutional factors and policies had a more profound influence on the nature of social relations than other proposed causes. The local cases were selected because of their comparability, as cities and in terms of the ethnic composition of their immigrant-origin populations. Their policymakers' reputations for their progressive responses to immigration rendered it easier to ascertain the impact of such interventions. In the eight cities ethnic conflict reached different levels and followed distinct patterns over time.

As suggested above, there was far less ethnic conflict on the ground than might reasonably have been expected, given the stakes, the shrill political rhetoric, and the profound socioeconomic trials facing Germany, the Netherlands, and Belgium during the period in question. Social relations could hit very rough patches, and issues would come along that riled residents and followed ethnic contours. Overt clashes were few. Ethnic conflict showed itself to be more localized and cyclical than typically portrayed. By itself, higher structural or political-cultural disconnection did not necessarily lead to conflict. Nor did congruence always yield harmony. In fact, greater political-cultural congruence could produce more ethnic "noise" when it occurred in the context of structural disconnection.

Reliable measures for ethnic conflict are hard to come by. Integration is notoriously difficult to gauge as well. Every way of measuring both phenomena has its advantages and disadvantages and can lead to highly idiosyncratic findings. Segregation, residential concentration, crime, educational achievement, cultural and political participation—at what level should they be assessed? On which bases and following what logic should taxonomies be constructed? Quantifying the structural aspect of integration appears straightforward, but the available national and local statistics are only very broadly comparable. Congruence could represent positive improvement or stem from backsliding or slower rates of population increase among native-stock popu-

lations. Political-cultural integration is so difficult to appraise that many ana-
lysts have either not tried (see de Regge 2002) or have simply cataloged existing immigrant associations (see Martiniello and Kagné 1997).

When talk turns to immigrant integration, comparative analyses have con-
jured up reams of statistics. Alternatively, scholars have built their analysis on
the rights granted immigrants in host societies (Brubaker 1992; Esser and
Korte 1985). The Austrian Federal Ministry of Science and Transport has
funded a major ongoing research project that measures integration according
to legal status in a set of European countries. Plotting countries on a scale
between 0 (most liberal) and 1 (most restrictive), that assessment has the
Netherlands doing better than Belgium and Germany in terms of security of
residence, social rights and benefits (broadly construed), political rights, and
conditions governing the acquisition and loss of citizenship. Belgium scores
highest on civil rights and family reunification. Only when it comes to social
rights does Germany avoid a third-place showing, besting Belgium. The two
countries tie on political rights, both earning a dismal rating of .67, compared
to middling .50 for the Dutch (Çinar, Davy, and Waldrauch 1999, 8).

While interesting and illuminating, such subjectively derived indices lump
many factors together and pass over the local-level and diachronic variations
that have been the central preoccupation in the analysis here. Besides, reality
can deviate from formal rights; much can transpire between the lip and the
cup. Authorities at all levels of governance have enjoyed room for maneuver,
influencing how rights are converted into implemented policies. A revealing
example comes from Germany, where well-intentioned allies of the immigrants have promised a future of intercultural harmony, if only the country
would abandon its citizenship laws based on *jus sanguinis.* Ignored has been
the fact that even though legislation had loosened German nationality law
even prior to the reform in 2000, thousands of immigrant-origin youths who
met all of the stringent requirements for formal German citizenship had failed
to apply in previous years. Moreover, the two national groups on which the
analysis here has focused, Turks and Moroccans, have fewer political rights
than native-stock residents and those from elsewhere in Europe. But the economic, civil, social, and political rights that they do enjoy are substantial
and—thanks to bilateral treaties signed with the EC—more extensive than the
rights of other non-Europeans. Why, then, have they experienced high levels
of structural and political-cultural disconnection in so many places?

This study responds to the need for more qualitative, comparative, and
process-oriented analyses. It has compared immigrant integration trajectories
across critical national and local cases, measuring incorporation in terms of
trends over time between immigrant-origin and native-stock residents either
toward (congruence) or away from (disconnection) each other along both the
structural and political-cultural dimensions. Imperfect, although in truth no
more subjective than quantitative or rights-based studies, such an approach

has the benefit of allowing for (without assuming) subnational variations in integration. The local-level comparison suggests in which cities non-European immigrants' position in the labor market and housing markets and educational and vocational training systems approached those of native-stock residents in the context of an overall trend toward residential concentration. In the political-cultural realm the issue has been whether their cultural access, consultative possibilities, formal citizenship status, political rights and participation levels, and associational life were resembling those of residents from indigenous backgrounds. The focus has been the direction of movement even more than the achieved level of integration. Portrayed graphically, the results—which themselves paper over much nuance—show just how complex the issue of immigrant integration really is (see tables 6.2, 6.3, and 6.4).

Institutions and policies did much to determine the observed patterns and whether or not ethnic conflict was a by-product. Social relations hinged on the intensity with which officials instituted policies to facilitate immigrants' structural and/or political-cultural integration, in conjunction with their treatment of ethnicity and their sequence. Different policies marked out different boundaries around social groups. When efforts to advance integration proceeded on an ethnic basis, they gave a boost to ethnic identities. When political-cultural policies stressed ethnicity, and structural congruence was slow in coming, conditions were rife for the outbreak of quarrels that took on ethnic coloring.

Affecting both policies and outcomes was the broader issue of social welfare restructuring, which in Germany, the Netherlands, and Belgium entailed various amounts and forms of decentralization, privatization, and delegation to nonprofit associations and self-help groups. Institutional evolution did not leave the same room everywhere for notions of self-help and empowerment.

TABLE 6.2
Immigrant Concentration and Structural Integration Trends
1970s Compared to Late 1990s
Better = toward congruence.

City	Spatial Concentration	Labor Market	Housing	Education/ Training
Essen	Higher	Mixed	Better	Better
Nuremberg	Higher	Mixed	Better	Better
Bremen	Higher	Mixed	Better	Better
Berlin	Higher	Mixed	Better	Better
Rotterdam	Higher	Mixed	Better	Better
The Hague	Higher	Better	Better	Better
Liège	Higher	Mixed	Mixed	Mixed
Ghent	Higher	Mixed	Better	Mixed

TABLE 6.3

Immigrant Political-Cultural Integration Trends

1970s Compared to Late 1990s

Better = toward congruence

City	Culture	Consultation	Naturalization	Political Rights	Associations
Essen	Neutral	Worse	Better	Neutral	Better
Nuremberg	Better	Neutral	Better	Neutral	Better
Bremen	Better	Better	Better	Neutral	Better
Berlin	Better	Neutral	Better	Neutral	Better
Rotterdam	Better	Better	Better	Better	Better
The Hague	Better	Better	Better	Better	Better
Liège	Neutral	Worse	Better	Neutral	Neutral
Ghent	Better	Better	Better	Neutral	Better

TABLE 6.4

Indicators of Conflict by Late 1990s

City	Far Right Political Strength	Highest Level of Ethnic Conflict	Associational Estrangement	Crime/ Insecurity
Essen	Low	Low	Moderate-High	Low
Nuremberg	Low-Moderate	Low	Low-Moderate	Low
Bremen	Moderate	Low-Moderate	Low	Moderate
Berlin	Low	Moderate	Low	Moderate
Rotterdam	Moderate-High	Low-Moderate	Low	Moderate
The Hague	Low-Moderate	Low	Low	Low
Liège	Low	Low	High	Moderate
Ghent	High	Low	Moderate-High	Low-Moderate

They did not apply to immigrant-origin populations or kindle ethnic identities in identical fashion across the cases.

Cross-national divergence was significant. Federal German authorities engaged in structural integration policies and studiously avoided ethnic targets. Simultaneously, however, they encouraged the "clientelization" of immigrants by the corporatist social welfare nonprofits—Caritas, Diakonisches Werk, and Arbeiterwohlfahrt—which organized them ethnoreligiously and vigilantly controlled their interactions with the host society. Politically, the foreigners' auxiliary councils, whether or not the opportunities they offered for consultative participation were meaningful, ordinarily followed ethnonational lines as well. They combined with social work practices to stimulate ethnic leadership and identities that surfaced with the reorganization of the German welfare state. That process led to a downward transference of responsibilities without the commensurate financial wherewithal.

The Netherlands, on the contrary, stressed ethnic identities openly and insistently from an early date, in the interests not of exclusion but of inclusion. Dutch social policies encouraged self-help and empowerment among immigrants, but decentralization transferred control over implementation (if not funding) more to municipal policymakers than to autonomous nonprofit and immigrant associations. The ethnic minorities policy and the social work sector did encourage bottom-up mobilization, and it emerged in the form of ethnic self-assertion. Internecine quarreling among ethnoreligious groups eventually gave pause to national officials, who borrowed a page from France's traditional republican model of individual integration and territorialized structural strategies.

It was just such a Jacobin approach that characterized French Belgium, where ethnic identities had no currency and political-cultural integration took a back seat to packages of neighborhood-based, indirect structural integration policies. As in some area of Germany, Walloon policies lent meaning to nonethnic collective categories. In Dutch Belgium, meanwhile, policymakers moved after a slow start to "minoritize" immigrants along ethnic lines like their Dutch cousins, discounting the structural dimension. Flemish officials' stimulation of self-organization was later and weaker than in the Netherlands, and it was stultified by the labyrinthine Belgian institutional system. Welfare state decentralization intensified centrifugal forces that magnified regional policy divergence, including the role ascribed to self-help groups. Some movement toward convergence was visible by the end of the 1990s, as Flemings and Walloons drew lessons from each other.

Local variation could be considerable as well. Cities like Essen and Nuremberg, envied or mocked in Germany for being quiet or boring, sooner or later played down ethnic identities in their approaches to immigrant integration, except in the area of education. Liège escaped ethnic turbulence by pushing that strategy even further, only to experience a higher crime rate and multiethnic disturbances that evoked France's suburban crisis. In Essen and Liège working-class and neighborhood identities that mitigated ethnic difference were promoted through general policies aimed at structural and, only secondarily, political-cultural integration. Ethnic conflict never presented a problem for authorities, yet the immigrants' detachment from institutional life substituted for it as a source of concern. Many of their needs were going unmet, and questions about the legitimacy of local democracy were raised. In Liège the Socialist-led administration adopted French-style urban and educational tactics pointed toward social exclusion and rooted in territorially delineated zones. Social policy and social work under such a scheme had more to do with maintaining top-down control than building capacity and self-reliance from the bottom up. Belying its location in the middle of stingy and hidebound Bavaria, Nuremberg was among the pioneers in according political and cultural access to immigrants and in encouraging their ethnic mobilization. It blanched at the resultant tensions, despite their rather modest proportions, and turned toward general policies that backed away from ethnic organizing and put the accent on individual and structural integration.

Urban centers renowned for being ethnically discordant locales, such as Berlin and Rotterdam, turned out to be those where higher crime rates had become associated with specific nationalities. Those cities and Ghent were characterized by a stress on political-cultural integration and an acceptance of self-help, empowerment, and ethnic identities. Those concepts retained their cachet in Ghent, where the Flemish Bloc's successes lent the false impression of a fractious and closed city, but bureaucratic bottlenecks kept them in check. National German structural policies took the edge off ethnic tensions in the German capital. Both it and, diffidently, Rotterdam were accentuating structural integration and playing down ethnic difference by century's end. The Dutch city's commitment to the new path firmed after Pim Fortuyn's triumph in 2002.

The two-city state of Bremen and the Dutch capital of The Hague, finally, blended strong support for ethnic based self-help organizing with equal insistence on structural integration and central management. Policymakers both generated and resolved interethnic conflict through their choice of interlocutors and dispersal of subsidies. The stronger flow of central state monies and nonnationals' more extensive political rights made it somewhat easier to perform the balancing act in the Dutch city. Under the shadow of a seemingly eternal budget crisis, Bremen's endeavors to fit in its immigrant-origin minorities went into a holding pattern. Hague officials were able to pursue their policy mix, by contrast, and even managed to withstand the Pim Fortuyn juggernaut that rocked their southern neighbors in Rotterdam.

As private-sector management techniques seeped into public-sector policymaking, five-year plans, benchmarks, and self-evaluation procedures became fixtures of the process. The heads of municipal agencies responsible for work with immigrant-origin populations and leaders of local immigrant and other associations were obliged to scramble for grants from state, provincial, regional, and national governments. Accountability and autonomy grew accordingly, as did paperwork and confusion. Funded in dribs and drabs, promising policies occasionally died on the vine. Others developed into models for national and even European policies. The impression one gains is of effervescence and mayhem in more or less equal measure.

Immigrants and the Welfare State

In the 1960s, the social welfare state tallied with a global project to resolve social problems in a comprehensive manner over the long term. By the 1990s, the discussion was more commonly about "approaches." The new outlook did not involve laws and structural budgets as much as experiments. Run by social workers and funded through the competitive grants process, they could be evaluated, limited in time, and abandoned at the drop of a hat. With no guarantee of survival, competition heated up among service providers and between them and other institutions (Ahkim 1998). Yet instead of favoring the dismantling of public services, these developments were more likely to promote their reconfiguration. Local social policy became a more complicated game.

Timing and historical ties had influenced immigration policies to create immigrant-origin populations of assorted sizes and combinations of ethnic backgrounds in (and within) Germany, the Netherlands, and Belgium. A maze of different legal statuses and privileges fragmented them, and local authorities and agencies expended an inordinate amount of time keeping track of changes and informing people. Nationality laws and naturalization procedures meant that there were host societies where the immigrant-origin population was comprised largely of nonnationals (Germany) and others where there were significant numbers of naturalized ethnic minorities (the Netherlands). Naturalization rates varied widely across the country cases and time: in Germany from 0.3 percent in 1986 to 1.1 percent in 1997; in Belgium from 1 percent to 2.7 percent in 1997; and in the Netherlands from 3.3 percent to 11.4 percent (Eurostat 2000; SOPEMI 1998).

As an employer, the public sector was slow to open to nonnationals, more so in Germany and Belgium than the Netherlands. Naturalization was required for most civil-service employment, notwithstanding a host of programs that tried to finesse that restriction. Even naturalized immigrants and the nonnationals who enjoyed limited suffrage in the Netherlands were not incorporated enough into the civil service or the welfare state's personnel rolls to constitute a full-fledged pressure group or regime of ethnic relations management. At most, there were pockets of ethnic minority voter strength in certain Dutch and Belgian urban districts. Local-level officials were charged with guaranteeing social order and seeing to the needs of all residents. Where immigrant suffrage was not permitted, authorities time and again put considerable effort into devising consultative institutional setups that offered some possibility of both learning what immigrants wanted and shaping their relationship with the rest of the population. The immigrant associations that interacted with such institutions provided ersatz employment opportunities for the better educated and served as something of a compensatory mechanism for limited possibilities in the local administration.

The immigrant elite that emerged was eager to speak on behalf of all immigrant-origin residents yet had no mandate to do so. Only a small segment of the population was brought in; the bulk fell further from involvement. A trend toward political-cultural disconnection was present in many of the case cities. Unease with the implications for democracy and social order led policymakers in all of them, albeit with varying degrees of zeal, to devote more energy toward fostering participation among immigrant-origin residents by the early 2000s. The co-optation that some have associated with the African American experience with the U.S. welfare state was thus not yet as evident in Germany and Belgium, nor even in the Netherlands. The relationship between the welfare state, ethnicity, and immigrant integration proved far more complex and changeable.

There were moves everywhere to bundle local policies and tailor them to specific neighborhoods as authorities endeavored to replace earlier ad-hoc, scattered, and duplicated efforts with more systematic, coordinated, and efficient policies. There was interest in rationalizing the approaches taken to immigrant-origin populations, so as to address their special needs without "problematizing" their presence. The terms employed to refer to immigrant-origin populations changed over the years. In their variety and variability, they bore witness to their ambiguous position in the host societies.

In Germany and the Low Countries, the people who were once referred to as "foreigners" and "guest workers" gradually became known as "immigrants" and "migrants," except on the part of those who felt that immigrants were not bona fide members of the local society. Talk in Germany was not always of "foreigners"; nor was it only political correctness that accounted for deviations from that term (compare Koopmans 1999, 634). The hands-down favorite in progressive policymaking circles in Germany was "foreign co-citizens" (*ausländische Mitbürger*), which mixed exclusion and inclusion in a telling manner. By century's end, immigrants were even being called "ethnic minorities" (*ethnische Minderheiten*) or "Turkish-stock" (*türkischstämmig*) citizens once in a while, but there was no clear pattern, even among the immigrants themselves (AESSW 1997a; ALB 2001, 11; ASB 1998, 10).

In the Low Countries, backers and opponents of multiculturalism more consciously wielded language as a tool. The qualitative change in Dutch policy in the mid-1980s was evident in a change of terminology, as "minorities policy" (*migrantenbeleid*) replaced "foreigner policy" (*vreemdelingenbeleid*). Following on the heels of this switch was the official adoption of the designation "nonindigenous person" (*allochton*). Local officials used the same language as their national-level counterparts, evidence of the top-down quality of Dutch policymaking in general. Flanders used "*allochtonen*," too, but policymakers in Ghent took pains to refer to "ethnic-cultural minorities" (*etnisch-culturele minderheden*) when discussing the immigrant-origin component of that diverse group. In Liège, by contrast, the city's Socialist and republican traditions came through in expressions like "personnes étrangères ou d'origine étrangère" (foreign or foreign-origin people). Only the far right talked of "guest workers" by the late 1990s in Belgium and the Netherlands, although concerns about Muslim immigrants manifested themselves in jesting references in Dutch-speaking areas to the "*Allah-chtonen*."[1]

It has become the fashion in much of the scholarly literature on immigration and social policy recently to ascribe explanatory power to the politics of symbolic interaction, public philosophies, policy "framing," and constructed discourses.[2] Running against that trend, the argument here is that the labels attached to immigrant-origin populations served as a signal of underlying policies, ideological positions, and power relations, rather than as a shaper of policy debates and choices or the glue holding together an elite consensus. In other words, language—discourse—followed politics and policies. More often than not, there was a wide gap between what went on at the street level and the discourse of politicians, educators, and social workers.

Similarly, the print and broadcast media helped set the tone for policy deliberations but did not direct them. At the national level they habitually equated immigrant-origin populations with crime and insecurity and perpetuated notions that they posed a problem for the host society and a threat to social order and cohesion. They employed the sorts of "hydraulic" metaphors—with immigrant flows and waves crashing against Europe's borders—familiar to North Americans. Ideology and partisan political affiliation often dictated media depictions of immigrants and their role in the labor market, society, schools, and politics.

All eight case cities included public relations work in their plans to facilitate immigrant integration. Several had full-blown media policies. Local officials, sometimes in collaboration with their state and national counterparts, met with local print journalists and editorial boards to encourage sensitivity and fairness. They urged advertisers not to forget the immigrant-origin components of their customer base. They worked with local radio and television to expand their coverage of issues of concern to all residents and to accentuate the positive aspects of diversity whenever possible. Public-access cable television and independent radio gave immigrants a chance to present themselves and their "normal" lives in the host society on their own terms, as well as to keep homeland cultures alive. Shows and publications in German, Dutch, French, and the "mother" tongues proliferated from the late 1980s on. As the 1990s drew to a close, cities like Nuremberg, Berlin, and Rotterdam were developing intercultural internet policies.

Multiculturalism and Civil Society

The integration policy story has much to say about multiculturalism in its variegated manifestations and practices in Europe. As policy in the case countries and cities, it took several forms, each of which had its limitations and dysfunctional aspects. In Penninx and Slijper's formulation (1999), Germany, the Netherlands, and Belgium all began with essentially a liberal national approach toward immigrants, emphasizing their individual rights and assimilation. In Essen and Liège the movement was then toward liberal neutrality (dealing with immigrants as individual citizens in the public realm) with as yet only hints in certain policy sectors of liberal multiculturalism or the pursuit of equality while accepting targeted policies on a provisional basis. Bremen and Nuremberg—after its flirtation with techniques that safeguarded ethnic identities—swung toward acceptance of liberal multiculturalism. Berlin blended it with elements of cultural pluralism (defining ethnonational identity as constitutive of immigrants in the public realm). So, too, did Rotterdam, The Hague, and Ghent, which all even toyed with aspirations toward communitarian pluralism (where an Islamic pillar would become an emancipating variant of preexisting consociational arrangements). When European officials veered toward that end of the multicultural continuum, they were likely to define integration (in other words, congruence) less as immigrants fitting in to the host society and more as immigrants fitting themselves into host societies that were transformed in turn. Nevertheless, the bottom line for host-society officialdom everywhere by the early 2000s was set in terms of the local language—German, Dutch, French—as a lingua franca, a basic set of responsibilities that all residents owed to the community, and civil liberties cast in individualistic terms that dovetailed with those ensconced in the international human rights regime. Liberal multiculturalism appeared to be ascendant nearly everywhere.

From European experiences with multiculturalism flowed implications for immigrants' position in civil society. Integrally associated with the notions of empowerment and self-help was the belief in the liberating benefits of "self-organization." Under liberal nationalism it was designed to take place within native organization's auspices, while under liberal neutrality it was a private-sector activity that the public sector should ignore. Cultural pluralism and communitarian pluralism, on the contrary, welcomed ethnic self-organization, the former because it offered a way to represent immigrant interests and the latter because identity-based activities were deemed vital to anyone's sense of well-being. For liberal multiculturalism, the pole toward which many progressive German, Dutch, and Belgian policymakers seemed drawn by the early 2000s, ethnic associations filled a temporary, instrumental function. They facilitated immigrants' cultural and social integration, yet with the goal of ensuring equality of opportunity and their own eventual relegation to the private sphere.

The idea was to legitimate immigrant-origin minorities by formally associating them with local-level consultative structures and social welfare delivery. Like the earlier incorporation of religious and linguistic minorities and economic interest groups (in particular radical syndicalist movements), which transformed them into state-affirming entities, the emerging patterns of cooperation would lead to a "deprimordialization" of ethnic-based groups. Ethnic-group "corporatism" would guarantee immigrants a presence and a right to be heard in policy deliberations, giving them a stake in the system and reducing tendencies toward alienation. It would thus put the brakes on ethnic group demands for the sake of social peace or even turn their constituencies into the beneficiaries of political and economic payoffs to such a degree that ethnic consciousness would be weakened (Safran 1994).

Just as the trade unions or the confessional nonprofits had earlier spoken on their behalf, so, too, were immigrant associations supposed to become non-citizens' representatives. Not surprisingly, then, immigrants astonished and frustrated Europeans when they did not form organizations that corresponded to the prevailing model. Instead, immigrant associational life was rent by ideological, religious, ethnic, regional, and generational divisions. Public subsidy schemes could aggravate ethnic-based associations' weaknesses by creating a distance between their co-opted leaders and the rank and file. Competition and fragmentation arose whenever subsidies were doled out selectively. Only in cohesive Bremen did a peak immigrant associational federation form, although officials compelled the construction of less unified, less inclusive, and less bottom-up organizations in Essen, Liège, Rotterdam, The Hague, and Ghent.

Islam

Muslims and their organizations likewise bore out the contradictions of official responses to them. The far right's efforts to work up Islam into an obstacle to immigrant integration worked better in Rotterdam and Flanders, where integration policies embraced ethnicity and overwhelmingly concerned the political-cultural realm, than in places where structural integration tended to be more important. In their attempts to defuse tensions, authorities in the former areas wound up going further in their financial and other institutional support for Islam. In none of the case cities, even so, did the religion create extreme anxiety. Across the cases, Muslims were treated like any other ethnic group, like members of a monolithic religious tradition, like members of their respective national or subnational groups, like individual residents, and/or like a possible threat to domestic security—depending on where they settled.

Organizationally, they responded to such variable structuring. That responsiveness should not be too surprising. Islam had to have been flexible and adaptable to survive and spread under the most wide-ranging of conditions. Before immigrating to Europe, Muslims lived in countries in which their faith received dramatically different treatment. In their homelands Islam's diversity was impossible to ignore. In Turkey, where the staunchly secular Kemalist establishment has had to cope with a popularly elected Islamist government, the wearing of headscarves by parliamentarians and even male politicians' spouses has aroused even more impassioned debate than in Europe (see Kenes 2003). So far only a potential threat to Europeans, Islamist movements and parties have already shaken North African regimes to their foundations. Islamism managed to establish a toehold on the continent in no small measure because of European policymakers' decision to allow or even encourage Muslim instructors and religious leaders to immigrate. It was disappointment with existing social, political, and economic integration policies and their inability to reach Muslim youths that led some of them to turn to Islam as a source of identity and a locus of political mobilization. In the vast majority of its manifestations, European Islam proved a benign, even positive force.

Radical Islam did generate fear. Even before September 2001, police periodically dismantled an armed Islamist group or recruiting network. Afterward, there was a rise in anti-Muslim rhetoric and actions, as well as harsh responses on the part of some police and policymakers. In the eight case cities, there was a dramatic political reaction and change of tone—but, tellingly, not of policy—only in Rotterdam. Most European countries had witnessed the emergence of Islamist groups from the 1970s on, with the variance across them attributable to differences in the composition and size of their Muslim immigrant-origin populations, their colonial past (or lack thereof), and the extent of public recognition and state support they accorded to Islam. Recently, movements like Abou Jahjah's European Arab League have gained notoriety in Belgium and the Netherlands. Nevertheless, only a very small minority of Europe's Muslims has ever been involved in violent, radical groups or activities (see Ireland 1998).

A bigger concern in the cities examined here was the lack of cohesive Muslim associations. National officials' labors to structure a domestic and domesticated "European" Islam met with discouraging results. They ran against far stronger effects of institutional structuring along national and subnational ethnic lines. Local policymakers did what they could to integrate mosque associations into consultative structures. In the pair of Dutch cities, municipal and regional officials used their higher levels of control to fashion peak Islamic associations. In Europe's urban centers the relationship between local institutions and immigrant associations—both formal organizations and looser groupings, as well as secular groups and religious ones—was critical in determining the nature of ethnic relations. In the eight cities figuring here, local interethnic networks were, as a general rule, strong enough to weather the trends toward separatism and conflict that the introduction of market forces, spatial concentration, ethnic identities, and self-help and empowerment notions tended to engender. These conclusions dovetail with research on Northern Ireland by John Darby and his colleagues (1990) and on India by Ashutosh Varshney (2001) that has added nuance and caveats to unbridled optimism about the role of civil society.

Europe

Enthusiasm about European-level developments needs to be similarly tempered. Immigration practices and policies have undergone "Europeanization" over the past couple of decades. Collaboration was long fairly loose and ad hoc, and supranational authority has been strongest by far in the area of freedom of movement for member-state nationals within the EU. The Amsterdam

Treaty, signed in 1997 and effective in 1999, signaled the transition from informal intergovernmental cooperation to incorporation within European-level policymaking structures: immigration was to become a matter for actions adopted by the EU Council of Ministers based on EU Commission proposals (Geddes 2000). The EU heads of state and government followed up their Amsterdam agreement with personal commitments at their European Council meeting in Tampere in 1999 to enter into partnerships with the immigrants' countries of origin, control immigration flows, and fight against immigrant smuggling networks.

The European Commission has since worked toward a common legal framework for admission and residence by means of draft directives. They have dealt with such issues as crime prevention, border controls, labor market access, equal treatment in the workplace, and the admission of students and others entering the EU for nonremunerated purposes. A pair of instruments to combat undocumented immigration won formal European Council approval in October 2002, and political agreement was reached on several dossiers on asylum in January 2003. A month later, the European Council reached similar consensus on a draft directive concerning the right to family reunification. Like the others, that draft directive stuck with vague, nonbinding references that allowed member states to relax certain conditions if they wished.

Policy harmonization has been even slower in the area of immigrant integration, where, as with social policy in general, talk has prevailed over action. Long missing was any push to coordinate national policies, except in developing pan-European rules to cover the nationality of stateless children and refugees (Hansen and Weil 2001). The drive to stimulate immigrant political participation through a Migrants Forum has run aground on corruption scandals. That said, an agenda of immigrant inclusion has started to take shape at the EU level, allied with the promotion of economic and social cohesion. The Treaty of Amsterdam contained provisions for police and justice cooperation to deal with racism and xenophobia. Among the commitments made in Tampere was a vow to devise dynamic policies to ensure the integration of third-country nationals residing legally in an EU member state (CCE 1999). In 2000, a package of antiracism measures was adopted by the Council of Ministers. It consisted of a directive on ethnic discrimination and a directive on discrimination in employment, followed soon after by a European Community action program. Over the next two years, the European Commission presented two communications in which it recommended a common approach to immigration management that took into account the economic and demographic development of the EU, each member state's capacity for reception, and conditions in immigrants' homelands.

Those European-level initiatives grew in importance over the decades in the case countries and cities. Local officials looked to EU-level policies when formulating their own. Particularly in Germany, but also in Belgium, references to Europe could serve as a counterweight to more stringent national-level positions. When Article 13 of the Amsterdam Treaty came into effect in July 2000, it became the first binding, explicit law in Germany that forbade ethnic-based discrimination in the workplace, education, social security, and access to goods and services (BMI 2002). For immigrants from Turkey and North Africa, it was treaties between their homelands and the European Communities, enforced and broadened in their application by the European Court of Justice in Luxembourg, that guaranteed "their" workers in the EU equal civil, economic, and social rights. The European Court of Justice has repeatedly reaffirmed that workers from Algeria, Morocco, Tunisia, and Turkey must be treated like national workers in the field of social security (see Ireland 1995). The EU's membership dance with Turkey and its heightened interest in the Mediterranean basin has had an impact on national and local officials and immigrant-origin communities. On the one hand, the attention has awakened Europeans to the significance of immigrants' homelands and generated respect. On the other, residents with ties to Turkey and the Arab world have reacted angrily whenever their homelands have not received similar respect from Brussels. The EU's palpable discomfort when dealing with issues related to Islam can color the atmosphere in the neighborhoods (see Ireland 1998).

European funding has gained a higher profile. As the EU creeps toward harmonized, or at least coordinated, integration policies, its solidarity with immigrants has been expressed primarily through the structural funds. They do not constitute a single source of financing in the EU budget; each covers a specific thematic area. The two most important to immigrant integration have been the European Regional Development Fund (which finances infrastructure, job creation, local development projects, and aid to small firms) and the European Social Fund (which promotes reintegration of the unemployed and disadvantaged into the workforce, primarily through training and recruitment aid). Immigrants and refugees have become a priority, although policies have normally targeted them as part of a broader group, such as poor people or women, or specific geographical areas, such as disadvantaged neighborhoods and decaying urban centers.[3]

A related source of support has been the networks of European cities that the European Commission has cultivated and in which Rotterdam, The Hague, Ghent, Liège, and Berlin—and the other German cities to a lesser extent—have participated. Serving as forums in which to compare policies and determine best practices, three partially overlapping networks have fit within the Local Integration/Partnership Action (LIA) program, focusing on different aspects of integration: a network known as Elaine, overseen by the European Center for Work and Society, has worked on ethnic minorities policies; Eurocities, on urban policies; and Neighborhoods in Crisis, on local-level renewal. Hundreds of pilot projects, conferences, and workshops received assistance under the aegis of the LIA, which was co-funded directly by the European Commission between 1996 and 1999 and indirectly thereafter. The successful effort in Rotterdam to increase Moroccans' and Turks' turnout in the 1998 municipal election was a LIA project, for example, executed by a nonprofit organization. In The Hague an LIA project helped to develop inner-city Schilderswijk and Transvaalwijk, with their many immigrant-origin residents and institutions, into a multicultural shopping area and tourist attraction (see LIA 1999). Those and similar success stories in Belgium and Germany notwithstanding, the LIA was hard-pressed to meet its express objective of encouraging network building, public-private partnerships, and the multiplier effects of local initiatives. EU-backed projects have suffered from short time horizons, unrealistic expectations, limited and intermittent funding, intrusive bureaucratic oversight, and rapidly shifting priorities. The Elaine network was dissolving by the end of the 1990s.

Many of the proposals winning LIA and EU backing have operated along ethnic lines, and they have featured the participation of ethnic minority associations and ethnically defined "target groups" and the notion of empowerment. It went without saying that "migrant and ethnic minority businesses" played a key role in local socioeconomic development and represented the best means to social inclusion (ECWS/Elaine 1999). Countries like Belgium and Germany that imposed special legal requirements on immigrant entrepreneurs were called on to enforce equal treatment. European-level officials frequently advised their local-level colleagues to "consult all of the ethnic communities" in their city, without explaining whom that meant and how such contacting would proceed (LIA 1999).

The impact of European policies on immigrant integration, in sum, has been growing but remains partial and ambiguous. Amid the welter of policies and programs and despite the EU's unwillingness to impinge on national prerogatives, the outlines of a liberal multicultural consensus have been coming into view. Policymakers in Brussels celebrate diversity and welcome expressions of ethnic identity. Of late, they have also been stressing the need to set down and harmonize rules on immigrants' rights and responsibilities. The EU has begun to argue that government services and voluntary associations play a crucial role in immigrant integration. Equal access is vital to having immigrants avoid social exclusion, but some types of service provision intensify it, isolating immigrants from the rest of the community and hindering their integration into the educational system and the labor market ("European Union" 2003). As in the case countries and cities, there is a dawning agreement that their obligations include respect for as yet largely undefined fundamental host-society values and a readiness to learn host-society languages. Ethnic identities and associations, it appears, will eventually find their proper place in the purely private realm.

The United States

The policy debates over immigrant integration in Europe should raise American eyebrows. For the direction of policy change, if not the liberal multicultural goal, has generally been in the opposite direction across the Atlantic—namely, from extreme decentralization and nonprofit delegation to a greater central (federal) role. In the process, Americans and Europeans have come to wrestle with many of the same issues. Gary Klass (1985) has noted that for a long time the United States had been unique in disposing of such a short time frame to deal with the problems posed by mass immigration and the cultural differences associated with it. European societies had had centuries to stabilize and mitigate their internal cultural differences before the onset of social legislation. In contrast to the American settler society, which built itself with voluntary and forced immigration, the struggle to incorporate immigrants in Europe began after their permanent presence had already become irrefutable.

If, as the late Abdelmalek Sayad (1997) observed, to think about diversity is to think about the state, then American settlement policies could be seen as the sign of a weak, decentralized, and regionalized political system. The frequent use of private and nonprofit associations to accomplish public purposes has earned the American state such monikers as the "franchise" (Wolfe 1975) or the "enabling" state (Kramer 1981). National governments have acted as a partner, patron, financier, and purchaser of services of voluntary organizations whose reliance on governmental support has ebbed and flowed.

Nowhere did this relationship hold more firmly than in the area of immigrant integration. For most of the country's history, there were few federal programs with immigrants' social, economic, or civic integration as an explicit aim (Glazer 1998). The United States had neither a full-fledged urban policy, minority policy, or immigrant assimilation policy (Weir 1998). Policymakers relied on the voluntary engagement of faith-based charities, urban political machines, immigrants' own mutual aid associations, and state and local governments, which were responsible for the emerging public school system. The Americanization movement in the interwar period gave a coercive twist to that approach. After it receded with the immigration quotas of the 1920s, however, the United States returned to its earlier ways. Even with most immigration cut off, state and local institutions and associations served to absorb migrants moving within the country: the Great Migration of African Americans from the South to the North, the "Okies" from the Dust Bowl to California, and Puerto Ricans to the cities of the East Coast (Martin 1999).

It has been the tragic distinctiveness of the African American experience that has given "bite" to issues of multiculturalism and diversity in the United States (Glazer 1999). During the social turbulence of the 1950s and 1960s, immigrant issues found their spot at the table. Coalitions emerged among civil rights and labor groups that led to linkages between community activists and government programs. The first enforcement of federal antidiscrimination laws in housing and public accommodation, in fact, followed from violations against temporary workers *(braceros)* from Mexico. The civil rights movement helped fashion a framework of policy reform, best seen in Congress' decision to drop the *bracero* program and to eliminate the national origins quota in the mid-1960s.

Heavier and more diverse inflows of refugees and asylum seekers hastened the shift toward federal involvement in the 1960s. The institutional response to the hemorrhage from Cuba wound up establishing a federal-state relationship that endured into the 1980s. It entailed direct federal assistance to a targeted national group and a targeted region, South Florida (Bach 1993). The federal government soon assumed responsibility for helping all refugees to integrate. The Department of State negotiated with nonprofit agencies, many of them church related, to act as surrogate "sponsors" for admitted refugees. The Department of Health and Human Services provided transitional assistance, and some public benefits not available to immigrants (Supplementary Security Income, Transitional Assistance to the Needy, and food stamps) were extended (Martin 1999).

That relationship between the public and nonprofit sectors underwent restructuring with the New Federalism of the Ronald Reagan years as the government in Washington withdrew from local programs and turned responsibilities for settlement and other policies to municipal and state authorities. Consequently, the latter become de facto interest groups that competed against each other for necessary resources, which they would then use to assist voluntary associations working with refugees. Financing remained highly centralized, therefore, even as policy formulation and implementation returned to more typical decentralization and nonprofit delegation. By the 1980s, this trend had led subnational officials to institute settlement programs that represented a sort of "refugee-ization" of integration programs for labor immigrants. Inequality widened among regions and groups under the pressure of resource competition. That development, in turn, stirred up pressures for more intense central state tutelage during the two Clinton administrations (Edmonston and Passel 1994; Gans 1997).

Influxes from across the developing world and the heated political reactions that they have unleashed have further thrown makeshift arrangements and the laissez-faire attitude underpinning them into crisis in recent years. The United States has been transformed from a European-based population to a multicultural "world nation." Many of the newcomers have held to elements of their cultures of origin and have thus been perceived as unwilling to dissolve into American culture. As people of color, many have also faced discriminatory barriers limiting opportunities and inhibiting integration. Some scholars of

American immigration have responded to growing concerns over social cohesion with assessments of immigrants' contributions to the economy (Borjas 1999) and the role of ethnic capital and ethnic entrepreneurship (Foner, Rumbaut, and Gold 2000; Portes 1995). Others have jumped into the debate that has opened over the advisability of developing full-fledged integration policies (Aleinikoff 1998; DeSipio and de la Garza 1998).

In fact, the country has not faced such widespread reconsideration of its immigration and integration policies since just after the turn of the twentieth century, the period that saw the spread of nativism and the Dillingham Commission recommend that Congress reduce the overall level of immigration. There have been signs that recent "assimilation anxiety" has prompted a new willingness to reconsider the meaning and path to incorporation and integration in the United States (Waldinger 1996). Most prominently, the U.S. Commission on Immigration Reform, headed by the late U.S. Representative Barbara Jordan of Texas, posed a series of thorny questions in its report to Congress in 1997 that closely resembled those nagging at Europeans:

> Are we, as some contend, on the verge of developing new notions of citizenship and community, ones that successfully weave together our multiple allegiances from the local to the universal? Should the notion of individual membership in a single nation-state be replaced by an emphasis on group representation, cultural rights, and membership in multiple countries? Or would such new notions of transnational and multicultural citizenship threaten basic principles of American democracy? Will the shared civic identity that makes both self-governance and the protection of rights possible suffer if these changes come to pass? (Pickus 1998, 7).

In its report, *Becoming American: Immigration and Immigrant Policy,* the commission put the accent on the controversial theme of Americanization. It was described as a "heroic struggle" involving Americans and immigrants alike in a two-way "process of cultivating a shared commitment to the values of liberty, democracy, and equal opportunity" (Pickus 1998, 7). A two-pronged approach to the management of diversity had taken root in the United States: to celebrate but not legally enshrine diversity in American culture, and to strive for the "political incorporation of both immigrants and indigenous minorities into the liberal polity as equal individuals" (DeSipio and de la Garza 1992, 202).

Yet in both the structural and political-cultural realms, the approach to integration adopted in the United States has helped to structure ethnic identities. Although its institutions were never designed to advance an ethnically or racially conscious program, even the small, fragmented American welfare state has had differential effects on ethnic groups. Whereas it purports to protect equality of opportunity, the American model recognizes ethnoracial differences, allowing identities based on them to coexist and thrive (Patterson 1997). That course of action can both point at group-based inequalities that might otherwise go unnoticed and discourage divisions by laying down universalistic rules (Kymlicka 1995). Then again, it can also sanction segregation and inhibit integration by perpetuating those very inequalities.

Immigrant integration has been coming under federal purview more than before, and those policies have done little to discourage ethnic and racial identities. That movement has run into and been channeled by changes in social policy more broadly. In recent years, the trend within America's already modest welfare state has been toward more reliance on the market and voluntary associations, above all those organized along ethnic and religious lines, and more public-private partnerships (Smith and Lipsky 1993).

The upshot of those interacting developments has been consistently higher levels of structural and political-cultural disconnection, residential segregation, and ethnic conflict in the United States than in Europe. The attacks of September 2001 only exacerbated existing fears of ethnic balkanization. It would take local-level comparative analysis to ascertain whether American cities with more extensive integration policies, such as New York City and Miami, produced outcomes that ran counter to that general rule and achieved movement toward congruence.

The mounting interest in immigrant integration argues for placing the American experience in a cross-national comparative analytical perspective wide enough to encompass more than just other settler societies with liberal welfare states (compare Pearson 2001; Stasiulis and Yuval-Davis 1995). Likewise, Britain's more centralized liberal welfare state has been credited with producing fewer opportunities for discriminatory treatment and smoother minority incorporation than its decentralized American counterpart. Nonetheless, British policy has converged on an American-style "race relations" approach that has yielded relatively high levels of ethnic conflict (compare Lieberman 1998 with Favell 1998). Comparisons with more comprehensive continental European welfare states promise to make it easier to see how institutional and policy changes, the power of which this study has demonstrated, affect such conflict.

Conclusion

Europeans often shudder when contemplating ethnic relations in America. Their disquiet stems from their immigration myths and histories and their nation-building experiences. They have left the continent with a far lower tolerance for ethnic diversity and disorder than the United States. To illustrate, the level of ethnic-based discord that was reached in Nuremberg when its leaders decided to mix integration policies into broader, sectorially organized social policies would have barely raised a red flag in a large American "gateway" city—Chicago, Houston, Los Angeles, Miami, New York, or San Francisco—

with an even more diverse immigrant-origin population. Unemployment has been much higher in Europe since the 1980s, yet immigrants' concentration and segregation and their educational and training deficits have been lower than in the United States. Even after their restructuring, European social welfare states have provided more extensive protections and social control than their American counterpart. Although crimes against property in some urban areas have surpassed rates in the United States, Europe is still nowhere near as violent.

Regardless, the presence of immigrant-origin residents has provoked upset and clashes there. Pushed by the growing differentiation of immigrant-origin populations, European policymakers have proceeded from a wide array of starting points. Their policy responses are still far from converging, even if there were indications by the early 2000s of an emerging consensus on liberal multiculturalism. Everywhere, progress has been hard won and painstaking, and not infrequently fraught with political risk.

In a selection of progressive cities in three consensual democracies, however, that risk has been run. The same holds true in a range of other urban areas in Belgium, Germany, the Netherlands, and across Europe that were not selected for this study for methodological reasons. In a number of locales, the outlines are visible of a struggle to find the appropriate balance between individual and collective rights and obligations. By process of trial and error, officials have discovered policies that work in a number of sectors—from bilingual assistant teachers to accompany immigrant-origin cohorts through their classes, to apprenticeships in ethnic businesses, to teamwork with Muslim communities to develop sensitive solutions to issues like ritual slaughtering and distinctive burial practices.

The story centers on the hard work, frustrations, personality conflicts, gossiping, minor victories, and absence of recognition and material rewards that are the stuff of everyday ethnic relations in the neighborhoods. Such microlevel developments are not the subject of attention-grabbing headlines. They can add up to major changes, all the same. In helping to bring them about, residents of immigrant origin have been contesting established forms of citizenship and contributing to the revitalization of European civil society. By becoming "uncomfortable" for their host societies, they have posed a highly constructive challenge, forcing a search for solutions to social problems that also affect many poor of native stock (Hollands 1998). Immigrants have asserted values that the majority might assume or take for granted, just as their predecessors shaped the development of the trade union movement and social work in the nineteenth century (Baxter 1999). They have, in short, jolted policymaking systems, forcing a needed reconsideration of social welfare, education, housing, and other policies.

This challenge is on the whole a peaceful one that does not directly endanger the prevailing social order. Several of the neighborhoods discussed in this study have gained notoriety as crucibles of Europe's immigration dilemma: Droixhe in Liège, Tenever in Bremen, Delfshaven in Rotterdam, and, of course, Kreuzberg in Berlin. The reality is not as uniformly bleak as regularly believed: alongside all of the troubles facing such areas is evidence of solidarity, dynamism, and hope. By the same token, these heavily immigrant-origin neighborhoods are not especially picturesque or serene. It is misguided to picture the multicultural society as a paradise in which every group lives exactly as it sees fit. Social cohesion should not be confused with consensus. Nor should the co-optation of immigrant-origin elites, rarely representative of the populations for whom they claim to speak, be seen as guaranteeing integration or social control. The key is to find means of dealing with conflicts and differences of interest in such a way as to allow for the airing of alternative views and the development of a resolution acceptable to all parties.

Not all of the policies that officials devised in the case countries and cities worked as intended. Yet European policymakers did react. Learning by doing, they managed now and then to concoct finely tuned, effective strategies. The significance of such conclusions should be indisputable, given the centrality that both immigration and the welfare state promise to play in the continent's foreseeable future. At a time when Europe appears to be pulling up the drawbridge, it is reassuring to see that some policymakers there have taken to heart the warning issued by Johann Wolfgang von Goethe: "The country that does not protect its foreigners soon goes under."[4] As time passes, in fact, those foreigners are becoming Europe.

NOTES

Chapter 1. Introduction

1. "Nationality" here denotes the legal status of recognized membership in the state, or formal citizenship. "Citizenship" in a more general sense relates to members' rights and duties in the civic, political, economic, and social realms (see Feldblum and Klusmeyer 1999). To reduce confusion, I will refer to "immigrants" (nonnationals) or "immigrant-origin populations" (nonnationals and nationals together), except when use of another term might help illuminate policy differences or emphases in a particular context.

2. See, among others, Jupp and Kabala (1993), Adelman (1994), and Reitz (1998). Somewhat analogous arguments have been made with reference to the settled Finnish minority in Sweden (Skutnabb-Kangas 1983).

3. A perusal of the articles on the welfare state and immigrants that have appeared in the *International Migration Review,* the flagship journal of the field, will confirm the prevalence of the political economy dimension.

4. For comparative analyses of this phenomenon, see Kramer et al. (1993); Salamon and Anheier (1997); and Powell and Clemens (1998).

5. Self-help movements have drawn criticism from traditional Socialists and the trade unions, among others, who have denounced them as the province of the bourgeois and academic classes (Deimer, Jaufmann, and Pfaff 1987).

6. In some political science studies, "empowerment" becomes shorthand for the advantages for democracy that local, grassroots participation is hypothesized to generate (see Nylen 2002).

7. For more on empowerment, see Cannan, Berry, and Lyons (1992), Simon (1994), Shera and Wells (1997), and Henry, East, and Schmitz (2002).

8. On this issue compare, among others, Etzioni (1993), Putnam (1993, 2000), and Fukuyama (1999).

9. Yasemin Soysal, quoted in Joppke and Lukes (1999, 11).

10. This "official" figure leaves out sizable numbers of naturalized citizens in the Netherlands, which has traditionally had generous legislation in this regard and large numbers of former colonials.

Chapter 2. Germany

1. Five years earlier, the one-millionth guest worker overall to arrive in Germany, a Portuguese man, had received a flower wreath and a moped at the Cologne station (Özoguz 1999).

2. Most policymaking power remained with the Ministry of the Interior, which consulted frequently with counterpart ministers of the federal-states.

3. German law has distinguished between entitled naturalization, used primarily by spouses of German nationals, and discretionary naturalization, employed in the regular accession of immigrants to German nationality.

4. The SPD's trajectory took it from supporting "linguistic and cultural integration that necessitates a majority German presence" to arguing for multiculturalism as an "element of cultural policy in a democracy" and an "opportunity" for the "German majority and the ethnic minorities" (Grudzielski 1990, 40–41).

5. A reform in the legislation regulating local governments in October 1984 allowed nonnationals across the country to work in an advisory yet nonetheless official capacity as "expert residents" in municipal commissions (Sen 1996).

6. The benefits available to asylum seekers depended on a separate scheme.

7. For examples, see AWO Bundesverband (1991), Boll and Povedano-Sánchez (1991), Bastin (1993), and Filtzinger and Häring (1993).

8. With a total of some 190,000 foreigners, the GDR had had a total population that was merely 1.2 percent immigrant in 1989 (Ireland 1997).

9. They could also be placed in educational and training schemes *(Fortbildung- und Umschulungsmassnahmen).*

10. Alevites themselves are quite variegated, and Kurds are even more diverse: speaking some fifteen Indo-European dialects related to Farsi, they belong to a number of religions, sects, and cultural groups (see Can and Can-Engin 1997).

11. There might well have been more Turkish secret service agents in Germany, long a major field of operations, than radical Turkish Islamists. Turkish travel agencies, pro-government associations, small businesses, and banks have served as important sources of information for authorities in Ankara (Solmaz 1999).

Chapter 3. German Cities and City-States

1. Forms of municipal organization vary across the country. City-states like Berlin and Bremen blend local and state authority and thus enjoy relative autonomy. North Rhine–Westphalia, which British troops occupied after the war, has enshrined the elected municipal council as the locus of local political authority. The council elects an executive body of honorary mayors, sometimes overseen by a lord mayor, while similarly indirectly elected civil servants run the administration. Having been under American postwar control, Bavarian cities have a local system of checks and balances, with a directly elected lord mayor who has a vote in the municipal council and stands at the head of the local administrative apparatus (see Gunlicks 1986).

2. Legally charged with providing in-kind assistance to asylum seekers, local authorities enjoyed discretion in determining the specific mix of benefits.

3. It would be removed officially in 2003, when immigrants (but not refugees) won the explicit right to choose which institution to contact for social counseling (RAA 2003).

4. Much background information in this section came from personal interviews in Essen at the Geschäftsstelle für Kommunale Ausländerangelegenheiten in June 1993 and with officials at the regional Büro für Interkulturelle Arbeit in March 1997.

5. Personal interview with AWO members, Essen, November 1997.

6. Public forum, "20 Jahre Ausländerbeirat Nürnberg," Scharrer Gymnasium, Nuremberg, November 12, 1993. The state of Bavaria cut its budget for integration projects by 250,000 deutsche marks in 1993 (Santoso 1994).

7. Personal interview at the Inter-Kultur-Büro in the Amt für Kultur und Freizeit, March 1999. The Inter-Kultur-Büro is the municipal agency dealing with immigrants' cultural and political integration.

8. It was also from the ports of Bremen and Bremerhaven that seven million Germans and other Central Europeans left for America in the nineteenth century.

9. The index was derived from twenty-seven indicators, including the social assistance rate, housing conditions, and the size of the immigrant population under age eighteen. The number of asylum seekers was on a steady upswing by the late 1970s, later joined by an influx of ethnic Germans (SJS 1991).

10. Personal interview at the Arbeiterwohlfahrt Kreisverband Bremen, November 1992.

11. Personal interviews at the Dachverband der Ausländer-Kulturvereine, Bremen, August 1992 and April 1999.

12. Since the previous election, the state assembly had shrunk from one hundred to eighty-three deputies, and Bremen City's municipal assembly from eighty to sixty-seven (Gerling and Dohle 2003).

13. Personal interview at the Berliner Institut für Vergleichende Sozialforschung (BIVS), Berlin, November 1996.

14. Once it had proved its viability, it became eligible for state financial aid in 1999.

15. Personal interview at the BIVS.

Chapter 4. The Netherlands

1. Nationally controlled social service provision ended for former colonials around the same time, taken over by new, government-subsidized foundations.

2. In the Dutch context, minority status connotes a situation of residential segregation, cultural marginalization, and the accumulation of negative socioeconomic characteristics over the course of more than one generation (TWCM 1995).

3. The Labor Party received most of the minority vote, but the Christian Democrats also had their supporters. Ethnic-based parties were not common, but in neighborhood elections in Rotterdam in 1984, a Turkish-Islamic party, Hakyol, did receive more than 40 percent of Turkish voters' backing (Böcker 1994b).

4. In the Dutch system there are generally twelve years of "basic" education, followed by several levels of intermediate and secondary education.

5. A Dutch newspaper discovered that Haselhoef had never undergone imam training and that he was not a consultant to Islamic organizations, as he had claimed (SAMS Den Haag 2001b:6–7). In April 2002 a Rotterdam court acquitted imam Khalil el-Moumni on the charges of discrimination, finding that his remarks fell within the scope of the freedom of religion ("Acquittal of Imam" 2002).

6. To add further to the incongruities, the forward to the reissue of Pim Fortuyn's book *(Against) The Islamization of the Netherlands,* out in November 2001, was written by Abdullah Haselhoef.

7. Ironically, the elections had been necessitated by the resignation of Wim Kok's government that April over the publication of an official report on the role of the two hundred Dutch soldiers assigned by the UN to safeguard the Bosnian Muslim population of Srebrenica. The city fell to the Bosnian Serbs in July 1995, and some 7,500 Muslims subsequently disappeared and were presumed massacred.

8. The Crown appoints the mayors of the Netherlands' 647 local governments to a six-year term. Each mayor presides over a team of adjuncts and a municipal council. The latter can range in size from seven to forty-five seats. Members of the councils, the real locus of power, hold their directly elected office for four years (Obdejin 1994).

9. Personal interview at the Stedelijke Adviesraad Multiculturele Stad, Rotterdam, November 1999.

10. To read a letter rejecting a subsidy for the Kurdish Youth Association based on these criteria, see BDH (1998a).

11. The SAMS expressed reservations about the questionnaires employed to generate the data and suggested that The Hague study Rotterdam's Minorities Monitor (SAMS Den Haag 1998, 4).

12. SAMS Den Haag 2001b; and personal interview at the Stedelijke Adviesraad Multiculturele Stad, The Hague, November 1999.

Chapter 5. Belgium

1. Communists suffered under intense police repression in general, foreign ones even more so than native Belgians.

2. Later renamed the Consultative Council for Populations of Foreign Origin, it ended its mandate in 1991, although it continued to meet for several years thereafter.

3. Personal interview at the Centre pour l'Égalité des Chances et la Lutte contre le Racisme, Brussels, October 1997.

4. The Dutch Community eventually merged with the Flanders region, a fusion that did not occur between the French Community and Wallonia.

5. Out of 73,000 registered Muslim voters—representing a community of more than 350,000 total—only 45,000 went to the polls, dissuaded by a very short election campaign, problems with the campaign information and ballots, and an insufficient number of polling places (Akarkach 1999).

6. Unlike their Dutch counterparts, Belgian regions and cities can add to or subtract from the personal income tax. Local sales and property taxes may be levied in both countries.

7. Personal interview at the Service des Relations Interculturelles, Liège, April 1999.

8. The PSC became the less confessional Democratic Humanist Center in 2002.

9. Personal interview at the Stedelijk Migrantencentrum, Ghent, April 1999.

10. Ghent did not see the large, noisy Kurdish demonstrations that Brussels and Genk did.

11. Personal interview at the Provinciaal Integratiecentrum Oost-Vlaanderen, Ghent, April 1999.

12. Personal interview at the Stedelijk Migrantencentrum, Ghent, April 1999.

Chapter 6. Conclusion

1. Personal interview at the Stedelijk Migrantencentrum, Ghent, April 1999, and at the Service des Relations Interculturelles, Liège, April 1999.

2. Prominent examples include Entzinger (1996), Favell (1998), and Koopmans and Statham (2000) on immigration; and Cox (2001) and Schmidt (2002) on social policy.

3. Personal interview at the Centre pour l'Égalité des Chances et la Lutte contre le Racisme, Brussels, October 1997.

4. Quoted in *Stimme* (DAB, Bremen), vol. 7, no. 71 (1993): 28.

REFERENCES

Abrahamson, Peter, John Anderson, Jan Peter Hendriksen, and Jørgen Elm Larsen. 1988. *Poverty-Unemployment-Marginalization,* Research Report no. 1. Copenhagen: University of Copenhagen, Department of Sociology.

"Acquittal of Imam." 2002. *Migration News Sheet,* no. 230 (May): 19.

Adelman, Howard. 1994. *Immigration and Refugee Policy: Australia and Canada Compared.* Vol. 2. Toronto: University of Toronto Press.

Afdeling Bestuursondersteuning (ABO). 1997. *Leefbaarheidsmonitor.* The Hague: Gemeente Den Haag.

Afdeling Voorlichting en Externe Betrekkingen (AVEB). 1998. *Den Haag in cijfers.* The Hague: Gemeente Den Haag.

Afdeling Woonbeleid (AWB). 2000. *Het emancipatiebeleid naar allochtonen en erkende vluchtelingen.* Brussels: Vlaamse Gemeenschap.

Ahkim, Ahmed. 1998. "La médiation interculturelle dans les hôpitaux." *Osmoses* (July–September): 17–19.

Akarkach, Hassan. 1999. "L'élection de l'Exécutif des Musulmans de Belgique." *Osmoses* (April–June): 4–5.

Akinbingöl, Faruk, Steven Broers, Greetje Luif, Antonio Silva, and Albert Tahaparij. 1996. *Veiligheidsbeleving van allochtonen in Kralingen-Crooswijk.* Amsterdam: Vrije Universiteit Amsterdam.

Aksoycan-de Bever, I. 1987. *Mediterrane Nederlanders.* Nijmegen: SUN.

Aleinikoff, T. Alexander. 1998. *Between Principles and Politics: The Direction of U.S. Citizenship Policy.* Washington, D.C.: Carnegie Endowment for International Peace.

Algemene Planningsdienst (APD). 1993. *VFIK—Migranten anno 1993 cijfers voor het vlaamse gewest en de gemeenten.* Brussels: Ministerie van de Vlaamse Gemeenschap, Departement Algemene Zaken en Financiën.

Amt für Entwicklungsplanung, Statistik, Stadtforschung und Wahlen (AESSW). 1997a. "Informationen zur Lebenssituation nichtdeutscher Einwohnerinnen und Einwohner in Essen." *Informationen und Berichte zur Stadtentwicklung,* no. 91. Essen: Stadt Essen.

———. 1997b. "Konzept interkulturelle Arbeit: Dokumentation der Auftaktveranstaltung." *Informationen und Berichte zur Stadtentwicklung,* no. 92. Essen: Stadt Essen.

Amt für Kultur und Freizeit (AKF). 1994. *Nürnberg: Ausländerprogramm.* Nuremberg: Stadt Nürnberg, Referat für Stadtentwicklung, Wohnen, und Wirtschaft.

239

———. 1997. "Konzept Migration und Alter." Nuremberg: Seniorenamt.

———. 2003. *Jahreskontrakt 2003*. Nuremberg: Stadt Nürnberg.

Amt für Stadtforschung und Statistik (ASFS). 1997. *Statistisches Jahrbuch der Stadt Nürnberg*. Nuremberg: Stadt Nürnberg.

———. 1999. *Statistisches Jahrbuch der Stadt Nürnberg*. Nuremberg: Stadt Nürnberg.

———. 2002. "Dr. Maly (SPD) gewinnt." *Nürnberger Statistik Aktuell* (March 17): 1.

Andrew, Caroline, and Michael Goldsmith. 1998. "From Local Government to Local Governance—and Beyond?" *International Political Science Review* 19, no. 2 (April): 101–17.

Anheier, Helmut K., Eckhard Priller, Wolfgang Seibel, and Annette Zimmer, eds. 1998. *Der dritte Sektor in Deutschland*. Berlin: Wissenschaftszentrum Berlin.

Ankowitsch, Christian. 1993. "Arm dran: Studie zur sozialen Lage in der Hansestadt." *Die Zeit*, May 28, p. 17.

Arbeiterwohlfahrt (AWO) Bundesverband. 1991. *Aufnahme und Integration von Zuwanderern als politische Aufgabe*. Bonn: Arbeiterwohlfahrt Bundesverband.

Attar, Rachida. 1994. "Après les Polonais, les Italiens et les Grecs, les Marocains," in *L'annuaire de l'émigration*, ed. Kacem Basfao and Hinde Taarji, 20–21. Rabat: Fondation Hassan II.

Ausländerbeauftragte Berlin and Senator für Gesundheit, Soziales und Familie (AB/SGSF), eds. 1985. *Miteinander Leben: Bilanz und Perspektiven*. Berlin: SGSF.

Ausländerbeauftragte des Landes Bremens (ALB). 2001. *Grundsätzliche Aufgabenstellung und Bericht über Aktivitäten*. Bremen: Land Bremen.

———. 2002. "Alles, was nicht in das Bild passt." *Statements der Ausländerbeauftragten des Landes Bremen*. Bremen: Freie Hansestadt Bremen.

Ausländerbeauftragte des Senats Berlin (ASB). 1991a. "'Ich hab' nichts gegen Ausländer, aber.'" Berlin: Senatsverwaltung für Soziales.

———. 1991b. *Zur Lage der jungen Ausländergeneration*. Berlin: Senatsverwaltung für Inneres.

———. 1992. *Türkische Berliner—Berlini Türkler*. Berlin: Senatsverwaltung für Soziales.

———. 1998. *Bericht zur Integrations- und Ausländerpolitik 1996/1997*. Berlin: Senat von Berlin.

———. 2001. *Deutsche Jugendliche in Berlin zu Einwanderungs- und Integrationsfragen*. Berlin: Senatsverwaltung für Arbeit, Soziales und Frauen.

———. 2002. *Repräsentativumfrage zur Lebenssituation türkischer Berlinerinnen und Berliner*. Berlin: Senatsverwaltung für Arbeit, Soziales und Frauen.

Ausländerbeirat der Stadt Essen (ASE). 1996. "Miteinander für Gerechtigkeit: Veranstaltungen in Essen." Essen: Stadt Essen, Geschäftsstelle Ausländerbeirat Essen.

Ausländerbeirat der Stadt Nürnberg (ASN). 1993. "20 Jahre Ausländerbeirat Nürnberg." Nuremberg: Stadt Nürnberg.

———. 1997. "Die Arbeit des Ausländerbeirates der Stadt Nürnberg, 1990–1996." Nuremberg: Ausländerbeirat der Stadt Nürnberg.

———. 2000. *Dokumentation der bayerischen Projektbörse*. Nuremberg: Ausländerbeauftragte der Stadt Nürnberg.

Ausländerbeirat des Bezirkamtes Wedding (ABW). 1992. "Leitlinien zur Ausländerarbeit im Bezirk Wedding." In *Integration von Ausländern in die Regelversorgung eines Wohlfahrtsverbandes*, ed. Britgitte Döcker, 213–34. Berlin: Arbeiterwohlfahrt Berlin Kreisverband Wedding.

"Ausländerbeirat kleiner." 1996. *Nürnberger Nachrichten*, October 10, p. 13.

"Ausländer-Extremismus ist in Berlin besonders gefährlich." 1996. *Berliner Morgenpost*, November 18, p. 12.

"Ausländer in Berlin am 31. Dezember 1996." 1997. *Berliner Statistik: Statistische Monatsschrift*. No. 2:53–57. Berlin: Statistisches Landesamt.

"Authorities' Mishandling of Affair." 2003. *Migration News Sheet,* no. 238 (January): 53–54. Electronic version.

Bach, Robert L. 1993. "Recrafting the Common Good: Immigration and Community." *Annals,* vol. 530 (November): 155–70.

Bade, Klaus, ed. 1993. *Deutsch im Ausland—Fremde in Deutschland.* Munich: C. H. Beck Verlag.

———. 1994. *Ausländer, Aussiedler, Asyl.* Munich: C. H. Beck.

Baggio, Gildo. 1993. "Les étrangers en Allemagne." *Migrations-Société* 5, no. 27 (May–June): 14–24.

Bakas, Adjiedj, and Sjoerd Groenewold Dost. 1995. *Vers gebrand.* Lelystad: Stichting IVIO.

Baldas, Eugen, Konrad Deufel, and Helmut Schwalb, eds. 1988. *Isolation oder Vernetzung? Ausländerorientierte Sozialarbeit.* Freiburg: Lambertus Verlag.

Bals, Christel. 1991. "Konzepte, Theorien und empirische Ergebnisse zur Eingliederung von Ausländern." *Information zur Raumentwicklung,* no. 7/8: 513–22.

Barras, Christine, N. Nisolle, and Jean-Pierre Pourtois. 1998. *Les projets de lutte contre l'exclusion dans les Zones d'action prioritaire.* Mons: Université de Mons-Hainaut.

Barry, Brian. 2001. *Culture and Equality.* Cambridge: Harvard University Press.

Bartels, Edien. 2000. "Dutch Islam: Young People, Learning, and Integration." *Current Sociology* 48, no. 4: 59–73.

Barth, Fredrik, ed. 1969. *Ethnic Groups and Boundaries.* London: Allen and Unwin.

Barwig, Klaus, and Wolfgang Hinz-Rommel. 1995. *Interkulturelle Öffnung sozialer Dienste.* Freiburg: Lambertus Verlag.

Basfao, Kacem, and Hinde Taarji, eds. 1994. *L'annuaire de l'émigration.* Rabat: Fondation Hassan II.

Bastin, Klaus-Dieter. 1993. "Soziale Dienste für Migranten." *Infodienst Migration des Diakonischen Werkes,* no. 4: 54–61.

Bauer, Rudolph. 1993. *Intermediäre Nonprofitorganisationen in einem neuen Europa.* Rheinfelden/Berlin: Schäuble.

———. 1998. "Sozialarbeit und Migration." *Information zur Ausländerarbeit,* no. 1: 16–23.

Bauer, Rudolph, and Hartmut Diessenbacher, eds. 1984. *Organisierte Nächstenliebe.* Opladen: Westdeutscher Verlag.

Baumann, G., and Thijl Sunier, eds. 1995. *Post-Migration Ethnicity.* Amsterdam: Het Spinhuis.

Baxter, Quentin. 1999. *Indigenous Rights.* Wellington: Institute for Policy Studies, Victoria University.

Bayerisches Staatsministerium für Arbeit und Sozialordnung (BSAS). 1988. *Initiativen der Ausländerarbeit in Bayern.* Munich: BSAS.

Beauftragte für Migration und Integration (BMI). 2002. *Bericht zur Integrations- und Ausländerpolitik in Berlin 2000.* Berlin: BMI des Senats von Berlin.

Bechmann, Ulrich, and Petra Pfänder. 1994. *Ausländerbeiräte in Nordrhein-Westfalen.* Düsseldorf: Ministerium für Arbeit, Gesundheit und Soziales.

"Belgium." 2002. *Migration News Sheet,* no. 237 (December): 20. Electronic version.

Berger, Hartwig. 1987. "Arbeitswanderung im Wandel der Klassengesellschaft." *Migration* 1, no. 1: 7–19.

Berger, Maria, Meindert Fennema, Anja van Heelsum, Jean Tillie, and Rick Wolff. 2001. "Politieke participatie van etnische minderheden in vier steden." Amsterdam: Universiteit van Amsterdam, Instituut voor Migratie en Etnische Studies.

Berjonneau, Jean-François. 1997. "La contribution des églises." *Migrations-Société* 9, no. 50–51 (March–June): 39–42.

Bestuurdienst Den Haag (BDH). 1997. *Marokko in de wijk, de wijk in Marokko.* The Hague: Gemeente Den Haag.

————. 1998a. *Experimentenfonds Multi-culturele Stad, 1999.* The Hague: Gemeente Den Haag.

————. 1998b. *Samen verder naar een ongedeelde stad: Plan Multiculturele Stad, 1998–2001.* The Hague: Gemeente Den Haag.

————. 2000. *Nota herijking integratiebeleid.* The Hague: Gemeente den Haag.

————. 2002. *Haags interculturalisatie-diversiteitsbeleid, 1976–2001.* The Hague: Gemeente den Haag.

Bestuurdienst Rotterdam (BDR). 1998. *Effectief Allochtonenbeleid.* Rotterdam: Gemeente Rotterdam.

Bitter-Witz, Hannelore. 1992. *Ausländersozialdienste der Arbeiterwohlfahrt Bremen e.V.* Bremen: AWO.

Blaise, Pierre. 1994. "Conseils consultatifs communaux des immigrés." In *L'annuaire de l'émigration,* ed. Kacem Basfao and Hinde Taarji, 47. Rabat: Fondation Hassan II.

————. 1995. "Entre prévention et répression: Les contrats de sécurité." *Travailler le social,* no. 12: 70–89.

Blaise, Pierre, and Albert Martens. 1992. "Des immigrés à intégrer." *Courrier Hebdomadaire,* no. 1358–1359. Brussels: Centre de Recherche et d'Information Socio-Politiques.

Blanc, Maurice. 1991. "Von heruntergekommenen Altenquartieren zu abgewerteten Sozialwohnungen." *Information zur Raumentwicklung,* no. 6/7: 447–57.

Blanchard, Marie-Madeleine. 1998. "Médiation familiale en contexte interculturel." *Osmoses* (July–September): 13–16.

Blaschke, Jochen. 1987. "Die Bedeutung von Flüchtlingen für die Institutionalisierung der türkischen Immigranten-Community in Berlin." Berlin: Berliner Institut für Vergleichende Sozialforschung.

Blommaert, Jan, and Marco Martiniello. 1996. "Ethnic Mobilization, Multiculturalism, and the Political Process in Two Belgian Cities." *Innovation in the Social Sciences* 9, no. 1: 51–74.

Böcker, Anita. 1994a. "Op weg naar een beter bestaan: De ontwikkeling van de maatschappelijke positie van Turken in Nederland." In *Het demokratisch ongeduld,* ed. Hans Vermeulen and Rinus Penninx, 145–76. Amsterdam: Het Spinhuis.

————. 1994b. *Turkse migranten en sociale zekerheid.* Amsterdam: Amsterdam University Press.

Body-Gendrot, Sophie. 2000. *The Social Control of Cities?* Oxford: Blackwell Publishers.

Body-Gendrot, Sophie, and Marco Martiniello, eds. 2000. *Minorities in European Cities.* New York: St. Martin's Press.

Boelhouwer, P. J. 1997. *Concentratie, Segregatie en Probleemcumulatie in den Haag.* Delft: Delftse Universitaire Pers.

Böhm, Andrea. 1999. "Die Mischung macht's." *Die Zeit,* February 18, no. 8, pp. 13–16.

Böhm, Otto. 1999. "Über Multikultur, deutsche Leitkultur und Toleranz." *Multikulturelles Nürnberg—Zeitung des Ausländerbeirates,* no. 7 (June): 1–2.

Bolesch, Cornelia. 1994. "Auf Streife bis zur Spritgrenze." *Süddeutsche Zeitung,* July 14, p. 3.

Bolkestein, Frits. 1997. *Moslem in de polder.* Amsterdam: Uitgeverij Contact.

Boll, Fritz, and Thomas Olk, eds. 1987. *Selbsthilfe und Wohlfahrtsverbände.* Freiburg: Lambertus Verlag.

Boll, Rudolf, and José Povedano-Sánchez. 1991. "Multikulturelle Gesellschaft und soziale Arbeit im DPWV." *Deutsche Zeitschrift für Sozialarbeit,* no. 4: 92–94.

Bolt, Gideon. 2001. *Wooncarrières van Turken en Marokkanen in ruimtelijk perspectief.* Utrecht: Universiteit van Utrecht.

Bolt, Gideon, and Ronald van Kempen. 2000. "Concentratie en segregatie in Nederlandse steden." In *Segregatie en concentratie in Nederlandse steden,* ed. Ronald van Kempen and Gideon Bolt, 13–34. Assen: Van Gorcum.

Bommes, Michael. 1993. "Ethnizität als praktische Organisationsressource." In *Die Dritte Welt und Wir,* ed. Mohsen Massarrat, Birgit Sommer, György Széll, and Hans-Joachim Wangel, 355–65. Freiburg: Informationszentrum Dritte Welt Verlag.

Bonacich, Edna. 1988. "The Social Costs of Immigrant Entrepreneurship." *Amerasia Journal* 14, no. 1: 119–28.

Boos-Nünning, Ursula, and Thomas Schwarz. 1991. *Traditions of Integration of Migrants in the Federal Republic of Germany.* Berlin: Berliner Institut für Vergleichende Sozialforschung.

Borjas, George. 1988. *International Differences in the Labor Market Performance of Immigrants.* Kalamazoo: W. E. Upjohn Institute.

———. 1999. *Heaven's Door.* Princeton: Princeton University Press.

Bortolini, Massimo. 1996. "La presse et les immigrés en Belgique en 1995." *Migrations Société* 8, no. 44 (March–April): 109–22.

———. 1997. "Le prix de l'oubli." *Écarts d'identité,* no. 81 (June): 4–8.

———. 1999. "Belgique." *Migrations-Société* 11, no. 64/65 (July–October): 41–55.

Bougarel, Xavier. 1992. "Allemagne: Assimilation ou préservation des spécificités?" In *Immigrés en Europe: Politiques locales d'intégration,* ed. Didier Lapeyronnie, 19–54. Paris: La Documentation Française.

Bousetta, Hassan. 2000. "Political Dynamics in the City." In *Minorities in European Cities,* ed. Sophie Body-Gendrot and Marco Martiniello, 129–44. New York: St. Martin's Press.

Breckner, Ingrid, and Klaus M. Schmals. 1989. "Armut im Schatten der Moderne." In *Armut im Reichtum,* ed. Ingrid Breckner, Heinelt Hubert, Michael Krummbacher, Dieter Oelschlägel, Thomas Rommerlspacher, and Klaus M. Schmals, 111–230. Bochum: Germinal Verlag.

Breeger, Norbert. 2000. "Selbst ist der Migrant." *Stimme* 14, nos. 7–8 (July–August): 6–7.

Bremische Bürgerschaft. 1987. *Sachregister und Sprechregister für die 11. Wahlperiode (1983–1987).* Bremen: Senat Bremens.

———. 1991. *Sachregister und Sprechregister für die 12. Wahlperiode (1987–1991).* Bremen: Senat Bremens.

———. 1995. *Sachregister und Sprechregister für die 11. Wahlperiode (1991–1995).* Bremen: Senat Bremens.

———. 1997. *Landtag, 14. Wahlperiode, Drucksache 14/857,* October 23.

———. 1999. *Landtag, 14. Wahlperiode, Drucksache 14/1382,* February 16.

Breton, R. 1964. "Institutional Completeness of Ethnic Communities and the Personal Relations of Immigrants." *American Journal of Sociology,* no. 70: 193–205.

Brown, Michael K., and Steven P. Erie. 1981. "Blacks and the Legacy of the Great Society." *Public Policy,* no. 29 (Summer): 299–330.

Brubaker, W. Rogers. 1992. *Citizenship and Nationhood.* Cambridge: Harvard University Press.

Buijs, Frank J. 1998. *Een moskee in de wijk.* Amsterdam: Het Spinhuis.

Bukta, Susanne. 2000. "Der lange Weg—Islamischer Religionsunterricht in Deutschland." *Stimme* 14, no. 5 (May): 6–9.

Bundesvereinigung der Deutschen Arbeitgeber (BDAG). 1972. "Kommunistische Infiltration." *Information zur Ausländerbeschäftigung,* no. 12: 19.

Buttler, Günter. 1992. *Der gefährdete Wohlstand.* Frankfurt: Fischer Taschenbuch.

Can, Murat, and Hatice Can-Engin. 1997. *De zwarte tulp: De positie van Turken in Nederland.* Utrecht: Uitgeverij Jan van Arkel.

Cannan, Crescy, Lynne Berry, and Karen Lyons. 1992. *Social Work and Europe.* New York: Macmillan.

Castles, Stephen. 2002. "Migration and Community Formation under Conditions of Globalization." *International Migration Review* 36, 4: 1143–68.

Center for Equal Opportunities and Opposition to Racism (CEOOR). 2002. *Data Collection Employment*. Brussels: Kingdom of Belgium.

Centrum voor Onderzoek en Statistiek (COS). 1994. *Prognose ethnische minderheden Rotterdam 2008*. Rotterdam: COS.

———. 1995. *Deelgemeenten vergeleken*. Rotterdam: COS.

———. 1998a. *De bevolkingsgroep "overige arme landen" in Rotterdam*. Rotterdam: COS.

———. 1998b. *Statistisch Jaarboek Rotterdam en Regio*. Rotterdam: COS.

Cesari, Jocelyn. 2000. "Islam in European Cities." In *Minorities in European Cities*, eds. Sophie Body-Gendrot and Marco Martiniello, 88–99. New York: St. Martin's Press.

Chattou, Zoubir. 1998. *Migrations marocaines en Europe*. Paris: L'Harmattan.

Çinar, Dilek, Ulrike Davy, and Harald Waldrauch. 1999. "Comparing the Rights of Non-Citizens in Western Europe." In *Research Perspectives on Migration*, 8–11.Washington, D.C.: Carnegie Endowment for International Peace.

Cohen, James. 1999. "Intégration: Théories, politiques et logiques d'État." In *Immigration et intégration*, ed. Philippe Dewitte, 32–42. Paris: Éditions La Découverte.

Cohn-Bendit, Daniel, and Thomas Schmid. 1993. *Heimat Babylon*. Hamburg: Hoffmann und Campe Verlag.

Collège des Bourgmestres et Échevins (CBE). 2001. *Communiqué de presse du 20 décembre*. Liège: Ville de Liège.

Commissie Allochtone Leerlingen in het Onderwijs (CALO). 1992. *Ceders en de tuin*. Zoetermeer: Ministerie van Onderwijs en Wetenschappen.

Commissie Stedelijke Vernieuwing, Sociale Vernieuwing, Volkshuisvesting en Allochtonenbeleid (CSV). 1999. *Verslag van de bijzondere commissievergadering uitvoeringsprogramma's*. Rotterdam: Gemeente Rotterdam.

Commissie voor Welzijn, Gezondheitszorg, Sport en Recreatie Den Haag (CWGSR). 1998. *Evaluatie Stichting Islamitisch Haags Platform*. The Hague: Gemeente Den Haag.

Commission des Communautés Européennes (CCE). 1999. *Conclusions de la Présidence*. Brussels: CCE.

Conseil Communal de la Ville de Liège. 1995. *Liège contre le racisme*. Liège: Ville de Liège.

Conseil Économique Wallon (CEW). 1960. *L'Économie de la région liégeoise*. Liège: CEW.

Cooke, P., ed. 1989. *Localities*. London: Sage.

Coronel, Mercita. 1998. "Revolutie aan de Maas." *Migranten Informatief*, no. 128 (October): 20–25.

Cox, Robert H. 1993. *The Development of the Dutch Welfare State*. Pittsburgh: University of Pittsburgh Press.

———. 2001. "The Social Construction of an Imperative." *World Politics* 53, no. 3 (April): 463–98.

Crawford, Beverly. 1998. "The Causes of Cultural Conflict: An Institutional Approach." In *The Myth of "Ethnic Conflict,"* ed. Beverly Crawford and D. Lipschutz, 98:3–43. Berkeley: University of California Press, University of California International and Area Studies Digital Collection.

Crul, Maurice. 2000. *De sleutel tot succes—over hulp, keuzes en kansen in de schoolloopbanen van turkse en marokkaanse jongeren van de tweede generatie*. Amsterdam: Het Spinhuis.

Dachverband der Ausländer-Kulturvereine in Bremen. 1992. "Kapitulation der Politik." *Stimme* 6, no. 61 (September): 6.

Darby, John, Nicholas Dodge, and A. C. Hepburn, eds. 1990. *Political Violence: Ireland in Comparative Perspective*. Belfast: Appletree Press.

Das, P., and H. Arslan. 2000. *Kleur in het middenveld*. Rotterdam: Erc. Research.

Dashort, Hyacintha, and Milana van der Werf. 1995. *Tussen djellaba en disco: Marokkaanse meisjes aan het woord*. Haarlem: Stichting Kleur in 't Werk.

Dassetto, Felice. 1998. "Naar een belgische Islam?" In *Belgische toestanden,* ed. Marc Swyngedouw and Marco Martiniello, 143–50. Antwerp: Standaard Uitgeverij.

Debuisson, Marc, Thierry Eggerickx, and Michel Poulain. 1993. "Démographie des grandes agglomérations urbaines en Wallonie." *Courrier Hebdomadaire,* nos. 1422–23. Brussels: Centre de Recherche et d'Information Socio-Politiques.

DEGRIN. 1992. *Initiativ werden.* Nuremberg: DEGRIN.

Deimer, Klaus, Dieter Jaufmann, and Martin Pfaff. 1987. "Komparative Evaluation sozialpolitischer Trägersysteme und Leistungsformen." In *Staat, intermediäre Instanzen und Selbsthilfe,* ed. Franz-Xaver Kaufmann, 255–72. Munich: R. Oldenbourg Verlag.

de Jong, Wiebe. 1986. *Interetnische verhoudingen in een oude stadswijk.* Delft: Eburon.

———. 1996. "Achterstandswijken." *Migranten-studies* 12, no. 2: 72–78.

Delcroix, Catherine. 1992. "Pays-Bas: Une volonté de 'discrimination positive.'" In *Immigrés en Europe: Politiques locales d'intégration,* ed. Didier Lapeyronnie, 145–64. Paris: La Documentation Française.

Deloy, Corinne. 2003. "The Socialists and Liberals in Power Win the Belgian General Elections." Paris: Fondation Robert Schuman.

De Mas, Paolo, and Rinus Penninx. 1994. "L'islam dans une société laïque et multiconfessionnelle." In *L'annuaire de l'émigration,* ed. Kacem Basfao and Hinde Taarji, 540–44. Rabat: Fondation Hassan II.

de Regge, Martine, ed. 1997. *Stedelijke integratiedienst Gent.* Ghent: Stad Gent.

———. 2002. *Minderhedenbeleidsplan 2003–2005.* Ghent: Stad Gent, Schepen Sociale Zaken, Huisvesting en Emancipatie.

de Rudder, Véronique, and Christian Poiret. 1999. "Affirmative action et 'discrimination positive.'" In *Immigration et intégration,* ed. Philippe Dewitte, 397–406. Paris: Éditions La Découverte.

Deschamps, Luk, and Koenraad Pauwels, eds. 1992. *Bibliografie: eigen organisaties van migranten.* Brussels: Ministerie van de Vlaamse Gemeenschap.

DeSipio, Louis, and Rodolfo O. de la Garza. 1992. "Making Them Us: The Political Incorporation of Culturally Distinct Immigrant and Non-Immigrant Minorities in the United States." In *Nations of Immigrants,* ed. Gary P. Freeman and James Jupp, 202–16. Oxford: Oxford University Press.

———. 1998. *Making Americans, Remaking America: Immigration and Immigrant Policy.* Boulder: Westview Press.

Deslé, Els. 1993. *Immigratie van vreemdlingen in de stad.* Brussels: Vrije Universiteit Brussel, Interuniversitaire Attractiepool 37.

———. 1996. *Arbeidsbemiddeling en/of werklosencontrole.* Brussels: Vrije Universiteit Brussel.

———. 1997. "Brussel 1968–1995: De politieke constructie van een migrantenprobleem." In *Migrantenpolitiek in Brussel,* ed. Els Deslé, Alain Meynen, and Kristel Vandenbrande, 7–23. Brussels: Vrije Universiteit Press.

Deutscher Caritasverband. 1992. *Arme unter uns.* Freiburg: Lambertus Verlag.

Devillé, Anne. 1996. "La réforme de la loi relative aux étrangers." *Courrier Hebdomadaire,* no. 1538. Brussels: Centre de Recherche et d'Information Socio-Politiques.

Dienst Welzijn, Facetbeleid Migranten (DWFM). 1993. *Afspraken 1994 Multi-culturele Stad.* The Hague: Gemeente Den Haag.

Dinse, Jürgen. 1992. *Zum Rechtsextremismus in Bremen.* Bremen: Edition Temmen.

Direction Bijstandszaken (DBZ) Den Haag. 1997. *Stimuleringsproject turkse en marokaanse jongeren.* The Hague: Ministerie van Sociale Zaken en Werkgelegenheid.

"Discussion." 1992. In *Schutzgesetze gegen ethnische Diskriminierung,* ed. Ausländerbeauftragte des Senats Berlins, 140–78. Berlin: Senatsverwaltung für Soziales.

Döcker, Brigitte, ed. 1992. *Integration von Ausländern in der Regelversorgung eines Wohlfahrtsverbandes.* Berlin: Arbeiterwohlfahrt Berlin Kreisverband.

Doering, Martina. 1996. "Keiner wollte den Job." *Berliner Zeitung,* November 13, p. 3.

Dominguez Martinez, S., S. M. Groeneveld, and E. W. Kruisbergen. 2002. *Integratiemonitor.* Rotterdam: Erasmus Universiteit and Sociaal Cultureel Planbureau Rotterdam.

Doomernik, Jeroan. 1995. "The Institutionalization of Turkish Islam in Germany and the Netherlands." *Ethnic and Racial Studies* 18, no. 1 (January): 46–63.

Échevinat des Relations Interculturelles (ERI). 2002. *Répertoire des associations interculturelles liégeois.* Liège: Ville de Liège.

Eddaoudi, Ali. 1998. *Marokkaanse jongeren: Daders of slachtoffers?* Rotterdam: Donker.

Edmonston, Barry, and Jeffrey S. Passel. 1994. *Immigration and Ethnicity: The Integration of America's Newest Arrivals.* Washington, D.C.: Urban Institute Press.

Effinger, Herbert. 1985. *Selbsthilfe und Arbeitsmarkt in Bremen.* Bremen: Netzwerk Selbsthilfe Bremen-Nordniedersachsen, Zentrum für Europäische Rechtspolitik, and Angestellten-kammer Bremen.

"Die Einbürgerung." 1994. *Stimme* 8, no. 72 (February): 10–11.

Engbersen, G., A. Hemerijck, and W. Bakker, eds. 1994. *Zorg in het europese huis: Grenzen van nationale verzorgingsstaten.* Amsterdam: Uitgeverij Boom.

Engel, Jürgen. 1982. *Die Arbeitsmarkt im Land Bremen und Gewerkschaftliche Strategien.* Bremen: Deutsche Gewerkschaftsbund.

"Entschädigung auch für AusländerInnen." 1994. *Stimme* 8, nos. 77–78 (September–October): 13.

Entzinger, Han B. 1984. *Het minderhedenbeleid: dilemma's voor de overheid in Nederland en zes andere immigratielanden in Europa.* Amsterdam: Uitgeverij Boom.

―――. 1996. "Minderheden of medeburgers?" In *Etnische minderheden en wetenschappelijk onderzoek,* eds. Henk Heeren, Patricia Vogel, and Hans Werdmölder, 80–97. Amsterdam: Uitgeverij Boom.

Erie, Steven P. 1987. "Rainbow's End: From the Old to the New Urban Ethnic Politics." In *Urban Ethnicity in the United States,* ed. Lionel Maldonado and Joan Moore, 249–75. Beverly Hills: SAGE.

Esping-Andersen, Gøsta. 1991. *The Three Worlds of Welfare Capitalism.* Cambridge: Polity Press.

―――. 1999. *Social Foundations of Postindustrial Economies.* Oxford: Oxford University Press.

Es-Saida, Malika. 1994. "L'enseignement de l'arabe à Bruxelles." In *L'annuaire de l'émigration,* ed. Kacem Basfao and Hinde Taarji, 41–43. Rabat: Fondation Hassan II.

Esser, Hartmut. 1983. *Ausländerintegration im Ruhrgebiet.* Essen: Kommunalverband Ruhrgebiet.

Esser, Hartmut, and H. Korte. 1985. "Federal Republic of Germany." In *European Immigration Policy,* ed. Tomas Hammar, 165–205. Cambridge: Cambridge University Press.

Etzioni, Amitai. 1993. *The Spirit of the Community: Rights, Responsibilities and the Communitarian Agenda.* New York: Crown.

European Center for Work and Society (ECWS)/Elaine. 1999. *Thematic Report, 1996–1999.* Maastricht: ECWS.

European Commission. 2002. *Impact Evaluation of the European Employment Strategy—Technical Analysis.* Brussels: European Commission, Directorate-General for Employment, Industrial Relations, and Social Affairs.

"European Union." 2003. *Migration News Sheet,* no. 241 (April): 45–46. Electronic version.

Eurostat. 2000. *European Social Statistics: Migration.* Luxembourg: Office for Official Publications of the European Communities.

Facklam, Rolf-Gerhard, and Peter Sakuth. 1984. *Ortsamtsbeiräte in Bremen.* Bremen: Senator für Inneres.

Faist, Thomas. 1994. "Immigration, Integration, and the Ethnicization of Politics." *European Journal of Political Research* 25: 439–59.

———. 1998. "International Migration and Transnational Social Spaces." Working Paper No. 9. Bremen: Universität Bremen, Institut für Interkulturelle und Internationale Studien.

Favell, Adrian. 1998. *Philosophies of Integration.* London: Macmillan Press.

Feldblum, Miriam, and Douglas Klusmeyer. 1999. "Immigrants and Citizenship Today." *Research Perspectives on Migration,* 1–4.Washington, D.C.: Carnegie Endowment for International Peace.

Fennema, Meindert, and Jean Tillie. 2000. "Civic Communities in a Multicultural Democracy: Ethnic Networks in Amsterdam." Amsterdam: Institute for Migration and Ethnic Studies, Universiteit van Amsterdam.

———. 2001. "Civic Community, Political Participation, and Political Trust of Ethnic Groups." *Connections* 24, no. 1: 26–41.

Fichter, Dorota. 1998. "Bericht über die Wohnsituation der Ausländer." *Multikulturelles Nürnberg—Zeitung des Ausländerbeirates,* no. 6 (October): 3.

Filsinger, Dieter, Franz Hamburger, and Dieter Neubert. 1983. "Die Verwaltung der Ausländer." In *Sozialarbeit und Ausländerpolitik,* ed. Franz Hamburger, Maria-Eleonara Karstan, Hans-Uwe Otto, and Helmut Richter, 44–61. Darmstadt: Luchterhand.

Filtzinger, Otto, and Dieter Häring, eds. 1993. *Von der Ausländersozialberatung zu sozialen Diensten für Migranten.* Freiburg: Deutscher Caritasverband.

Fischer-Brühl, F. 1981. "Der Ausländerbeirat der Stadt Nürnberg." *Informationsdienst zur Ausländerarbeit,* no. 1: 80–82.

Foner, Nancy. 1997. "The Immigrant Family: Cultural Legacies and Cultural Changes." *International Migration Review* 31, no. 4 (Winter): 961–74.

Foner, Nancy, Rubén Rumbaut, and Steven Gold, eds. 2000. *Immigration and Immigration Research in the United States.* New York: Russell Sage Press.

Forbes, H. D. 1997. *Ethnic Conflict: Commerce, Culture, and the Contact Hypothesis.* New Haven: Yale University Press.

Francq, Bernard. 1992. "Belgique: Une situation transitoire." In *Immigrés en Europe: Politiques locales d'intégration,* ed. Didier Lapeyronnie, 55–82. Paris: La Documentation Française.

Freeman, Gary P., and James Jupp, eds. 1992. *Nations of Immigrants: Australia, the United States, and International Migration.* Oxford: Oxford University Press.

Friedrichs, Jürgen, Harmut Häussermann, and Walter Siebel, eds. 1986. *Süd-Nord Gefälle in der Bundesrepublik?* Opladen: Westdeutscher Verlag.

Fröhlich, Felix. 1993. *Entwicklung, Stand und Probleme der ausländischen Bevölkerung in Nürnberg.* Erlangen-Nuremberg: Friedrich-Alexander-Universität.

Fukuyama, Francis. 1999. *The Great Disruption: Human Nature and the Reconstitution of Social Order.* New York: Free Press.

Gaf, Friedrich W. 1990. "Bedingungen der Toleranz." *Evangelische Kommentare* 23, no. 1: 10–13.

Gaitanides, Stefan. 1992. "Die multikulturelle Gesellschaft." *Die neue Gesellschaft/Frankfurter Hefte* 39, no. 4: 316–22.

———. 1998. "Qualifizierung der sozialen Arbeit in der multikulturellen Einwanderergesellschaft." *Information zur Ausländerarbeit,* no. 2: 58–62.

Gans, Herbert J. 1997. "Toward a Reconciliation of 'Assimilation' and 'Pluralism'." *International Migration Review* 31, no. 4 (Winter): 875–92.

Garson, Jean-Pierre. 1997/98. "Opening Mediterranean Trade and Migration." *OECD Observer* 209 (December–January): 21–24.

Geddes, Andrew. 2000. *Immigration and European Integration.* Manchester: Manchester University Press.

Geelen, Henk, Alice van Unen, and Guido Walraven. 1994. *Services Integration for Children and Youth at Risk in the Netherlands.* The Hague: Sardes.

Geisser, Vincent. 1997. *Ethnicité républicaine: Les élites d'origine maghrébine dans le systéme politique française.* Paris: Presses de la Fondation Nationale des Sciences Politiques.

Geissler, Heiner. 1991. "Die bunte Republik—Multikulturelles Zusammenleben im neuen Deutschland und das christliche Menschenbild." *Zeitschrift für Ausländerrecht und Ausländerpolitik* 11, no. 3: 107–13.

Gemeente den Haag. 1995. *Onderwerp: Gemeentelijk emancipatiebeleid.* The Hague: Gemeente den Haag.

Gemeente Rotterdam. 1978. *Nota Migranten in Rotterdam.* Rotterdam: Gemeente Rotterdam.

———. 1983. *Moskeegroepen als zelforganisaties.* Rotterdam: Gemeente Rotterdam.

———. 1992. *De nieuwe Rotterdammers.* Rotterdam: Gemeente Rotterdam.

Gemeentelijk Allochtonen Overleg (GAO). 1996. *Vooruit bewegen in roerige tijden.* Rotterdam: Gemeente Rotterdam.

Gerling, Wigbert, and Christian Dohle. 2003. "Scherf trifft ins Schwarze." *Weser-Kurier,* May 26, p. 1.

Gidron, Benjamin, Ralph M. Kramer, and Lester M. Salamon, eds. 1992. *Government and the Third Sector.* San Francisco: Jossey-Bass.

Glazer, Nathan. 1998. "The Incorporation of Immigrants in the United States." In *Temporary Citizens or Future Citizens?* ed. Myron Weiner and Tadashi Hanami, 56–76. New York: New York University Press.

———. 1999. "Multiculturalism and American Exceptionalism." In *Multicultural Questions,* ed. Christian Joppke and Steven Lukes, 183–98. Oxford: Oxford University Press.

"Gleiche Rechte für alle Bürger." 1993. *Nürnberger Zeitung,* December 11, p. 16.

Gosseau, Chantal. 1998. "Les conseils représentatifs des centres régionaux ont dégagé leurs priorités d'action." *Osmoses* (October–December): 17–19.

Gramberg, J., J. Reverda, and R. Kleinegris. 1992. *Segregatie en bouwbeleid.* The Hague: Gemeente Den Haag, Afdeling Planologie.

Greve, Martin, and Tülay Çinar. 1998. *Das Türkishe Berlin.* Berlin: Ausländerbeauftragte des Senats Berlin and Senatsverwaltung für Soziales.

Groth, Klaus-Martin, and Johann Müller-Gazurek. 1983. *Ausländer-Sozialrecht.* Frankfurt: Metzner.

Grottian, Peter, Freidrich Kotz, and Michael Lütke. 1986. "Die Entzauberung der Berliner Sozialpolitik." *Leviathan,* no. 7: 201–12.

Groupe de Sociologie Wallonne. 1994. *Citoyenneté et gestion locale.* Louvain-la-Neuve: Université Catholique de Louvain.

Grudzielski, Stany. 1990. *Immigrés et égalité des chances en Europe.* Brussels: European Centre for Work and Society.

Gunlicks, Arthur B. 1986. *Local Governments in the German Federal System.* Durham: Duke University Press.

Gürtler, Christoph. 1985. *Rahmenplan Sozialwesen Ausländerprogramm der Stadt Nürnberg.* Nuremberg: Arbeitsgruppe Nürnberg-Plan.

Gutenberger, Ingo. 1993. "Stadt muss für Etat Rücklage auflösen." *Westdeutsche Allgemeine Zeitung,* July 10, p. 3.1.

Haelsterman, Wim, and Manuel Abramowicz. 1997. "La représentation électorale des partis d'extrême droite." *Courrier Hebdomaduaire,* nos. 1567–68. Brussels: Centre de Recherche et d'Information Socio-Politiques.

Hafez, Kai. 1996. "Das Islambild in der deutschen Öffentlichkeit." *Die neue Gesellschaft/Frankfurter Hefte,* no. 5 (May): 426–32.

Hanesch, Walter. 1992. "Armut und Armutsberichterstattung in Kommunen." *Theorie und Praxis der Sozialen Arbeit,* no. 1: 20–26.

———. 2001. "Armut und Integration in den Kommunen." *Deutsche Zeitschrift für Kommunalwissenschaften,* no. 1: 27–47.

Hannemann, Volker. 1997. "Ausländer in Bremen—Migration und Integration." *Niedersächsisches Jahrbuch für Landesgeschichte,* vol. 62: 101–24.

Hansen, Randall, and Patrick Weil, eds. 2001. *Towards a European Nationality.* London: Palgrave Macmillan Publishers.

Hardin, Russell. 1995. *One for All: The Logic of Group Conflict.* Princeton: Princeton University Press.

Hauptamt Essen. 1992. "Einrichtung einer Projektgruppe zur Überprüfung und Fortschreibung eines Konzeptes für die zukünftige Ausländerarbeit in der Stadt Essen." *Mitteilungsblatt der Stadtverwaltung Essen* 80, no. 9 (May 15): 220.

Häussermann, Hartmut, and Walter Siebel. 2001. "Integration und Segregation—Überlegungen zu einer alten Debatte." *Deutsche Zeitschrift für Kommunalwissenschaften,* no. 1:68–79.

Heijs, Eric. 1995. *Van vreemdeling tot Nederlander.* Amsterdam: Het Spinhuis.

Hein, Jeremy. 1993. "Immigrants, Natives, and the French Welfare State." *International Migration Review* 25, no. 3: 592–609.

Heinelt, Hubert, ed. 1997. *Modernisierung der Kommunalpolitik.* Opladen: Westdeutscher Verlag.

Heitmeyer, Wilhelm, Joachim Müller, and Helmut Schröder, eds. 1997. *Verlockender Fundamentalismus.* Frankfurt: Suhrkamp Verlag.

Heitmeyer, Wilhelm, Helmut Schröder, and Joachim Müller. 1997. "Desintegration und islamischer Fundamentalismus." *Aus Politik und Zeitgeschichte,* No. B7–8: 17–31.

Heller, Daniel. 1992. "Für eine qualitative Stärkung der direkten Demokratie." *Neue Zürcher Zeitung,* July 24, p. 21.

Henry, Sue, Jean East, and Cathryne Schmitz, eds. 2002. *Social Work with Groups.* Binghamton, N.Y.: Haworth Press.

Hermans, Philip. 1994. "Les centres d'intégration en Flandre." In *L'annuaire de l'émigration,* ed. Kacem Basfao and Hinde Taarji, 43–45. Rabat: Fondation Hassan II.

———. 1995. *Opgroeien als Marokkaan in Brussel.* Brussels: Cultuur en Migratie.

Hetzel-Burghardt, Elke, and Mechthild Schirmer. 1990. "Das niederländische Modell der Ausländerberatung." *Informationsdienst zur Ausländerarbeit,* no. 2: 67–68.

"Higher Number of Elected Councilors Who Belong to Ethnic Minorities." 2002. *Migration News Sheet,* no. 231 (June): 26.

Hinz-Rommel, Wolfgang. 1998. "Interkulturelle Öffnung sozialer Dienste und Einrichtungen." *Information zur Ausländerarbeit,* no. 1: 36–41.

Hockert, Reinhard, and Klaus Liebe-Harkort, eds. 1996. *Zur Kurdenfrage in der Türkei.* Frankfurt: Gewerkschaft Erziehung und Wissenschaft.

Hoffmann, Lutz. 1986. *Beiräte—Wahlrecht—Bürgerrecht.* Frankfurt: Dagyeli.

———. 1997. *Vom Gastarbeiterparlament zur Interessenvertretung ethnischer Minderheiten.* Wiesbaden: Arbeitsgemeinschaft der Ausländerbeiräte Hessen.

Hoge Raad voor de Volksontwikkeling (HRV). 1992. *Advies: Een cultureel beleid voor migranten.* Antwerp: HRV.

Hollands, Marlie. 1998. *Integratie als avontuur.* Utrecht: Uitgeverij Jan van Arkel.

Honeyford, Ray. 1988. *Integration or Disintegration?* London: Claridge Press.

Hooper, John. 2002. "The Twisty Politics of a Far-Right Showman." *Guardian,* May 7, p. 1.

Hotz, Dieter. 1987. "Arbeitslosigkeit, Sozialhilfeausgaben und kommunales Investitionsverhalten." *Information zur Raumentwicklung,* nos. 9/10: 593–610.

Huber, Berthold. 1990. "Multikulturelle Gesellschaft und Grundgesetz." *Die neue Gesellschaft/ Frankfurter Hefte* 37, no. 10: 914–22.

Huh, Suzanne. 2002. *Vortrag: Freiwilliges Engagement und Selbstorganisationen von MigrantInnen.* Frankfurt: Institut für Soziale Infrastruktur Sozialforschung.

Huntington, Samuel P. 1996. *The Clash of Civilizations and the Remaking of World Order.* New York: Simon and Schuster.

Huth, Suzanne. 2002. *Vortrag: Freiwilliges Engagement und Selbstorganisationen von MigrantInnen im Kontext wissenschaftlicher Diskussion.* Frankfurt am Maim: Institut für Soziale Infrastruktur und Sozialforschung.

Iletmis, Gule, and Brigitte Heimannsberg. 1993. "Das Boot ist leer." *Stimme* 7, no. 69 (August): 8.

Infodienst der Landesarbeitsgemeinschaft der Kommunalen Migrantenvertretungen (LAGA). 2001. "Integrationskonzepte in NRW." *Migration,* no. 13 (June): 1–25.

Institute for Migration and Ethnic Studies (IMES). *Annual Report 1996.* Amsterdam: IMES.

Institut für Stadtteilbezogene Soziale Arbeit und Beratung (ISSAB), ed. 1989. *Zwischen Sozialstaat und Selbsthilfe.* Essen: Klartext Verlag.

Ireland, Patrick. 1994. *The Policy Challenge of Ethnic Diversity.* Cambridge: Harvard University Press.

———. 1995. "Migration, Free Movement, and Immigrant Integration in the European Union." In *European Social Policy,* ed. Stephan Leibfried and Paul Pierson, 231–66. Washington, D.C.: Brookings Institution.

———. 1996. "Vive le Jacobinisme! Les Étrangers and the Durability of the Assimilationist Model in France." *French Politics and Society* 14, no. 2 (Spring): 33–46.

———. 1997. "Socialism, Unification Policy, and the Rise of Racism in Eastern Germany." *International Migration Review* 31, no. 119 (Fall): 541–68.

———. 1998. "Europe's Río Grande? The Mediterranean Basin, Islam, and the EU's Southern Strategy." Research Paper no. 54. Athens: Research Institute for European and American Studies.

———. 2000. "Reaping What They Sow: Institutions and Immigrant Political Participation in Western Europe." In *Challenging Immigration and Ethnic Relations Politics,* ed. Ruud Koopmans and Paul Statham, 233–82. Oxford: Oxford University Press.

Irwin, Galen, and Joop van Holsteyn. 1997. "Where to Go from Here? Revamping Electoral Politics in the Netherlands." *West European Politics* 20, no. 2 (April): 93–118.

Jacobson, David. 1996. *Rights across Borders.* Baltimore: Johns Hopkins University Press.

Jacquier, Claude. 1992. *Les quartiers américains, rêve et cauchemar.* Paris: Éditions L'Harmattan.

Jaedicke, Wolfgang, Kurt Ruhland, Ute Wachendorfer, Helmut Wollmann, and Holger Wonneberg. 1991. *Lokale Politik im Wohlfahrtsstaat.* Opladen: Westdeutscher Verlag.

Janssen, Nanco. 1995. *Volkshuisvestingbeleid an 'etnische minderheden'.* Utrecht: Onderzoeksverlag Utrecht.

Jennings, E. T., Jr. 1983. "Racial Insurgency, the State, and Welfare Expansion: A Critical Comment and Reanalysis." *American Journal of Sociology* 88 (6): 1220–36.

Jensen, Leif. 1989. *The New Immigration: Implications for Poverty and Public Assistance Utilization.* Westport, Conn.: Greenwood Press.

John, Barbara. 1995. *Towards a Tolerant and Peaceful, Democratic European Town.* Berlin: Ausländerbeauftragte des Senats Berlin.

Johnson, Norman. 1987. *The Welfare State in Transition.* Amherst: University of Massachusetts Press.

Joppke, Christian, and Steven Lukes, eds. 1999. *Multicultural Questions.* Oxford: Oxford University Press.

Junger, Tas J. 1995. "Preventie van criminaliteit in theorie en pratijk." *Sociale interventie* 4, nos. 3/4: 109–21.

Junger-Tas, J., G. Terlouw, and M. Klein, eds. 1994. *Delinquent Behavior among Young People in the Western World*. Amsterdam: Kugler Publications.

Jupp, James, and Marie Kabala, eds. 1993. *The Politics of Australian Immigration*. Canberra: Australian Government Publishing Services.

Kalpaka, Annita. 1992. "Rassismus und Antirassismus." In *Es geht auch anders!* ed. Gabriele Pommerin-Götze, Bernhard Jehle-Santoso, and Eleni Bozikake-Leisch, 93–101. Frankfurt: Dagyeli Verlag.

Kämper, H. 1987. "Arbeitslosigkeit im strukturschwachen Ruhrgebiet am Beispiel Essen." *Informationen zur Raumentwicklung*, nos. 9/10: 557–60.

Kanther, Manfred. 1996. "Deutschland ist kein Einwanderungsland." *Frankfurter Allgemeine Zeitung*, no. 265 (November 13): 11.

Kapphan, Andreas. 1995. "Nichtdeutsche in Berlin-West." *Berliner Statistik: Statistische Monatsschrift*. Berlin: Statistisches Landesamt. No. 12: 198–209.

Karapin, Roger. 1998. "Explaining Far-Right Electoral Successes in Germany." *German Politics and Society* 16, no. 3 (Fall): 24–61.

Karbach, Peter. 1990. *Nürnberg: Organisation und Struktur des städtischen Lebens*. Fürth: Wissenschaftlich-Publizistischer Verlag.

Kardoff, Ernst von. 1989. *Selbsthilfe und Krise der Wohlfahrtsgesellschaft*. Munich: Minerva Verlag.

Kassner, Bernd. 1993. "Nachbarn halten Nachtwache für türkische Bürger." *Westdeutsche Allgemeine Zeitung*, July 5, p. 3.1.

Kastoryano, Riva. 1996. *La France, l'Allemagne et leurs immigrés*. Paris: Armand Colin.

Katz, Michael B. 1995. *Improving Poor People*. Princeton: Princeton University Press.

Kaufmann, Franz-Xaver. 1987. "Zur Einführung." In *Staat, intermediäre Instanzen und Selbsthilfe*, ed. Franz-Xaver Kaufmann, 9–40. Munich: R. Oldenbourg Verlag.

Kayser, Muriel. 1996. "Les fonctions sociales des associations de quartiers populaires et les immigrés." *Migrations-Société* 8, no. 45 (May–June): 49–60.

Kenes, Bülent. 2003. "Veiled Resistance of Status Quo Against Reform Steps." *Turkish Daily News*. April 27, p. 5.

Kieselbach, Thomas, and Fauke Klink, eds. 1991. *Arbeitslosigkeit und soziale Gerechtigkeit*. Bremen: Angestelltenkammer.

King, Desmond, and Gerry Stoker, eds. 1996. *Rethinking Local Democracy*. London: Macmillan.

———. 1999. *In the Name of Liberalism*. Oxford: Oxford University Press.

Kirbach, Roland. 1999. "Patchwork der Kulturen." *Zeitpunkte*, no. 2 (February): 26–27.

Klass, Gary M. 1985. "Explaining America and the Welfare State." *British Journal of Political Science* 15, no. 4 (October): 427–50.

Klingst, Martin. 1992. "Präsenz auf der Strasse ist Gebot." *Die Zeit*, November 27, p. 3.

Klonovsky, Michael. 1994. "Streitfall Ausländerkriminalität." *Focus Magazine*, February 7, 68–73.

Kloosterman, Robert, Joanne van der Leun, and Jan Rath. 1997. *Over grenzen—Immigranten en de informele economie*. Amsterdam: Het Spinhuis.

Knauf, Diethelm, and Helga Schröder, eds. 1993. *Fremde in Bremen—Auswanderer, Zuwanderer, Zwangsarbeiter*. Bremen: Edition Temmen.

Knaust, Manfred, and Lutz Linnemann. 1984. *Das Bremer FAN-Projekt*. Bremen: Senator für Jugend and Soziales, Referat Jugendforschung.

Kommunalverband Ruhrgebiet (KRG). 1983. *Ausländerintegration in Essen-Katernberg*. Essen: KRG.

Kom-Pas. 2002a. "Spot op—Intercultureel Netwerk Gent." *Kom-Pas@gent.be*, vol. 2, no. 3: 1–3.

————. 2002b. "Spot op: Team vorming—Stedelijke Integratiedienst." *Kom-pas@gent.be,* vol. 3, no. 1: 1–3.

Koninglijk Commissariat von het Migrantenbeleid (KCMB). 1989. *Integratie(beleid): Een werk van lange adem.* Brussels: Koninkrijk België.

————. 1990. *Voor een harmonische samenleving.* Brussels: Koninkrijk België.

————. 1991. *Samen op weg in een multi-etnische samenleving.* Brussels: Koninkrijk België.

————, ed. 1993. *Tekenen voor gelijkwaardigkeid.* Brussels: Inbel.

Koopmans, Ruud. 1999. "Germany and Its Immigrants: An Ambivalent Relationship." *Journal of Ethnic and Migration Studies* 25, no. 4 (October): 627–47.

Koopmans, Ruud, and Paul Statham. 2000. *Challenging the Politics of Immigration and Ethnic Relations.* Oxford: Oxford University Press.

Kosok, Elisabeth. 1991. *Hundert Jahre Gewerkschaft Metall Essen.* Essen: Klartext Verlag.

Kowalski, Matthias, and Christian Reiermann. 1994. "Soziale Sicherung: Das Ende der Verschwendung." *Focus Magazine,* no. 36 (September 5): 206–13.

Kramer, Ralph M. 1981. *Voluntary Agencies in the Welfare State.* Berkeley: University of California Press.

Kramer, Ralph M., Håkon Lorentzen, Willem B. Melief, and Sergio Pasquinelli. 1993. *Privatization in Four European Countries.* New York: M. E. Sharpe.

Kreisjugendring Nürnberg-Stadt. 2001. "Neues Projekt für Migranten in Nürnberg." *Live Dabei,* no. 29 (February–March): 1–2.

Kriebisch, Friedhorst, Rainer Stubbe, Margot Dolls, and Viola Hammetter. 1978. *Neuorganisation der Sozialen Dienste.* Bremen: Senatskommission für das Personalwesen and Institut für Sozialarbeit und Sozialpädagogik.

Krummbacher, Michael. 1989. "Armut und kommunale Sozialpolitik im Ruhrgebiet." In *Armut im Reichtum,* ed. Ingrid Breckner, Heinelt Hubert, Michael Krummbacher, Dieter Oelschlägel, Thomas Rommerlspacher, and Klaus M. Schmals, 231–73. Bochum: Germinal Verlag.

————. 1998. "Zur Partizipation von Migranten als Ressource nachhaltiger Stadtentwicklung." *Information zur Ausländerarbeit,* no. 3–4: 16–21.

Kulbach, Roderich, and Norbert Wohlfahrt. 1994. *Öffentliche Verwaltung und soziale Arbeit.* Freiburg: Lambertus Verlag.

Kullberg, J. 1996. Aanbodmodellen geïnventariseerd. Ph.D. diss., Delftse Universitaire Pers, Delft.

Kulturladen Gröpelingen. 1992. *Von Istanbul nach Gröpelingen.* Bremen: Kulturinitiative Gröpelingen.

Kupfer-Schreiner, Claudia. 1992. "Es geht auch anders!—Zweisprachige Erziehung in der Regelklasse." In *Es geht auch anders!* ed. Gabriele Pommerin-Götze, Bernhard Jehle-Santoso, and Eleni Bozikake-Leisch, 349–71. Frankfurt: Dagyeli Verlag.

Kymlicka, Will. 1995. *Multicultural Citizenship.* Oxford: Oxford University Press.

La Grotta, Luigi. 1999. "Zeit der Versprechen: Bürgerschaftswahl in Bremen." *Stimme* 13, no. 6 (June): 7–11.

La Grotta, Luigi, and Claudia Schmidt. 1999. "15 Jahre DAB." *Stimme* 13–14 (December–January): 18–21.

Landman, Nico. 1992. *Van mat tot minaret.* Amsterdam: VU-uitgeverij.

Lang, Kirsty. 2002. "Maverick Dutch Rightwinger Poised for Success." *Guardian,* May 8, p. 1.

Lapiower, Alain. 1997. *Total Respect: La génération Hip Hop en Belgique.* Brussels: Éditions EVO and Fondation Jacques Gueux.

Laytouss, Brahim. 1999. "El-Markaz et-Tarbawi." *El-Meydaan* 3, no. 3: 6.

Leclercq, Colette. 1998. "Les plans sociaux intégrés sous la loupe de deux journées de réflexion." *Osmoses* (October–December): 4–6.

Leefbaar Rotterdam. 2002. *Coalitie akkoord.* Rotterdam: Leefbaar Rotterdam.

Le Galès, Patrick, and Alan Harding. 1998. "Cities and States in Europe." *West European Politics* 21, no. 3 (July): 120–45.

Leggewie, Claus. 1991. *Multi Kulti: Spielregeln für die Vielvölkerrepublik.* Berlin: Rotbuch Verlag.

Leggewie, Claus, and Zafer Senocak. 1993. *Deutsche Türken: Das Ende der Geduld.* Hamburg: Rowohlt Verlag.

Leibfried, Stephan, and W. Voges. 1992. "Armut im Wohlfahrtsstaat." *Kölner Zeitschrift für Soziologie und Sozialpsychologie,* no. 32. Special issue.

Leicht, Robert. 2001. "Lieber den Bock als Gärtner." *Die Zeit,* no. 24 (October 31): 4.

Leman, Johan. 1991. "The Education of Immigrant Children in Belgium." *Anthropology and Education Quarterly* 22, no. 2 (June): 140–53.

———. 1994. *Kleur bekennen.* Tielt: Uitgeverij Lannoo.

Lesage, Dieter. 1998. *Zwarte gedachten over België.* Antwerp: Dedalus.

Lesthaeghe, Ron. 2000. *Communities and Generations.* Brussels: Vrije Universiteit Brussel Press.

Levy, Jonah D. 1999. *Tocqueville's Revenge.* Cambridge: Harvard University Press.

Li, Wei. 1998. "Anatomy of a New Ethnic Settlement: The Chinese 'Ethnoburb' in Los Angeles." *Urban Studies* 35: 479–501.

Lieberman, Robert. 1998. *Shifting the Color Line.* Cambridge: Harvard University Press.

Liebermann, Patrick. 1996. "La discrimination positive pour repenser les processus d'intégration." *Osmoses* (October–December): 8–10.

Lijphart, Arend. 1975. *The Politics of Accommodation.* Berkeley: University of California Press.

Lill, Dagmar. 2001. "Vorwort." In *Migration und Integration 2000,* ed. Frank Meng, 3. Bremen: Ausländerbeauftragte des Landes Bremen.

Linders, D., M. van Rhee, and H. van Lith. 2002. *Analyse Gemeenteraadsverkiezingen Rotterdam, 6 maart 2002.* Rotterdam: Centrum voor Onderzoek en Statistiek.

Lindo, Flip. 1994. "Het stille succes: De sociale stijging van Zuideuropese arbeidsmigranten in Nederland." In *Het demokratisch ongeduld,* ed. Hans Vermeulen and Rinus Penninx, 117–44. Amsterdam: Het Spinhuis.

Lindsiepe, Sabinde. 1993. "Miteinander leben." *AWO Post,* no. 19 (September–October): 8.

Llorens, José. 1993. "Eine politische Bilanz." In *20 Jahre Ausländerbeirat Nürnberg,* ed. Ausländerbeirat der Stadt Nürnberg, 22–45. Nuremberg: Stadt Nürnberg.

———. 1998. "Chronik des Ausländerbeirats." *Multikulturelles Nürnberg—Zeitung des Ausländerbeirates,* no. 6 (October): 4–5.

Local Integration/Partnership Action (LIA). 1999. *Thematic Sub-Report: Promoting the Participation of Migrants and Ethnic Minorities in the Local Political Life.* Brussels: LIA.

Loeffelholz, Hans-Dietrich von, and Dietrich Thränhardt. 1996. *Kosten der Nichtintegration ausländischer Zuwanderer.* Düsseldorf: MAGS-Nordrhein-Westfalen.

Lucassen, Jan, and Rinus Penninx. 1994. *Nieuwkomers, Nakomelingen, Nederlanders.* Amsterdam: Het Spinhuis.

Lüsebrink, Hans-Jürgen. 2002. "L'Allemagne, une métropole sans empire?" *Migrations-Société* 14, nos. 81–82 (May–August): 73–82.

Lutz, Helma. 1992. "In zwei Welten denken und handeln: Migrantinnen in der Migrantinnensozialarbeit." In *Fremde Frauen,* ed. Marion Schulz, 64–80. Frankfurt: Verlag für Interkulturelle Kommunikation.

Lux-Henseler, Barbara. 1997. "Ausländer in Nürnberg." *Statistische Nachrichten der Stadt Nürnberg.* No. 1: 3–22. Nuremberg: Stadt Nürnberg, Amt für Stadtforschung und Statistik.

Mahnig, Hans. 1995. "'Gelijkheid' of 'respect voor verschil'?" *Migranten-studies* 11, no. 1: 39–48.

Manço, Altay. 1997. "Intégration des jeunes turcs: Deux enquêtes pour quel constat?" *Osmoses* (January–March): 14–17.

Manço, Ural. 1998. "Een turkse Luikenaar." In *Belgische Toestanden,* ed. Marc Swyngedouw and Marco Martiniello, 169–70. Antwerp: Standaard Uitgeverij.

Mandel, Ruth. 1991. "Identity and Ethnic Constructions in the Context of Migration." In *Ethnicity, Structured Inequality, and the State in Canada and the Federal Republic of Germany,* ed. Robin Ostrow, Jürgen Fijalkowski, Y. Michael Bodemann, and Hans Merkens, 137–56. Frankfurt: Peter Lang Verlag.

Margolina, Sonja. 1998. "Wer zu spät kommt." *Die Zeit,* no. 25 (June 10): 13.

Marinelli, Vera. 1999. "Une politique en faveur des minorités ethniques." *Migrations-Société* 11, nos. 64–65 (July–October):169–80.

Martin, Susan Forbes. 1999. "Comparing the Rights of Non-Citizens in Western Europe." In *Research Perspectives on Migration,* 5–8. Washington, D.C.: Carnegie Endowment for International Peace.

Martiniello, Marco. 1995. "The National Question and the Political Construction of Immigrant Ethnic Communities in Belgium." In *Racism, Ethnicity, and Politics in Contemporary Europe,* ed. Alec G. Hargreaves and Jeremy Leaman, 131–44. Aldershot: Edward Elgar.

———. 1998. "Les élus d'origine étrangère à Bruxelles." *Revue européenne des migrations internationales* 14, no. 2: 123–49.

Martiniello, Marco, and Bonaventure Kagné. 1997. "City Template Liège: Basic Information on Ethnic Minorities and Their Participation." Liège: Université de Liège.

Marty, Martin E. 1997. *The One and the Many.* Cambridge: Harvard University Press.

Massey, Douglas S. 1986. "The Settlement Process among Mexican Migrants to the U.S." *American Sociology Review* 51, no. 5: 685–89.

Massey, Douglas S., and Nancy A. Denton. 1993. *American Apartheid.* Cambridge: Harvard University Press.

Meinhardt, Rolf. 1989. "Minderheitenpolitik in den Niederlanden." *Informationsdienst zur Ausländerarbeit,* no. 3: 65–67.

Meng, Frank. 2001. *Migration und Integration 2000.* Bremen: Ausländerbeauftragte des Landes Bremen.

Messina, Anthony M. 1996. "The Not So Silent Revolution." *World Politics* 49, no. 1 (October): 130–54.

Messina, Anthony M., Luis R. Fraga, Laurie A. Rhodebeck, and Frederick D. Wright, eds. 1992. *Ethnic and Racial Minorities in Advanced Industrial Democracies.* Westport, Conn.: Greenwood Press.

Meyer, Astrid. 1995. "The Institutionalization of Islam in the Netherlands and in the UK: The Case of Islamic Schools." *New Community* 21, no. 1: 37–54.

Meys, Werner. 1986. "Stadt Essen—Die Eingliederung von Türken am Beispiel einer Stadt." In *Zukunft in der Bundesrepublik oder Zukunft in der Türkei,* ed. Werner Meys and Faruk Sen, 103–16. Frankfurt: Dagyeli.

Meys, Werner, and Faruk Sen, eds. 1986. *Zukunft in der Bundesrepublik oder Zukunft in der Türkei?* Frankfurt: Dagyeli.

Minister für Gesundheit und Soziales (MGS). 1990. *Berufsbildungsbericht Nordrhein-Westfalen.* Düsseldorf: Minister für Arbeit.

Minister van Binnenlandse Zaken (MBZ). 1983. *Minderhedennota.* The Hague: MBZ.

Minister voor Grote Steden- en Integratiebeleid (MGSIB). 2002. *Integratie in het perspectief van immigratie.* The Hague: MGSIB.

Ministerie van Sociale Zaken en Werkgelegenheid (MSZW). 1993. *Het stichtingsakkoord over etnische minderheden in de praktijk.* The Hague: MSZW.

———. 1994. *Integratiebeleid etnische minderheden, Tweede Kamer, 1993–1994.* The Hague: MSZW.

Ministerium für Arbeit, Gesundheit und Soziales and Landesamt für Datenverarbeitung und Statistik (MAGS/LDVS). 1982. *Ausländische Arbeitnehmer in Nordrhein-Westfalen.* Düsseldorf: MAGS/LDVS.

———. 1992. *Ausländer, Aussiedler und Einheimische als Nachbarn.* Düsseldorf: MAGS/LDVS.

Ministerium für Arbeit, Soziales und Stadtentwicklung, Kultur und Sport (MASSKS) des Landes Nordrhein-Westfalen. 1999. *Selbstorganisationen von Migrantinnen und Migranten in NRW.* Düsseldorf: MASSKS.

Modolo, Claudio. 1997. "Le Centre pour l'Égalité des Chances." *Osmoses* (January–March): 4–6. Special issue.

Modood, Tariq, Sharon Beishon, and Satnam Virdee. 1994. *Changing Ethnic Identities.* London: Policy Studies Institute.

Müller, C. Wolfgang, ed. 1993. *Selbsthilfe: Ein Einführendes Lesebuch.* Weinheim: Beltzverlag.

Müller, Martina. 1993. *Afrikaner in Berlin.* Berlin: Ausländerbeauftragte des Senats.

Multiculturele Instelling "Het Kruispunt." 1997. *Verslag van het gesprek tussen een aantal Marrokaanse jongeren, vertegenwoordigers van de politie en de gemeente Den Haag.* The Hague: Gemeente Den Haag.

Münz, Rainer. 2000. "Europe and Its Immigrants." Paper presented at Symposium on Governance, Globalization, and the European Union: What Europe for Tomorrow? Österreichische Akademie der Wissenschafter, Vienna, September 28–30.

Münz, Rainer, and Ralf Ulrich. 1999. "Immigration and Citizenship in Germany," *German Politics and Society,* vol. 17, no. 4 (Winter): 1–33.

Murphy, Richard C. 1982. *Gastarbeiter im deutschen Reich.* Wuppertal: Peter Hammer Verlag.

Musterd, Sako, and Wim Ostendorf, eds. 1998. *Urban Segregation and the Welfare State.* London: Routledge.

Muus, Philip. 2001. "International Migration and the European Union." *European Journal on Criminal Policy and Research,* no. 9: 31–49.

Nationaal Instituut voor de Statistiek (NIS). 1990. *Regional Statistisch Jaarboek.* Brussels: Ministerie van Economische Zaken.

———. 1996. *Regional Statistisch Jaarboek.* Brussels: Ministerie van Economische Zaken.

Nederlands Centrum Buitenlanders (NCB). 1995. *Allochtonen over Nederland(ers).* Utrecht: NCB.

Neef, Rainer. 1992. "The New Poverty and Local Government Social Policies." *International Journal of Urban and Regional Research* 16, no. 2 (June): 202–21.

"New Belgian Parliament." 2003. *Migration News Sheet,* no. 243 (June): 60. Electronic version.

Noelle, Thorsten. 1996. "Empowerment in der niederländischen sozialen Arbeit." *Soziale Arbeit* 45, nos. 9–10: 318–25.

Norman, Peter. 1998. "German Job Crisis Hits Turks Harder." *Financial Times,* February 13, p. 2.

"Notizen." 1998a. *Stimme* 12, no. 4 (April): 2.

———. 1998b. *Stimme,* vol. 12, no. 6 (June): 2.

Nylen, William R. 2002. "Testing the Empowerment Thesis." *Comparative Politics* 34, no. 2 (January): 127–45.

Obdejin, Herman. 1994. "Marocains et Hollandais au cours de l'histoire." In *L'annuaire de l'émigration,* ed. Kacem Basfao and Hinde Taarji, 478–84. Rabat: Fondation Hassan II.

Oberndörfer, Dieter. 1992. "Vom Nationalstaat zur offenen Republik." *Aus Politik und Zeitgeschichte,* no. B9 (February 21): 21–28.

Ögelman, Nedim. 1999. Organizations, Integration, and the "Homeland Hangover." Paper presented at the Annual Meeting of the American Political Science Association, September 2–5, Atlanta, Ga.

O'Laughlin, John, and Jürgen Friedrichs, eds. 1996. *Social Polarization in Post-Industrial Metropolises.* New York: Walter de Gruyter.

Olk, Thomas, and Hans-Uwe Otto, ed. 1989. *Soziale Dienste im Wandel.* Neuwied: Luchterhand Verlag.

Oostindie, Gert. 1997. *Het paradies overzee.* Rotterdam: Bert Bakker.

Osenberg, Hanno. 1987. "Kleinräumige Wohnungsmarktbeobachtung auf kommunal-statistischer Basis." *Information zurRaumentwicklung,* nos. 11/12: 735–48.

Otto, Jeannette. 1999. "Lernziel Integration." *Zeitpunkte,* no. 2 (February): 64–66.

Ouali, Nouria. 1994. "La politique d'intégration." In *L'annuaire de l'émigration,* ed. Kacem Basfao and Hinde Taarji, 28–29. Rabat: Fondation Hassan II.

———. 1998. "Nationalité belge: Stratégie identitaire ou stratégie professionnelle des jeunes d'origine étrangère?" *Osmoses* (October–December): 5–8. Special issue.

Özcan, Ertekin. 1989. *Türkische Immigrantenorganisationen in der Bundesrepublik Deutschland.* Berlin: Hitit Verlag.

Özdamar, Tuncay. 2000. "Hände weg von meiner Muttersprache." *Stimme* 14, nos. 7–8 (July–August): 8–9.

Özoguz, Aydan. 1999. "Zäher Fortschritt." *Zeitpunkte,* no. 2 (February): 16–21.

Panafit, Lionel. 2000. "En Belgique, les ambiguïtés d'une représentation 'ethnique.'" *Le Monde Diplomatique* (June): 12–13.

Panayotidis, Gregorios. 1989. "Die gemeinsame Geschichte von Deutschen und Ausländern." In *Leben in einer multikulturellen Gesellschaft,* 3:24–25. Landezentrale für Politische Bildung. Bremen: Steintor.

Parmentier, Marc. 1999. "Les centres régionaux entre missions et priorités." *Osmoses* (April–June): 6–8.

Patterson, Orlando. 1997. *The Ordeal of Integration.* New York: Civitas/Counterpoint.

Pauwels, K., and L. Deschamps. 1993. *Organisations immigrées en Flandre.* Sybidi-Papers, no. 14. Louvain-la-Neuve: Éditions Académia.

Pearson, David. 2001. *The Politics of Ethnicity in Settler Societies.* New York: St. Martin's Press.

Penninx, Rinus, and Kees Groenendijk. 1989. "Auf dem Weg zu einer neuen Einwanderungspolitik in den Niederlanden?" *Zeitschrift für Ausländerrecht und–politik,* no. 4: 169–74.

Penninx, Rinus, and Boris Slijper. 1999. *Voor elkaar? Integratie, vrijwilligerswerk en organisaties van migranten.* Amsterdam: Universiteit van Amsterdam, Instituut voor Migratie en Etnische Studies.

Pfleghar, Michael. 1992. "Arbeitsimmigranten und –immigrantinnen und ihre Familien in Berlin nach 1961." *Geschichtswerkstatt,* 51–63. Braunschweig: Arbeitskreis Andere Geschichte Braunschweig.

Phalet, Karen. 2000. *Islam in de multiculturele samenleving.* Utrecht: European Research Centre on Migration and Ethnic Relations.

Phalet, Karen, and Barbara Kiekels. 1998. "Immigratie en integratie." In *Belgische Toestanden,* ed. Marc Swyngedouw and Marco Martiniello, 151–61. Antwerp: Standaard Uitgeverij.

Pickus, Noah M. J. 1998. *Becoming American/America Becoming.* Durham: Duke University, Terry Sanford Institute of Public Policy.

Picque, Charles. 1992. "Table-Ronde-Débat: Les villes européennes face à leurs minorités immigrées." In *Agence pour le Développement des Relations Interculturelles (ADRI),* 115–33. Vol. 2, *L'Intégration des minorités immigrées en Europe.* Paris: ADRI.

Pierson, Paul. 1995. "The New Politics of the Welfare State." Zentrum für Sozialpolitik (ZeS) Working Paper no. 3. Bremen: ZeS, Universität Bremen.

———. 1996. "The New Politics of the Welfare State." *World Politics* 48, no. 2 (January): 143–79.

———, ed. 2001. *The New Politics of the Welfare State.* Oxford: Oxford University Press.

Plücker, Holger, and Martin Weber. 1990. *Stand und Entwicklungsbedarf der Ausländerarbeit in Bremen.* Bremen: Senator für Jugend und Soziales.

"Polizeichef lobt Kontakt zu Türken." 1993. *Westdeutsche Allgemeine Zeitung,* July 13, p. 3.

Polizeidirektion Nürnberg. 1995. "Gegen die Jugendkriminalität." *Multikulturelles Nürnberg —Zeitung des Ausländerbeirates,* no. 5 (February): 7.

Pommerin-Götze, Gabriele, Bernhard Jehle-Santoso, and Eleni Bozikake-Leisch, eds. 1992. *Es geht auch anders! Leben und Lernen in der multikulturellen Gesellschaft.* Frankfurt: Dagyeli Verlag.

Popp, Friedrich. 1992. "Multikulturelle Gesellschaft zwischen Utopie und Wirklichkeit." In *Es geht auch anders!* Ed. Gabriele Pommerin-Götze, Bernhard Jehle-Santoso, and Eleni Bozikake-Leisch, 30–59. Frankfurt: Dagyeli Verlag.

Portes, Alejandro. 1995. *The Economic Sociology of Immigration.* New York: Russell Sage Foundation.

Portes, Alejandro, and R. G. Rumbaut. 1996. *Legacies.* Berkeley: University of California Press.

Poulain, Michel. 1994. "Migrations en Belgique." *Courrier Hebdomadaire,* nos. 1438–39. Brussels: Centre de Recherche et d'Information Socio-Politiques.

Poulain, Michel, and Thierry Eggerickx. 1990. "De demografische kenmerken van de vreemde bevolking in de Belgische staden (1983–1988)." *Bevolking en Gezin,* no. 1: 77–92.

Powell, Walter W., and Elisabeth S. Clemens. 1998. *Private Action and the Public Good.* New Haven: Yale University Press.

Premdas, Ralph R. 1997. "Public Policy and Ethnic Conflict." UNESCO Discussion Paper Series, no. 12. Geneva: UNESCO.

Presse- und Informationsamt (PIA). 1997. *Nürnberg in Zahlen.* Nuremberg: Stadt Nürnberg, Amt für Stadtforschung und Statistik.

Prey, Hedwig. 1989. *Die Unruhen in Berlin-Kreuzberg.* Berlin: Berliner Institut für Vergleichende Sozialforschung.

Prigge, Rolf. 1998. "Umbau des öffentlichen Sektors und Reform des politischen Systems." In *Bremens Selbstständigkeit,* ed. Heiner Heseler, Rudolf Hickel, and Rolf Prigge, 70–96. Bremen: Edition Temmen.

Pritzkuleit, Klaus. 1989. "Eingliederung auf Zeit." *Der Ueberblick,* no. 4: 31–33.

Projectbureau Geïntegreerd Veiligheidsbeleid (PGVB). 1998. *Rotterdam, veilig idee?* Rotterdam: Gemeente Rotterdam.

Puskeppeleit, Jürgen. 1989. "Entwicklungslinien und perspektiven der Sozialdienste." *Informationsdient zur Ausländerarbeit,* no. 1: 14–19.

Puskeppeleit, Jürgen, and Dietrich Thränhardt. 1990. *Vom betreuten Ausländer zum gleichberechtigten Bürger.* Freiburg im Breisgau: Lambertus-Verlag.

Putnam, Robert D. 1993. *Making Democracy Work.* Princeton: Princeton University Press.

———. 2000. *Bowling Alone: Civic Disengagement in America.* New York: Simon and Schuster.

Radtke, Franz-Olaf. 1990. "Multikulturell—Das Gesellschaftsdesign der 90er Jahren?" *Informationsdienst zur Ausländerarbeit,* no. 4: 27–34.

Rainwater, Lee. 1991. "The Problem of Social Exclusion." In *Human Resources in Europe at the Dawn of the Twenty-first Century,* ed. Eurostat, 401–14. Luxembourg: Eurostat.

Ramadan, Tariq. 1999. *Être musulman européen.* Lyons: Éditions Tawhid.

Rath, Jan. 1991. *Minorisering: De sociale constructie van etnische minderheden.* Amsterdam: Sua.

———. 1995. "Beunhazen van buiten—De informele economie als bastaardsfeer van sociale integratie." In *Sferen van integratie,* ed. G. Engbersen and R. Gabriëls, 74-109. Amsterdam: Uitgeverij Boom.

Rath, Jan, Kees Groenendijk, and Rinus Penninx. 1993. "De erkenning en institutionalisering van de Islam en België, Groot Britannië en Nederland." *Tijdschrift voor sociologie* 14, no. 1: 53–76.

Rath, Jan, Rinus Penninx, Kees Groenendijk, and Astrid Meyer. 1996. *Nederland en zijn islam.* Amsterdam: Het Spinhuis.

"Razzia im Kurdentreff." 1993. *Nürnberger Nachrichten,* November 6–7, p. 14.

Rea, Andrea. 1996. "Violences urbaines, discrimination et injustice." *Agenda interculturel,* no. 142 (March): 10–13.

Reed, Adolph, Jr. 1995. "Demobilization in the New Black Political Regime." In *The Bubbling Cauldron,* ed. Michael Peter Smith and Joe R. Feagin, 182–208. Minneapolis: University of Minnesota Press.

Regiegroep Stedelijk Jeugdbeleid Rotterdam (RSJBR). 1997a. *Ogroeien in Rotterdam.* Rotterdam: Gemeente Rotterdam.

———. 1997b. *Stedelijk jeugdbeleid Rotteram.* Rotterdam: Gemeente Rotterdam.

Regionale Arbeitsstelle zur Förderung van Kindern und Jugendlichen Zuwandererfamilien (RAA). 2003. *Soziale Beratung und Betreuung in Essen.* Essen: Stadt Essen.

Regionale Arbeitsstelle zur Förderung van Kindern und Jugendlichen Zuwandererfamilien (RAA)/Büro für Interkulturelle Arbeit (BIA). 2000. *Konzept für die interkulturelle Arbeit in der Stadt Essen.* Essen: Stadt Essen.

———. 2001. *Zweiter Umsetzungsbericht zum Handlungskonzept für die interkulturelle Arbeit.* Essen: Stadt Essen.

———. 2002. "Finanzierung des Gesamtkonzepts Sprachförderung in 2002." *Anlage zur Drucksache 5/1159/2002.* Essen: Stadt Essen.

Reiniger, Wolfgang. 1999. "Einführungsrede." Essen: Stadt Essen, Rathaus.

Reinsch, Peter, ed. 2001. *Measuring Immigrant Integration.* Aldershot: Ashgate.

Reitz, Jeffrey. 1998. *Warmth of the Welcome.* Boulder: Westview.

Reitz, Jeffrey, and R. Breton. 1994. *The Illusion of Difference.* Toronto: C. D. Howe Institute.

Renaerts, Monique. 1997. "L'Exécutif des Musulmans de Belgique." *Osmoses* (January–March): 6–9.

Rex, John. 1996. *Ethnic Minorities in the Modern Nation State.* London: Macmillan Press.

Richmond, Anthony H. 1988. *Immigration and Ethnic Conflict.* London: Macmillan Press.

Richter, Helmut. 1983. "Subkulturelle Segregation zwischen Assimilation und Remigration." In *Sozialarbeit und Ausländerpolitik,* ed. Franz Hamburger, Maria-Eleonara Karstan, Hans-Uwe Otto, and Helmut Richter, 106–25. Darmstadt: Luchterhand.

Rittstieg, Helmut. 1992. "Einbürgerung als eigene Angelegenheit der Bundesländer." In *Doppelte Staatsbürgerschaft—Ein europäischer Normalfall?* ed. Ausländerbeauftragte des Senats Berlins, 131–40. Berlin: Senatsverwaltung für Soziales.

———. 1996. "Minderheitenrechte oder Menschenrechte?" *Blätter für deutsche und internationale Politik,* no. 8 (August): 993–1004.

Roché, Sebastian, ed. 2003. *Sociologie de l'insécurité.* Paris: Éditions Armand Colin.

Rocheron, Yvette. 1999. "Les mariages mixtes, un indice anthropologique de l'assimilation?" In *Immigration et intégration,* ed. Philippe Dewitte, 205–11. Paris: Éditions La Découverte.

Roelandt, Theophil, and Justus Veenman. 1994. *Onzeker bestaan: De maatschappelijke positie van Turken, Marokkanen, Surinamers en Antillanen in Nederland.* Amsterdam: Boom/ISEO.

Rooijendijk, Lambert, and Jan Hendrik Somme. 2000. *Interculturalisatie.* Baarn: Uitgeverij H. Nelissen B.V.

Röpke, Karin. 2003. "Ergebnisse des Integrations-Konzeptes." *Stimme* 14, nos. 3–4 (March–April): 12–13.

Roseman, D., D. Laux, and G. Thieme, eds. 1996. *EthniCity.* Savage, Md.: Rowman and Littlefield.

Rumbaut, Rubén C. 1977. "Paradoxes (and Orthodoxies) of Assimilation." *Sociological Perspectives* 40, no. 3: 483–551.

Runge, Irene. 1993. *Vom Kommen und Bleiben: Osteuropäische jüdische Einwanderer in Berlin.* Berlin: Ausländerbeauftragte des Senats.

Sackmann, Rosemarie. 2001. "Integration von Zuwanderern in Frankreich und in den Niederlanden." *Deutsche Zeitschrift für Kommunalwissenschaften,* no. 1: 80–96.

Safran, William. 1994. "Non-Separatist Policies Regarding Ethnic Minorities: Positive Approaches and Ambiguous Consequences." *International Political Science Review* 15, no. 1 (January): 61–80.

Salamon, Lester. 1993. "The Global Associational Revolution: The Rise of the Third Sector on the World Scene." Occasional Paper no. 15. Baltimore: Johns Hopkins University, Institute for Policy Studies.

Salamon, Lester M., and Helmut Anheier, eds. 1997. *Defining the Nonprofit Sector: A Cross-National Analysis.* Manchester: Manchester University Press.

Santel, Bernhard. 2002. "Aussen vor? Zur politischen Partizipation von Zuwanderern in Deutschland." In *Integration und Partizipation in der Einwanderungsgesellschaft,* ed. Marianne Krüger-Potratz, Hans Reich, and Bernhard Santel, 11-25. Osnabrück: Akademie für Migration und Integration der Otto-Benecke-Stiftung.

Santoso, Saskia Soeria. 1994. "AGABY auf der Durststrecke." *Multikulturelles Nürnberg—Zeitung des Ausländerbeirates,* no. 4 (July): 6.

Sayad, Abdelmalek. 1997. "L'immigration et la pensée d'État." Comments at the colloquium "Être étranger, un crime?" Louvain-la-Neuve: Université Catholique de Louvain.

Schain, Martin. 1999. "Minorities and Immigrant Incorporation in France." In *Multicultural Questions,* ed. Christian Joppke and Steven Lukes, 199–223. Oxford: Oxford University Press.

Schmalz-Jacobsen, Cornelia. 1992. *Daten und Fakten zur Ausländersituation.* Bonn: Beauftragte der Bundesregierung für die Belange der Ausländer.

———. 1995, "Gemeinsames zuhause Bundesrepublik Deutschland." In *Interkulturelle Öffnung sozialer Dienste,* ed. Klaus-Barwig and Wolfgang Hinz-Rommel, 23–35. Freiburg im Breisgau: Lambertus Verlag.

Schmidt, Georg. 1989. *Als Bremen amerikanisch war.* Bremen: Johann Heinrich Döll Verlag.

Schmidt, Vivien. 2002. "Does Discourse Matter in the Politics of Welfare State Adjustment?" *Comparative Political Studies* 35, no. 2 (March): 168–93.

Schmitter Heisler, Barbara. 1983. "Immigrant Minorities in West Germany: Some Theoretical Concerns." *Ethnic and Racial Studies* 6, no. 3 (July): 308–19.

———. 1992. "New Poverty in the Welfare State: Institutional Dimensions of Social Exclusion and the Formation of an Underclass in the Netherlands and Germany." Paper presented at the Eighth International Conference of Europeanists, March 27–29, Chicago.

———. 2000. "The Sociology of Immigration." In *Migration Theory: Talking across Disciplines,* ed. Caroline B. Brettell and James F. Hollifield, 77–96. New York: Routledge.

Schneider, Wolf. 1991. *Essen—Abenteuer einer Stadt.* Düsseldorf: ECON Verlag.

Scholz, Ludwig. 1998. "Ein spannungsfreies Miteinander." *Multikulturelles Nürnberg—Zeitung des Ausländerbeirates,* no. 6 (October): 1.

Schröder, Gerhard. 1992. "Wir brauchen Zuwanderer." *Der Spiegel* 46, no. 11: 59–68.

Schröter, Hiltrud. 1997. *Arabesken: Studien zum interkulturellen Verstehen im deutsch-marokkanischen Kontext.* Frankfurt: Peter Lang Verlag.

Schulämter Nürnbergs. 1998. *Bericht über die Situation der ausländischen Schülerinnen und Schüler.* Nuremberg: Schulämter Nürnbergs, Referat IV.

Schul- und Kulturreferat (SKR). 1992. "Kulturmosaik." Pamphlet. Nuremberg: Stadt Nürnberg.

Schwarz, Thomas. 1987. "Ethnische Koloniebildung und die Organisationen des Sports türkischer Zuwanderer in Berlin." *Migration* 1, no. 1: 159–78.

———. 1992. *Zuwanderer im Netz des Wohlfahrtsstaats.* Berlin: Editions Parabolis.

Seidel-Pielen, Eberhard. 1999. "Halbherzige Offenheit." *Zeitpunkte,* no. 2 (February): 22–25.

Sen, Faruk. 1996. *Ausländerwahlrecht, doppelte Staatsbürgerschaft und politische Partizipation.* Essen: Zentrum für Türkeistudien.

———. 1998. "Islam in Deutschland." *Information zur Ausländerarbeit,* nos. 3–4: 86–89.

———. 1999. "Eine saubere Bilanz." *Zeitpunkte,* no. 2 (February): 52–57.

———. 2002. "Euro Islam." *Stimme* 16, nos. 9–10 (September–October): 8–10.

Senat Bremens. 1989. Drucksache 12/461. *Mitteilungen des Senats vom 21. Februar 1989: Ursachen, Auswirkungen und Lage des Rechtsextremismus.* Bremen: Senat Bremens.

Senator für Arbeit Bremen (SAB). 1979. *Konzeption zur Integration der ausländischen Arbeitnehmer und ihrer Familienangehörigen im Lande Bremen.* Bremen: Freie Hansestadt Bremen.

Senator für Arbeit, Frauen, Gesundheit, Jugend und Soziales (SAFGJS). 2000. *Grundsätze, Leitlinien und Handlungsempfehlungen für die bremische Integrationspolitik.* Bremen: Freie Hansestadt Bremen.

Senator für Gesundheit und Soziales (SGS). 1987. *Bericht über die räumliche Situation der islamischen Gemeinden in Berlin.* Berlin: Senat Berlin.

Senator für Gesundheit, Soziales und Verbraucherschutz (SGSV). 2002. *Armut und soziale Ungleichheit in Berlin.* Berlin: Land Berlin.

———. 2003. "Pressemeldung: Berliner Landesbeirat für Integration und Migration Konstituiert sich." Berlin: Land Berlin.

Senator für Inneres Bremen. 1989. *Beiräte nach der Reform 1989.* Bremen: Freie Hansestadt Bremen.

Senator für Jugend und Soziales (SJS). 1986. *Bericht über die Vergabe von Zuschüssen aus Wettmitteln 1986 für die Sozialarbeit in Ausländervereinen.* Bremen: SJS.

———. 1991. *Zweiter Sozialbericht für die Freie Hansestadt Bremen.* Bremen: Freie Hansestadt Bremen.

Senator für Schule, Jugend und Sport (SSJS). 2001. *Handreichung für Lehrkräfte an Berliner Schulen.* Berlin: Land Berlin.

Senatsverwaltung für Inneres Berlin (SIB). 1999. "Positionspapier Ausländerpolitik in Berlin." Berlin: Grundsatzangelegenheiten der Innenpolitik und Planung.

Senatsverwaltung für Soziales. 1993. *Horizon in Berlin: ein Beispiel europäischer Sozialpolitik.* Berlin: Senat Berlin.

Service Public Fédéral (SPF)—Sécurité Sociale. 2001. *Tout ce que vous avez toujours voulu savoir sur la Sécurité sociale.* Brussels: Royaume de la Belgique.

Shachar, Ayelet. 1999. "The Paradox of Multicultural Vulnerability." In *Multicultural Questions,* ed. Christian Joppke and Steven Lukes, 87–111. Oxford: Oxford University Press.

Shadid, W. A. R., and P. S. van Koningsveld. 1997. *Moslims in Nederland.* Houten and Diegem: Bohn, Stafleu, Van Loghum.

Shera, Wes, and Lillian Wells, eds. 1997. *Empowerment in Social Work.* New York: Columbia University Press.

———. 1999. *Empowerment Practices in Social Work.* Toronto: Canadian Scholars' Press.

Simon, Barbara Levy. 1994. *The Empowerment Tradition in American Social Work.* New York: Columbia University Press.

Skutnabb-Kangas, T. 1983. "Research and Its Implications for the Swedish Setting." In *Multicultural Education in Immigrant Countries,* ed. T. Husen and S. Opper, 127–40. Oxford: Pergamo Press.

Smith, Steven Rathgeb, and Michael Lipsky. 1993. *Nonprofits for Hire: The Welfare State in the*

Age of Contracting. Cambridge: Harvard University Press.

Sociaal-Economische Raad van Vlaanderen (SERV). 1998. *De sociaal-economische belangengemeenschap Vlaanderen/Brussel.* Brussels: SERV.

Sociale Zaken en Wekgelegenheid (SZWG) Rotterdam. 1997. *Vrijwilligersbeleid in Rotterdam.* Rotterdam: Gemeente Rotterdam.

Solmaz, Ali. 1999. "Deutschland als zentrales Operationsfeld des türkischen Geheimsdienstes MIT." *Geheim* (April): 1–8.

Sommer, Marie-Luise. 1988. *Aktivitäten von Ausländern mit Ausländern für Ausländer in Nürnberg.* Nuremberg: Stadt Nürnberg, Amt für Kulturelle, Freizeitsgestaltung.

Sommer, Theo. 1998. "Der Kopf zählt, nicht das Tuch." *Die Zeit,* no. 30 (July 16): 3.

———. 1999. "Ein langer Weg." *Zeitpunkte,* no. 2 (February): 3–6.

SOPEMI (Continous Reporting System on Migration). 1998. *Trends in International Migration.* Paris: Organization of Economic Cooperation and Development.

Soysal, Yasemin N. 1994. *Limits of Citizenship.* Chicago: University of Chicago Press.

Sozialdemokratische Partei Deutschlands (SPD) Berlin. 2001. *Koalitionsvereinbarung.* Berlin: SPD Berlin.

SPD-Ratsfraktion Essen. 1986. *Bilanz: Rechenschaftsbericht 1984–1986* (Essen: SPD).

Spiewak, Martin. 1999. "Neue Heimat Islam." *Zeitpunkte,* no. 2 (February): 34–39.

Spohn, Margaret. 1994. *Langfassung des Berichts zur internationalen UNESCO-Tagung des Zentrums für Türkeistudien: "Migranten in der Europäischen Union, Neue Integrationsansätze und Fremdenfeindlichkeit."* Essen: Zentrum für Türkeistudien.

Spoo, Eckart. 1992. "Gewalt gegen Minderheiten beklagt." *Frankfurter Rundschau,* October 22, p. 36.

Sprinkhuizen, F. J. P., and C. H. M. van Oosterwijk. 1996. *Jeugdige delictplegers in de regio Haaglanden.* The Hague: Politie Haaglanden.

Stad Gent. 2001. *Bestuursakkord 2001–2006.* Ghent: Stad Gent.

Stadt Essen. 1984a. *Handlungsprogramm zur Integration der ausländischen Arbeitnehmer und ihrer Familienangehörigen aus den Anwerbeländern,* vol. 1. Essen: Amt für Entwicklungsplanung.

———. 1984b. *Handlungsprogramm zur Integration der ausländischen Arbeitnehmer und ihrer Familienangehörigen aus den Anwerbeländern,* vol. 2. Essen: Amt für Entwicklungsplanung.

———. 1999. *Interkulturelles Konzept.* Essen: Stadt Essen.

Stad Nürnberg. 2003. *Ausländerbeiratswahl 2003.* Nuremberg: Wahlamt.

Stallmayer, Tina, and Margaret Heckel. 2001. "Migranten gegen das Minus." *Financial Times Deutschland,* May 30, p. 1–2.

Stark, Wolfgang. 1996. *Empowerment.* Freiburg: Lambertus.

Stasiulis, Daiva, and Nira Yuval-Davis, eds. 1995. *Unsettling Settler Societies.* London: Sage.

Stasz, Andrew. 1992. "Progress through Mischief." *Politics and Society* 20, no. 4 (December): 521–28.

Statistisches Landesamt Berlin (SLBE). 1998. *Sozialhilfe in Berlin.* Berlin: Senat des Landes Berlin.

Statistisches Landesamt Bremen (SLHB). 1997. *Jahrbuch 1997.* Bremen: Freie Hansestadt Bremen.

———. 1998. *Jahrbuch 1998.* Bremen: Freie Hansestadt Bremen.

———. 1999. *Statistische Mitteilungen: Wahl der Bremischen Bürgerschaft.* Vol. 100. Bremen: Freie Hansestadt Bremen.

Stedelijke Adviesraad Multiculturele Stad (SAMS) Den Haag. 1995. *Advies notitie "uitwerking motie algemeen/categoriaal."* The Hague: Stedelijke Adviesraad Multiculturele Stad.

———. 1998. "Reactie op plan MCS, 1998–2001." The Hague: Gemeente Den Haag.

———. 2001a. *SAM—Nieuwsbrief* 2 (November).

————. 2001b. *SAM—Nieuwsbrief* 4 (December).

————. 2002a. *Beknopte geschiednis van de Haagse adviesraden.* The Hague: SAMS den Haag.

————. 2002b. *SAM—Nieuwsbrief* 12 (September).

————. 2002c. *SAM—Nieuwsbrief* 13 (October).

————. 2002d. *Reactie op "Programme Interculturalisatie en Diversiteit 2003."* The Hague: Stedelijke Adviesraad Multiculturele Stad.

————. 2002e. *Woonruimteverdeling.* The Hague: Stedelijke Adviesraad Multiculturele Stad.

————. 2003. *Werkplan 2003.* The Hague: Stedelijke Adviesraad Multiculturele Stad.

Stedelijke Adviesraad Multiculturele Stad (SAMS) Rotterdam. 1999. *Advies over de Rijksnota integratiebeleid.* Rotterdam: SAMS Rotterdam.

————. 2001. *Divers in emancipatie.* Rotterdam: SAMS.

————. 2002. *Met hen niet zonder hen.* Rotterdam: Stedelijke Adviescommissie Multiculturele Stad.

————. 2003. *Werkplan 2003 en jaarsverslag 2002.* Rotterdam: Stedelijke Adviescommissie Multiculturele Stad.

Stedelijke Integratiedienst (SID). 1999a. *Jaarverslag 1998.* Ghent: Erkend Regionaal Integratiecentrum Gent.

————. 1999b. *SIF—beleidsplan 2000–20002.* Ghent: Erkend Regionaal Integratiecentrum Gent.

————. 2001. *Beleidsplan etnisch-culturele minderheden.* Ghent: Stad Gent.

————. 2002. *Omgevingsanalyse 2003–2005.* Ghent: Stad Gent.

Stein, Jörg. 1998. "Vorbild Hessen?" In *Schlusslicht oder Vorbild?* ed. Referat Ausserschulische Massnahmen/Fort- und Weiterbildung, 14. Düsseldorf: Ministerium für Arbeit, Soziales und Stadtentwicklung.

Steunpunt Werkgelegenheit, Arbeid en Vorming (WAV). 1999. *De arbeidsmarkt in Vlaanderen.* Louvain: Steunpunt WAV.

Stratman, Friedrich. 1984. "Zwischen Bürokratischem Eigeninteresse und Selbsthilfeanspruch." In *Organisierte Nächstenliebe,* ed. Rudolph Bauer and Hartmut Diessenbacher, 9–25. Opladen: Westdeutscher Verlag.

Stroobants, Jean-Pierre. 2002. "Aux Pays-Bas, les populistes font leur entrée au gouvernement." *Le Monde,* July 23, 2.

Strooij, Henry. 1997. "Stilaan in beeld: Kaapverdianen in Rotterdam." *Migranten Informatief,* no. 122 (February): 3–7.

Stüwe, Gerd. 1996. "Migranten in der Jugendhilfe." *Migration und Soziale Arbeit,* nos. 3–4: 25–29.

Sunier, Thijl. 1996. *Islam in beweging: Turkse jongeren en islamitische organisaties.* Amsterdam: Het Spinhuis.

Targosz, Patricia. 1998. "Les conseils représentatifs des centres régionaux: Esquisse d'un outil capital." *Osmoses* (January–March): 9–12.

Tesser, P. T. M., F. A. van Dugteren, and A. Merens. 1996. *Rapportage Minderheden 1996.* Rijswijk and The Hague: Sociaal en Cultureel Planbureau and Vuga.

Tesser, Paul, and Carlo van Praag. 1996. "Ruimtelijke segregatie en maatschappelijke integratie van allochtonen." *Migranten-studies* 12, no. 2: 60–71.

Thränhardt, Dietrich. 1983. "Ausländer im Dickicht der Verbände." *Neue Praxis,* pp. 62–78. Special issue.

————, ed. 1994. *Landessozialbericht—Ausländerinnen und Ausländer in Nordrhein-Westfalen.* Münster: Institut für Politikwissenschaft der Westfälischen Wilhelms-Universität.

————. 1998. "Between State and Market: Local Governments and Immigration." *German Politics and Society* 16, no. 4 (Winter): 68–86.

———. 2000. "Einwanderer und soziales Kapital." in *Einwanderer-Netzwerke und ihre Integrationsqualität in Deutschland und Israel,* ed. Dietrich Thränhardt and Uwe Hunger, 15-51. Vol. 11, Studien zu Migration und Minderheiten. Münster: Lit Verlag.

Thyré, Annick. 1998. "Travaux d'intégration au C.E.S.R.W." *Osmoses* (January–March): 18.

Tijdelijke Wetenschappelijke Commissie Minderhedenbeleid (TWCM). 1995. *Kaderadvies: Eenheid en verscheidenheid.* Amsterdam: Het Spinhuis.

Tillie, Jean. 1998. "Explaining Migrant Voting Behavior in the Netherlands." *Revue européenne des migrations internationales* 14, no. 2: 71–95.

Tocqueville, Alexis de. 1969. *Democracy in America.* 2 vols. Garden City, N.Y.: Doubleday.

Toonen, Theo A. J. 1996. "On the Administrative Condition of Politics." *West European Politics* 19, no. 3 (July): 609–32.

"Türkisch als Abiturfach." 1993. *Gazette—Die Deutsch-Türkische Zeitung aus Nürnberg* 1 (October): 10.

Uchatius, Wolfgang. 1999. "Einer für alle." *Zeitpunkte,* no. 2 (February): 72–74.

Uebel, Cornelia. 1999. "Die zweite Öffentlichkeit." *Zeitpunkte,* no. 2 (February): 94–97.

Ullman, Claire F. 1998. *The Welfare State's Other Crisis.* Bloomington: Indiana University Press.

United Nations. 2000. *Replacement Migration.* New York: United Nations Population Division.

van Amersfoort, Hans. 1982. *Immigration and the Formation of Minority Groups—The Dutch Experience.* Cambridge: Cambridge University Press.

Vandenbrande, Kristel. 1995. *Het Vlaams-Brussels migrantenbeleid bestaat niet.* Brussels: Vrije Universiteit Brussel, Interuniversitaire Attractiepool 37.

van den Brande, Luc, and Luc Martens. 1998. *Besluit van de Vlaamse regering betreffende de erkenning en subsidiëring van de centra en diensten voor het Vlaamse minderhedenbeleid.* Brussel: Vlaamse Regering.

Vanderkam, Michel. 1997. "Une brochure brosse le portrait des projets FIPI wallons." *Osmoses* (July–September): 14–17.

van der Molen, Esmé. 1998. "Rotterdam moet trots worden op z'n diversiteit." *Migranten Informatief,* no. 129 (December): 10–13.

van der Valk, Ineke. 1996. *Van migratie naar burgerschap.* Amsterdam: Instituut voor Publiek en Politik.

van der Zwaard, Jake. 1998. "Kategorisieren oder Differenzieren." *Information zur Ausländerarbeit,* no. 1: 31–35.

van Dugteren, F. 1993. *Woonsituatie minderheden.* Rijswijk: Sociaal en Cultureel Planbureau.

van Kempen, Ronald, and H. Priemus. 2001. "De Nederlandse sociale huursector." *Tijdschrift voor de volkshuisvesting* 7, no. 3 (May): 12–18.

Vanneste, D. 1985. *Gent, een geografische gids.* Louvain: Acta Geographica Lovaniensia.

van Peer, C., and F. Lammertyn. 1990. *De welzijnszorg ten behoeve van migranten, vluchtelingen en woonwagenbewoners.* Louvain: Katholieke Universiteit Leuven, Sociologisch Onderzoeksinstitut.

van Rhee, Martin. 2002. *Analyse van de opkomst bij de gemeenteraadsverkiezingen in Rotterdam.* Rotterdam: Centrum voor Onderzoek en Statistiek.

van Thijn, Ed, ed. 2000. *Racisme in Nederland.* Amsterdam: De Balie.

Varshney, Ashutosh. 2001. "Ethnic Conflict and Civil Society." *World Politics* 53, no. 3 (April): 362–98.

———. 2003. "Nationalism, Ethnic Conflict, and Rationality." *Perspectives on Politics* 1, no. 1 (March): 85–99.

Veelkleurige Stad (VKS). 2002. "Uitvoeringsprogramma Veelkleurige Stad, 1998–2002." Rotterdam: Gemeente Rotterdam.

Veenman, Justus, ed. 1996. *Keren de kansen? De tweede-generatie allochtonen in Nederland.* Assen: Van Gorcum and Compagnie.

Verband der Initiativen in der Ausländerarbeit (VIA). 1987. "Initiativgruppen in der Ausländerarbeit Bayern." *VIA-Magazin.* Bonn: VIA. No. 5: 1–7.

Verdurmen, Jolanda, Paul van Wensveen, and Corrine Oudijk. 1997. *Tabellenboek en onderzoeksverslag leefbaarheidsmonitor Den Haag.* Rotterdam: Centrum voor Onderzoek en Statistiek.

Verfassungsschutz Rheinland-Pfalz. 1995. *Islamistische Extremisten.* Mainz: Ministerium des Innern und für Sport.

Vermeulen, Hans, ed. 1997. *Immigrantenbeleid voor de multicultuele samenleving.* Amsterdam: Het Spinhuis.

Vermeulen, Hans, and Rinus Penninx, eds. 1994. *Het demokratisch ongeduld.* Amsterdam: Het Spinhuis.

Vesting, Bettina. 2003. "Bayern fordert schärfere Gesetze gegen Islamisten." *Berliner Zeitung,* May 3, p. 1.

Villan, Michel. 1996. "Un décret historique pour une politique cohérente d'intégration." *Osmoses* (October–December): 5–7.

Ville de Liège. 2000. "Programme de politique générale, 2000–2006." Liège: Ville de Liège.

———. 2002. *Rapport annuel—Année 2001.* Liège: Ville de Liège.

Visser, Jelle, and Anton Hemerijck. 1997. *A Dutch Miracle.* Amsterdam: Amsterdam University Press.

Vlaams Fond voor de Integratie van Integratiekansarmen (VFIK). 1995. *Migranten op 1 Januari 1994.* Brussels: Ministerie van de Vlaamse Gemeenschap, Administratie Planning en Statistiek.

Vlaams Parlement. 2002. "Ontwerp van Decreet betreffende het Vlaamse inburgeringsbeleid." Stuk 1229 (2001–2002), no. 2.

Voogt, Peter W. 1994. *In de buurt: Participatie van migranten bij buurtbeheer.* Rotterdam: Rotterdams Instituut Bewonersondersteuning.

"Wählen nur noch Nicht-EU-Bürger den Ausländerbeirat?" 1996. *Nürnberger Nachrichten,* September 21–25, p. 15.

Waldinger, Roger. 1996. *Still the Promised City: African Americans and New Immigrants in Postindustrial New York.* Cambridge: Harvard University Press.

Walzer, Michael. 1997. *On Toleration.* Cambridge: Harvard University Press.

Waters, Mary. 1999. *Black Identities.* New York: Russell Sage Foundation.

Wehrmann, Elisabeth. 1997. "Ein Modell ist gefährdet." *Die Zeit,* no. 17 (April 25): 5.

Weiner, Myron. 1995. *The Global Migration Crisis.* New York: Harper Collins.

Weir, Margaret. 1998. *The Social Divide.* Washington, D.C., and New York: Brookings Institution and Russell Sage Foundation.

Werkgroep Waardenburg. 1983. *Religieuze voorzieningen voor etnische minderheden in Nederland.* Rijkswijk: Ministerie van Welzijn, Volksgezondheid en Cultuur.

Werkstatt. 1993. *Selbsthilfe Wegweiser Essen.* Essen: Informationsstelle für Essener Selbsthilfegruppen, Initiativen und Projekten.

Wertenschlag, Rudolf. 1980. *Grundrechte der Ausländer in der Schweiz* (Basel: Universität Basel).

Westin, Charles. 2003. "Striking a Balance between Diversity and Social Cohesion." Stockholm: Stockholm University National Europe Center. Paper no. 74.

Wetenschappelijke Raad voor Regeringsbeleid (WRR). 1979. *Ethnic Minorities.* The Hague: WRR.

Wieviorka, Michel. 1996. *Une société fragmentée?* Paris: La Découverte.

Wilensky, Harold L. 1981. Foreword to *Voluntary Agencies in the Welfare State,* ed. Ralph M. Kramer, xiv–xxii. Berkeley: University of California Press.

Willeke, Stefan. 1999. "Im fremden Land Almanya." *Zeitpunkte*, no. 2 (February): 10–15.

Willett, Cynthia, ed. 1998. *Theorizing Multiculturalism*. Oxford: Blackwell.

Wilpert, Czarina. 1991. "Ethnic Identification and the Transition from One Generation to the Next among Turkish Migrants in the Federal Republic of Germany." In *Ethnicity, Structured Inequality, and the State in Canada and the Federal Republic of Germany*, ed. Robin Ostow, Jürgen Fijalkowski, Y. Michael Bodemann, and Hans Merkens, 121–36. New York: Peter Lang.

Wilson, William Julius. 1987. *The Truly Disadvantaged*. Chicago: University of Chicago Press.

———. 1996. *When Work Disappears*. New York: Alfred A. Knopf.

Wimmer, Andreas. 1997. "Explaining Xenophobia and Racism." *Ethnic and Racial Studies* 20, no. 1 (January): 17–41.

Wolfe, Alan. 1975. *The Limits of Legitimacy: Political Contradictions of Contemporary Capitalism*. New York: Free Press.

Wolff, Rick, and Jean N. Tillie. 1995. *"In principe zijn de lijnen kort"—Een onderzoek naar het minderhedenbeleid en de minderhedenvoorlichting*. Amsterdam: Gemeente Amsterdam.

Wuertz, Karen. 1994. *Stad en stedeling*. Rotterdam: Gemeente Rotterdam, Project Geïntegreerd Veiligheidsbeleid.

Zaimoglu, Feridun. 1995. *Kanak Sprak*. Berlin: Rotbuch Verlag.

Zaptçioglu, Dilek. 1998. *Der Mond isst die Sterne auf*. Stuttgart: K.-Thienemanns-Verlag.

Zegers de Beijl, Roger. 1992. "Wenn auch gleich vor dem Gesetz." In *Schutzgesetze gegen ethnische Diskriminierung*, ed. Ausländerbeauftragte des Senats Berlins, 65–114. Berlin: Senatsverwaltung für Soziales.

van Zelm, E. A. 1996. *Sturen met twaalf kapiteins*. Rijswijk: Ministerie van Volksgezondheid, Welzijn en Sport.

Zelnhefer, Siegfried. 2002. "Integration ist keine Einbahnstrasse." *Nürnberg Heute* 73: 1–6.

Zentralstelle für die Integration von Zugewanderten. 1992. *"Wir" Inländer und "die" Ausländer*. Bremen: Ausländerbeauftragte des Landes Bremen.

Zentrum für Türkeistudien (ZfT), ed. 1993. *Migration Movements from Turkey to the European Community*. Brussels: Migrants Forum of the European Communities.

———, ed. 1994. *Ausländer in der Bundesrepublik Deutschland*. Opladen: Leske and Budrich.

Zuwanderungskommission. 2001. *Zuwanderung gestalten, Integration fördern*. Berlin: Bundesministerium des Innern.

"Zwarte scholen doen het goed." 1999. *Rotterdams Dagblad*, April 22, p. 12.

Newspapers

Berliner Morgenpost (Berlin)

Berliner Zeitung (Berlin)

De Gentenaar (Ghent)

Haagsche Courant (The Hague)

La Meuse (Liège)

Nürnberger Nachrichten (Nuremberg)

Nürnberger Zeitung (Nuremberg)

Neue Ruhr Zeitung (Essen edition)

Rotterdams Dagblad (Rotterdam)

Tagesspiegel (Berlin)

Tageszeitung (Bremen and Berlin editions)

Weser-Kurier (Bremen)

Westdeutsche Allgemeine Zeitung (Essen edition)

INDEX